Advances

in COMPUTERS
VOLUME 55

Advances in
COMPUTERS

EDITED BY

MARVIN V. ZELKOWITZ

Department of Computer Science
and Institute for Advanced Computer Studies
University of Maryland
College Park, Maryland

VOLUME 55

ACADEMIC PRESS

A Harcourt Science and Technology Company

San Diego   San Francisco   New York   Boston
London   Sydney   Tokyo

Academic Press
A Harcourt Science and Technology Company
525 B Street, Suite 1900, San Diego, California 92101-4495, USA
http://www.academicpress.com

Academic Press
A Harcourt Science and Technology Company
Harcourt Place, 32 Jamestown Road, London NW1 7BY, UK
http://www.academicpress.com

International Standard Book Number 0-12-012155-7

Contents

CONTRIBUTORS iv
PREFACE xv

The Virtual University: A State of the Art

Linda Harasim

1. Introduction 2
2. A Powerful New Phenomenon: Online Collaborative Learning in
   Virtual Classrooms. 6
3. Canada's Virtual-U 15
4. Establishing a First-Rate Virtual University 27
5. Defining the Virtual University: What It Is and Should Be 31
6. Conclusions: Implications for Pedagogical and Technological
   Developments 39
7. Research Directions and Questions 39
   References. 45

The Net, the Web and the Children

W. Neville Holmes

1. Introduction 50
2. The Net. 51
3. The Web 57
4. The Children 64
5. The Possibilities 75
6. Conclusion 81
   References. 82

Source Selection and Ranking in the WebSemantics Architecture Using Quality of Data Metadata

George A. Mihaila, Louiqa Raschid, and Maria-Ester Vidal

1. Introduction 89
2. A Motivating Example 91
3. WebSemantics Architecture for Publishing and Locating Data
   Sources 92
4. Describing Source Content and Quality Metadata. 96
5. Queries for Discovering, Selecting and Ranking Sources 100

6. Efficient Manipulation of Scqd's 104
7. Related Research 113
8. Summary and Future Work 115
   References... 116

Mining Scientific Data

Naren Ramakrishnan and Ananth Y. Grama

1. Introduction 120
2. Motivating Domains................................ 122
3. Inductive Mining Techniques......................... 134
4. Data Mining as Approximation and Lossy Compression 143
5. Putting It All Together 151
6. Future Research Issues............................. 156
7. Concluding Remarks 161
   References... 162

History and Contributions of Theoretical Computer Science

John E. Savage, Alan L. Selman, and Carl Smith

1. Introduction 172
2. A Brief History 173
3. Theory in the Practice of Computing 174
4. Contributions to Other Disciplines..................... 178
5. Foundational Research.............................. 179
6. Summary... 182
   Acknowledgements.................................. 183
   References... 183

Security Policies

Ross Anderson, Frank Stajano, and Jong-Hyeon Lee

1. What Is a Security Policy?............................ 186
2. The Bell–LaPadula Policy Model....................... 190
3. Examples of Multilevel Secure Systems.................. 199
4. The Biba Integrity Model 207
5. The Clark–Wilson Model 209
6. The Chinese Wall Model............................. 211
7. The BMA Policy 212
8. Jikzi 214
9. The Resurrecting Duckling 216
10. Access Control.................................... 219
11. Beyond Access Control.............................. 222
12. Automated Compliance Verification..................... 227

13. A Methodological Note.   228
14. Conclusions   230
    Acknowledgements   230
    References   231

Transistors and IC Design

Yuan Taur

1. Introduction to CMOS VLSI   238
2. MOSFET Scaling Theory   242
3. CMOS Device Issues below 0.25 μm   251
4. 25-nm CMOS Design   266
5. Interconnect Issues   273
    References   278

AUTHOR INDEX   281

SUBJECT INDEX   289

CONTENTS OF VOLUMES IN THIS SERIES   297

COLOUR PLATE SECTION BETWEEN PAGES 142 AND 143

Contributors

Ross Anderson leads the security group at the Computer Laboratory, University of Cambridge, where he is Reader in Security Engineering. He is a Fellow of the Institution of Electrical Engineers and of the Institute of Mathematics and Its Applications. He has well-known research publications on a number of security policy topics including medical privacy and banking systems, as well as on the underlying technologies such as cryptography and tamper resistance. He is the author of the book *Security Engineering—A Guide to Building Dependable Distributed Systems*.

Ananth Y. Grama received his Ph.D. in computer sciences from the University of Minnesota in 1996. Since then, he has been an assistant professor of computer sciences at Purdue University. His research interests span the areas of parallel and distributed computing infrastructure and applications, large-scale data analysis and handling, and data compression. He has co-authored several papers and a textbook, *Introduction to Parallel Computing—Design and Analysis of Algorithms*, with Kumar, Gupta, and Karypis (Benjamin Cummings/Addison-Wesley, 1994). He has been the recipient of several awards—the Vice Chancellor's Gold Medal (University of Roorkee, 1989), the Doctoral Dissertation Award (University of Minnesota, 1993), the NSF CAREER Award (1998), and the Purdue University School of Science Outstanding Assistant Professor Award (1999).

Linda Harasim is the Network Leader and CEO of Canada's TeleLearning Network of Centres of Excellence (http://www.telelearn.ca), which was established under the Networks of Centres of Excellence program in July 1995 with funding of $26.2 million to March 2002 and plans are underway for Phase 2 funding. The TeleLearning NCE is a national collaboration linking Canadian researchers and client communities involved in the development, application, and evaluation of advanced education technologies based on collaborative learning and knowledge building. She leads the Virtual-U research projects, involving the largest field trials of post-secondary education in the world, and is recognized internationally as a pioneer in designing, testing, and delivering online education and for demonstrating the effectiveness of teaching and learning online. In 1983, she completed a Ph.D. in educational theory at the University of Toronto. She has produced three books: *Online Education: Perspectives on a New Environment* (Praeger, 1990), and *Global Networks: Computers and International Communications* and

Learning Networks: A Field Guide to Teaching and Learning Online (both MIT Press, 1995) (http://mitpress.mit.edu).

W. Neville Holmes graduated in electrical engineering from Melbourne University and worked the first two years after graduation as a patent examiner. Joining IBM Australia in 1959, he worked in technical positions within Australia and overseas for the next 30 years, including stints at the World Trade Systems Center in Poughkeepsie, NY and the European Systems Research Institute in Geneva. He took a Masters degree in cognitive science from the University of New South Wales in 1989 and moved to Launceston in Tasmania where he took up a teaching position in what is now the School of Computing at the University of Tasmania.

Jong-Hyeon Lee holds a Ph.D. in computer science from the University of Cambridge, UK. He worked for years as a senior researcher in the Electronics and Telecommunications Research Institute in Korea and currently runs Filonet Corporation, Vancouver, Filonet Korea Incorporated, Seoul, and Filonet Singapore Pte. Ltd., Singapore. His research interests include computer security, reliable long-term document management, and middleware for Web-based applications.

George Mihaila obtained a Bachelor of Science in computer science from the University of Bucharest in 1991. He received a Master of Science and a Ph.D. in computer science in 1996 and in 2000, respectively, from the University of Toronto. His thesis research was on publishing, locating, and querying networked information sources. He served on the faculty of the University of Bucharest from 1991 to 1993 and worked in industry as a systems analyst from 1991 to 1994. He has been a visiting researcher at the French National Institute for Research in Computer Science and Control (INRIA), the University of Maryland Institute for Advanced Computer Studies (UMIACS), and Compaq's Systems Research Center (SRC), and has been a research assistant in the Department of Computer Science at the University of Toronto. He joined the research staff of the IBM T. J. Watson Research Center in December, 2000.

Naren Ramakrishnan received his Ph.D. in computer sciences from Purdue University in August 1997. Since August 1998, he has been an assistant professor of Computer Science at Virginia Tech. His research interests include recommender systems, problem solving environments, data mining, and topics that lie at the intersection of artificial intelligence and computational science. He received an MIT Technology Review TR100 nomination in April 1999 and a National Science Foundation Faculty Early Career Development Award in August 2000.

Louiqa Raschid received a Bachelor of Technology in electrical engineering from the Indian Institute of Technology, Madras, in 1980, and a Ph.D. in electrical engineering from the University of Florida, Gainesville, in 1987. She is an associate professor at the Smith School of Business, the Institute for Advanced Computer Studies, and the Department of Computer Science, University of Maryland. She has been a visiting scientist at the French National Laboratories for Information Sciences (INRIA), Hewlett–Packard Research Labs, and Stanford Research Institute. She currently serves on the Technical Advisory Board of Common Object Inc., a service provider for online business-to-business transactions. Her research interests include scalable architectures for wide area computation with heterogeneous information servers, query optimization and evaluation techniques, and publishing and locating sources using the WWW and XML. Papers that she has co-authored have been nominated for Best Paper at the 1996 International Conference on Distributed Computing Systems and the 1998 International Conference on Cooperative Information Systems.

John E. Savage earned Sc.B., Sc.M., and Ph.D. degrees from MIT. After employment at Bell Telephone Laboratories he joined Brown University in 1967. He co-founded its Computer Science Department in 1979, serving as its second chairman. He is a Guggenheim Fellow, a Fellow of the ACM, IEEE, and AAAS, and a member of the MIT Corporation Visiting Committee for the Department of Electrical Engineering and Computer Science. He has done research on information theory and coding, analysis of algorithms, complexity theory, parallel computation, and high-performance computing. His latest book, *Models of Computation: Exploring the Power of Computing*, was published in 1998.

Alan L. Selman received a B.S. from City College of CUNY in 1962, an M.A. from the University of California, Berkeley in 1964, and a Ph.D. from the Pennsylvania State University in 1970. He held faculty positions at Florida State, Iowa State, and Northeastern universities prior to joining the University at Buffalo in 1990, where he served as chairman of the Computer Science Department from 1990 to 1996. He is a Fellow of the ACM, has been a Senior Fulbright Scholar, and is a member of the editorial boards of the *Chicago Journal of Theoretical Computer Science, Journal of Computer and System Sciences*, and *Theory of Computer Systems*. He founded the IEEE Conference on Structure in Complexity Theory and served as its conference chairman 1985–1988. His book *Computability and Complexity Theory*, co-authored with Steven Homer, will be published this year.

Carl H. Smith earned a B.S. from the University of Vermont and an M.S. and a Ph.D. from the State University of New York at Buffalo, and was habilitated at the University of Latvia. He held a faculty position at Purdue University before joining the University of Maryland. He was a Fulbright Scholar and a Foreign Member of the Latvian Academy of Science. He serves on the editorial board of *Journal of Computer and Systems Sciences*, *Theoretical Computer Science*, *International Journal of the Foundations of Computer Science*, and *Fundaments Informaticae*. His latest book *Theory of Computing, a Gentle Introduction*, with Efim Kinber, was published by Prentice Hall in the summer of 2000.

Frank Stajano holds a Dr. Ing. in electronic engineering from La Sapienza University of Rome, Italy and a Ph.D. in computer science from the University of Cambridge, UK. He worked for many years as a research scientist at AT&T Laboratories Cambridge (formerly ORL). His research interests include security, ubiquitous and wearable computing, scripting languages (particularly Python), object oriented programming, communications, and multimedia. After a year in Japan as a Toshiba Fellow he will take up the ARM Lectureship in Ubiquitous Computing at the University of Cambridge.

Yuan Taur received a B.S. degree in physics from National Taiwan University, Taipei, Taiwan, in 1967 and a Ph.D. degree in physics from University of California, Berkeley, in 1974. From 1975 to 1979, he worked at NASA, Goddard Institute for Space Studies, New York. From 1979 to 1981, he worked at Rockwell International Science Center, Thousand Oaks, California. Since 1981, he has been with the Silicon Technology Department of IBM Thomas J. Watson Research Center, Yorktown Heights, New York. His recent work and publications include Latchup-free 1-μm CMOS, Self-aligned TiSi2, 0.5-μm CMOS and BiCMOS, Shallow trench isolation, 0.25-μm CMOS with n+/p+ poly gates, SOI, Low-temperature CMOS, and 0.1-μm CMOS. He has been Manager of Exploratory Devices and Processes and is a Fellow of the IEEE. He is currently the editor-in-chief of *IEEE Electron Device Letters*, and has authored or co-authored over 100 technical papers and holds 10 U.S. patents. He has received four Outstanding Technical Achievement Awards and six Invention Achievement Awards over his IBM career. He co-authored a book, *Fundamentals of Modern VLSI Devices*, published by Cambridge University Press in 1998.

Maria Esther Vidal received a Bachelor of Technology in computer engineering (1988), a Masters in computer science (1991), and a Ph.D. in computer science (2000), from Universidad Simon Bolivar, Caracas, Venezuela. She is the first graduate of their doctoral program and her thesis received an Award of Excellence. She is an associate professor in the Department of Computer Science, Universidad Simon Bolivar. She was a research scientist at the Institute of Advanced Computer Studies, University of Maryland, from 1995 to 1999. Her research interests include mediator data models to describe the contents and capabilities of Web accessible sources (WebSources); cost models, query planning, and plan generation for WebSources with limited query capability; and locating WebSources based on metadata describing their content and quality of data. She has received the following honors: Recognition as an Outstanding Master's Student in 1991 from Universidad Simon Bolivar, and the Award of Excellence in 1991 from Fundacion Gran Mariscal de Ayacucho, Venezuela—this award is given to outstanding scholars in Venezuela.

Preface

In this 55th volume in this series, we present seven papers that present a variety of new technologies that will affect computer users and the general population alike, as computers take on an increasingly important role in our lives. Continuously published since 1960, *Advances in Computers* has presented the ever-changing impact computers make on our day-to-day living and has described the best new technologies that should affect us in the near future.

We begin with two papers that show the impact that computers have on our educational system. In Chapter 1, Linda Harasim writes on "The Virtual University: A State of the Art." The advent of the World Wide Web in the 1990's greatly changed the role of online education. Its ease of use made the Internet accessible to the general public, and its powerful graphic capabilities expanded the range of disciplines that could be offered totally or partially online. Dr. Harasim discusses urgent technological and pedagogical issues that must be addressed if the field of online education is to mature and to meet the high expectations of the population that expects to benefit by participating in it.

In Chapter 2, Neville Holmes writes on "The Net, the Web, and the Children." This chapter takes a slightly different view from Chapter 1. Rather than calling the World Wide Web a revolutionary development, he explains the Web as simply an evolutionary development of human communication and human information encoding systems. He makes the case that the use of the Net and the Web is associated with, if not assisting, the accelerating gap between the rich and the poor nations of the world, and between the rich and the poor within nations. Those most severely disadvantaged by all this digital technology are the world's children. They are also the ones that could benefit most, and suggestions are made for changes that could help bring these benefits about.

Continuing with the WWW theme, in Chapter 3, "Source Selection and Ranking in the WebSemantics Architecture Using Quality of Data Metadata" by George A. Mihaila, Louiqa Raschid, and Maria-Esther Vidal, the authors discuss some of the problems of using the Web effectively, especially how to find the information you are looking for. The World Wide Web has become the preferred medium for the dissemination of information in virtually every domain of activity. However, access to data is still hindered by the difficulty of locating data relevant to a particular problem.

In order to solve this problem, the authors discuss WebSemantics, a method for maintaining metadata about source content and quality of data. They use a data model for representing metadata similar to those used in a data warehouse environment.

Chapter 4 by Naren Ramakrishnan and Ananth Y. Grama entitled "Mining Scientific Data" discusses another aspect of discovering relevant information in large databases. The recent past has seen rapid advances in high-performance computing and tools for data acquisition. Coupled with the availability of massive storage systems and fast networking technology to manage and assimilate data, these have given a significant impetus to data mining in the scientific domain. Data mining is now recognized as a key computational technology, supporting traditional analysis, visualization, and design tasks. In their chapter, they characterize the nature of scientific data mining activities and identify dominant recurring themes. They discuss algorithms, techniques, and methodologies for the effective application and summarize the state-of-the-art in this emerging field.

Chapter 5, "History and Contributions of Theoretical Computer Science" by John Savage, Alan Selman, and Carl Smith, presents an overview of the contributions made by theoretical computer science. In most computer science departments in academia, students traditionally steer away from the "theory" courses and instead want to learn about the Web, Java, OO design, and other programming tasks. Theory is often viewed as too hard or irrelevant. However, theoretical computer science has had a major impact on practical computing concepts. In this chapter, the authors discuss some of the results that the theory community has made toward the more practical aspects of computing.

Chapter 6 by Ross Anderson, Frank Stajano and Jong-Hyeon Lee is entitled "Security Policies." With the growth of the Web and the concept of ubiquitous computing, there is a growing need to ensure that access to personal data is controlled and monitored. A security policy is a high-level specification of the security properties that a given system should possess. It is a means for designers, domain experts, and implementers to communicate with each other, and a blueprint that drives a project from design through implementation and validation. This chapter presents a survey of the most significant security policy models in the literature, showing how security may mean different things in different contexts.

In the final chapter, "Transistors and IC Design" by Yuan Taur, the author discusses the development of the computer chip. Everyone knows that computers seem to continually get faster and cheaper over time. In this chapter, the author discusses how this is being accomplished. The chapter focuses on CMOS transistors and their design principles, the basic building blocks of today's computer chips. After reviewing the evolution of CMOS transistors and why they now become the prevailing IC technology in the microelectronics industry, Dr. Taur discusses the elementary guidelines of CMOS scaling—the more a transistor is scaled, the higher becomes its packing density, the higher its circuit speed, and the lower its power dissipation.

I hope that you find these chapters of interest. If you have any further suggestions on topics to cover in future volumes, or if you wish to be considered as an author for a future chapter, contact me at mvz@cs.umd.edu.

MARVIN V. ZELKOWITZ
University of Maryland and Fraunhofer Center for Empirical Software
Engineering,
College Park, Maryland

The Virtual University: A State of the Art

LINDA HARASIM

TeleLearning Network of Centres of Excellence
Simon Fraser University at Harbour Centre
515 West Hastings Street, Time Centre, 7th floor
Vancouver, British Columbia V6B 5K3
Canada
linda@telelearn.ca

Abstract

Educational interest in the Internet is exploding among instructors, learners, and educational institutions internationally. The advent of the World Wide Web in 1992 was a watershed in the development of online education. Its ease of use made the Internet accessible to the general public, and its powerful graphic capabilities expanded the range of disciplines that could be offered totally or partially online (by enabling virtual labs, studios, animations, etc.). The invention of the Web thus coincides with the growth spurt in online education.

Nonetheless, there are urgent technological and pedagogical issues that must be addressed if the field of online education is to mature and to meet the high expectations of the population that expects to benefit by participating in it. Much of the online post-secondary education available at the end of the 20th century had been created piecemeal. Despite rapidly growing interest, proliferation of software rather than proof or evidence of the methods that produce the best results characterized the field. Knowledge about the most powerful pedagogical models and technological environments to support effective online education and best practice remained limited.

This chapter begins with a discussion of the state of the art of online education today, especially online post-secondary education. Then it focuses on the Virtual-U, a Web-based environment designed to provide a flexible integrated framework to support active collaborative learning and knowledge construction in a wide range of disciplines. The chapter describes the basic architecture of the system and the results of four years of Virtual-U field trials in 14 institutions with more than 450 courses taught by 250 faculty to a total of 15 000 students.

Finally, it describes alternative forms of virtual universities and issues in their implementation, while many university faculty and instructors are beginning to adopt Web-based instruction in their course offerings. Virtual universities are a distinct phenomenon. The discussion includes the implications of the Virtual-U results for the pedagogical and technological developments needed to establish engaging, effective, and productive virtual universities.

1. Introduction   2
   1.1 Traditional Distance Education Courses   4
   1.2 Interaction Using the Internet   4
   1.3 Attributes of Online Interaction   5
2. A Powerful New Phenomenon: Online Collaborative Learning in Virtual
   Classrooms   6
   2.1 Pedagogical Design   7
   2.2 Early Efforts to Use Education Principles in Networked Learning   8
   2.3 Early Findings in Networked Learning   9
   2.4 Technological Design: The Need for Software Environments Customized for
       Educational Use 10
   2.5 New Solutions, New Problems: Technological Cornucopia, Education
       Conundra 11
3. Canada's Virtual-U 15
   3.1 Virtual-U Research Base and the TeleLearning Initiative 15
   3.2 The Virtual-U 17
   3.3 Virtual-U Design Principles and Processes 18
   3.4 Spatial Metaphor 18
   3.5 Virtual-U Tools 19
   3.6 Results of the Virtual-U Field Trials 21
   3.7 Virtual-U Field Trials 21
   3.8 The Virtual Professor 21
   3.9 The Virtual Learner 22
   3.10 The Virtual Course 24
4. Establishing a First-Rate Virtual University 27
   4.1 Faculty Credentials 27
   4.2 The Role of the University and Faculty 28
   4.3 Pedagogies and Instructional Design 29
   4.4 Number of Courses and Class Size 30
   4.5 Costs 30
5. Defining the Virtual University: What It Is and Should Be 31
   5.1 Pedagogic and Administrative Models for a Virtual University 32
6. Conclusions: Implications for Pedagogical and Technological Developments 39
7. Research Directions and Questions 39
   7.1 VU Research Database 40
   7.2 VU DataMiner 40
   7.3 VUCat 41
   References 45

1. Introduction

Educational adoption of computer networking began in the mid-1970's, following closely upon the invention of packet-switched networks in 1969 [1] and of e-mail and computer conferencing in 1971 [2]. Many of the scientific researchers involved in early networking experiments, such as DARPA (Defense Advanced Research Project Agency), were also academics, and they began to use these new tools in their courses. The technological experimentation by these professors and their students coincidentally generated social and educational innovation: network technologies opened unprecedented new opportunities for educational communication, interaction, and collaboration.

As access to and use of these computer networks grew, the development of new applications contributed significantly to the emergence of the new field of online learning and helped to shape cyberspace into a human space, an area for social contact and knowledge building. Certainly the 1980's witnessed the rise of online education and learning networks at all levels of education, from public schools to colleges and universities, and its introduction into workplace training and programs for continuing education [3].

The online educational revolution is especially evident in the field of postsecondary education. It is driven by the tremendous public appetite for access to college and university programs created by the changing nature of work. More and more, an undergraduate degree is seen as basic certification for employment in the knowledge economy. Students, employers, and workers are recognizing the need for lifelong learning and continuing professional development as their jobs change. The availability of virtual university offerings that take advantage of the flexibility of the Internet is of particular interest to them.

This revolution comprises three interrelated trends—the rapid growth of online learning, the development of new corporate universities, and the extreme competitiveness of the job market (for employers as well as qualified employees) at a time of relatively low unemployment. International Data reported that in 1998 nearly 710 000 students were enrolled in at least one online course and predicted a figure of 2.2 million by 2002. Businesses large and small are beginning to see that internal educational facilities have the potential of training employees quickly and cost effectively and also of helping attract and retain more skilled individuals. Traditional universities and colleges will lose large numbers of students to new institutions unless they significantly alter their instructional methods to keep pace with developments spurred by the Internet. They must examine the educational undertakings of competitors (public, private, and corporate), understand their own strengths and reputation among the public, and customize teaching methods to the different age groups of students [4].

The customization of the Internet for educational delivery has enabled an entirely new modality of education to emerge—online education—profoundly distinct from yet clearly related to traditional distance and classroom education [5].

1.1   Traditional Distance Education Courses

In traditional distance education courses, learners receive a self-contained set of print materials by mail and then work alone on the course package and a set of assignments with a certain amount of access to a tutor by telephone or mail for clarification or further direction. Over the years, some of these courses have added elements such as broadcast radio, television programs, audio- and videocassettes, and CD-ROM multimedia disks. The use of teleconferencing or e-mail groups in some courses allows a degree of discussion and opportunities to connect with other students directly, but distance or correspondence education is essentially based on individualized learning. Distance education courses typically use the Web in a similar way. Students may receive and submit material and comments electronically, but the instructor is still operating on a one-to-one (individualized) or one-to-many (broadcast/lecture) basis, with limited opportunities for group interaction and collaborative learning.

D. Keegan [6] identified six key elements of distance education:

- Separation of learner and teacher,
- Influence of an educational organization,
- Use of media to link teacher and learner,
- Two-way exchange of communication,
- Learners as individualized rather than grouped, and
- Educators as an industrialized form.

Traditional distance education often has high dropout rates especially for those institutions with very flexible schedules for course completion. Studies show that they are related to the isolation of the distance learner and other socio-affective motivational issues related to individualized learning. Providing connections to their peers have been major factors in improving completion rates.

1.2   Interaction Using the Internet

The new network technologies have provided powerful new opportunities for teaching and learning at a distance. These technologies may be categorized by how their key attributes affect social interaction. Two main types of interaction divide the field, although each has several variations:

1.2.1   Same time/different place interaction

Same time/different place technologies (synchronous communication) include audio teleconferencing, audiographics, teleconferencing, video conferencing, and real-time chatrooms. While they vary in terms of cost, complexity of use, and type of technology employed, they all provide communication channels that link individuals or groups of people at multiple sites for live two-way communication and interaction. The educational approach is similar to the face-to-face lecture, except that students are at a distance from the lecturer and from one another.

1.2.2 Different time/different place interaction

Different time/different place (asynchronous communication) interaction refers to technologies that support or enable interaction among users (either instructor–learner or among the learners) at times that best suit them as individuals. Since the early 1980's, these technologies have been referred to as CMC (computer-mediated communication).[1] While e-mail is used widely in distance and online education activities, it is computer conferencing that provides the powerful many-to-many group communication element.

1.3 Attributes of Online Interaction

Computer conferencing enables communication or interaction best described as a form of discourse-in-writing.

Five attributes distinguish such communication in online educational environments and provide a conceptual framework to guide design and implementation of online course delivery:

- Many-to-many (group communication),
- Any place (place independence),
- Any time (asynchronicity, time independence),
- Text-based (enhanced by multiple media), and
- Computer-mediated messaging.

Electronic mail systems, even group mail services, make possible the first four characteristics; however, e-mail systems do not *organize* many-to-many communication. Computer conferencing was expressly invented for this purpose [2], and it excels as a groupware and enabler of collaborative

---

[1] Although the category can also include technologies that provide learner–machine interaction as in computer-assisted instruction (CAI), computer-based training (CBT), and so forth, it is the first, CMC technologies—e-mail, listservs, and computer conferencing systems—that are discussed in this chapter.

learning. Levinson [7] notes that subtle differences in technology affect the social educational environment: "The importance of social factors suggests that 'computer conferencing' may be a better name for the process than is 'computer-mediated communication'; the term 'conferencing' accentuates the inherent 'groupness' of this educational medium" (p. 7).

2. A Powerful New Phenomenon: Online Collaborative Learning in Virtual Classrooms

Since the early 1980's, university professors have experimented with different ways of conceptualizing, designing, and delivering courses online by computer conferencing. Their work has contributed toward the advance of a powerful new phenomenon: network-mediated online collaborative learning in virtual classrooms [3, 8–12].

Collaborative learning refers to an interactive group knowledge-building process in which learners actively construct knowledge by formulating ideas into words. They then develop these ideas/concepts as they react and respond to other students' comments on the formulation [13–18]. The instructor carefully structures the learning activities using defined social roles and procedures, and focuses on particular content and student work. Thus, knowledge building is the process of progressive problem solving whereby students are encouraged to create intellectual property and to acquire expertise.

Why have students worked together in groups? The underlying pedagogical rationale is based on the view that learning is inherently a socio-dialogical process and, hence, that there is a need for instructional environments and activities to promote discourse, exchange, and reflection. A vast number of studies involving both teaching and learning have examined ways collaboration is used in the learning process. The purposes of groupwork have ranged from providing variation in classroom activities and teaching students to cooperate and engage in productive and satisfying teamwork, to sharing the workload to enable large projects, to promoting peer tutoring and supporting constructivist goals and principles, such as sharing alternative viewpoints (multiple perspectives), challenging existing perspectives, and co-laboring to define various points of view and methods for identifying or creating the best of a variety of "right" answers [19–21].

Critical to all collaborative education is the question: How does the design of the pedagogy and the design of the technological environment best support collaborative learning? This crucial question is addressed in the next major section of the chapter.

2.1 Pedagogical Design

The five attributes of online education presented in 1.3 enable new teaching and learning options. They apparently offer almost unlimited methods of presenting virtual university courses, but they also place unique constraints on designing and managing the online educational environment.

Since the 1980's, computer conferencing has been a prime delivery environment for online post-secondary courses, and at present it remains the "heart and soul" of online education. Presumably a discourse focus will always exist, for education is essentially about interaction, conceptual change, and collaborative convergence.

Of all networking media available to educators in the 1980's and 1990's, conferencing systems were the most amenable to instructional design. Conferences could be thought of as "spaces" that could be shaped to form an educational forum. Structuring and sequencing the topics into an environment for educational interaction required significant input by the teacher. Just as in classroom education, online education required the instructor to organize the learning events according to topic, task, group, and timeline to support group discussions, activities, and assignments. However, the design requirements of the computer conferencing medium were different, in important ways, from face-to-face communication.

To illustrate, both formats support group communication exchange. However, for seminars, discussions, debates, and group projects to function online, they must be reconceptualized to fit within the attributes of the computer conferencing environment. In a typical group project, there are certain givens, such as a meeting or a series of meetings to plan and implement a task. However, an online group has different "givens." Its asynchronous qualities increase access and expand opportunities for discussion, interaction, and reflection. Increased access (temporal and geographical) and the motivation of working with a group can stimulate very active input by learners.

On the other hand, managing group tasks among team members located in different locations working at different times and possibly even different time zones and coordinating the workflows in a compressed time period is also a complex organizational challenge. Designs to structure and organize student input are clearly needed because the asynchronous and place-independent characteristics create problems of coordination and convergence. Some participants may lag behind others or even "disappear" for a time. Moreover, text-based discussion can be voluminous and soon overwhelm even an enthusiastic reader. The ability to organize messages and focus the discussion is important for managing the information flows and supporting a process of conceptual convergence.

2.2   Early Efforts to Use Education Principles in Networked Learning

Online courses use a variety of activities based on collaborative learning. Some may start and end with a set of plenary activities (i.e., full group discussions) to build the sense of group identity and community. They then use seminars, small group discussions, and group assignments to engage students in the course topics and to move from divergent to convergent processes of conceptual change.

Courses designed and offered in the mid to late 1980's at the Ontario Institute for Studies in Education (OISE) illustrate this approach. They were 13-week graduate level credit courses, with a limit of about 25 students (although some courses were considerably smaller and a few significantly larger). Topics leading into week one were designed as ice-breakers, such as conferences for self-introductions, setting personal and class learning objectives, and engaging in a "Great Debate" to initiate student interaction and to facilitate student comfort in the online environment. Thereafter, the online courses moved into a series of group discussions and projects related to the curriculum.

These courses employed a fairly complex instructional design; between 35 and 60 computer conferences and subconferences were used to create the environment over the course of a semester. The shape of the environment changed each week; one topical conference would close, as the conference space for the subsequent week's seminar was opened.

Conference spaces were also defined by the size of learning group. Plenary (full group) discussions were used to launch the course, so that students interacted with everyone, to create a sense of community. Informal conferences, such as the "course café" and "mutual help" were also designed as plenary sessions. In a large class (more than 20 students) or where there were distinct special interest or work groups, week-long small group discussions helped manage the volume. Group assignments and tasks had two to four persons per group. Dyads or learning partnerships were also used for online group work. In this design, two students are partnered either for a specific task/assignment or for peer support.

The OISE online courses were distinguished by active peer-to-peer discussion of ideas and exchanges of information. In them, students contributed 85 to 90% of the messages, a level of student participation and interaction high even for face-to-face graduate seminars. The collaborative nature of the conferences is also illustrated by the quality of the interaction. Analysis of selected contents of the online courses indicates that learners formulated positions and responded to their peers with active questioning, elaboration, and/or debate. Transcript analysis of online seminars and small group activities showed that students built on one another's ideas by posing and answering questions, clarifying ideas, and expanding on or debating points raised by others [22]. Message map analysis of interaction patterns in selected online discussions also demonstrated that students refer to one another's messages, adding on and building to the ideas posed [23]. Peer interaction, in which students are exposed to multiple perspectives on a particular topic as well as challenged by questions or requests to expand of their own ideas, is a valuable opportunity for knowledge building and developing critical thinking skills [18]. Online activities were found to facilitate such collegial exchange.

Online interaction thus displayed fewer of the extremes typical of face-to-face class activity, such as excessive or dominating input by a few and little or no participation by everyone else in the class. Online environments do not entirely eliminate domination by a few more vocal participants. What was new was that asynchronous conferencing ensured the air time for everyone to have input.

2.3 Early Findings in Networked Learning

Over a decade of research at OISE and elsewhere yielded valuable insights into the strengths and difficulties of using networks for online course delivery and course enhancement. System-generated data continued to show that students regularly contributed large amounts of original text, generating a rich database of information. Not only was the overall volume of messaging high, but it was also fairly evenly distributed among the students. Students attributed the increased participation to the expanded opportunities for access afforded by the asynchronous, place-independent environment.

Group interaction also motivated students. Student and instructor interviews emphasized that it was intellectually stimulating and fun and that as a result they worked harder and produced higher quality work online. Many online courses developed strong communities of friendship. Students also benefited from the exposure to a diverse range of perspectives in the group learning design: they read and considered input from all other students, rather than hearing only the ideas of the instructor.

In the early weeks of online discussions, students often reported communication anxiety and feeling "lost in space." Nonetheless, most soon learned how to direct their comments to the appropriate conference and reported increased confidence after 8+ hours of using the system. Having conferences for different topics and types of activities helped to orient students to the course curriculum and facilitated their navigation through the conferencing system.

These early field studies on networked learning and environments suggested that if participants form mental models of the "spaces" where they are working—the virtual seminar, the virtual project room, the virtual laboratory, the café for social interactions, and so forth—they will learn to apply appropriate "social factors" to their interactions [24].

2.4 Technological Design: The Need for Software Environments Customized for Educational Use

Nonetheless, despite research demonstrating the potential of net-worked technologies to support active collaborative learning and interaction [10, 15, 25], important problems with using generic network-ing tools like e-mail, computer conferencing, and newsgroups also became evident. They imposed significant overhead costs on the user because they were not specifically designed to support educational activities [12, 15, 26]. Instructors had to expend significant effort to reformulate their traditional classroom activities for the asynchronous communication spaces and then also "shape" the text-based computer conferences into "virtual" learning environments. This process involved substantial administrative, organizational, and pedagogical challenges and costs. Many experiments failed, and early enthusiasts were discouraged.

A basic key problem in using generic environments for educational purposes included the fact that they did not have easy-to-use integrated or integratable tools. Customized educational network environments were urgently needed with tools to:

- provide effective access and navigation and assist instructors in designing the curriculum for the Web environment;
- manage the course (calendars, gradebooks, easy uploading and downloading of multiple media files for all users);
- support cognitive activities that employed techniques such as message representation, visualization, and concept mapping; and
- provide group and personal work spaces.

A lack of tools to scaffold key learning approaches such as seminars, debates, role plays, hypothesis generating, and collaborative convergence was identified as a significant issue as well [15, 25, 25].

Discipline-specific tools were also needed to expand the types of course content that could be delivered over networks, especially in those fields that required lab and studio instruction, such as computer and engineering sciences, health, medicine, and the cultural and fine arts.

Hitherto, online education had been largely limited to discourse-oriented disciplines (the humanities, social sciences, education) or applications with significant focus on group discussions and written projects. In addition to circumscribing the disciplines that could participate in online education, the lack of multimedia capacity had limited development of tools to support new discourse patterns. The advent of the Web, with its ability to present graphics, sound, and animation, fueled an explosive growth in educational adoption of the Internet, both to augment face-to-face courses and to deliver courses totally online.

2.5   New Solutions, New Problems: Technological Cornucopia, Education Conundra

Ironically, the technological solutions provided by the Web also introduced new problems and exacerbated existing ones in the field of online education. While the invention of CMC had launched an unprecedented level of social interaction, communication, and collaboration, the invention of the Web fuelled an unprecedented level of publishing. Two basic models of learning thus emerged: one based on collaborative learning and interaction, and the other based on publishing information (posting course materials, lecture notes, student assignments, etc. online).

The former promoted online educational interaction and collaboration and developed from post-secondary applications of the Internet in the 1980's. Initially, many involved in online post-secondary education could be described as having a "build it ourselves" or "do it ourselves" attitude [27], and several universities are commercializing their home-grown systems. However, Dataquest, an IT market research and consulting firm and a division of GartnerGroup, has reported a decline in this trend: "Universities are moving away from home-grown electronic instructional systems and moving toward commercially developed systems" [28]. A very large pool of potential open source contributions among all of the home-grown educational software are within institutions around the world. Many of the authors of this software would be encouraged to contribute to a well-organized educational open source movement. This represents a large untapped potential for specialized educational software such as modules developed through university research projects. Difficulties with the home-grown approach became apparent as external costs accrued and it became necessary for the university (or sometimes a department) to become a publishing house, to provide user support, to invest in developing and testing, and to ensure that its system does in fact support state-of-the art pedagogies and effective educational delivery.

The second model, Web publishing, is based on the old paradigm of education—transmission of information rather than active and interactive construction of knowledge. Thus, many Web-based learning activities in the late 1990's were based on the lecture mode. Course materials were posted on the Web for students to download and to study on an individualized basis. This format is possibly more efficient than traditional correspondence distance education, but it falls far short of realizing the educational potential of collaborative learning and knowledge construction that the Web can offer the 21st century knowledge society.

So while technological developments and new opportunities have increased educational interest and adoption, the ratio of signal to noise is low. Ways of maintaining educational quality remain a major concern. Unfortunately, however, educators, university administrators, and the public must scramble to filter the facts from the hype, with little empirical evidence or guidelines to illuminate the issues. While early-state standards such as IMS (IEEE-LOM) are emerging for technological and educational accepted standards, these are inadequate for designing or selecting online education systems or course offerings. Currently, inferring "compliance" with these standards is simply a marketing exercise as interoperability of different so-called compliant systems cannot yet be established, and there are as yet few significant research results that can provide evidence of success and efficiency.

At the turn of the 21st century, the state of the art of Web-based learning is thus characterized by a proliferation of commercial products and services rather than distinctive educational progress, excellence, or advances. The marketplace is being flooded with toolsets with similar features and software where differences lie more in design than in use.

There is little distinctiveness or differentiation among commercial Web-based education software.

Web-based products intended for the general educational marketplace may follow the route of other content providers, such as undergraduate textbooks producers, in which a great deal of money is spent identifying and marketing to the average needs of the market rather than the real needs of individual courses and specific subject areas.

2.5.1 Open source and educational environments

An entirely new approach to technology development is suggested by the open source movement. Open source advances depend upon the willingness of programmers to freely share their program source code so that others can improve upon it. The Internet was itself the product of a process of networked collaboration. The source-sharing tradition of the Unix world was famous for its friendliness in allowing others to reuse the code. Linux (an operating system "produced" by thousands of programmers who collaborated over the Internet) has taken this tradition to its technological limit, with terabytes of code generally available [29, p. 33]. The open source code strategy holds promise for educational software development and distribution. Chief among its potential advantages is the possibility of encouraging innovations that will ignite the desire to create educational advances and push the envelope of educational opportunities.

In the commercial world, open source software is gaining momentum as developers begin to release high-quality applications for business-to-business e-commerce and other areas. Traditionally viewed as a cheap alternative to better applications, open source is now seen as a viable option even at the higher end. Companies are emerging with business models that aim to profit from it. E-commerce growth is expected to make open source software an important part of online trading and bring more business users to the open source movement [30].

Raymond [29] distinguished between the "cathedral style" and the "bazaar approach" to software development. The cathedral style assumes "a certain critical complexity above which a more centralized, *a priori* approach was required. It believed that the most important software needed to be built like cathedrals, carefully crafted by individual wizards or small bands of mages working in splendid isolation, with no beta released before its time" (p. 29). This approach, which characterizes most software development to date, is the opposite of Linus Torvald's open source style of development: "release early and often, delegate everything you can, be open to the point of promiscuity" (p. 30). Unlike the reverential cathedral building approach, the open source "Linux community seemed to resemble a great babbling bazaar of differing agendas and approaches (aptly symbolized by the Linux archive sites, which would take submissions from *anyone*) out of which a coherent and stable system could seemingly emerge only by a succession of miracles" (*ibid.*).

The cathedral approach has for the most part yielded "look alike" Web-based learning environments, all with a similar sets of basic tools and few distinguishing features except for the size of the marketing budget. Concern with market share has leveled the playing field: companies that have achieved a significant market share are now investing in marketing rather than innovation. Open source development requires a community mindset and budgets that are not primarily dedicated to sales. Open source innovators invite a far larger group of creative educators, designers, and technical experts to become involved.

There is nevertheless a significant risk in using the open source approach. Profound common and complementary social and technological motivations underlie online education and open source. This is very positive. At the same time, it is far from adequate. The potential for positive and negative is tremendous. As is discussed in the Conclusions, creating virtual universities requires much more than skill in technological design. The educational considerations must come first: How can and do these environments enhance cognitive activities?

2.5.2   Faculty concerns with online teaching

Many educators who strongly support face-to-face education have gladly updated unwieldy classroom equipment, replacing projectors with Power-Point presentations, mimeographs with photocopies, and typewriters with computers, and most appreciate having e-mail to supplement or replace inconvenient office hours and playing telephone tag with students and colleagues alike. Even those who use or recommend materials available on the Web only as enhancements to traditional classroom activities are generally aware that new online databases can greatly speed up and improve bibliographical and other searches, and so interest is expanding exponentially.

For many, the possibility of using the Web for course delivery, in part or whole, holds a powerful appeal. Students can work at a time and pace convenient to them and appropriate to the course; they can participate from home or work, or while traveling; they can actively engage with peers and with instructors to build knowledge and understanding collaboratively; and they can take time to reflect on ideas, compose their thoughts, and participate throughout the week, not just at set class times. Faculty appreciate similar access advantages and find not only that course materials can be reused but also that students can build upon the transcripts and discussion of previous classes, networking and constructing knowledge geographically, temporally, and historically.

Despite such possibilities, the majority of faculty members are still genuinely confused about what it means to adopt and adapt the Web for teaching purposes. The interest in enhanced learning opportunities is being clouded by political and financial battles that ignore educational issues. A heated debate has emerged with the two sides using broad brushstrokes to promote or condemn these technologies, and it has left faculty and educators confounded and bruised.

On one side are government and business, enthusiastic to achieve the financial savings they believe will accrue from using online learning. The opposite camp argues that the same technologies will debase the value of educational credentials and decries the creation of what they term "digital diploma mills." In fact, the promoters and the critics seem to share a common and naive view of online learning as machine driven rather than learning driven, with both sides focusing on the technology and ignoring the pedagogy. Both perceive online or network environments as monolithic, indistinguishable from one another, and apparently immune to different technological designs and instructional models, applications, and exigencies.

Many who hold negative views on online education are reacting to fears of job loss—some because they feel they cannot adapt to the new methods, others because they believe universities will hire more part-time, lower-paid instructors to implement online courses consisting of canned content designed elsewhere. Most faculty, however, are genuinely concerned with the social issue of equal access to education and with the quality of the evidence thus far produced on the results of online learning.

3.   Canada's Virtual-U

The goal of the system now known as Virtual-U (http://www.vu.vlei.com) was to provide a flexible framework to support advanced pedagogies based on principles of active learning, collaboration, and knowledge building that would employ various instructional formats, including seminars, tutorials, group projects, and labs. Its flexibility and focus on teaching and learning based on educational principles and research differentiate it from other virtual universities.

It is set apart from the traditional model of distance education in two main ways. First, courses are designed so that the instructor acts as a facilitator and moderator; students collaborate in gathering, organizing, and analyzing information. Second, students work asynchronously—that is, they do not have to be online at a specified time to take part in the class. Classes have scheduled times by which messages or assignments must be received, but students can prepare and send their work at whatever time of the day or night is convenient to them.

The Virtual-U is also unique in having a vast array of data available on the environment, courses, and tools it has produced.

3.1   Virtual-U Research Base and the TeleLearning Initiative

In the 1980's and early 1990's, research on online education emphasized participation—viewed as the *active writing* of messages—in educational computer conferencing. This work was important because students can and do generate a great deal of text-based collaborative discourse with important cognitive benefits. Writing online is supported by the tools available; producing messages is fairly straightforward.

At the same time, research suggested that although computer conferences supported divergent thinking (brainstorming, idea generation, and input), they did not provide specific means to achieve convergent thinking [25]. There were no tools, for example, to support *active reading*, which emphasizes retrospective analysis and thoughtful processing of the ideas generated and archived in computer conferencing systems. Such tools should be integrated with the conferencing system to support retrieval and organization of the stored archive.

The Information Manager prototype was developed in 1990–1991 to provide such an educational customization of generic computer conferencing systems by integrating a hypertext tool (HyperCard) to facilitate access to and reuse and reorganization of conference archives [22]. The purpose was to add educational value by customizing computer conferencing to facilitate active reading as well as active writing and, especially, to support the process of conceptual change through collaborative participation and convergent thinking.

In late 1993, the author joined forces with colleagues to design and embed various network learning tools that supported the adoption of the collaborative learning in online educational activities. This prototype took ideas from the Information Manager to a far more ambitious level, seeking to create a virtual environment by integrating some off-the-shelf tools with a conferencing system. A multidisciplinary research team of educators, HCI specialists, engineers, computer scientists, database designers, and instructional designers initially intended to produce a design based on networked workstations and a Unix server in order to provide multimedia components and an architecture, campus spaces, and tools that would help shape the environment specifically for online learning.

The result was the Virtual-U (VU), an online environment with tools customized to support instructors and learners in the delivery or enhancement of university courses. By 1994, with the dramatic developments of multimedia on the Web, the Virtual-U team decided to develop the Virtual-U as a Web-based system.

In 1995, the Virtual-U became one of the key research applications within the TeleLearning Network of Centres of Excellence (TL•NCE), http://www.telelearn.ca. This national collaborative program links Canadian researchers and client communities involved in the development, application, and evaluation of advanced education technologies based on collaborative learning and knowledge building. The TL•NCE supports a variety of large and smaller-scale projects related to telelearning research, development, and commercialization efforts. Virtual-U continues to participate in this collaborative program, contributing the largest known field trials of online post-secondary education in the world and, most recently, encouraging global partnerships and open source initiatives.

3.2   The Virtual-U

Virtual-U is a Web-based networked learning environment customized for post-secondary and/or workplace education (Fig. 1). It is a course management system that provides a framework for designing, delivering, and managing individual courses or entire programs.

Virtual-U is a cross-platform application, with an integrated set of CGI-based Web applications built upon industry-standard Web server architectures. It also supports all types of multimedia files, so instructors can choose to upload course resources that require specific plug-ins and/or client applications, even those with high bandwidth requirements.

Security is managed on the server. It authenticates all those who access the system from a browser and allows them custom access to the resources and utilities in the courses in which they are enrolled. This model also enables the application to maintain a consistent state on the server so that the participants' resources, personal options, and viewing preferences are carried with them as they access the Virtual-U campus from different computers.

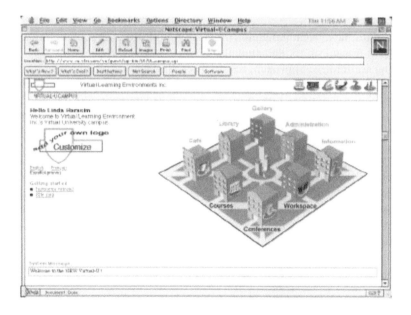

FIG. 1.

There is no need for multiple user IDs or access mechanisms. In fact, a person can be enrolled in one course as a student while participating as an instructor in another one. When they add content and/or messages within the VU environment, participants can also easily link to other WWW resources as well as to specialized VU resources and activities. They do not have to have any knowledge of markup language in order to interact with the system.

3.3   Virtual-U Design Principles and Processes

The development of the Virtual-U is based on designing a technology that supports advanced educational principles of collaborative learning and knowledge building. Unlike most commercial educational software available on the market, Virtual-U has a research base that directly informs its ongoing development. In 1996, the research project launched field trials to meet the following objectives:

- to develop and study state of the art Web-based technology for post-secondary online course delivery;
- to conceptualize teaching and learning models applicable to Virtual-U; and
- to illuminate models and methods for all instructors interested in utilizing the Web.

So far, data have been gathered from a corpus of 450 courses taught by 250 faculty to a total of 15 000 students.

Using an iterative approach, research results feed into the development of Virtual-U tools and drive the design of refinements that enhance learning and teaching activities. For example, research demonstrated the need for tools to assist instructors in conceptualizing courses and for learner support in how to conduct collaborative projects, how to analyze information from various perspectives, how to organize threads of an argument, and so on (Fig. 2). In response, VU developers are working on specific embedded supports to facilitate course design (by providing a case library of course exemplars and employing case-based reasoning tools), collaborative learning (by creating activity templates in VGroups), and knowledge building by different visual representations of VGroups (by using continuous zoom algorithms and visualization tools).

3.4   Spatial Metaphor

Until the invention of the Web, online learning environments were completely text based. Participants formed their own image of the virtual

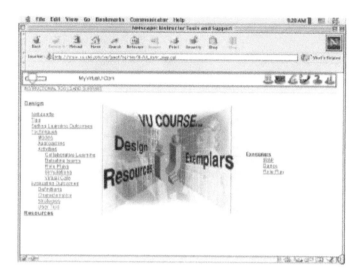

FIG. 2.

environments as they do when reading prose. With multimedia, it became possible to provide explicit orientation cues, both for navigating around the virtual environment and for setting social norms about the appropriate behavior expected in each virtual space.

In Virtual-U's spatial metaphor, users navigate using images of university buildings, offices, and study areas (see Fig. 3). While the key spaces are instructional, the Virtual-U environment also includes spaces for administrative activities, a library, social exchange (the virtual café), and other information resources (including a gallery).

Observations of the early versions of Virtual-U suggest that a spatial metaphor provided a sense of place and was thus a useful mental model to assist navigation. While it is helpful to new students learning how to navigate, more experienced users sometimes find it inefficient. Therefore, there are now four alternative ways of navigating Virtual-U and accessing tools: spaces (graphic imagery), a navigation map, menus, and a course control panel.

3.5 Virtual-U Tools

Virtual-U provides the following integrated tools:

VGroups conferencing system: An asynchronous communication medium that gives instructors or moderators the ability to set up collaborative groups easily and to define structures, tasks, and objectives. Any user can learn to moderate conferences and to create subconferences.

FIG. 3.

VU-Chat: A real-time (synchronous) communication medium that enables users to chat in "rooms" that they create for the purpose. VU-Chat allows multimedia to be incorporated in the messaging options.

Course structuring tool: Templates that prompt instructors for relevant information, such as weekly overviews, required readings, grading standards, and group conferencing assignments. The tool allows them to create courses without having programming knowledge.

Gradebook: Database of students' grades displays text and graphical representations of student performance, including personal grades and distribution of marks for evaluated activities.

Personal workspace: A home space where users can access their own calendars, course syllabi, and resources and upload or access their own files.

System administration tools: Functions that assist the system administrators in installing and maintaining Virtual-U, for example, creating and maintaining accounts, defining access privileges, and establishing courses on the system.

Upload features: Tools that allow instructors and learners to send multimedia files from their local machines to the Virtual-U server. Learners electronically submit their assignments, and the instructors organize and comment on these submissions.

3.6   Results of the Virtual-U Field Trials

The Virtual-U field trials are generating powerful data on instructional designs, impacts on instructor and learner workload, user satisfaction and practice, quality of learning, assessment issues, and student completion rates. The findings provide significant guidance in the design and implementation of more effective online education models and environments.

Evidence from instructors and learners alike confirms that the formal educational environment provided by the Virtual-U encourages more serious online course work. Instructors report improvements in their own teaching as well as in students' grasp of course concepts and their ability to write and talk about them at a deeper level. Students strongly value the frequent feedback and support from other students and the freedom to study at their convenience.

Elsewhere, educational adoption of the WWW is predominantly characterized by a casual "enhanced mode" in which students surf the Web for information. Virtual-U courses are distinguished by formal learning application of the Web for total or mixed mode delivery. Significantly, 26% of VU courses are taught entirely online, not by distance education institutions but by traditional universities and colleges, indicating a trend towards this new mode of delivery.

3.7   Virtual-U Field Trials

These data culled from the field trials have begun to create a composite picture based on empirical evidence. They are, admittedly, first steps and not conclusive results, but they do yield a profile of this emergent field, particularly some of the key successes and challenges, and some of the new roles and organizational forms that are being generated: the virtual professor, the virtual learner, the virtual classroom, and (various forms of) the virtual university. Below we synthesize selected data analyses.

3.8   The Virtual Professor

The virtual professor is an educator who actively chooses or prefers to teach online instead of or in addition to teaching traditional classes. Contrary to the general image of online instructors as young and male, we found that three-quarters of the professors adopting the Virtual-U were senior faculty and over one-third were female, and the majority taught in the social sciences, humanities, and health sectors, along with engineering and computing science. Their complaints generally related to workload and lack of technical support. These educators reported a powerful "rejuvena-tion" in their motivation and satisfaction with their accomplishments. It is clear that university administrators that decide to embrace online learning will have to find the resources to provide instructors with assistance from instructional designers, technical experts, and support personnel.

The instructors' major complaint was the high initial workload. They reported that online teaching consumed much more time than classroom teaching or distance education. A typical novice-to-expert learning curve was evident as instructors learned to deal with new expectations and demands. With experience, they became more comfortable. Both class-room instructors and distance educators reported that the second offering was somewhat easier and that the third offering required a "similar workload."

Instructors said they felt more intellectually stimulated because their online students were more engaged with learning and developed a sense of group. Several instructors reported better learning outcomes than in face-to-face classes. In their opinion, students produced better written and more reflective assignments because others provided a variety of perspectives. They felt that the conferences helped students grasp more concepts as they engage in more meaningful analyses. In addition, instructors believe that experience online with collaborative learning approaches improved their face-to-face teaching style.

Instructors reported major changes in their instructional roles as they moved from face-to-face to online modalities. Principally, instructors and students became more interactive when they moved from the one-to-many lecture model $(1-n)$ to the many-to-many group discourse model $(n-n)$. In particular, the instructor had to learn how to facilitate throughout a course rather than to lecture (and/or entertain) as students became more active. Therefore, the instructor became less of a provider and more of a participant as the students took more responsibility for generating input, references, and examples.

3.9   The Virtual Learner

Another new entity is the virtual learner, the student who prefers to take all or some courses totally online. Some choose this mode because they have family or job responsibilities, but many also prefer the enhanced interaction and educational quality that an online course can offer.

A large majority of the students surveyed reported satisfaction—more than 85% would take another online course—and the gender difference was insignificant (81% of females and 77% of males were positive about the experience). Students particularly appreciated the improved opportunities for peer interaction and communication, the increased control, and the ability to manage their time better.

The major problems students encountered were not related to their workload but rather to technical difficulties and slow network times. Many also experienced communication anxiety initially, that is, insecurity about the appropriateness of the messages they sent and whether they were sent to the appropriate "conference." Feedback helped alleviate student concerns as they gained skills and confidence in navigating the online classroom and learned its new socio-technical requirements.

Learning online, in virtual environments, dramatically changes the patterns of interaction and supports an unprecedented level of learner input, interaction, and exchange.

- Participation in an online or mixed mode course is 7 days/week, 24 hours/day (24/7).
- Students are typically very active in posting, reading, and responding to messages.
- Peer interaction is typically high.
- In face-to-face classes, instructors uses approximately 80%+ of air time; online, students input about 85% of messages.
- There is a far more equitable spread of communications among students than in face-to-face courses, but there were some differences among disciplines. For example, in humanities and health sciences, 50% of students sent 90% or more of the messages, while in business and statistics, 50% of students sent 65 to 75% of messages.

An in-depth analysis of 32 courses shows some differences in levels of user activity between totally online and mixed mode offerings, but overall, the level of student interaction and discourse is significantly high.

Of the 13 totally online courses with 18 instructors and 166 students, usage data analysis shows that:

- 85% of the students logged on 5 or more times per week.
- 77% of the students logged on at least 10 times per week.
- On average, students logged on 6.5 times and posted 3 messages per week.
- Distribution of communications is measured by percentage of the total message that is generated by the 50% of students who posted the most. The average distribution of communications is 72.3%.
- Peer-responsiveness is measured by the percentage of total messages that are reply messages. The average peer-responsiveness was 44%.

Even in mixed mode, the level of active student participation and interaction is significant. Analysis of usage data from 19 mixed mode courses with 28 instructors and 206 students shows that:

- 43% of the students logged on 5 or more times per week.
- 26% of the students logged on 10 or more times per week.
- On average, students logged in 4.5 times and posted 2 messages per week.
- The average distribution of communications for the 19 courses is 71%.
- The average peer-responsiveness of the 19 courses was 49%.

The high level of user activity suggests that environments such as the Virtual-U motivate students to actively engage in discourse and conceptual change, and contribute to convergent knowledge construction.

The level of student completion in the Virtual-U field trials has to date far surpassed that of traditional distance education offerings and that of online offerings by traditional distance education institutions and suggests that active engagement and collaboration motivates them.

Analysis of 36 online courses shows that Virtual-U course completion rate was 90%.

3.10   The Virtual Course

Virtual university courses offer an unprecedented new opportunity for enhancing educational effectiveness, by offering 24/7 access to peer discussion, collaboration, and knowledge building. Research indicates that collaborative learning has become widely adopted as the "webagogy" of choice. Collaborative learning characterizes virtual university course offerings. Nonetheless, it is more true of some designs than others, depending upon the instructional design and the importance of the Web to the course goals.

3.10.1   Collaborative learning

Of the 100 VU courses researched in depth, 100% incorporated collaborative learning approaches (discussion, group projects, debates, etc.).

Data on assessment strategies show the kinds of approaches that instructors employed in assessing the online learning activities.

- 21% of the courses had assignments completed in groups (e.g., papers or reports where a grade is assigned to a group).
- 48% of the courses used individual assignments (e.g., papers or reports).

- 25% of the instructors graded online participation (quantity and/or quality).
- 13% of the course grading schemes list process (e.g., cooperation, quality of development of issue) as a criterion. They exclude "participation" as measured in terms of quantity.
- 12% of the courses included exams in the grading scheme.

Virtual course activity is becoming ubiquitous; traditional lecture classrooms and distance education delivery are increasingly incorporating some type of online interaction. As a result, virtual coursework may be characterized by its use of one of three modes of delivery: adjunct use, to enhance traditional classroom or distance education; mixed mode delivery, in which a class employs networking as a significant but not total part of instructional activity; and totally online mode.

3.10.2 Adjunct use

Adjunct mode approaches can be a valuable enhancement to traditionally delivered courses, and they are a good way for instructors to begin to explore the use of Web-based learning. Adjunct mode typically refers to optional activities for students, although these activities may be formally integrated into the curriculum and form a small part of the grading process. This approach is the most widespread form of networking in higher education around the world. It is also historically one of the first educational applications of computer networks at the university level.

Adjunct mode use of networks allows students to communicate with their instructors and with other students outside of normal classroom or office hours for such purposes as encouraging research using the Internet search engines, accessing online resources, increasing access to instructors for "office hours," submitting and/or exchanging class assignments, and expanding opportunities for informal group discussion and social interaction. In distance education courses, networking is used to enhance tutor–learner contact, for educational support, information exchange, submitting assignments, and providing feedback. Networking also introduces opportunities for learner–learner interaction and collaborative learning approaches in distance education.

3.10.3 Mixed mode

In mixed mode delivery, the online environment is a principal (but not the only) environment for educational interaction. Mixed mode is distinguished from adjunct mode because networking is fully integrated as a significant portion of the curriculum, with up to one half or more of the activities and part of the assigned grades related to online work. Networking is used in one or more major assignments or activities, such as role plays, simulations, small group discussions or seminars, collaborative research, and group writing projects.

The use of online seminars in a face-to-face class is yet another illustration of mixed mode delivery. This approach has been used with undergraduate and graduate courses in communication at Simon Fraser University, Canada. Six weeks of a 13-week course are conducted online as student-led seminars; the other seven weeks are held as face-to-face lectures and tutorials. Online, students participate in seminar groups of about 15 people (there may be three or more such groups in a course). Six topics, one each week, are discussed in each seminar group. Students have two roles: as seminar leader for one week, and as seminar discussant for five weeks. As seminar leaders, students work in small teams, with one to two peers, to prepare and present the topic, moderate the discussion for a week (synthesize, focus, and advance the interaction), and summarize that week's activities and major discussion points.

While face-to-face seminars are often restricted to small classes of advanced students, the online approach has been valuable even with second-year students, encouraging active engagement in formulating and developing arguments and analyses. Online seminars enable all students to have a voice and participate: something not possible in a face-to-face classroom, even with small numbers, and certainly impossible in large undergraduate classes.

Student participation is distinct from typical classroom discourse, in which the instructor dominates most of the class. Not only is the overall volume of messaging high, but it also is fairly evenly distributed. Most students submit comments most of the time, sending several messages each week. A few students participate irregularly, sending few or no messages some weeks. However, in no case did a student not contribute at all during an online course.

In addition to enabling active learner participation and time to reflect before responding, students are positive about asynchronous weekly seminars because they motivate them to keep up with the readings and interaction with peers helps them think through the issues, but it is the opportunity to lead a seminar, while the most difficult and even intimidating, that students typically rate as the most enjoyable and best learning opportunity.

3.10.4   Online mode

Online courses use the Web or networks as the *primary* environment for course discussion and interaction. Course activities such as presentation of information, class interaction and discussion, and group work are undertaken online (although media such as textbooks, telephones, or even occasional face-to-face meetings may be integrated as part of the instructional design).

Simon Fraser University's *Dancing in Cyberspace* is a choreography course that introduces students to the creative potential of the virtual body in cyberspace. Students use *Life Forms*, a 3-D human animation software program, to explore human movement through experientially designed sequences. They use the Virtual-U learning environment to interact and collaborate on assignments, thereby increasing their ability to analyze and integrate the information.

- Students are required to purchase a *Life Forms* software package or use the *Life Forms* software also available in the SFU computer labs.
- Students must log on to the Virtual-U three times a week (for 30 minutes each time), to send messages, upload files (*Life Forms* animation assignments), post topics assignments, and read postings from class members and the tutor-marker/course supervisor.
- *Life Forms* assignment preparation and time for topics readings are independent of the log on requirement to the Virtual-U.

The online classroom is open 24 hours a day, seven days a week for uploading assignments, responses, and questions to class members and the tutor-marker/course supervisor at any time. Sessions are asynchronous (not in real time) and each lasts one week.

4. Establishing a First-Rate Virtual University

Now that we have reviewed the typical qualities of the virtual professor, virtual learner, and virtual course, we should summarize what it would take to establish a first-rate virtual university before looking at several existing models.

4.1 Faculty Credentials

The interest in enhanced learning opportunities is being clouded by political and financial battles that ignore educational issues. Both the promoters and the critics of online learning seem to share a common and naive view that it is machine driven rather than learning driven, with both sides focusing on the technology and ignoring the pedagogy. Many faculty who hold negative views on online education believe universities will hire more part-time, lower-paid instructors to implement online courses consisting of canned content designed elsewhere.

In many ways, university policy regarding the role of faculty will determine the level of public and academic acceptance or approval of virtual university offerings. A virtual university needs prestigious full-time faculty members who will provide opportunities for first-rate learning opportunities. They must be provided with professional status. For example, they should establish who will control the curricula and what the role of research will be, be able to attend academic meetings, and to do research and publish.

4.2   The Role of the University and Faculty

Bruffee [35] argues that the fundamental role of college and university education is to help students renegotiate their membership in the knowledge communities from which they come while assisting them to reacculturate themselves into the academic communities they have chosen to join (p. 231). The notion of discourse is central: "The point of departure is the notion of 'knowledge communities' itself and the ways in which human beings negotiate and renegotiate knowledge within and among those communities." Knowledge is viewed as a construct of the community's form of discourse, constructed and maintained by local consensus and subject to endless conversation and of learning as a social, negotiated, consensual process. T. Kuhn similarly argued that scientific knowledge changes as scientists revise the conversation among themselves and reorganize the relations among themselves [32, pp. 199–203, 209–10].

What in fact is the authority of colleges and universities and justifies their existence? Bruffee [31] points out that the stature and vitality of a university and the rationale for its establishment is a product of the authority of those who teach there. The authority, nature, and goals of post-secondary institutions thus depend on what professors and instructors think they know, how they know it, and what they consider knowledge to be:

> In every case, college and university professors ... are members of an authoritative community ... whom the community charges with the respon-sibility of inducting new members. In accepting this responsibility, professors set out to help students acquire fluency in the language of those communities, so that they become, if not necessarily new professionals, then people who are "literarily minded," "mathematically minded," "sociologically minded," and so on. That is, students learn more than disciplinary jargon. Their education is reacculturation involving intense, flexible linguistic engagement with members

of communities they already belong to and communities to which they do not yet belong [31, p. 154].

Bruffee goes so far as to argue that the survival of academic and professional disciplines depends upon this process of collaborative discourse among students and between students and the academic as a process of conceptual change, reacculturation, and collaborative convergence. "Knowledge communities cannot get along without members who are committed to teaching, because without teachers communities die as soon as their current members die. Their knowledge ceases to exist. When there are no new mathematicians, physicians, lawyers, and classicists, pretty soon there is not mathematics, medicine, law or classics" [31]. Turoff [33] argues that an institution cannot teach a subject one way to its regular students and choose to offer a completely different alternative to the distance students. "If a topic can be taught by software and there is no need for human communication, then it is no longer worthy of a university course, but is what we have commonly come to view as training and the acquisition of skills."

Hence the potential of a virtual university is not as a mechanization or automation of educational delivery but as an enhancement and advance to the profound civilizational discourse that represents and constitutes the university and the conversion of that knowledge community. The attributes of the virtual university imply many challenges but these might well be viewed as secondary to the unique and unprecedented opportunities for enhancing and expanding the discourse of knowledge communities and thereby profoundly contributing to the most fundamental role of faculty and the university.

4.3 Pedagogies and Instructional Design

Powerful, innovative, and proven pedagogies are critical for academic success and user satisfaction. Pedagogies based on advanced learning models such as collaborative learning and knowledge building are essential. The key to quality programming is faculty training and support in a virtual university webagogy: they must know how to design and develop online courses, how to deliver them, and how to engage learners in knowledge work activities. Also they must have the technical advice and assistance that allows them to focus on the courses themselves. Investment in significant and systematic training is currently almost nonexistent on most campuses where faculty are initiating online courses. This reality is perhaps the single weakest link in the investment chain for success.

4.4 Number of Courses and Class Size

About 20 different majors (400 unique course) or degree offerings seems to be the average at successful institutions, although the number of majors in a given area will vary greatly. The critical factor is having enough students in a given degree (even with multiple majors) so that the students can form a community and undertake various activities as a collaborative group.

Collaborative learning involves a class size of 25 or fewer in an undergraduate degree course (for one semester) or possibly fewer students in a shorter course timeline. Working teams should involve 3 to 7 students each, depending on the type and duration of the tasks, while group assignments may involve at least three to five teams in a class. In addition, a class of 20 to 25 students is likely to generate a reasonably active discussion. As students progress to upper division and to graduate courses, the critical mass for good discussion goes down as each student becomes more of an expert in the subject matter and has more inherent incentive to participate. Courses offered on a shorter time frame (6 to 8 weeks, rather than 13+ weeks) would likely benefit from small class size (8 to 12 students).

Research and field experience yield the same conclusion: the technology is not a mechanism for generating large class sizes nor for increasing the efficiency of the educational process. It is really a means of increasing effectiveness. This is not a message that administrators as yet understand.

4.5 Costs

Data show that success in virtual universities involves shifting funds from the physical plant to the faculty. Turoff [33] argues that the same investment that might be proposed for a new building on an existing campus could launch a virtual university that is made up of a faculty of far higher quality on average than that of most existing institutions.

The University of Phoenix Online found that success was possible and even profound, but that savings in the plant needed to be invested in learner support services and staff. The University of Phoenix Online has approximately three times the number of support staff than the physical University of Phoenix.

While specific network and computer architectural requirements and costs are outside the scope of this report, here we set out some general requirements to frame the overall vision. The educational model is one of small group learning entirely online, using a traditional semester model and tenured high-quality faculty. Costs for a cohort model or the use of part-time faculty are not included.

A ballpark figure is that the costs and effort required to set up a first-class academic program for 2 000 students with students and faculty collaborating from around the world would cost less than the addition of a single classroom building on a physical college campus (approximately $15 million Cdn). Costs include:

- Non-faculty personnel costs,
- Physical equipment costs,
- Computer equipment and software, and
- Faculty.

The costs presented reflect a teaching-oriented program, although the need for a virtual university to offer research orientation and graduate programming should be positively considered. The model proposed is based on offering three semesters a year (summer being a third semester) and allowing faculty to vary which of the three semesters they elect as vacation leave.

5.   Defining the Virtual University: What It Is and Should Be

Finally, this chapter examines what distinguishes existing virtual university model(s) according to the learning technologies and learning approaches employed.

What is not considered to be a virtual university here? The definition employed excludes approaches that emulate traditional lecture halls by using synchronous technologies (videoconferencing, real-time chat rooms) and/or traditional distance education and individualized machine-based approaches such as computer-based training (individualized self-paced learning), nor does it consider models that use the Web primarily for publishing instructional or student materials with perhaps some e-mail connection between faculty and student.

In this chapter, we consider a virtual university to be one that encourages the acculturation of students into the discourse of the discipline through interaction among peers and the professor. Students discuss, debate, and change their concepts, moving individually and collectively to increasing convergence with one another and with the larger knowledge community [35]. Typically, such convergences occur through collaborative discourse in online courses, via networks such as the Internet or Intranets, using asynchronous technologies, such as computer conferencing (First Class, Lotus Notes, Convene, etc.) or Web-based technologies especially customized for education (LearningSpace, WebCT, Virtual-U, etc.). These learning technologies enable and support active, collaborative learning approaches, and the software provides tools for:

- designing courses and developing an interactive course syllabus,
- conducting individual and group learning activities, and
- recording and accessing evaluations and grades.

Field research and practice demonstrates that substantial educational success is possible with a virtual university learning technology and approach, but it is related to pedagogical factors (appropriate instructional design, a learner-centered approach, and peer learning) [3], administrative investment and support (see [34]), and strong marketing (see [35]).

What should a virtual university model include and constitute? The virtual university must be viewed as high quality if it is to succeed in both meeting local needs and competing internationally. Today, any virtual university is by default global. Hence, issues of quality will be a key competitive advantage.

5.1 Pedagogic and Administrative Models for a Virtual University

A synthesis of emergent models for virtual universities includes the following:

- Prestigious virtual university: Group/semester model,
- Prestigious traditional and virtual university combo,
- Professional virtual university: Group/cohort model,
- Best of breed virtual university (networked), and
- Niche virtual university.

Before looking at these models, we should briefly compare them to the traditional university. Virtual and physical universities have unique attributes that determine major aspects of instructional design and delivery.

Table I below distinguishes them in a variety of aspects, but the key to the differences lies in the following:

- The traditional (physical) university is group oriented, synchronous (time dependent), place dependent, and multimedia oriented (although the core communication channel is audio-based).
- The virtual university is group oriented, asynchronous (time independent), place independent, computer mediated, and multimedia oriented (although the core communication channel is text-based).

TABLE I

Input	Traditional university	Prestigious virtual university	Professional virtual university	Niche virtual university
Philosophy	Students come to campus	Campus goes to students	Campus goes to students	Campus goes to students
Mission	Defined by level of instruction	Defined by level of instruction	Degree-centered, workforce focused	Workplace, professional focused
Curricula	Relatively stable and comprehensive	Relatively stable and comprehensive	More flexible, adult oriented, focused on workplace	More flexible, focused on workplace
Instruction	Most courses are lecture-based	Most courses are based on group learning and seminars	Courses based on group learning, use of student experiences	Greater variety of methods and use of student experience
Faculty	Primarily full-time academics	Primarily full-time academics	Usually part-time faculty with professional experience	Usually part-time faculty with professional experience
Learning technology	Enhances lecture-oriented instruction	Supports group learning and extended access	Supports group learning and extended access	May support some individualized as well as group learning
Physical facilities	Extensive physical plant	Minor physical plant (for non-academic staff)	Minor physical plant (for non-academic staff)	Minor physical plant (for non-academic staff)
Productivity outcomes	Student credit hours and degrees	Student credit hours and degrees	Student credit hours and degrees	Student credit hours and degrees

Note. The combo and best of breed virtual university inputs are the same as those of the prestigious virtual university.

5.1.1 Prestigious virtual university:
Group/semester model

A virtual university is like a physical university in its mission and educational processes. A virtual university offers a wide variety of credit courses that lead to a particular area of specialization and degree or diploma. It might offer only undergraduate programs or both undergraduate and graduate. The courses are taught by full-time academic faculty who engage with students to develop their expertise, skills, and understanding in specific bodies of knowledge and employ curricula, resources, and assessment of the learning processes and outcomes. Course credits are based on demonstration of mastery of the course objectives. Typically, participation in activities such as group discussions, seminars, debates, simulations, and individual and/or group projects, all mediated through the online learning environment, would characterize a virtual course. Hence, to a remarkable degree, the activities are similar to those in a physical university course, although they are mediated differently. Students in a virtual university typically interact with faculty, peers, and curricula through a computer conferencing system, which is integrated with other course design and course management tools in the virtual learning environment. Course resources may be online (readings, video clips, animations, graphs, spreadsheets, etc.) in the learning environment or in a CD-ROM or simulation software or offline, such as a course textbook.

The principal difference is student access. Students in the virtual university can gain access to the course(s) from anywhere, at any time convenient to them and appropriate to the course. They engage in the class discourse throughout the week, usually about three to five times. Students in the physical university engage in similar activities and assignments (with less peer interaction and collaboration), taking part in the class by traveling to a room in a building by public or private transportation at a specific time and for a specific time each week.

Nonetheless, it is essential to emphasize that ease of access should not be developed at the expense of quality of learning. The virtual university should not be regarded as "second class" or "last resort" learning options, a reputation that plagues most distance education providers. What is essential is the importance of real and perceived quality of learning, and access must mean access to active intellectual interaction and unparalleled opportunities for engagement and collaborative convergence.

To meet the criterion of quality programming, a virtual university must employ top quality faculty and instructional staff, produce high-level academic curriculum and resources, use group discussion and project activities for most if not all the coursework, produce demonstrable results, support research, and provide integrated coherent and cohesive degree/diploma programs, not just assorted courses.

5.1.2 Prestigious traditional and virtual university combo

In the combined traditional and virtual university model, a traditional university offers a complete or partial version of its programming entirely online. Students can take their degree entirely face-to-face or entirely online or through some combination. By the early 21st century, most universities offered some courses online, but most were undertaken as initiatives by individual faculty rather than having administrative encouragement or support. As a result, totally online offerings of a degree or certificate, together with requisite administrative and instructional support systems for students and instructors, are still rare.

Those that do offer totally online degrees or diplomas, such as traditional classroom, or distance and open universities that have moved into online delivery, are meeting a profound societal and economic need. An example is the University of Illinois Online (UI-Online). It is not a separate degree-granting virtual university. All of the courses, programs, and public resources offered under the UI-Online umbrella are grounded in the academic programs of the three campuses of the University of Illinois, "taught and managed by the same faculty and subject to the same quality controls. Although on-campus students occasionally enroll in UI-Online courses, these Internet-based programs are expected to primarily benefit a new, direct access to on-campus programs" [36].

It is important to note that UI-Online positions itself very strongly as part of the university's overall mission; the title of the article quoted is "UI-Online: The Realization of the 21st Century Land-Grant University." The focus is on high-quality service, and the programming is in strategic, visible curricular areas. Moreover, UI-Online is administered through the Office of the Vice President for Academic Affairs, and the initiative is thus supported at the highest academic level.

UI-Online is not an educational provider but an administrative enabler: it coordinates and helps to plan strategic online programming, but primarily it funds campus departments and colleges to create and manage courses and programs offered under the UI-Online umbrella. UI-Online also provides grants for faculty, departments, and colleges to acquire and support their own hardware or to purchase comparable services from campus-level providers.

In the combo model, the faculty of the virtual university are typically the same and teach similar course loads whether the courses are offered online or face-to-face. UI-Online, however, provides special grants to campus departments to cover one-time costs of converting existing campus-based programs to an online format. "These costs include faculty release time and summer salaries, employment of graduate and undergraduate assistants, compensation of programmers and technical support staff during the development phase, and purchase of hardware and software" [34].

This is a powerful model, and variations on the traditional–virtual university can be expected to become increasingly prevalent as universities seek to respond to demands for increased and flexible student access, to global market opportunities, and to local and global needs for knowledge workers. The virtual university component would not compete with but rather complement on-campus offerings.

5.1.3 Professional virtual university: Group cohort model

The professional virtual university is based on group learning. This is a basic tenet of adult education and online it is expressed in asynchronous group learning activity. In this way, it is very similar to the virtual university programming presented in 5.1.1 and 5.1.2 above.

However, it is distinct and innovative in scheduling. Rather than being organized in the typical three semesters, the offerings follow a continuous learning cycle. As soon as the requisite number of students register, the "bus" leaves the station, and the next "bus" pulls in. This delivery sequence primarily targets working adults who need the ease of entry for course progression and who prefer a concentrated period of course activity (6 to 8 weeks), taking perhaps two to three courses at a time, rather than the traditional route of five courses per 12-week semester with months between course offerings.

There are other differences in the organization of the professional (working adult-oriented) university, in both distance education and virtual mode. They tend to employ part-time professional faculty and offer a centralized curriculum. Their working professional adult students seem to agree that the curriculum is as good as if not better than that in traditional universities.

This is especially true in adult and continuing education, as the following example illustrates:

> Dr. Raye Bellinger, a cardiologist who manages a seven-physician practice in Sacramento, CA, has gone back to school without abandoning his business. He signed up for a University of Phoenix M.B.A. over the Internet, paying his fees by credit card. On the first day, he logged on and downloaded the syllabus

(textbooks available for purchase over the Internet). He also read his professor's lecture on technology management. A week later, he handed in his first assignment—a 13-page paper on his practice's patient management system. "They insist that you write about things you are doing in your own job," says Bellinger.

He then posted his paper to a class forum and over the next several days got responses from both classmates and his professor. Think of the system as a time-shifting classroom where students discuss topics as their schedules permit [37].

Arguments flourish as to whether professional and working adults benefit from a "profession" practice-based curriculum and faculty. Some argue that institutions employing part-time faculty represent an academic sweatshop where underpaid lumpen intellectuals slave for a pittance. Others respond that most faculty in these institutions hold a master's or doctoral degree and that some do research and publish books and papers.

However, in this model most instructors, like their students, have full-time jobs in the professions they teach, and they argue that this keeps them in touch with current issues and trends in their specialties. Accounting courses, for instance, are taught by practising CPAs. Finance courses are taught by MBAs. For these faculty, teaching is a source of extra income or stimulation.

Academic scholarship may or may not be distinct from professional knowledge building, but certainly arguments can be made that more flexible learning opportunities are worthy of consideration.

Whether tenured faculty would accept teaching in continuous cycles is not known.

5.1.4 Best of breed virtual university: Network or consortium model

This is a model in which selected universities and education providers collaborate to provide courses and/or programs for the lifelong learning market.

A critical issue is whether "name brand" universities would choose to collaborate with lower level universities, which they might consider a dilution of the overall brand and perception of quality. It is most likely that top international universities will employ models 1 and 2; that is, they will provide their own prestigious virtual university offering. They will (try to) go it alone!

So, how can consortia among top-level universities be encouraged? What is the value-added? This is not an easy question to answer and requires further study. However, there seem to be major benefits in terms of leveraging of scarce resources for technological infrastructure, faculty training, support, curricular integration, and so on, especially in settings where academic institutions and populations are small.

The advantages of this model include the following:

- Linking "best of breed" university providers encourages a collaborative rather than competitive model,
- Most universities have fewer resources and faculty than top or even middle level U.S. universities. Networking and leveraging is therefore essential for such universities if they are to participate effectively in online offerings,
- There are significant cost savings in linking the best in specified fields, and undertaking common marketing, training, and other initiatives,
- Students appreciate the ability to select minors from a variety of programs, and
- Faculty can share experiences, leverage successes and resources, and so forth.

Some disadvantages include the following:

- Motivating the best to participate may be difficult,
- Demonstrating value of involvement to top institutions is a challenge, and
- Persuading political forces to support cross-boundary networking can be a difficult challenge.

Requirements include the following:

- Ensuring value-added, i.e. common credentialing, common user interface, and tracking of credits,
- Ensuring common approaches: common user interface, common pedagogical approaches, and common technologies, at least at the department/discipline level, and
- Ensuring common resources: training certification, and technical and pedagogical support.

5.1.5 Niche Virtual University

The niche virtual university may fit into any of the other models, although it is most likely to be found in smaller traditional universities with departments or faculties that are widely known for distinctive programs and high achievements. It is distinguished by the focus on discipline/market distinction and need and often targets mid-career working adults. A niche VU targets specific areas of high demand, for example, public service education, information technology areas, continuing medical (and/or health) education, telecommunications engineering, business administration, and computer science.

6. Conclusions: Implications for Pedagogical and Technological Developments

Online education can equal or surpass the satisfaction and effectiveness of face-to-face instruction, but the environment is sensitive, and the enormous financial savings in physical plant must be reinvested—at least initially—in significant learner support.

University programs and policies must enshrine principles of quality educational programming and delivery in online programming by:

- Ensuring the professional status of faculty;
- Ensuring that the virtual university is client- or learner-centered, not faculty-centered, and that the focus is on teaching excellence and accessibility;
- Addressing issues of quality seriously by investing significant and adequate funding for faculty, training, and technology; and
- Deliberately seeking out prestigious faculty and providing higher wages to attract and keep the best minds (which could reverse the brain drain) and support the view that the virtual university is an attractive and prestigious alternative to the physical university.

Online education that adheres to these principles can help address the three challenges for higher education identified by S. Ehrmann [38]:

1. Accessibility, especially how to reach and educate the full range of adults who deserve a chance at an education, despite their location, schedules, cultural differences, or physical disabilities;
2. Quality, especially learning for the 21st century: how to improve the life chances of each of their adult learners, as individuals and as members of economic, cultural, and political communities; and
3. Dealing with the first two challenges when money and political support are in short supply.

7. Research Directions and Questions

The findings on user activity raise important research questions related to the impact of instructional design on when, how, how much, and which students participate and/or interact. By providing full transcripts of the user discourse and usage statistics and conference headers, Virtual-U online courses enable far deeper study of educational interactions, progress, and the relationship between factors such as instructional design, role of the moderator, and student activity. Virtual-U researchers and developers have identified three key methodologies and tools to advance understanding of teaching and learning online. The first two are researcher tools, while the third (VUCat) is a tool that has been customized to enable VU users to track online course activities from many perspectives.

7.1   VU Research Database

The VU Research Database has been designed to host various types of data related to VU courses, enrollment, users, VU field sites, and administration. It also hosts computer-generated usage data and research results. Its purpose is to provide easy and accurate information retrieval and updates and to support research inquiries, course and field site management, and VU system administration.

Features include the following:

- It is a distributed database system, containing a set of databases hosting different categories of data.
- It has built-in forms for easy data entry.
- It has predefined queries for routine calculations and information retrievals.
- A data warehouse is built on top of the database to support structured and/or ad hoc queries, analytical reporting, and decision support.

Ways it is/can be used include the following:

- as a research data bank,
- as a repository storing historical data and data analysis results,
- for data update and retrieval, and
- to support structured and ad hoc queries.

7.2   VUDataMiner

Using current technology, VUDataMiner provides VU researchers with a powerful tool to study user behavior and various aspects of teaching/learning processes. They can examine the communication, participation, and interaction patterns among students and the instructors, and their trends over time. In addition, it provides system administrators and designers with a tool for monitoring and optimizing system performance.

Features include the following:

- Basic summary: It produces summary statistics and provides views of the results from different perspectives. For example, it can give the descriptive statistics of the participation of a class in terms of total number of logins and messages written per day of the week or per hour of the day.
- Classification analysis: It builds a model for each class based upon features in the log data and generates classification rules from such models. For example, the classification of user groups according to their different navigation behavior can help refine the user interface.
- Association analysis: It discovers association/dependency relationships from a set of data. For example, some access patterns may be associated with certain user characteristics.
- Time-series analysis: Analysis of data collected along time sequences assists discovery of time-related patterns, characteristics, trends, similarities, periodicity, and so on.
- Data visualization: It gives graphical data display for effective interpretation.

Ways it is/can be used include the following:

- to provide in-depth analysis of user behavior, especially in conjunction with other discourse analysis methods (e.g., latent semantic analysis),
- to set up a typical user model, and
- to discover usage and access trends over time.

7.3   VUCat

VUCat stands for VU course analysis tool. This tool provides online instructors with a window for monitoring students' participation and their contribution in different parts of a course and their performance in a course as a whole. It provides basic statistics of individual student or group performance.

Features include the following:

- Table summary of the number of logins, postings, and total time spent for individual students or group of students,
- Access statistics on individual conferences and/or a complete course, and
- Graphical display of summary data.

Ways it is/can be used include the following:

- to help the instructors recognize where and when students participate,
- to inform individual students who are behind in a discussion or activity,
- to identify individual students who might be encountering technical and/or learning difficulties and provides them with help, and
- to provide a means of formative evaluation of student performance.

Future plans for research and development of the Virtual-U build on the findings to date and are interrelated with the larger national research program of the TeleLearning Network of Centres of Excellence.

- Develop structures and templates to scaffold and study the use of advanced pedagogy by continuing research into models of collaborative learning, creating a case library of knowledge objects and course exemplars, and developing tools that will provide for measures of different dimensions of online learning.
- Conceptualize, implement, and evaluate tools to support the management of instruction and collaborative learning; research and prototype tools to facilitate progressive group communication, problem-solving, and instructional design and organization of group learning. Prototype tools that scaffold and support knowledge-building processes, organize discourse into meaningful knowledge spaces by users, and visualize discourse from multiple perspectives, as well as support annotation.
- Validate and customize advanced research tools and methods related to discourse analysis and data mining. Adapt or develop and implement researcher and instructor level tools that collect and analyze computer-generated usage data, conference transcripts, online polling data, capture of user interactions with interface via keyboard and mouse, and virtual artifacts.
- Develop advanced technology testbed for software platform research, enabling integration of distributed objects and XML experimentation for user interface development. This open architecture will allow institutions and educational software developers to enhance or extend the core Virtual-U functionality by integrating custom software components. This will also enable cutting-edge research and development projects that concentrate on more specialized areas of online education to easily integrate within an entire online educational framework.
- Study user interaction in virtual learning environments by evaluating and refining the user interaction aspects of new pedagogical tools for

presentation of content as they are developed and tested in the "Advanced Testbed" before inclusion in the working version of Virtual-U. Address the question of what constitutes an engaging and effective virtual learning environment (VLE) by building on other research on virtual environments to investigate what features or scaffolds can enhance (and hasten) engagement in different environments and how engagement relates to learning.

● Address delivery and quality aspects to determine what system resources are required to successfully operate a Virtual-U course or program by performance analysis. Improve the performance of multimedia delivery, such as streaming video, when the users access the system via connections with different bandwidth capabilities. The project continues to investigate how telelearning applications such as Virtual-U function in networked environments. The intent is to evaluate the quality of service (QoS) obtainable with different course parameters, network configurations, and network protocols. This method allows us to determine where the bottlenecks in the system performance are and to predict the system capacity. We can also predict the effect on the system performance of adding more (perhaps a lot more) multimedia content and users to online courses.

In order to serve the client community properly, it is critical that the telelearning environment support network connections at a variety of speeds. Techniques for dealing with requests for content at differing resolutions will be investigated. The project will compare techniques such as embedded coding and multiple resolution representation and look at tradeoffs such as storage requirements and processing delays at the server.

We will also study ways of layering and prioritizing different media (text, audio, images, and video) so that information can be transmitted seamlessly as link capacities change. We will evaluate the effectiveness of the different strategies through computer simulation (QoSim) and user tests on the Advanced Testbed platform. The system will be integrated into a "multimedia-rich" Virtual-U. We will also test Internet protocols that allow intermediate nodes to throw away low-priority data when congestion is detected or there is a local low-speed connection.

Finally, we consider the issue of open source development as a strategy for Virtual-U and other telelearning software. One of the major challenges of telelearning software development has been the cost of commercialization, whereby interesting and important innovations are arrested by unending need to address the specific needs of current and potential users. Open source suggests a possible way of transcending this conundrum.

Raymond [29] identifies this as a core issue distinguishing cathedral building from the open source bazaar style:

> In the cathedral-builder view of programming, bugs and development problems are tricky, insidious, deep phenomena. It takes months of scrutiny by a dedicated few to develop confidence that you've winkled them all out. Thus the long release intervals, and the inevitable disappointment when long-awaited releases are not perfect.
>
> In the bazaar view, on the other hand, you assume that bugs are generally shallow phenomena—or, at least, that they turn shallow quickly when exposed to a thousand eager co-developers pounding on every new release. Accordingly you release often in order to get more corrections (p. 42).

Raymond goes on to note that this large group approach was much the same as the "Delphi approach" discovered many years ago by sociologists. The Delphi effect occurs when group input is averaged, and successive representations ultimately yield a convergence, a common set of responses. "It appears that what Linus has shown is that this applies even to debugging an operating system—that the Delphi effect can tame development complexity even at the complexity level of an operating system kernel" (p. 42).

It is noteworthy that the so-called "Linus Law" builds upon a social tenet that earlier generated the technology of computer conferencing, which this chapter has termed as the "heart and soul" of online education and virtual universities. The motive force behind the invention of computer conferencing, according to Turoff, was to extend and enable nation-wide Delphi methods, using computer networks [39]. Turoff's first online Delphi system, Emisari, was the prototype for his conferencing system.

Opportunities and challenges will occur as computer scientists and learning scientists begin collaborating to create new learning environments and supports. Raymond notes that in the open source movement "every good work of software starts by scratching a developer's personal itch" [29, p. 32]. Yet he also advises programmers that "treating your users as co-developers is your least-hassle route to rapid code improvement and effective debugging" (p. 37). This comment is especially true for applications developers, most of whom have had little or no experience with open source approaches. Working with other developers is not only about reducing "hassle"; it is also about enabling powerful advances and solutions that take into account programming expertise and the equally critical subject/application area knowledge.

Frameworks for collaboration are necessary preconditions for building effective online environments, especially as applied to education. First, open source approaches recognize that one cannot originate a project, that is, code, from the ground up in bazaar style. The open source "nascent developer community needs to have something runnable and testable to play with. When you start community-building, what you need to be able to present is a plausible promise. Your program doesn't have to work particularly well. It can be crude, buggy, incomplete, and poorly documented. What it must not fail to do is (a) run, and (b) convince potential co-developers that it can be evolved into something really neat in the foreseeable future" [32, pp. 57–58].

It is perhaps here where educational research and online educational tools and environments can begin to interface with open source programmers. A number of possibilities exist. Here are some examples from the Virtual-U situation.

- Modularize and release existing parts of the Virtual-U software as open source, with documentation.
- Release partially complete (post-prototype) tools, such as VUCat and VUDataMiner.
- Release incomplete (preprototype) tools, with conceptual frameworks and materials and design specifications. These releases might include course activity templates and learning assessment tools.

In the above examples, the tools would have significant evidence-based design based on advanced educational principles and extensive research, and thus they would provide a powerful potential framework for collaboration. Such a framework would support principled design by both programmers and educators and thereby catalyze a wave of solid online educational invention and innovation.

The creation of "good work" in online learning environments is an immense programming challenge, but it is an equally profound educational one. If it can be solved, it will be the result of educators and programmers learning to communicate and collaborate on this invitation to alter our civilization's method of education.

REFERENCES

[1] Hafner, K. and Lyon, M. (1996). *Where Wizards Stay up Late: The Origins of the Internet.* Simon and Shuster, New York.
[2] Hiltz, R. and Turoff, M. (1978). *The Network Nation: Human Communication via Computer.* Addison–Wesley, Reading, MA.
[3] Harasim, L., Hiltz, R., Teles, L. and Turoff, M. (1995). *Learning Networks: A Field Guide to Teaching and Learning Online.* MIT Press, Cambridge.
[4] *Financial Times*—Business Education, 3 April 2000.
[5] Harasim, L. (1989). "Online education: A new domain". In *Mindweave: Computers, Communications and Distance Education* (R. Mason and T. Kaye, Eds.), pp. 50–62. Pergamon Press, Oxford.

[6] Keegan, D. (1980). "On defining distance education". *Distance Education*, **1**(1), 13–36.

[7] Levinson, P. (1990). "Computer conferencing in the context of the evolution of media". In *Online Education: Perspectives of a New Environment* (L. Harasim, Ed.), p. 7. Praeger, New York.

[8] Hiltz, R. and Wellman, B. (1997). "Asynchronous learning networks as a virtual classroom". *Communications of the ACM*, **40**(9), 44–49.

[9] Bradsher, M. (1996). "Making friends in the global village: Tips on international collaborations". *Learning and Leading with Technology*, **23**(6), 48–50.

[10] Hiltz, R. (1994). *The Virtual Classroom: Learning without Limits via Computer Networks*, Human–Computer Interaction Series. Ablex, New Jersey.

[11] Khan, B. (1997). *Web-Based Instruction*. Educational Technology, Englewood Cliffs, NJ.

[12] Feenberg, A. (1993). "Building a global network: The WBSI executive education experience". In *Global Networks: Computers and International Communication* (L. Harasim, Ed.). MIT Press, Cambridge.

[13] Anderson, S., Rolheiser, C. and Bennett, B. (1995). "Confronting the challenge of implementing cooperative learning". *Journal of Staff Development*, **6**(1), 32–39.

[14] Bouton, C. and Garth, R. Y. (1983). *Learning in Groups: New Directions in Teaching and Learning*, p. 14. Jossey-Bass, San Francisco.

[15] Harasim, L. (Ed.) (1993). *Global Networks: Computers and Communication*. MIT Press, Cambridge.

[16] Sharan, S. (1980). "Cooperative learning in small groups: Recent methods and effects on achievement, attitudes, and ethnic relations". *Review of Educational Research*, **50**(2), 241–271.

[17] Slavin (1983). *Cooperative Learning*. Longman, New York.

[18] Webb, J. (1989). "Peer interaction and learning in small groups". *International Journal of Educational Research*, **13**(1), 21–29.

[19] Cunningham, D. J., Duffy, T. and Knuth, R. (1993). "The textbook of the future". In *Hypertext: A Psychological Perspective* (C. McKnight, A. Dillon and J. Richardson, Eds.), pp. 19–50. Forwood, Colchester.

[20] Savery, J. R. and Duffy, T. M. (1995). "Problem-based learning: An instructional model and its constructivist framework". *Educational Technology*, **35**(8), 101–112.

[21] Sharan, S. and Sharan, Y. (1992). *Expanding Cooperative Learning Through Group Investigation*. Teacher's College Press, Columbia University, New York.

[22] Harasim, L. (1991). "Designs and tools to augment collaboration in computerized conferencing systems". In *Proceedings of the Hawaiian International Conference on Systems Science*, Vol. 5, pp. 379–385.

[23] Winkelmans, L. C. (1988). *Educational Computer Conferencing: An Application of Analysis Methodologies to a Structured Small Group Activity*. Unpublished M.A. thesis, University of Toronto.

[24] Feenberg, A. (1990). "Social factor research in computer-mediated communications". In *Online Education: Perspectives on a New Environment* (L. Harasim, Ed.). Praeger, New York.

[25] Harasim, L. (Ed.) (1990). "Online education: An environment for collaboration and intellectual amplification". *Online Education: Perspectives on a New Environment*, pp. 39–66. Praeger, New York.

[26] Smith (1988). "Teaching special relativity through a computer conference". *American Journal of Physics*, **56**(2), 142–147.

[27] Bacsich, P. (1997). "Re-engineering the campus with web and related technology for the virtual university: Insights from my work in Europe analysed in the context of developments in the US". School of Computing and Management, Sheffield Hallam

University, Sheffield, UK. Available at http://www.cms.shu.ac.uk/public/events/flish97/bacsich-paper.htm.

[28] Business Wire, 15 June 1999; www.businesswire.com.

[29] Raymond, E. S. (1999). The Cathedral and the Bazaar, pp. 32, 33, 37, 42, 57, 58. O'Reilly, Sebastopol.

[30] Investor's Business Daily, 19 June 2000.

[31] Bruffee, K. A. (1999). Collaborative Learning: Higher Education, Interdependence, and the Authority of Knowledge, 2nd edn., pp. 154 and 231. Johns Hopkins Univ. Press, Baltimore.

[32] Kuhn, T. (1970). The Structure of Scientific Revolutions, 2nd ed., pp. 199–203, 209–210. Univ. of Chicago Press, Chicago.

[33] Turoff, M. (1997). "Costs for the development of a virtual university". Journal of Asynchronous Learning Networks, 1(1). Available at URL: http://www.aln.org.

[34] Oakley II, B. (1998). UI-OnLine: Status report. A report for the University of Illinois, Bloomington, IL. Available at http://www.online.uillinois.edu/annual_report/index.html.

[35] Massey, C. and Curry, J. (1999). Online post-secondary education: A comparative analysis. A report for Industry Canada, Ottawa, Canada.

[36] Manning, S., Oakley II, B. and Ward, L. (1998). UI-OnLine: The realization of the 21st century land-grant university. A report for the University of Illinois, Bloomington, IL. Available at http://www.online.uillinois.edu/about.uionline.html.

[37] Gubernick and Eberling (1997). "I got my degree through e-mail". Forbes Magazine Inc., June.

[38] Ehrmann, S. C. (1994). Responding to the triple challenge: Facing post-secondary education: Accessibility, quality, costs. A report for the Organization for Economic Cooperation and Development, Center for Educational Research and Innovation. Washington, DC.

[39] Turoff, M. (1996). Alternative futures for distance learning: The force and the darkside. Available at URL: http://eies.njit.edu/~turoff/Papers/darkaln.html.

The Net, the Web, and the Children

W. NEVILLE HOLMES

School of Computing
University of Tasmania
Launceston 7250
Australia

Abstract

The Internet and the World Wide Web are explained as simply evolutionary developments of human communication and human information encoding systems. A case is made that the use of the Net and the Web is associated with, if not assisting, the accelerating gap between the rich and the poor nations of the world, and between the rich and the poor within nations. Those most severely disadvantaged by all this digital technology are the world's children. They are also the ones that could benefit most, and suggestions are made for changes that could help bring these benefits about.

1.	Introduction	50
2.	The Net	51
	2.1 Origins	51
	2.2 Recent Development	56
3.	The Web	57
	3.1 Origins	58
	3.2 Books	60
	3.3 The Advance of the Web	63
4.	The Future	64
	4.1 The Future of the Net	65
	4.2 The Future of the Web	69
	4.3 The Future for Children	73
5.	The Children	75
	5.1 The Politics	76
	5.2 The Net	77
	5.3 The Web	80
6.	Conclusion	81
	References	82

1. Introduction

In this chapter it is my purpose to discuss three of the most important features—perhaps aspects would be a better term—of our present civilization, to draw attention to certain disturbing trends in the development of each, and to consider the possible methods of reversing those trends.

The first of my three aspects is the technology of *immediate* communication. This technology that was born when spoken language was first developed and is now most splendidly evident in the Internet. This Internet is now so pervasive in the technologically favored fraction of our civilization, from which the readership of this book is drawn, that I am in no danger of being misunderstood if I simply call it "the Net" from here on.

The second of my three aspects is the technology of *delayed* communication, a technology that was born when written language was first developed and that is now flourishing as the World Wide Web. Again, the World Wide Web is well enough known to my readers here that I can safely call it merely "the Web."

The Web is extremely useful because the Net makes it so immediately available, but the two entities are quite distinct. The technology underlying the Net is that of digital communications. The technologies underlying the Web are those of the encoding of information as digital data, and of the storage and retrieval of digital data.

The third of my three aspects is not technological, but social. My third aspect is our children—that part of the world's population that is, by reason of their recent birth, more or less completely dependent on, and shaped by, the rest of the population.

My overall thesis is simply that the world's children being, and always having been, the most significant part of its population, the Net and the Web could be of enormous benefit to our children instead of being, as they are, directly or indirectly, the source of most of the misery and hardship visited on the children of the world.

My overall approach is to fill in the background to the Net and the Web so that their profound significance may be better appreciated, and their immense potential for improving our society better understood. That such potential is being grossly perverted is then argued by briefly reviewing the sad state of the world, a world in which far too many children are being robbed of their health, their culture, and their humanity by inequitable use of technology, technology that is largely digital. Finally, some few measures that, if adopted, might begin to reverse the tragic worsening of the lot of the world's children are suggested.

2. The Net

There is a popular perception that the Net is revolutionary, that its use will transform our society almost overnight, and even that the Net will make possible a new economy that will suddenly bring prosperity for all [1]. Well, almost all.

The Net is an instrument for the very swift transport of messages. The messages convey information—instructions, requests, news, descriptions, identifications, quantities, and so on.

Human civilizations have been able to develop, and be destroyed, because they have developed better and better techniques for using signals of some kind to send messages in a timely fashion. The need to transport messages did not arise as the Net was being developed.

Similar revolutions have been touted in the past. The Railways Revolution of mid-19th century Britain was expected to bring in a new economy, with prosperity for all. It didn't [2]. The introduction of railways had many effects, but, looking back, it can be seen as part of the evolution of material transport, preceded as it was by dredging of natural waterways, and the construction of networks of canals and metaled roads, and followed by development of vast highway and airway systems.

It is certain that in a century or so, providing our climate change hasn't destroyed our civilization completely [3], the Internet "Revolution" will be seen as just one stage in the evolution of message transport. If that stage is not to turn out as wasteful as the Railways Revolution did, our leaders and planners, and educated people at large, need to see clearly now that the Net is evolutionary, and that we should control its evolution rather than let it run where its promoters thrust it.

Let us therefore look now at the evolution of human communication, of which the Net is only the most recent stage.

2.1 Origins

It is natural to think of communication as being primarily vocal. Many animals exchange information by vocal utterance. It is fascinating, and perhaps sobering, to reflect on the possibility that dolphins do it so much more fluently than humans do that we have not yet been able to detect their meaning [4].

Speech is itself only one aspect of normal human communication, which is greatly enriched by gesture—body language. Indeed, some researchers are convinced that speech evolved from gestural communication [5]. We instinctively resort to gesture and mime when trying to communicate with someone who doesn't speak a language we know, or when loud noise prevents speech from being heard. Furthermore, now that the larger community no longer tries to stop them from doing so, communities of deaf people use remarkably complex and effective sign languages that are quite unrelated to the spoken language of the surrounding community.

It is curious that communication with computers, or at least the transmission of data from human to machine, is primarily gestural, whether using keyboard or mouse. Indeed, given that most of the world's computing power is, and will for some time remain, devoted to videogames, gestural use of the world's computers will persist.

However, speech is the main feature of human communication, and there is a real prospect of, and already some reality in, speech-controlled computers and even conversational computers [6].

2.1.1 Speech

Speech is a complex behavior that we learn as children. We use it mainly to exchange ideas with one another. Its usefulness depends on our perceptual systems being able to make out standard words and phrases in other people's speech and match them to words and phrases that we ourselves know how to utter.

Communication by speech depends on being able to ignore variations in how different people say the same words, and even how the same word may be differently spoken by the same person at different times. Perception of words in an utterance enables us to infer the kind of thoughts the speaker wishes us to have as a result of the utterance.

Thus there are three components to any speech act: the thoughts and intentions of the speaker, the speech itself, and the thoughts and reactions of the listener. It is conventional, and even an international standard, to refer to the thoughts (or at least the meaningful content of the thoughts) as *information*, and to refer to the speech mediating the transfer or induction of thoughts as *data*.

For a speech act to be in some way successful, the thoughts engendered in the mind of the listener by the speech act must bear some relationship to what the speaker intended them to be. These engendered thoughts are given particularity by the state of mind of the listener and by the listener's past experience. No two people will have exactly the same thoughts when listening to the same utterance. Information is usually vague, varying, and ill-formed. Speech data are not.

The words and phrases of speech are perceived as encoding of standard ideas. We have a limited number of words and phrases in our vocabularies to choose from when we construct an utterance, although the combinatory possibilities are huge in number. It is precisely the limitation of vocabulary that enables us to perceive standard words and phrases despite variations in the way they might be uttered and in the way we might hear them.

The point I am making here is that encoding thoughts in speech can only capture a small and transient portion of the richness of consciousness. Any encoded representation of information can only convey a small part of the richness of the thought that momentarily holds the meaning as it is being represented.

2.1.2 Language

The combination of vocabulary and rules for using it shared by a community or culture is called a language. In the past, communities and cultures have been identified by and with their languages, even quite small communities, so that in many multicultural regions it was usual to be able to speak more than one language.

Nowadays, languages are dying out faster than animal and plant species as standard language use is actively promoted by governments and commercial interests for ease of control and lowering of costs. Imposition of a standard language by a government is nothing new, and governments have often acted purposefully to quash the language of minorities, particularly of conquered minorities. In countries that have in the past sustained a wide variety of regional variation and local dialects, migration for employment, education in a standard language, and above all the press and television, have been smoothing out linguistic variation.

Whether varied or not, particular languages are shared by communities large and small as their means of communication.

The difficulty with communication by speech is that it is only useful for communicating with someone within earshot. There are three main ways around this difficulty, all of which involve signaling, that is, the transmission of some abstraction or transfiguration of the messages to be communicated. Each of these is, to a greater or lesser degree, an adaptation of spoken language.

2.1.3 Signaling by assisting speech

The first means of communicating over long distances is by overcoming the weakening experienced by speech over distance in normal conversational circumstances. The simplest way of doing this is to shout, and messages have been transmitted in favorable circumstances by chains of shouters, who can be greatly assisted by simple loud-hailers, or, nowadays, megaphones.

More subtle is the use of speaking tubes, which have been used on rail trains and on ships to allow dispersed crew to communicate easily. Such tubes overcome the attenuation of sound, caused by its spreading its energy spherically from the speaker, by running it down a tube. The attenuation is greatly reduced in much the same way as it is for signals imposed on light waves by running those light waves down optical fibers [7].

Even more subtle is the technique of imposing the patterns of speech on top of signals that have greater carrying power than speech. Many cultures have used drums in this way by imitating speech—there is enough redundancy in speech for the imitation to be understandable without the imitation having to be very precise.

Cultures in mountain regions such as New Guinea, parts of Turkey, and the Canary Islands have in some cases developed *whistled languages*, in which speech is superimposed over whistling by people such as shepherds and goatherds so that they can conduct conversations across and along deep valleys [8]. The method of superimposing one signal onto another to give the first signal the carrying power of the second is nowadays known as *modulation*, and it makes possible modern methods of signal transmission. The method was also used in developing radio broadcasting and telephony.

The sound waves of speech can be conducted along taut cords or wires with relatively little loss—a technique well-known in the 1930s and 1940s to schoolchildren, like myself, who would make bush telephones from tin cans and string. We were unaware that this technique had been used with wire as early as 1796 by a German called Huth, who named his device the "Telephon" [9].

The logical conclusion to this line of development was the electrical telephone. The advent of the electrical telephone so greatly extended the practical range of this signaling technique that it became a popular success. A sequence of technical developments gave rise to the growth of huge telephone systems.

2.1.4 Signaling by messenger

A second means of long-distance communication is to have an agent memorize a message, or to provide the agent with a record or other memory aid, and have the agent travel to deliver the message. The messengers do not even have to be people, birds such as homing pigeons having been trained in many countries to carry messages swiftly, a great advantage in a messenger. An elaboration of this is to have a succession of messengers who pass the message along.

This use of messengers has been common to all civilizations, ranging from pre-European Australia where message sticks were used as *aides memoires* [10], to the modern world-wide postal services.

Systematic use of messengers requires some convention for recording messages explicitly or indirectly, and came to depend on use of writing to record utterances. The direct recording of messages depended on the development of a system for writing in persistent form utterances that would otherwise be lost through the limitations of memory.

The disadvantage of signaling by messenger is twofold—the time the message takes in its travel, and the cost of the messengers and their traveling.

2.1.5 Signaling by code

A third way to communicate over long distances is to have a scheme for encoding a signal in such a way that it can be sent by creating a phenomenon, such as smoke or reflected sunlight, that can be perceived at a distance.

Very simple signals, for instance a notification of an expected event, require merely the presence or continuing absence of smoke or, at night, a fire. Australian aboriginal hunting groups lit smoking fires not only to signal a kill, but also to signal its location, so that their followers could butcher the meat while the hunters went after more prey.

Signals can be sent over long distances by using chains of signal stations. The opening scene of Æschylus's play "Agamemnon" of 458 BCE had a watchman on the roof of the palace at Argos receive news of the victory of the Greeks in Troy from the last of a chain of fire-signals.

More complex signals required timed sequences of symbols, and there is mention of the use of water clocks to synchronize signaling by flame for Hannibal in the fourth century BCE, but there is no description of the coding system. On the other hand, Polybios in the second century BCE describes an encoding of letters of the Greek alphabet into a two-digit quinary number system intended for signaling, but there is no evidence of its actual use [11].

Many systems of encoded signaling were used over the centuries, such as signal flags for passing messages between islands and ships, but they were limited by the ability of the human eye to see the signal. Although sighting tubes were used to improve perception, the real breakthrough in such signaling came with the use of the telescope. Means then had to be developed not only for encoding a message, but also for timing it and for managing the flow of a message by signal elements that were not part of the actual message. Although such coding and control methods were described and demonstrated by Sir Robert Hooke in the 1680s, practical optical telegraphy had to await improvements to the telescope, which were devised in the mid-18th century [12]. With the improved telescope, complex signals could be clearly seen a long distance away under favorable conditions.

As a result, sophisticated semaphore systems came into use in Europe in the late 18th century. Many different systems were proposed. In Scandinavia a scheme with six shutters was finally adopted, but elsewhere in Europe a system using a rotatable arm at each end of a rotatable beam at one stage linked, in today's geographical terms, Spain, France, Italy, Germany, Belgium, and Holland [13]. Semaphore systems were used in many parts of the world, including the Tamar Estuary of northern Tasmania where one of the signal stations is being rebuilt as a tourist attraction.

The problem with the semaphore was that it relied on a clear line of sight along the entire chain of signal stations, which were typically erected on the top of hills or tall buildings. The advantage of the semaphore was that there were no problems with owners of property between signal stations.

However, the electrical telegraph gradually superseded the semaphore. Its overwhelming advantage was that it worked as well in fog or at nighttime as it did in clear sunshine. The problem of getting permission to take telegraph wires across private property proved not to be a barrier, and lines were typically run alongside roads and the rail tracks that were being built during the 19th century. The electrical telegraph took over from the optical [14].

2.2   Recent Development

The recent history of international networked communications — over the past century and a half — is much more accessible and much better known than the history related in the preceding sections. An abbreviated account is therefore all that is needed to close this section.

The electrical digital telegraph systems developed in the 19th century were extended, both with cables and wireless, and were in use well into the 20th century both internationally and intranationally. The sound of Morse code was familiar to customers, and enjoyed by schoolchildren, in country post offices in Australia as late as the mid-1900s.

However, the convenience of the telephone system for direct personal communications was behind the evolution of telephone systems for the past hundred years — first electrical, then electronic, and now optical; first analog and now digital; first circuit switched manually, then automatically, and now moving to packet switched, particularly in mobile telephony.

Recent developments are usually depicted as revolutionary. Thus it is important to emphasize that, in the light of a more complete consideration of its history, networked communication systems have rather been steadily evolving, more or less in step with the development of electrical circuit manufacturing technology.

Particular hyperbole is usually attracted to descriptions of the Net. In fact, the networking of computers, which is the essence of the Internet, has also been steadily evolving in parallel with the development of digital computers themselves [15]. This should not occasion surprise, as digital computers are themselves far more basically short-range signaling machines in their internal functioning than they are computational.

Even before digital computers burgeoned there was widespread use of long distance data transmission by means of card-to-card, paper-tape-to-paper-tape, and, later, either of these to magnetic tape equipment, using ordinary telephone lines. In the 1960s remote teletype machines and RJE (remote job entry) systems became popular. The Net is simply an evolutionary outcome of these early systems, and in the evolution the computer mediated traffic has been growing faster than the voice traffic and now exceeds it. There really isn't anything to be surprised about (see [17] on [16]).

3. The Web

The Web is not the Net. The World Wide Web is the many stores of data held on millions of magnetic disks spread around the world, stores that are linked to each other in a web by pointers, often called *hyperlinks*. The pointers are in the stored data. It is the role of the Net to allow those pointers to be used to bring the data pointed to into the network terminal of a user, typically onto the display screen of the user [18].

Human civilizations have been able to develop because they have evolved better and better techniques for representing information, and for storing the data that represent that information. The need to store data did not arise as the Web was being developed.

The Web is, at the moment, a vast and chaotic collection of data of great variety—representing books and documents, newspapers and journals, diagrams and illustrations, paintings and photographs, music and movies, catalogs and encyclopedias, programs and statistics, and so on.

There is a common perception that the Web, like the Net on which it depends, is revolutionary, that its use will transform our society almost overnight, and even that the Web will make possible a new Renaissance that will bring knowledge and learning for all.

Similar revolutions have been touted in the past. The relatively recent rise of compulsory education in the rich countries of the world was supposed to usher in an era of happiness and prosperity for all. It was based on, among others things, the availability of inexpensive mass-produced books to serve as school readers and textbooks. The results of that revolution were never fully realized, and nowadays the level of illiteracy and innumeracy in rich countries is steadily rising.

It is certain that in a century or so, the "revolution" of the World Wide Web will be seen as just as evolutionary as that of the Net, just one stage in the evolution of our society's accumulation of recorded knowledge. If the benefits of that stage are not to turn out as illusory or inequitable as those of compulsory education, our leaders and planners, and educated people at large, need to see clearly now that the Web, like the Net, is evolutionary, and that we should control its evolution rather than let it run where its promoters thrust it.

Let us therefore look now at the evolution of which the Web is only the most recent stage, the evolution of our information encoding and data storage.

3.1   Origins

The alphabetic system of writing used to encode this book had its origins in southwest Asia 6000 years or so ago, as did most other alphabetic or syllabic writing systems in widespread use today. These systems developed to assist commerce.

In the beginning small baked clay tokens symbolizing certain kinds of property were kept as an inventory record. As commerce developed the procedure was adopted of enclosing an appropriate number of appropriate tokens in a dried clay ball that served as a kind of delivery docket to be broken open to verify correct delivery. Much later the further development of commerce led to the delivery details being recorded, for the benefit of intermediaries, also on the surface of the clay delivery docket by pressing tokens into it while it was still soft. Further slow stages of development were the omission of the tokens from inside the ball, and the use of a stylus to create the symbols previously made by imprinting with tokens.

Eventually the clay ball was reshaped to a more convenient tablet shape, and the symbolism refined to better record more complex inventories and transactions and, eventually, histories and myths. All this 3000 or 4000 years ago [19].

3.1.1 Manuscripts

Although writing as engravure persisted, for instance through the use of wax tablets and copperplate printing, superficial writing developed from the inscription of clay tablets through the use of dyes to mark plaster, and later inks to mark thin sheets of papyrus or hide. Handwriting developed so successfully that people have made professions as scribes, clerks, and copyists for many thousands of years until the very recent development of typewriters and copying machines.

Handwritten documents were always primarily used by an administrative few to control society for the benefit of the people at the top of the social hierarchy. The power of documents lies in the authority of their permanence—the word of authority made substantial. In Europe the development of the social power of the Christian churches was based on documentation. The documents of the churches were manufactured in establishments called *scriptoria* where barely literate scribes, illuminators, and binders worked under poor conditions to make books for the running of the churches.

In Europe the manuscripts were written onto parchment (lambskin originally shipped through Pergamon) or vellum (calfskin), originally as scrolls, later folded for convenience. Manuscripts were stoutly bound so that they could be chained down to discourage theft, and with stout clasps to prevent the parchment or vellum from buckling completely out of shape.

The development of universities in Europe in the 12th century caused the use of manuscripts to spread beyond the Church. The universities built up libraries, and stationers associated with the universities rented books out, section by section, to be copied by or for students. Learning began to be valued, by those who could afford it, for more than its administrative or commercial value.

3.1.2 Printing

The development of printing in Europe in the latter half of the 15th century is usually depicted as having sprung into being at Gutenberg's behest, Gutenberg being credited with the adoption of movable type. This picture is erroneous on several counts [20].

There was printing before Gutenberg. Outlines to guide illumination of manuscripts were often printed in manuscripts during their manufacture, devotional books were published with sacred pictures printed from woodblocks, and the key development on which text printing was based was the importation of paper manufacturing technology from East Asia.

Paper was so important in early printing not because it was cheap—it was actually very expensive—but because it could be relied on to lie flat, which vellum and parchment couldn't.

Another development necessary for the gradual adoption of text printing was methods for the manufacture of type. This was a triumph of metallurgy. The process involved cutting type punches from hard metal. The punches were used to shape a softer metal to serve as the end of a mould in which type were cast from a metal of lower melting point. The complexity of the process made the type quite expensive, and their useful life was rather limited.

The printing press itself was, for most of the history of printing, a simple screw-operated press with which skilled tradesmen were remarkably productive. The technology of the press of course evolved with the other technologies—such as paper making, ink, and type founding—but the development was expensive.

Standards evolved as part of the evolution of the technology. There was a great variety of type faces, although divided until very recently in some Latin alphabet countries between Renaissance-inspired Roman/Italic faces and traditional Gothic faces. However, details such as the various dimensions of the type slugs, their arrangement in cases so that type composition could be swift, and the size and folding of sheets of paper were gradually though sporadically standardized.

It is usual to depict the development of printing technology over the past century or so, machines such as Linotype and Mergenthaler typesetting machines, the large rotary presses used to print hundreds of thousands of newspapers in a shift, and more recently the digital typesetting and composing systems, as revolutionary. The appearance of rapid development comes partly from the accumulation of knowledge and skills, partly from an increase in the number of people exploiting that knowledge and those skills, and partly from the magnifying perspective of recency.

At any time when there are technological developments, current and recent developments are better known, their context better understood, and their novelty more obvious, than older ones. To people living in a hundred years time the developments of today will seem as relatively ho-hum as the developments of one hundred years ago seem to us today. In 200 years time, the developments of today will seem to have faded into the mists of time, if not altogether forgotten.

3.2 Books

Printing technology has long been used for many purposes, for stationery and cards, for pamphlets and leaflets, for posters and notices, for newspapers and magazines, and for books. All of these kinds of publications have osmosed to the Web.

However, the least ephemeral use of printing has been in the production of books. Books have been used to capture and perpetuate not only rules and facts both administrative and scientific to command and instruct, but also speculations and imaginings both informative and performative—philosophy, music, fiction, drama, commentary, and criticism. Books are intended to evoke a wide range of human emotion—joy, despair, humor, concern, curiosity, sympathy, anger, satisfaction, piety, wonder, and so on, and so on. They can do so across centuries and millennia [21].

3.2.1 The manufacture of books

Books have gone through a long evolution [22]. Lengthy strips of manuscript were often used rolled up as scrolls, as the Torah still is, and kept in cylinders such as post offices still sell, in some countries at least. Later it was found convenient to fold the manuscript strips up concertina fashion, and apply a stout cover for protection. When manuscript books were produced in the constructional style of present-day books, their covers were used to chain them to lecterns and to clamp them shut to discourage buckling of the parchment leaves and the consequent gross distortion of the book.

When books were first printed they were, to make them easier to sell, made as like manuscript books as possible, even to their illumination. Marginal markings and annotations such as used in manuscript books were typically imitated in print, although these were later developed into the endnotes and footnotes so beloved of many scholars, particularly historians [23], and most recently into the hyperlinks that form the basis for the Web.

The great expense of producing books in the early days of printing kept them simple and, because so much capital was tied up in keeping stocks of them, print runs were minuscule even by the standards of only a century or so later. For quite a long time it was the practice to sell books uncut and unbound, so that a bibliophile would take a newly purchased book straight to a bookbinder.

Two significant effects of the high cost of production of early books were first that the business of publishing fell into the hands of people such as stationers who had enough capital to be able to stock books, and second that the stationers did most of their business with, and under the protection of, universities and governments. Indeed the monopoly of copyright was originally, in England at any rate, granted to publishers on condition that they suppress any seditious or heretical publications [24].

A later effect was the popularity of notices and pamphlets, which, being small and very simple, could be printed and sold more quickly than books. These were, in effect, early examples of mass advertising.

As the technology of book production developed, books became cheaper and this made the ideal of universal literacy seem feasible in rich countries. Compulsory schooling in such countries, coupled with the availability of cheap textbooks, led to the attainment of very high levels of literacy indeed around the middle of the 20th century, levels not reached before or since. At about that time, too, the now ubiquitous paperback book became popular, and put more books into more homes than ever before.

3.2.2   The content of books

One great advantage in the printing of books was that the process ensured, accidents aside, that the text was the same in all copies of a particular edition. The hand copying of manuscripts led to the accumulation of errors, both through simple mistakes of semi-literate scribes and through gratuitous "correction" by doctrinal supervisors. Of course mistakes were made in setting up type, but it was relatively easy for the compositor to make changes to type already set up in formes or galleys, and the changes could be conveniently marked on a proof or galley print by a skilled and learned proof reader.

Manuscript books were either just text or text with illumination and possibly illustration. Early printed books, *incunables* from the cradle of printing, imitated this. Later books were additionally decorated in a variety of ways, to make it easier for both the binder and the reader. For example, page numbering, which made it easier for the binder to check folding and folio sequence, for the reader to keep track of progress in reading, and for other authors to exactly cite arguments and quotations, was a later introduction.

Other embellishments, taken up over a long period of history, were chapter divisions, page headings and footings, title pages, colophons, tables of contents, indexes, bibliographies, and advertisements. The practice of using endnotes and footnotes was brought over from manuscript times, as were certain conventions of punctuation [25], but these were developed as the technology of printing and publishing developed.

Some practices were adopted for a while and then dropped. In the 19th century chapters of popular books were often headed by a short summary of the action to be found in the chapter. Some common practices became uncommon. The use of very large capitals for the first letters of chapters was continued from manuscript days, and can be very decorative, but it is very rare in books nowadays, although it is occasionally seen in magazines—for example, in the *Scientific American*.

The lessening of the cost of books and booklets led also to an outpouring of "creative" writing, the Gothic novels of two centuries ago being overwhelmed in volume, for example, by the produce nowadays of writers such as Barbara Cartland. For ease of reading, or perhaps for ease of profit making, comic books have found an enormous market, and so have sporting, pornographic, and other magazines.

3.2.3   The storage of books

The accumulation and storage of books presents at least two major problems, one being the physical accommodation of the books, the other being the discovery and retrieval of a particular book from a collection [26].

Bound books store onto shelves much more easily than scrolls, although when books were first stored on shelves they were typically placed spine inwards, perhaps because their chains were attached alongside the clamp on the edge of the cover opposite to the spine. In such cases, books were identified for retrieval by labels secured across the edges of the paper and clamped into place.

When the adoption of paper for printing on rendered the clamps unnecessary, and the use of the inconvenient and expensive chains was phased out, books eventually came to be shelved spine out, and later the practice was adopted of embossing the title and the author's name on the spine.

Early libraries, a few exceptions like the library at Alexandria apart [21], were very small by today's standards. Where they had bookshelves these were usually associated with lecterns and the shelves were placed at right angles to the windowed walls to make the best use of available natural light. In larger libraries a list of the books in any shelf was posted up at the inward end of each doubled clamp of shelves.

The technology of storing books developed alongside the technology of printing them, most universities up till recently finding their steadily increasing collection of books an embarrassment to house, although modern lighting and ingenious systems of moving shelves have allowed more books to be crammed into the available space. Public libraries have experienced similar problems. The universities, at least in Australia, have had this problem solved for them partly by drastically reduced budgets, which has led to regular clearing out of books that their library's computing systems reveal to be rarely used, or at least rarely borrowed.

3.3   The Advance of the Web

The combination of the development of printing and publishing technology with the galloping increase in the number of people writing books of one kind or another has led to an enormous increase in book and newspaper production, an increase that has denuded the world of many of its forests.

There has been a lot of unobservant talk in the recent past of the paperless office, but the reality is that the development of digitally driven printers, from teletypes and typewriters through electromechanical line printers to copiers and laser printers, two functions now often provided by a single machine, has driven a steadily increasing consumption of paper.

The convenience and, for the time being, the cheapness of paper seem to ensure its persistent popularity. Electronic books have recently been espoused as the enemy of paper, but it is difficult to see them taking over, although they will undoubtedly find a market. Another market that will exist for a while is the book, with video clips and other glorifications, stored on CD-ROM, but, just as for videogames, the future for stored entertainment seems to be that of hyped-up television [27]. Such material will be brought into the homes of the well-off through optical fibers.

3.3.1 Bulk data storage

The most crucial technological expectation behind the wonderful visions of television loaded down into the home at will, or of vast amounts of text, pictures, and sounds, to be summoned into a multimedia virtual reality player at will, is very realizable. The capacity of the world's businesses, particularly the media companies, to store as much encoded data as they wish, is fast becoming a reality through recording techniques for almost unimaginably dense data storage coupled to increasingly cheap methods for manufacturing devices to do so.

Were it not for the parallel development of the Net, with the use of wavelength multiplexed optical fibers to give again almost unimaginably high rates of data transmission, these recording techniques would merely give rise to a burgeoning printing and publishing industry purveying ever more products of ever greater splendor and stimulation using optical disks or whatever comes to supersede them as they superseded the vinyl disks of the 1960s and 1970s.

However, the Web provides the possibility of storing all the world's publications, without exception and without the need for pruning out little-borrowed items, at various storage points from where they can be downloaded at will. The World Wide Web is a scheme with the potential to do just that, and to provide the world with a universal library in the style and philosophy of the tragically destroyed Alexandrian library, a library that anyone could use who can use the Net [28, 29].

4. The Future

The purpose of the preceding sections was to portray the two technological developments that are nowadays lauded to the skies—the Net and the Web—as the products of a natural and gradual evolution rather than as a juggernaut that cannot be opposed or even controlled and that can only be properly understood by the would-be technocrats who preach the gospel of this juggernaut [30].

The Net and the Web are, of course, controllable, given enough purpose and understanding by enough people, in particular by enough of those people holding themselves to be members of a computing profession. This purpose and understanding must come from an appreciation of the technological evolution described in the preceding sections, coupled to a consideration of the likely outcome of failing in that purpose and understanding [31].

The following subsections are intended to sketch the dangers inherent in uncontrolled, or, rather, purely commercially and bureaucratically controlled, development of the Net and the Web. The dangers are bad enough, but they are given added horror by the certainty that these dangers threaten the children of the world—present and future—far more than they threaten the adults.

Indeed, the circumstances of the present children of the world are already tragic enough, obscenely so. The computer on my desk shows me from the Web that, in this computer-driven new economy of a world, people are dying of hunger at the rate of one every 3.6 seconds. Bad enough, perhaps, but three out of four of those dying thus are children (*http://www.hunger-site.com/*), and many more, predominantly children, are dying of armed conflict and cheaply curable sicknesses (*http://www.unicef.org/*).

The Net and the Web could be used to improve conditions for the poor, the young, and the needy. They are unlikely to be used in this way unless the dominant commercial interests that promote the new economy rather than the old community are counteracted [32].

4.1   The Future of the Net

One thing is certain. The data transmission capacity of the Internet will be greatly increased, increased beyond our present imaginings [33–36].

What is this increase likely to be used for? The short answer, expanded in the following, is that it will be used for profit, and there is nothing wrong with that, particularly in the "developed" world so dominated by shares and taxes neither of which could exist in our "developed" society without profits being made. However, the less fortunate parts of our world and of our societies, especially their children, must not be overlooked in all this profit making.

A pessimist might predict that the benefits of the Net will be all too narrowly distributed. If that is the case, what should be done with the Net for the children, who make no profits?

4.1.1   The Net and the children

Of course there are profits to be made *from* children, who are at present exploited widely all over the world—typically by advertising and entertainment businesses in the first world, and by slavers and factory owners in the third—but these are the children, profitable but not profiting, who would gain most benefit from the Net. Moreover, there is little profit to be made from bringing the Net to the poor families of the second world.

The Net is superb for communicating, so the first use of the Net should be to support those who bring, or who might wish to bring, help to disadvantaged children and their parents. Much of the improvement in the lot of the world's poor is, in these days of government cost-cutting, being done by volunteer organizations, and the Net can be used, and is being used, to make both their gathering of donations and their managing of work more effective.

The first priority of such helping organizations is simply the maintenance of the life of their clients and the promotion of their clients' health, but such help is relatively ineffective in reducing the need for it— the best help will help the clients help themselves. Donated food and medicine is all very well, but people who are helped and taught to grow their own food, and to treat if not prevent their own sicknesses benefit most. This means volunteer teachers, a commodity in short supply, and especially teachers of teachers. Adults will need this teaching, but the teaching of children is more important and in the long run more effective.

Isolated teachers will be relatively ineffective, and their efforts likely to be wasted. Here the Net is of paramount importance as the basis for cheap and effective communication between volunteer teachers and their distant mentors and advisors, between volunteer teachers and their scattered local teachers, and, most importantly, between local teachers to support their cooperation and so foster their eventual independence. Communication using the Net thus can help volunteer teachers by enabling them to advise and supervise dispersed local teachers and volunteers, and by enabling dispersed locals to help one another.

All this would be indirectly in support of the disadvantaged children. Direct use of the Net by children would not be possible until enough prosperity is generated to support communications equipment in poor schools and communities, but very simple and cheap Net-enabled terminals could be of great benefit for children in poor schools through their support of discussion groups and "chat-rooms," always provided their local language was supported. This would give motivation and incentive for acquiring literacy.

None of this could happen unless the poor could be reached by the Net. The technology for it exists. The politics doesn't. Nor, yet, does the motivation among the poor, and the Net is not necessarily beneficent [37].

4.1.2 The entertainment industry

The main consumer of the Net's future capacity will be the entertainment industry. The great media companies are already gearing up to commandeer the Net—witness the Time/AOL merger. The capacity of broadcast entertainment, even when satellites are used, is vanishingly small compared to that provided by optical fibers, especially now that wavelength division multiplexing and optical switching are coming into practical use. Broadcast live television will fade before the onslaught of an almost unlimited choice of studio chat shows, sporting events, news channels, and sitcoms, and the Net's increasing capacity will lead to these entertainments becoming more and more interactive and attractive to the people being entertained.

Chat show audiences will sit at video consoles where they can applaud and vote and even have their pictures selected by an editor for inclusion in the transmitted show as they watch it. Top of the market shows will allow members of the audience to virtually attend, virtual reality technology letting them feel they are actually there without them having to go through the inconvenience of physically traveling to the show.

Sporting events anywhere in the developed world will be available as they are taking place. The armchair sportswatcher will be able to pick and choose at will, and, for popular events, even choose from a range of viewpoints. In due course, virtual reality technology supported by very powerful computation will provide the viewer with the illusion of actually being there.

News channels, for those in more serious mood, will allow viewers to vicariously visit at any time any of the world's trouble spots—where there are armed conflicts, accidents, massacres, scandals, riots, natural catastrophes, and so on. Remotely controlled armoured cameras will bring the viewer closer to the action, and powerful simulation programs will allow the viewer to see realistic reconstructions of tragedies that the cameras didn't reach in time.

The Net will be used to encourage gambling on the outcome of any of the entertaining events as they are being viewed so that the entertainment value will be heightened and the profit increased, and for those in search of the ultimate in entertainment, the Net will make possible highly elaborate and realistic participative games in which people will be able to kill one another without anyone in fact getting hurt. Physically hurt, that is.

This picture of the future for a Net-based entertainment industry is not fanciful. It is probably an understatement of what will happen in the course of time, just as the future of transport that could be envisioned by the railways investors of the mid-1800s fell far short of the highways and airways of today [2]. The effect of such entertainment on children is predictable in nature, although not perhaps in severity.

4.1.3 Commerce and industry

The entertainment industry is likely to be the main user of the Net in the future, but certainly not the only one [38]. The large global industries now forming will have many uses for the capacity of the Net [39].

Global enterprises are starting to use the Net to make doing business with one another more effective, cheaper, and swifter. Markets of various kinds— stock markets, financial markets, futures markets, commodities markets, and so on, and so on—are being set up by groups of large companies to provide 24-hours-a-day 7-days-a-week world-wide trading. Such schemes are part of what is being called B2B (business-to-business) e-commerce (electronic commerce).

This is being done at present by human operatives but programs are already being designed and written to allow trading to be entirely carried out by computer across the Net. This will make the large companies much more effective, and the reduction in labor costs (a process now called "disintermediation" [40]) will greatly increase their profit margins.

As the larger companies employ fewer and fewer people, the working time of those left in steady employment will become more and more expensive. Such highly paid executives will not want to waste their valuable time traveling even shortish distances to meetings, but will instead use the Net to host meetings virtually. The technology for this is already being developed [41]. Such virtual meetings will not use anywhere near as much of the Net's capacity as the entertainment industry, however.

What is likely to be a larger load on the Internet is in the second kind of e-commerce—B2C or business to consumer, otherwise known for the moment as "e-tailing". Although it is more conspicuous on the Web at present, and increasingly through e-mail on the Net, it is starting to be piggybacked on the entertainment industry. The entertainment industry is where almost all the advertising is done, so it is natural that in some countries black boxes are already being added to domestic television sets as "interactive TV" where the interactivity is focused on e-tail shopping through the domestic TV set. As digital television moves onto the Net, e-tailing seems certain to grow by leaps and bounds.

4.1.4 Private use of the Net

The future development of the Net will be dominated by the entertainment industry. Business use of the Net will also grow significantly. These uses will dwarf strictly private use of the Net, which will nevertheless grow rapidly through the adoption of mobile telephones.

The use of mobile telephones has been growing dramatically, particularly among the youth of developed countries, but the mobile telephone industry is now busy extending its handheld devices to enable them to be used as interfaces to the Net, and mobile telephones are already being sold complete with protocols like WAP and Bluetooth to enable them to be used for automated shopping.

This implies that the present dominant use of mobile telephones for interpersonal chatter will soon be overtaken by their use for retail marketing.

4.2   The Future of the Web

Another thing is certain. The data storage capacity of the world's computers that form the Web will be greatly increased, increased beyond our present imaginings [42].

What is this increased capacity likely to be used for? Again, the short answer is—for profit—and again, there is nothing inherently wrong with that, provided the less well-off in our world and in its many societies are not deprived of the benefits of the Web.

If the Web does become almost totally commercialized, as might be expected from the parallels with the development of television, then the poor and their children, who by definition live outside the commercial world, would be excluded from the Web. Freedom from a commercial Web could well be a cultural benefit, but what benefits might children expect to gain from an altruistic Web?

4.2.1   The Web and the children

The Web ideally does what, until very recently, only libraries could do— collect the encoded information that partially embodies the literate cultures of the world [29]. There are dangers in this—the distributed store is continuously changing [43], the storage media are typically obsolescent, and there are few controls over the Web's content—so the cultural stability and reliability of the Web's data are at least suspect.

These problems should not be insurmountable, and much has been written and demonstrated already about digital and virtual libraries [28]. To store textual and pictorial representations recording many of the world's cultures is feasible. If this were done, the teachers of the world's disadvantaged children would have a splendid and glorious resource to help them in acculturing their pupils.

It is the task of teachers to educate their pupils, where education means equipping them to survive and, ideally, prosper within their society. The Net and its Web could be of great help here, provided equipment to use it were available to the pupils who need it most. Even so, there are dangers.

Teachers, many of them, need to be trained to engender social skills in their pupils. This engendering can only be done in the society of the class under control of a trained teacher, and social skills can only be destroyed in the exclusive society of the Web terminal. Education is a social activity. Videogames and Web surfing are not.

Pupils need to be brought up in their own cultures. If the Web is to be used for such enculturing, then material of all cultures must be made available on the Web. This would be extremely difficult and costly to do, but the oligocultural world that an uncontrolled commercial Web threatens to bring would be fatal to the continued development of human society.

4.2.2 The entertainment industry

The foremost candidate for commercial use of the Web is VOD—video on demand. The video rental shops and the broadcast television networks are obsolescent, at least in the developed world. The gigantic media networks, on the other hand, can expect greatly increased business and profits.

- If people can buy whatever films and television shows they want whenever they want them, and whatever sporting events and pornography they want likewise, they will undoubtedly buy many more of them, and be prepared to pay extra for the convenience.
- If people are buying stored entertainment in ever greater quantities then the profitability of that stored entertainment will be greatly increased by boosting their advertising content, overtly or covertly. Now that overt advertising has almost reached saturation level, advertisers are paying to have their products put into view, or better still used by actors, during the breaks between the overt advertisements, and the power of computers is already being used to meld advertisements and products into video sequences live and recorded.
- The increased profits for the media companies from VOD will lead to mergers and globalization, which will be assisted by the ability to store a selection of sound tracks in different languages for both the entertainment and the advertisement.

Of course the profits will not be fully realizable unless the big companies are able to control fully the distribution of their entertainment—the use of intellectual property law is the key to this [44]. The present push, through the World Intellectual Property Organization, to extend dramatically the scope and the effective term of copyright protection throughout the world is evidence that the big media companies are aware of this. Further evidence is the effort, this time through the World Trade Organization, to have copyright laws more rigidly enforced.

A significant cameo of the push to extend control by copyright is the recent litigation against a company called Napster to prevent them from allowing their customers to exchange recorded music using their networking services. It is likely that exchange of educational material will also be brought more under commercial control by the use of copyright.

4.2.3 Commerce and industry

Commerce and industry will have many uses for their immensely increased data storage capacity. As their business comes more and more to be carried out using the Net, they will need the capacity to archive complete details of all their transactions.

The complete archival storage of all their business transactions will enable retailers to personalize their marketing. Programs will be able to compute for each customer what they buy, what they are prepared to pay for what they buy, how likely they are to spot overpricing or overcharging, and what marketing ploys are most effective for use on them. From records for each customer of what goods they have already purchased, when they have purchased them, and how they have already responded to replacement offers, programs will be able to compute the best times for sending other replacement offers.

Such practices are called "dynamic pricing" and have attracted some adverse comment [45], but their steady adoption seems inevitable though perhaps dependent on the development of more subtle forms.

The more subtle forms of dynamic pricing will depend on having huge archival storage of transaction data collected from many customers [46]. Such data can also be useful enough to be sold to other companies not directly competing with the company collecting the data. Traffic in personal data is also profitable for government bodies who collect data about their subjects (citizens they should no longer properly be called [47]).

The big companies will have great advantage in this kind of marketing [48]. The reduction in labor costs afforded by e-commerce, particularly in e-tailing, will lead to greater investment in marketing. The likely consequence of this, coupled with the importance of entertainment for marketing, is that the global e-tailing companies that are already beginning to form will move into the entertainment industry themselves, probably by taking over the smaller of the media companies.

The entertainment industry might not be completely taken over by commerce. The collection of news and the promotion of gambling seem likely to remain as distinct industries, although at least the news services will remain completely dependent on advertising revenues. On the other hand, social trends suggest that the pornography industry is likely to become officially sanctioned, later if not sooner, so that it will probably be taken over to support the retailing industry.

4.2.4 Private use of the Web

At present, private use of the Web is most significant. The common adoption of the HTTP protocol and of HTML coding [49] has made it easy for anyone to set up Web pages with the support of their ISP (Internet service provider). This wonderful development has been been greatly supported by companies such as Yahoo! and Alta Vista and Google (there are many more), which run search engines to produce continually updated indexes to the vast content of the Web. However, the success of these companies has led to them being used more and more for advertising and marketing, and this trend is likely to continue [50].

The accumulation of private Web pages is likely to continue and flourish, at least for the time being, but this activity is already being rivaled by commercial use. Commercial use demands more capability from the Web so that commercial pressure will force HTML, and eventually HTTP, into obsolescence and eventual elimination, along with the Web pages that depend on those standards. This development is clearly signaled by the recent worldwide adoption of the ebXML (significantly the *eb* stands for *electronic business*) standard as a replacement for HTML (*http://www.ebxml.org/*).

Private users and educators will need to convert to ebXML, and this should not present a problem, but there are indications that the development of Web material by private users and educators will not grow very much, and certainly not relative to commercial material.

- The increasing use and extension of copyright law by large companies to control as much as possible any textual, graphical, or musical material that can be developed or commandeered for sale over the Net will restrict more and more what private users can put into the Web pages [51]. Search engines can, and doubtless will, be used to hunt down copyright offenders [52], and this will act as a deterrent to people who would otherwise store personal and historical material on the Web for general use.

- The use of private materials on the Web cannot grow the way commercial use can because such use largely depends on the combination of literacy and speculative initiative in potential users. Both of these requisites are in a decline that is being accelerated by determined government cost-cutting in education and by the ministrations of the entertainment industry.

- The commercialization of search engine technology will lead to private Web pages being excluded from general indexing, an exclusion made easy by the adoption of ebXML.
- The widespread adoption of devices without archival data storage capacity, such as "thin clients" and Web-enabled mobile telephones and television sets, will greatly reduce, in relative terms at least, the number of people able to put their own material onto the Web.

4.3   The Future for Children

The future for children depends on the future for adults who are their parents and carers. There are two very significant factors here.

1. The use of the Net and the Web, and of the digital computing and communications technology underlying them, is helping to greatly increase the gap between rich and poor — both between rich and poor nations, and between rich and poor within nations (*http://www.undp.org/*). This gap is now often called *the Digital Divide* [53].
2. The widening gap is leading the poor nations, and the poor within nations, to have proportionately many more children than the rich, at least in part because the rich, unlike the poor, see having children as diminishing their standard of living.

Another and very disquieting factor is that commercial interests are trying to expand into Web-based training, a development that is being encouraged by governments wishing to reduce their spending on education [54].

4.3.1   *The digital divide*

The inherent competitiveness of human nature has ensured, and will continue to ensure, that some few in human societies will dominate the remainder both in property and power. It has always been thus [55] and doubtless always will be. The immorality, or obscenity in extreme cases, lies not in the existence of the gap between rich and poor, but in the size of the gap.

The gap between rich and poor has been conspicuous in recent history, particularly in times of industrial development, as writings of authors such as Charles Dickens have recorded. After the Second World War it seemed for a while as though the gap was being gradually narrowed largely because of a political and moral will to make it so.

Tragically, it would seem that the adoption of digital technology in computation and telecommunications 30 or 40 years ago has added so much to the competitive advantage of the rich that the gap between rich and poor—nations and people—has started widening, and indeed the widening seems to be accelerating.

> [From 1960 to 1980] per capita income grew by 73% in Latin America and by 34% in Africa. By comparison, since 1980, Latin American growth has come to a virtual halt, growing by less than 6% over 20 years—and African incomes have declined by 23%.
>   ... From 1950 to 1980 ... welfare policies added more than a decade of life expectancy to virtually every nation on the planet.... Since 1980 to today life ... has become brutish and shorter. Since 1985 the total number of illiterate people has risen, and life expectancy is falling in 15 African nations.... In the former Soviet states ... life expectancy has plunged, adding 1.4 m a year to the death rate in Russia alone [56].

Of course, coincidence doesn't prove causation, but it does give food for thought.

Nevertheless there are many writings proclaiming that in fact everything is getting better. Indeed, the world's economy is growing overall, and there are statistics to prove it. The economy could continue to grow indefinitely, the climate, the resources, and the state of society permitting. Several points should be remembered, however.

1. There is no contradiction between the growth of the economy and the growth of the gap between rich and poor. Both can happen at once, and that they do is simply evidence of the increased competitiveness conferred on the rich by their being able to exploit technology. Sooner or later an increasing gap would change the state of society dramatically.
2. The quoting of figures relating to the distribution of annual income in societies is essentially misleading as to wealth or poverty. Annual income is related not to property but to the rate at which property can be acquired. Mathematicians and engineers would call income the first differential coefficient of wealth. Unhappily that coefficient is not the gross income but the *nett* income, because some at least of the gross income must be used to sustain life. The poor have no nett income and therefore cannot accumulate wealth—most can barely survive and typically die much younger than the rich.
3. Statistical measures of the economy such as employment percentages only relate to that part of society that participates in the economy. The great majority of the world's population has never done so, and an increasing proportion of the population of so-called "advanced" countries fails to do so. "More than 700 000 Texans [more than 1%] are either in prison, on parole or on probation" [57].

The facts are plain. There is more poverty and misery than ever before, and there will be much more in future, at least for several decades to come. Further, the worsening coincides with the large-scale adoption of digital technology, and it is not fanciful to see more in this than mere coincidence [58, 59].

4.3.2 The infancy divide

Increasing poverty is bad enough. The real tragedy, though, is that the poverty is disproportionately visited on children. Rich people have fewer children, and those rich people who do have children tend to have them later in life.

The phenomenon is particularly obvious in rich countries without significant immigration, Japan for example, where the drastic aging of their population is seen as threatening economic growth. The Singapore government is now offering substantial payment for people who produce babies.

In some rich countries nuclear families are becoming rarer among the poor so that many of the children of the poor are reared under highly unstable conditions. Furthermore, the high unemployment rates now common in such countries for 30 years means that many children who are growing up in families are growing up in families where neither parent has ever had a job, or at least not a steady one. Also in some such countries unemployed girls have children so that they are eligible for the increased government support paid to single mothers.

A frontpage article in *The Mercury* appearing as this chapter was being finished, ironically on Friday October 13, stated "Several Tasmanian welfare agencies are facing total collapse, unable to cope with a flood of poverty-stricken families." Newly severe problems cited were drug-dependent babies, suicidal preschool children, and elderly grandparents on meager pensions as sole carers of children—all these in a prosperous developed country.

If this seems a sad story, it's much worse for children in poor countries. They are afflicted by war, famine, flood, sickness, and exploitation of every imaginable kind (e.g., [60], but see also the preamble to the References section below).

5. The Children

The Net and the Web could be developed into the basis for an enormous improvement in the lot of children if only some of the evident economic prosperity could be redirected to helping the poor and educating their children. That in fact the opposite is happening is a political issue.

5.1   The Politics

As long as the governments of economically developed nations are devoted to the growth of their economies rather than the welfare of their subjects, the gap between their rich supporters and their poor subjects will grow, as will the number of disenchanted and disenfranchised in their countries [61], and the gap between their countries' economies and those of the poor supplier countries will also continue to grow.

History tells us that there will be two results of such widening disparities, one relatively short-term, the other long-term. The short-term result is revolution, of which the usual outcome is the replacement of one unsatisfactory form of government by a more ruthless one. A succession of worse governments will lead eventually to the second result—mayhem and complete social disruption [62].

The Net and the Web may very well enable bad governments to survive longer than they otherwise would, but the effect will only be to make the eventual complete disruption worse than it would otherwise be.

If our developed countries are to avoid such a fate, then very-well-considered political action will need to be taken over a long period of time by well-educated idealistic subjects who wish to become citizens in a society of citizens [63]. Such political action is becoming unlikely because welfare and education systems are being steadily disabled by the governments of developed countries on the advice of such experts as economic rationalists [64]. Indeed computers and the Net are proclaimed to be most desirable in reducing the cost of education, but are in reality most effective in reducing the possibility of students being educated (*http://www.allianceforchildhood.net/*).

The prospect for undeveloped countries is even worse because the governments of developed countries are being required to consistently support G7 economic expansion [65]. "Free trade" is the catchcry, which translates into the freedom of the rich to use digital technology to exploit the resources of the entire world, and to ignore the needs of its poor [66].

Counteracting these trends is, of course, a political matter, and as such is not usually considered a proper topic for discussion in professional writings (but see [67, 68]). However, for computing professionals the issue *is* relevant because the products and services of the profession are being used in support of the economic "and thence political" ambitions of the rich [32].

5.1.1   Globalization

An important, though probably temporary, use of the Net is to help some of those who see the political problems organize to protest in the close vicinity of meetings of developed country alliances such as the World Bank and the International Monetary Fund, and alliances of the super-rich such as the World Economic Forum.

Such protests are being tolerated by host governments, probably because they are unlikely to have much effect. Indeed, they are wonderfully entertaining for television viewers, and media commentators can easily be used to denigrate the protesters.

The pity is that the protests are directed against globalization, which indeed is being used as the basis for G7 economic expansion [69]. While globalization in its present form is being used to widen the gap between rich and poor, a globalization that instead spreads the direct and indirect benefits of digital technology intercommunally and internationally is the only way of ameliorating the present social disparities and avoiding eventual social disruption.

Global action, both political and technological, is needed to reverse the acceleration of the gap between rich and poor nations and between the rich and poor in nations. It is not appropriate here to review the needed global and local political action, except to observe that undisruptive change can only be achieved by the persistent and careful efforts of informed and educated people working primarily outside the mire of party politics. Such work can be greatly assisted by the Net and the Web (for Oxfam's successful work against the MAI see *http://www.oxfam.org.uk/policy/ papers/mai_update/mai_update.html*).

The Net and the Web must be able to be used in support of these political efforts. Maintaining the right and capability of people at large to use the Net and the Web noncommercially must be a prime objective of these political efforts. It is encouraging that organizations such as the Electronic Frontier [70] and the Open Software Movement (*http://www.opensource.org/*) have just such an objective.

However, the conditions of the poor cannot be significantly improved in five or 10 or 20 years. The solution lies in persistent long-term striving, by this generation and by the next. Thus the amelioration will be greatly hastened if this generation concentrates on educating the next to take up the political struggle. The Net and the Web, in uncommercialized forms, have great potential for fostering this education.

The following sections offer some speculative suggestions about how the Net and the Web might be directed to support the children of the world.

5.2 The Net

The Net is the latest stage in the development of communication between people. It should be developed to provide easy and cheap communication between people all over the world, particularly for poor people, both to promote cooperation and understanding and to bring them support from professional people and from other people with useful knowledge and experience.

The commandeering of the Net to provide primarily advertising and its accompanying entertainment must be averted. To promote understanding, official agencies should be constrained to provide local, regional, and international information and news over the Internet on a noncommercial basis, and to provide it credibly, reliably and thoroughly.

5.2.1 Information from the Net

Such information and news will be useless unless it is valued. It will not be useful amongst the poor people to whom it is of most potential value unless enough schooling is given for the poor, particularly the poor children, to understand and make use of it. Children must be armed with knowledge and attitudes that enable them to resist advertising, blunt or subtle, designed to persuade them to gamble or to buy junk food, pornography, and other harmful products [71]. Such education can only come from teachers and parents [54] but the Net and its Web could be of great help to educators provided we learn from past mistakes [72].

For the poor to benefit from the Net and its Web they must be educated in the traditional sense. That is, they must be given social skills and altruistic attitudes [73]. Education is moving away from such objectives in developed countries, where education is designed to inculcate the "ideals" of competition, independence, and enrichment for those who can afford an education, and towards control and training by machines for those for whom the government must still pretend to maintain some modicum of responsibility.

In developed countries, such a turnaround will be difficult to attain, because children are more influenced by television than they are by whatever schools and families are left to them. This forms a vicious circle leading to the further neglect of community and family values and the adoption of competition and social isolation.

In undeveloped countries the challenge is to avoid the breakdown of family values and the adoption of consumerist values as some degree of prosperity is attained and as commercial entertainment and its built-in advertising become widely adopted.

In all countries the ready availability through the Net of rich and credible information from many cultures, and of advice and encouragement from volunteer educators throughout the world, would be of immense value to concerned parents and trained teachers in their struggle to preserve or restore community values.

5.2.2 Technical standards

For the widespread use of the Net by poor communities, measures will have to be adopted so that the Net will be, first, very cheap to use and, secondly, very widely useable.

- Standards must be adopted for a basic level of capability on the Net, providing for voice, text, graphics, and video applications at the transport layer level and above of the OSI protocol model. As soon as they are stable, the standards must be frozen except for incremental improvement. All network service providers must be required to support these standards. The purpose of this freezing is to avoid the continuing adoption of new features and capabilities that tend more to create a new market and diminish a previous market than to provide significant new benefit to users.

- Standards must be adopted for a wireless networking protocol suitable for providing Internet services to isolated areas cheaply, and these standards should be made as stable as possible. The purpose is to provide at least voice, text, and simple graphic Net services as cheaply as possible to areas otherwise with few or no electronic communications services.

- Standards must be adopted for hardware to support, on the one hand voice, and on the other hand combined voice, text, and simple graphics services, provided by the Net. As much capability as possible, particularly window control, should be designed into the standard so that the operating systems providing services to the various classes of users shall be as simple and reliable as possible. The operating system should also, as a corollary, be defined by the standard. The purpose of all this is to make it possible, if not necessary, for industry to manufacture reliable Internet terminal hardware very cheaply and widely.

5.2.3 Exploiting the standards

The adoption of standards like those suggested just above could only be achieved by concerted and clever political action by persons of strong will and good faith. Keeping such standards alive over the long period of time that would be necessary to get the most benefit out of them for the poor of the world will be even more difficult, as commercial interests make much more profit from continually changing circumstances.

Getting to the poor the benefit of a basic Net also depends on getting Net equipment into the hands of the poor, at first for local communications, then for bringing advice and expertise of people who could help the poor better support themselves both in their living conditions and in their education and that of their children.

In practice, ensuring such equipment can be cheaply made in the quantities needed, and getting it into the hands of the poor is not an impossible problem as similar problems have already been solved on a small scale [74]. One great difficulty lies in enlisting and marshaling the help of experts, most likely but not only volunteers in other time zones, and to deliver that help effectively. The Net is a very important part of the solution to this difficulty.

5.3   The Web

The Web is the latest stage in the development of the storage and retrieval of data to allow information to be disseminated and exploited. It should be developed to allow useful data to be collected in vast quantities, and to be as useful as possible to as many people as possible all over the world, particularly poor people, both to supply knowledge and to enrich advice to poor people and to support the education and training of the children of those people.

5.3.1   Technical standards

For the widespread use of the Web by poor communities, measures will need to be adopted so that the Web will be, first, very cheap to use and, secondly, very widely useable.

- The present trends in the definition and operation of copyright law should be reversed [75]. The complete elimination of intellectual property in copyright should be at least considered as it acts primarily to enrich the media companies at the cost of almost everyone else. Furthermore, the very nature of digital encoding of data makes reliable and repeated copying so simple that enforcing copyright law has become a rather sick joke, attended by largely circumventable protective measures that lessen the effectiveness and reliability of equipment embodying the measures and make that equipment much more costly.

- Standards should be adopted for efficient processing of text represented in the world's eight or ten most-used writing systems, and for easy transliteration between them as far as possible. The purpose is to provide effective encoding of text that allows the minor languages of the poor of the undeveloped nations to be simply encoded using the most appropriate available writing system. The Unicode standard is unsuitable for such a purpose as it provides, alarmingly, for each language to be separately and rather inefficiently encoded [76].

- Standards should be adopted to allow the simple marking up of text and illustrations using the major writing systems in a language-independent way. Such standards are necessary to allow people literate in minor languages to produce material for the Web.

- Standards should be adopted for the collation and marking up of verbal material in association with graphic material, and for the verbal selection of such material, in a great variety of natural languages. Such standards are necessary because so many of the world's poor, both in rich countries and in poor, are functionally illiterate. Such standards are also important for the development of voice recognition techniques and equipment able to deal with a great variety of minor languages, and to be used for Web-assisted training.

- A standard intermediate language needs to be developed and adopted and exploited to allow automatic or computer-assisted translation into minor languages. This can only be done practically by having such an intermediate language for which minor language automatic and assisted translation can be developed and in which human translators can be trained.

5.3.2 Exploiting the standards

The purpose of the standards suggested above is to enable the Web to be used by the teachers of the poor and of the children of the poor, and by the children themselves and their parents. The standards, if adopted and enforced, would not provide in themselves a technical fix for the widening gap between rich and poor. Rather they would in the first instance provide a basis for the necessary help for the teachers and other workers essential to attack the problem, and only later to provide direct assistance to the poor.

The political problems of getting standards appropriate to the poor accepted, and of getting help for the poor in the first place, can only be surmounted by concerted world-wide political activity for which the support of the Net and the Web is essential. As these problems are solved, then the help and the standards need to be exploited to solve the basic problems of informing and educating the poor. Cheap and effective communications equipment for exploiting the Internet, and abundant and relevant data to be made useful by the Web, then need to be developed.

The suggested standards are directed to supporting the accumulation and dissemination of data stored on the Web so that poor and their helpers are as usefully and beneficially informed as possible.

6. Conclusion

Of the three entities mentioned in the title of this chapter, *the children* are the primary concern, and *the Net* and *the Web* are simply means that could be used to the great benefit of the children and, through them, the world at large.

The Net and the Web are portrayed here as the latest stage in the development of human civilization. The children are depicted here and elsewhere as the most severely affected victims of the misuse and degradation of the Net and its Web. If this depiction is accepted, then the problem to be faced is how to turn the Net and the Web into instruments for the betterment of children, and for the eventual creation of a world less betrayed by inequity [77].

While some technological suggestions have been made in the immediately preceding sections, the problem of global inequity will not be solved by technology. The problem is a social and political one [64]. All that technology can do is to help those who work to slow and eventually reverse the growing gap between the rich and the poor.

Technology is not the answer to the world's social problems. Indeed it is often their source. The problems can only be solved by people, although their efforts in problem solving can be made much more effective if the harmful effects of technology are recognized and averted, and if the use of technology is turned to help the world's afflicted and those who would help them [78].

REFERENCES

A thorough bibliographic study for the unreasonably ambitious undertaking of this chapter would be a full-time work of years. The references given below, and cited in the text, are therefore offered as illustration and suggestion rather than as corroborative detail.

However, the heart-rending plight of children that motivates this attempt to publicize it is well documented in the daily and weekly press. That plight is worsening. The author will maintain for a little while a list of URLs, mainly from the BBC who often give onward links, about more conspicuous tragedies inflicted on children, at *http://www.comp.utas.edu.au/users/nholmes/nwch/*

[1] Comerford, R. (2000). "Technology 2000: The Internet". *IEEE Spectrum*, **37**(1), 40–44.
[2] Rolt, L. T. C. (1970). *Victorian Engineering*. Penguin Books, Harmondsworth, Middlesex.
[3] Karl, T. R. and Trenberth, K. E. (1999). "The human impact on climate". *Scientific American*, **281**(6), 62–67.
[4] Mastro, J. G. (1999). "Signal to noise". *The Sciences*, **39**(6), 32–37.

[5] Corballis, M. C. (1999). "The gestural origins of language". *American Scientist*, **87**(2), 138–145.
[6] Zue, V. (1999). "Talking with your computer". *Scientific American*, **281**(2), 40–41.
[7] Bane, P. W. and Bradley, S. P. (1999). "The light at the end of the pipe". *Scientific American*, **281**(4), 90–95.
[8] Busnel, R. G. and Classe, A. (1976). *Whistled Languages*. Springer-Verlag, Berlin.
[9] Warnke, G. (1995). "Naturwissenschaft und Technik in Zeitalter der Aufklärung". In *So weit das Auge reicht: die Geschichte der optischen Telegrafie* (K. Beyrer and B.-S. Mathis, Eds.), pp. 16–28. Museum für Post und Kommunikation/G. Braun, Frankfurt am Main.
[10] Carroll, B. (1992). *Australian Communications through 200 Years*. Kangaroo Press, Kenthurst, NSW.
[11] Schürmann, A. (1995). "Kommunikation in der alten Gesellschaft". In *So weit das Auge reicht: die Geschichte der optischen Telegrafie* (K. Beyrer and B.-S. Mathis, Eds.), pp. 7–15. Museum für Post und Kommunikation/G. Braun, Frankfurt am Main.
[12] Holzmann, G. J. (1995). "Die optische Telegraphie in England und anderen Ländern". In *So weit das Auge reicht: die Geschichte der optischen Telegrafie* (K. Beyrer and B.-S. Mathis, Eds.), pp. 116–130. Museum für Post und Kommunikation/G. Braun, Frankfurt am Main.
[13] Holzmann, G. J. and Pehrson, B. (1995). *The Early History of Data Networks*. IEEE Press, Los Alamitos, CA.
[14] Standage, T. (1998). *The Victorian Internet: The Remarkable Story of the Telegraph and the Nineteenth Century's On-Line Pioneers*. Walker, New York.
[15] Abbatel, J. (1999). *Inventing/Building? the Internet*. MIT Press, Cambridge, MA.
[16] Hafner, K. and Lyon, M. (1996). *Where Wizards Stay up Late: The Origins of the Internet*. Simon and Schuster, New York.
[17] Goeller, L. (2000). "Insomniac wizards revisited". *IEEE Technology and Society*, **19**(2), 6–9.
[18] Chakrabarti, S., Dom, B. E., Kumar, S. R., Raghavan, P., Rajagopalan, S., Tomkins, A., Kleinberg, J. M. and Gibson, D. (1999). "Hypersearching the Web". *Scientific American*, **280**(6), 44–52.
[19] Schmandt-Besserat, D. (1996). *When Writing Came About*. Univ. of Texas Press, Austin.
[20] Febvre, L. and Martin, H-J. (1958). *L'Apparition du livre*. Éditions Albin Michel, Paris. [Trans: *The Coming of the Book*, Verso, London, 1976.]
[21] Manguel, A. (1996). *A History of Reading*. Flamingo, HarperCollins, London.
[22] Johns, A. (1998). *The Nature of the Book: Print and Knowledge in the Making*. Chicago Univ. Press, Chicago.
[23] Grafton, A. (1997). *The Footnote: A Curious History*. Faber and Faber, London.
[24] McKeough, J. and Stewart, A. (1997). *Intellectual Property in Australia*. Butterworths, Sydney.
[25] Parkes, M. B. (1992). *Pause and Effect: An Introduction to the History of Punctuation in the West*. Scolar Press, Aldershot, Hants., U.K.
[26] Petroski, H. (1999). *The Book on the Bookshelf*. Borzoi, Knopf, New York.
[27] Macedonia, M. (2000). "Why digital entertainment drives the need for speed". *IEEE Computer*, **33**(2), 124–127.
[28] Fox, E. A. and Marchionini, G. (1998). "Toward a worldwide digital library". *Communications of the ACM*, **41**(4), 28–32.
[29] Chen, H-C. and Houston, A. L. (1999). "Digital libraries: Social issues and technological advances". *Advances in Computers*, **48**, 257–314.
[30] Postman, N. (1993). *Technopoly: The Surrender of Culture to Technology*. Vintage Books, London.

[31] Stefik, M. (1996). *Internet Dreams: Archetypes, Myths, and Metaphores.* MIT Press, Cambridge, MA.
[32] Gates, J. R. (1998). *The Ownership Solution: Towards a Shared Capitalism for the Twenty-First Century.* Penguin Books, Harmondsworth, Middlesex.
[33] Clark, D. D. (1999). "High-speed data races home". *Scientific American,* **281**(4), 72–77.
[34] Pelton, J. N. (1998). "Telecommunications for the 21st century". *Scientific American,* **278**(4), 68–73.
[35] Riezenman, M. J. (2000). "Technology 2000: Communications". *IEEE Spectrum,* **37**(1), 33–38.
[36] Roberts, L. G. (2000). "Beyond Moore's law: Internet growth trends". *IEEE Computer,* **33**(1), 117–119.
[37] Stoll, C. (1995). *Silicon Snake Oil: Second Thoughts on the Information Highway.* Pan Books, Macmillan, London.
[38] Press, L. (1994). "Commercialization of the Internet". *Communications of the ACM,* **37**(11), 17–21.
[39] Brynjolfsson, E. and Yang, S-K. (1993). "Information technology and productivity: A review of the literature". *Advances in Computers,* **43**, 179–214.
[40] Berghel, H. (2000). "Predatory disintermediation". *Communications of the ACM,* **43**(5), 23–29.
[41] Hardman, V., Sasse, M. A. and Kouvelas, I. (1998). "Successful multiparty audio communication over the Internet". *Communications of the ACM,* **41**(5), 74–80.
[42] Livingston, J. D. (1998). "100 years of magnetic memories". *Scientific American,* **279**(5), 80–85.
[43] Brewington, B. E. and Cybenko, G. (2000). "Keeping up with the changing Web". *IEEE Computer,* **33**(5), 52–58.
[44] Mann, S. (2000). "Existential education in the era of personal cybernetics". *Communications of the ACM,* **43**(5), 33–36.
[45] Streitfeld, D. (2000). "Amazon's price experiment on the Web sparks consumer wrath". *Guardian Weekly,* **163**(16), 37.
[46] Brodley, C. E., Lane, T. and Stough, T. M. (1999). "Knowledge discovery and data mining". *American Scientist,* **87**(1), 54–61.
[47] Saul, J. R. (1995). *The Unconscious Civilization.* Penguin Books, Harmondsworth, Middlesex.
[48] King, P. and Tester, J. (1999). "The landscape of persuasive technologies". *Communications of the ACM,* **42**(5), 31–38.
[49] Berghel, H. and Blank, D. (1999). "The World Wide Web". *Advances in Computers,* **48**, 179–218.
[50] Bosak, J. and Bray, T. (1999). "XML and the second-generation Web". *Scientific American,* **280**(5), 79–83.
[51] Lawton, G. (2000). "Intellectual-property protection opens path for e-commerce". *IEEE Computer,* **33**(2), 14–17, 21.
[52] Introna, L. and Nissenbaum, H. (2000). "Defining the Web: The politics of search engines". *IEEE Computer,* **33**(1), 54–62.
[53] Bolt, D. B. and Crawford, A. K. (2000). *Digital Divide: Computers and Our Children's Future.* TV Books, New York.
[54] Holmes, W. N. (1999). "The myth of the educational computer". *IEEE Computer,* **32**(9), 36–42.
[55] Johnson, A. W. and Earle, T. (1987). *The Evolution of Human Societies.* Stanford Univ. Press, Stanford, CA.
[56] Pallast, G. (2000). "IMF's shock cures are killing off the patients". *Guardian Weekly,* **163**(16), 14.

[57] *The Economist* (2000), September 9, p. 42.
[58] Mowshowitz, A. (1992). "Virtual feudalism: A vision of political organization in the information age". *Informatization and the Public Sector*, **2**, 213–231.
[59] Vallas, S. (1998). "Manufacturing knowledge: Technology, culture, and social inequality at work". *Social Science Computer Review*, **16**(4), 353–369.
[60] Boothby, N. G. and Knudsen, C. M. (2000). "Children of the gun". *Scientific American*, **282**(6), 40–45.
[61] de Swaan, A. (1997). "The receding prospects for transnational social policy". *Theory and Society*, **20**, 561–575.
[62] Fukuyama, F. (1999). "The great disruption". *Atlantic Monthly*, **283**(5), 55–80.
[63] Dyson, E. (1997). *Release 2.0: A Design for Living in the Digital Age*. Penguin Books, Harmondsworth, Middlesex.
[64] Galbraith, J. K. (1992). *The Culture of Contentment*. Penguin Books, Harmondsworth, Middlesex.
[65] Friedman, J. (2000). "Americans again, or the new age of imperial reason?" *Theory, Culture & Society*, **17**(1), 139–146.
[66] de Swaan, A., Manor, J., Øyen, E. and Reis, E. P. (2000). "Elite perceptions of the poor". *Current Sociology*, **48**(1), 43–54.
[67] Balabanian, N. (2000). "Controlling technology: Should we rely on the marketplace?" *IEEE Technology and Society*, **18**(2), 23–30.
[68] Tavani, H. T. (1998). "Information technology, social values, and ethical responsibilities: A select bibliography". *IEEE Technology and Society*, **17**(2), 26–40.
[69] Pieterse, J. N. (2000). "Globalization north and south". *Theory, Culture & Society*, **17**(1), 129–137.
[70] Barlow, J. P. (1991). "Electronic frontier: Coming into the country". *Communications of the ACM*, **34**(3), 19–21.
[71] Berdichevsky, D. and Neunschwander, E. (1999). "Towards an ethics of persuasive technology". *Communications of the ACM*, **42**(5), 51–58.
[72] Hargittai, E. (2000). "Radio's lessons for the Internet". *Communications of the ACM*, **43**(1), 50–57.
[73] Damon, W. (1999). "The moral development of children". *Scientific American*, **281**(2), 56–62.
[74] Yunus, M. (1999). "The Grameen bank". *Scientific American*, **281**(5), 90–95.
[75] Walker, T. J. (1998). "Free Internet access to traditional journals". *American Scientist*, **86**(5), 463–471.
[76] Holmes, W. N. (1998). "Towards decent text encoding". *IEEE Computer*, **31**(8), 108–109.
[77] Shneiderman, B. (2000). "Universal usability". *Communications of the ACM*, **43**(5), 84–91.
[78] Friedman, T. L. (1999). *The Lexus and the Olive Tree*. HarperCollins, London.

Source Selection and Ranking in the WebSemantics Architecture Using Quality of Data Metadata[1]

GEORGE A. MIHAILA

Department of Computer Science
University of Toronto
Toronto, Ontario M5S 3G4
Canada
georgem@cs.toronto.edu

LOUIQA RASCHID

Robert H. Smith School of Business and UMIACS
University of Maryland
College Park, MD 20742
USA
louiqa@umiacs.umd.edu

MARÍA-ESTHER VIDAL

UMIACS
University of Maryland
College Park, MD 20742
USA
Departamento de Computación y Tecnología de la Información
Universidad Simón Bolívar
Caracas 1080-A
Venezuela
mvidal@umiacs.umd.edu

Abstract

The World Wide Web (WWW) has become the preferred medium for the dissemination of information in virtually every domain of activity. Standards and formats for structured data interchange are being developed. However, access to data is still hindered by the challenge of locating data relevant to a particular

[1] This research was partially sponsored by the National Science Foundation grants IRI9630102 and DMI9908137, the Defense Advanced Research Projects Agency Grant 01–5–28838 and by CONICIT, Venezuela.

problem. Further, after a set of relevant sources has been identified, one must still decide which source is best suited for a given task, based on its contents or domain knowledge, and appropriately rank these sources. WWW sources typically may cover different domains and they may differ considerably with respect to a variety of quality of data (QoD) parameters. Examples of QoD parameters are completeness of the source contents and recency of update of the contents. In order to solve this problem of source selection and ranking, we maintain metadata about source content and quality of data—or scqd metadata. We use a data model for representing scqd metadata similar to those used in a data warehouse environment. The WebSemantics (WS) architecture (G. Mihaila *et al.*, 1998, in *Proc. 6th Int. Conf. On Extending Database Technology (EDBT)*, pp. 87–101; and G. Mihaila *et al.*, 2000, *Very Large Database Journal*, in press) was developed to solve the task of publishing and locating data sources using the WWW. We first present the WS architecture. We then describe extensions to the WS data model, catalog and query engine, to handle scqd metadata. The query language for source selection and ranking supports both strict and fuzzy matching of scqd metadata. Then we present some problems in the efficient management of the scqd metadata. We discuss how scqd metadata can be organized in partially ordered sets to support efficient query processing. Some queries cannot be answered by any single source. Thus, we must consider the task of combining multiple scqd's to select combinations of sources in the answer. We consider a number of techniques for combining scqd's. We compare the efficiency of these techniques, as well as possible loss of accuracy incurred due to some of the techniques, when combining scqd metadata.

1. Introduction 89
2. A Motivating Example 91
3. WebSemantics Architecture for Publishing and Locating Data Sources. 92
   3.1 Architecture. 92
   3.2 Publishing Data Sources in WS-XML 93
   3.3 WebSemantics Catalog. 95
4. Describing Source Content and Quality Metadata 96
   4.1 Model for Source Content and Quality Descriptions 97
5. Queries for Discovering, Selecting and Ranking Sources 100
   5.1 Discovering Data Sources 100
   5.2 Selecting and Ranking Data Sources 101
   5.3 The QoD Applet. 104
6. Efficient Manipulation of Scqd's 104
   6.1 Grouping Scqd's Using Partially Ordered Sets 105
   6.2 Computational Issues in Accessing Combination of Scqd's 108
   6.3 Finding Best Sources Using the Partially Extended Po-set 112
7. Related Research. 113
8. Summary and Future Work. 115
   References 116

1. Introduction

The World Wide Web has become the preferred medium for the dissemination of information in virtually every domain of activity. While most of this information is textual, we are witnessing an increasing interest in using this medium as a platform for publishing structured and semi-structured data, such as scientific data sets in various disciplines. For example, large collections of data about the environment are publicly available in online repositories [1−4].

The World Wide Web (WWW) is a system for sharing *documents*. In this system, documents are published and accessed via the HTTP protocol and HTML document format standards. Recently XML and XMLSchema [5, 6] have been proposed and widely adopted as a data exchange format and a model for exchanging structured data on the WWW. Online collections of structured data, e.g., scientific data sets, often comply with a standard for interoperability, e.g., the data are in a relational DBMS. The data may also conform to a common semantics; i.e., each item of data is precisely defined. The concept of sharing such information comes under the umbrella of the *Semantic Web* proposed by Berners-Lee in [7]. However, the sharing of information between scientists is still a very difficult process. Sharing is hindered by the lack of mechanisms for *describing and publishing* data sources, and for *discovering* the existence of data relevant to a problem.

Resource description languages and mechanisms for resource discovery have been proposed [8−12]. Much of this work has centered on bibliographic collections and resource discovery and information sharing among such specialized collections. There has been some work on extensions to other domains, for example, geo-referenced or geo-spatial data [11]. However, there is still little support for publishing and describing data sources for structured data on the WWW, and for resource discovery using the metadata of these sources.

In related research, we developed WebSemantics (WS), a system that permits publication and discovery of sources containing typed data, using the WWW and XML. WS extends the WWW with a specification for publishing the location, and optionally the metadata (types and domain knowledge) of sources, in WS-XML documents. The WS-XML specification is an instance of the XML [5] metalanguage. WS-XML assumes the use of XMLSchema to describe types and domain metadata. WS then provides a catalog and query language for discovering relevant (published) data sources. The language combines features for searching relevant WS-XML documents that publish data sources with features for searching over the metadata describing these sources. This approach smoothly integrates the functionality already existing on the WWW for searching documents with the WS extensions for searching over the metadata.

The research described in this paper addresses the task of selecting and ranking sources, assuming that they have been discovered and registered in the WS catalog. After a set of relevant sources has been identified, one still must decide which source is best suited for a given task and appropriately rank these sources. WWW sources typically may cover different domains and they may differ considerably with respect to the domain metadata about their *contents*. They may also differ based on the *quality of data* (QoD) parameters that describe their contents. Criteria for judging the quality of data in a source have been proposed in the literature [13]. In [14], we identified four QoD parameters: completeness, recency, frequency of updates, and granularity. These four parameters are a subset of the rich geo-spatial metadata standards that have been developed and widely accepted, including the ANZLIC (Australian New Zealand Land Information Council) standard [15] and the DIF (Directory Interchange Format) [16].

To solve the problem of source selection and ranking using QoD parameters, we maintain metadata about source content and quality of data—or scqd metadata. We present a data model for the *source content quality descriptions* (scqd's) that are used to describe the source metadata. The data model is similar to those used in a data warehousing environment, and is based on a set of dimension attributes, a set of measure attributes, domains, and a set of QoD parameters. The WS query language has been extended for source selection and ranking, using both strict and fuzzy matching of the scqd metadata. We present the features of the language by example.

The rich scqd data model must be searched efficiently to support source selection and ranking. The size of the search space is dominated by the size of the content descriptors, which may be very large. Further, when a single source cannot answer a query, multiple scqd's must be combined. Thus, we must consider techniques for the management of the scqd metadata. We discuss how scqd metadata can be organized in partially ordered sets (po-sets), and we describe how the po-set can be searched efficiently.

Some queries cannot be answered by a single source. Thus, we must consider the task of combining multiple scqd's to select combinations of sources in the answer. The number of possible combinations is also dominated by the size of the content descriptors. We consider a number of techniques for combining scqd's. The first is a naive online algorithm to enumerate all the scqd's and can be expensive. To avoid enumerating an exponential number of possible combinations, we propose a heuristic that gradually extends the associated po-set of scqd metadata toward a lattice. There is a potential tradeoff between the size of the po-set and the loss of accuracy of the scqd metadata, when combining multiple scqd's. The tradeoff depends on the particular technique that is chosen.

This paper is organized as follows: Section 2 provides a motivating example and Section 3 presents the WS architecture. Section 4 describes the data model for scqd metadata and Section 5 describes the query language extensions for source selection and ranking. Section 6 discusses techniques for the efficient manipulation of scqd's. Section 7 presents related work and Section 8 concludes.

2. A Motivating Example

Consider a collection of data sources containing meteorological data such as temperature, air pressure, and rainfall. These correspond to the measure attributes of a data warehouse. We can also consider some dimension attributes, e.g., time and location (or city). Suppose we visualize the data in several sources using the following relations: *Air(time, city, temperature, pressure)*, *Precipitation(time, city, rainfall)*, etc. These sources record measurements in the form of time series data at some given granularity, e.g., one tuple every hour.

Individual data sources will typically contain data only for a subset of these types for different domains. Sources may also differ on the time granularity of their measurement. A source may record one measurement every hour, or two measurements each day, etc. Finally, for some domain and time granularity, source S_1 may have *all* the temperature and pressure data for Toronto since 1990, while source S_2 may have 80% of all the temperature data, 50% of the pressure data and 90% of the rainfall data for Kingston for the current year, and source S_3 may have half of the rainfall and temperature data for Canada since 1950.

Another facet of data quality is its timeliness. Different sources may contain more (or less) recent data, and may be updated at various rates (daily, weekly, twice a month, etc.). In many cases data quality degrades over time so consumers will seek the most recent data for their applications.

Thus, we need to obtain source content and quality of data metadata, to assist the user in selecting and ranking sources best suited for some query. For example, a scientist who wants to study the evolution of temperature in Toronto over the past 50 years should be able to identify source S_3 as containing most of the relevant data.

3. WebSemantics Architecture for Publishing and Locating Data Sources

In related research [17, 18] we have presented the WS architecture to address the task of publishing and locating data sources. The WS architecture supports the following functions:

- An architecture that permits the publication and discovery of data sources containing structured data,
- A catalog that stores metadata about data sources in a specific application domain, and
- A query language that supports the discovery of data sources.

A description of a prototype implementation of the WS architecture, catalog, and query language is in [18]. In this section, we briefly review the WS architecture and the current prototype.

3.1 Architecture

The WS system has a layered architecture of interdependent components (see Fig. 1). The *data source layer* has two components, *data sources* and *wrappers*. Data providers create and manage collections of autonomous *data sources* that can be accessed over the Internet. These data sources can provide query capability ranging from full DBMS functionality to simple scanning of files. WS assumes uniform access to both kinds of sources, independent of the capability of the sources. This is accomplished using *wrapper* components.

The second layer is the *World Wide Web layer*. The WWW is used as a medium for describing and publishing sources. Thus, in order to publish a data source, a provider needs to create a WS-XML document describing the source.

The third layer is the *catalog layer*. A *catalog* is a specialized repository storing metadata about a collection of data sources in some application domain. For each source, the catalog maintains metadata characterizing the source, such as the set of types exported by the source, the domains for a subset of attributes of some types, a textual description of the data source, and the URL of the WS-XML document that published the source.

Finally, the WS *query processor* component, bound to a specific catalog, allows the user to discover and select sources based on the available metadata.

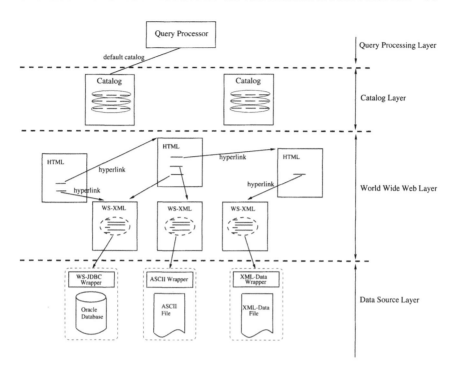

FIG. 1. The WebSemantics layered architecture.

3.2 Publishing Data Sources in WS-XML

Suppose a community of environmental scientists agreed on a common schema, EnvSchema, and an associated semantics for various measurements. The schema consists of a set of *types*, e.g., relational table names and attributes. While we use the relational data model to simplify our example, WS does not insist on the use of the relational model. In order to make the schema available to everyone, they publish it on the Web, in the XML file shown in Fig. 2. This file conforms to the XML-Schema conventions for describing strongly typed relational data [6]. It identifies a type Air, and attributes and data types, e.g., city of type string.

Consider a scientist who measures air quality parameters in Ontario. She measures the concentration of greenhouse gases in the atmosphere and stores the results of her daily measurements in a DB2 database. The schema of this database follows the shared semantics, EnvSchema. In order to make this data source known to WebSemantics users, she publishes a WS-XML document, as shown in Fig. 3. It specifies the connection information for the source, including the type or location of the wrapper, e.g., a JDBC

```
<xs:schema xmlns:xs="http://www.w3.org/1999/XMLSchema" version="1.0">

  <xs:element name="Air">
    <xs:complexType content="empty">
      <xs:attribute name="date"            type="timeInstant"/>
      <xs:attribute name="city"        type="string"/>
      <xs:attribute name="CO2percentage" type="float"/>
      ...
    </xs:complexType>
  </xs:element>

  <xs:element name="Rainfall">
    ...
  </xs:element>

</xs:schema>
```

FIG. 2. The `EnvSchema.xml` file: a shared schema for environmental data.

```
<?xml version="1.0"?>
<!DOCTYPE ws SYSTEM "wsxml.dtd">
<ws>
 <source>
  <sci>
     <wrapper wtype="JDBC"/>
     <repository rtype="DB2"
           rlocation="jdbc:db2://server.env.org/ontario"/>
  </sci>
  <metadata>
     <schema>http://www.env.org/EnvSchema.xml</schema>
     <type name = "Air"> ... </type>
     <type name = "Precipitation"> ... </type>
  </metadata>
  <desc> This repository contains daily measurements of air quality
        parameters in Ontario for the year 2000. </desc>
 </source>
</ws>
```

FIG. 3. Describing a data source in a WS-XML document.

driver for the DB2 DBMS, and the location of the data source. The document also identifies a subset of types from the shared schema (EnvSchema) that are available in this source. Optionally, additional metadata about the content and quality of each type can be specified, as will be discussed in Section 4.

3.3   WebSemantics Catalog

In the current prototype, we have implemented a centralized catalog for a small collection of data sources. The catalog currently supports catalog construction, querying, and simple maintenance tasks (deleting and updating individual sources). During catalog construction, when a new source is registered, the catalog downloads the corresponding WS-XML document and extracts types and domain metadata exported by each source.

During the catalog query phase, the catalog answers queries on sources, types, and domains, by accessing the data stored in the catalog. The query task is handled by the **ViewCat** applet (shown in Fig. 4). On

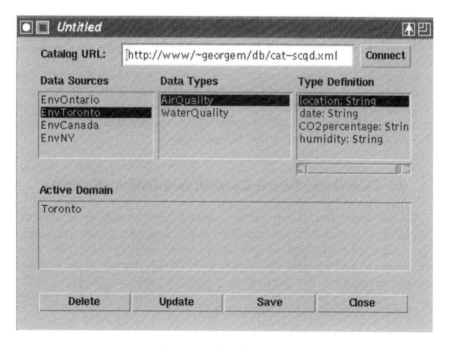

FIG. 4. The ViewCat applet.

startup, the applet connects to the catalog specified in the command line and displays a list of all the registered sources. Alternatively, users can connect to another WS catalog by typing its address in the **Catalog URL** text area and pressing the **Connect** button. There are two types of catalog addresses:

- a URL of a WS-XML file (e.g., "http://www.env.org/catalog.xml") and
- an RMI URL of a remote catalog (e.g., "rmi://www.env.org/Catalog").

In the first case, the built-in catalog loads and parses the specified file, registering all the sources described therein. In the second case, the applet contacts the specified remote catalog through the remote method invocation (RMI) protocol [19].

3.3.1 Viewing the catalog contents—the ViewCat applet

Upon selection of a source, the set of types available in that source is displayed in a listbox. The lower text area displays the connection information for that source. Upon selection of a type, the set of its attributes (and their data types) is displayed in the "Type Definition" listbox. Finally, the active domain of any attribute in the current source can be computed by selecting the attribute of interest from the list. For example, in Fig. 4, the domain for attribute "location" is displayed.

In Section 7, we have compared the WS approach with related work. One important aspect of such a comparison is the efficiency of the WS catalog in indexing WS-XML pages, and in supporting queries. We refer the reader to [20], which has some experimental results comparing the cost of accessing WS-XML pages versus using the WS catalog.

4. Describing Source Content and Quality Metadata

We introduce four quality of data parameters: completeness, recency, frequency of updates, and granularity, and then present a metadata model for source content (and) quality descriptions (scqd's), based on these parameters. We then describe extending the WebSemantics architecture to publishing metadata for the sources. Finally, we discuss extensions to the query language to support source selection and ranking using the metadata.

The four QoD parameters are as follows:

- Completeness: Suppose there is some ideal, possibly virtual, complete source that contains all the relevant data. Now, any particular source generally contains a fraction of the data (tuples) in the complete source. An estimate of the fraction of the data of the complete source that is in the particular data source represents its *completeness*. The completeness measure is useful in query evaluation to select sources that are most likely to contain relevant information. Completeness may be estimated using query feedback, for example, based on the queries that were successfully answered at this source, or may be provided by an administrator or expert user.

- Recency: Another important aspect of data quality is the *recency* of the data. One can imagine an environment where several data sources provide similar information, but some sources have older data than others. In many application domains data quality tends to depreciate over time so it makes sense whenever we have a choice to try to use the most recent data.

- Frequency of updates: A large class of sources are updated at fixed length intervals, e.g., weekly or daily. If the *frequency of updates* is available, it is reasonable to take it into consideration as an indication of the quality of a data source. Also, it can be used to estimate the recency, if the last update time is unknown.

- Granularity: An important class of data is "time-series" data consisting of periodic samplings of some time-varying measure attribute. Examples include meteorological information, stock closing prices, and currency exchange rates. A common characteristic of these data types is the presence of a time attribute in the type definition and a functional dependency of all the other (measure) attributes on this one. For this class of data, one can distinguish among sources based on the sampling granularity, e.g., hourly, daily, weekly.

4.1 Model for Source Content and Quality Descriptions

We introduce a metadata model for scqd's as follows:

- **SODA** is a set of dimension attributes, e.g., *city*, *time*.
- **SOMA** is a set of measure attributes, e.g., *temperature*, *pressure*.
- T_1, T_2, ..., T_n are relational types, where each type T_i has attributes A_{i1}, A_{i2}, ..., $A_{ik_i} \in$ **SODA** $\cup$ **SOMA**. Every attribute A_{ij} is associated with a domain $dom(A_{ij})$.
- A source S contains data for a subset of T_1, T_2, ..., T_n
- A source S may have several scqd's describing its contents.

An scqd is a triple $(t, cd, qods)$, where:

- t is a type,
- cd is a content descriptor that specifies domains for some of the dimension attributes of t, and
- $qods$ is a set of quality of data (qod) descriptors.

A qod descriptor is a tuple $(lcd, c, r, f, g, soma)$, where:

- lcd is a content descriptor corresponding to the contents of some specific source,
- the parameters c, r, f, g correspond to the QoD parameters *completeness, recency, frequency of updates* and *granularity*, respectively, and
- $soma \subseteq$ **SOMA** is a subset of the measure attributes of t.

The QoD parameters qualify the *soma* attributes in the source described by the *lcd*. They are as follows: c estimates the fraction of the data in the *complete type*[2] available in the source, r is the recency of the data, f represents the length of the intervals when the data are updated, and g specifies the granularity of some dimension attributes.

Example 4.1 The *scqd*'s for describing some sources that contain data corresponding to the types *Air* and *Precipitation* are as follows:

Air(time, city, temperature, pressure)
S_1 $scqd_{11}$: (Air, [(city, *CityInCanada*), (time, *YearSince1990*)], $\{qod_{111}\}$)
      qod_{111}: ([(city, {Toronto}), (time, *CurrentYear*)], 1.0, 5 days, _,
                  (time, 1 hour), {temperature, pressure})
S_2 $scqd_{21}$: (Air, [(city, *CityInUSA*), (time, *CurrentYear*)],
                  $\{qod_{611}, qod_{612}\}$)
      qod_{211}: ([(city, {NYC}), (time, *CurrentYear*)], 0.7, 3 days, _,
                  (time, 4 hours), {temperature})
      qod_{212}: ([(city, {NYC}), (time, *CurrentYear*)], 0.4, 3 days, _,
                  (time, 12 hours), {pressure})
S_3 $scqd_{31}$: (Air, [(city, *CityInCanada*), (time, *YearSince1950*)], $\{qod_{311}\}$)
      qod_{311}: ([(city, *CityInCanada*), (time, *YearSince1950*)], 0.5, 10 days,
                  _, (time, 24 hours), {temperature, pressure})
Precipitation(time, city, rainfall)
S_2 $scqd_{22}$: (Precipitation, [(city, *CityInUSA*), (time, *CurrentYear*)],
                  $\{qod_{221}\}$)

---

[2] The complete type is a possibly virtual relation that contains all the relevant data for the type.

qod_{221}: ([(city, {NYC}), (time, *CurrentYear*)], 0.9, 2 days, _,
(time, 12 hours), {rainfall})

S_3 $scqd_{32}$: (Precipitation, [(city, *CityInCanada*), (time, *YearSince1950*)],
{qod_{321}})

qod_{321}: ([(city, *CityInCanada*), (time, *YearSince1950*)], 0.5, 10 days,
_, (time, 24 hours), {rainfall})

Source S_1 contains *Air* data, for *city* in *CityInCanada* and *time* in
YearSince1990. The QoD values indicate that for *city* = Toronto and time in
CurrentYear, for measure attributes *temperature* and *pressure*, the completeness is 1.0 (100%), the recency is 3 days, and the granularity is once per
hour with respect to the dimension attribute *time*. The update frequency is
not specified, but we can estimate that the update frequency can be no better
than once in 3 days, since the recency is at least 3 days.

```
<?xml version="1.0"?>
<ws>
 <source>
  ... (source connection information as in Figure 3)
  <metadata>
     <scqd type = "Air">
        <domain attr="location"
                domtype="enumeration"
                values="Halifax Montreal Toronto Calgary Vancouver"/>
        <domain attr="time" domtype="range"
                minvalue="Jan 1, 1990" maxvalue="Dec 31, 2000"/>
        <qod>
          <subdomain attr="location" domtype="enumeration"
               values="Toronto"/>
          <subdomain attr="time" domtype="range"
               minvalue="Jan 1, 2000" maxvalue="Dec 31, 2000"/>
          <dimension name="completeness" value="1.0" />
          <dimension name="last_updated" value="Mar 1, 2000" />
          <dimension name="granularity" attr="time" value="1 hour" />
          <measure attrs="temperature pressure"/>
        </qod>
     </scqd>
      ...
  </metadata>
 </source>
</ws>
```

FIG. 5. Encoding QoD metadata in a WS-XML document.

For convenience, we refer to a user-defined hierarchy of the domain metadata, for the dimension attributes, e.g., (*city*, Toronto) is *included* in (*city*, *CityInCanada*).

Sources will publish their metadata information using the WWW. In Fig. 5, we encode this information in an XML file, using the WS-XML format [18]. Note that this is an extension of the WS-XML format presented earlier in Fig. 3. The extension allows for the publishing of scqd metadata.

5. Queries for Discovering, Selecting, and Ranking Sources

The WebSemantics Query Language (WSQL) [18] supports finding data sources that are published in WS-XML documents or that are registered in existing catalogs. The WSQL language integrates constructs borrowed from WebSQL [21] and OQL [22]. To introduce the functionality of the WS language, we first describe queries to discover data sources. Then we consider the WS query features to select and rank sources. We present the features of the language through examples.

5.1   Discovering Data Sources

Suppose that a scientist is interested in air quality data for his research. In order to locate data sources of interest, he can execute the following query:

Query 1 Find all the sources described in WS documents that mention the phrase "air quality".

select *s*
from   Document *d* **such that** *d* **mentions** "air quality",
              Source *s* **such that** *d* **describes** *s*;

A user can exploit additional information, for example, the home page of a particular research institute, to restrict the scope of the search to the pages reachable from that home page. The following query would build the desired collection of sources:

Query 2 Find all the sources described in WS-XML documents reachable from "http://www.env.org/" that contain the phrase "air quality" in their text.

select *s*
from   Document *d* **such that** "http://www.env.org/" $\rightarrow$ * *d*,
              Source *s* **such that** *d* **describes** *s*
where   *d.text* **contains** "air quality";

An alternative is to pick sources directly from specialized WS catalogs. For instance, going back to our example with environmental data, suppose one knows the addresses of several catalogs registering relevant data sources. One can select sources of interest from these catalogs with the following query:

Query 3 Find all data sources containing air quality information for Toronto, identified from a specific list of catalogs.

select s
from   Catalog c **in** {"rmi://alpha.env.org/WSCatalog", "rmi://rep.env.ca/
          Catalog"},
          Source s **in** $c.sources$,
          Scqd c **in** $s.scqds$,
          Qod q **in** $c.qods$
where $c.type =$ "Air"
          and $q.lcd \geqslant$ [(city, {Toronto})];

5.2 Selecting and Ranking Data Sources

We extend the WS query language to exploit QoD parameters to select among a collection of data sources and rank them. The language can express queries with both *strict* and *fuzzy* conditions on the QoD dimensions associated with specific content descriptions. Strict conditions are comparison predicates. Fuzzy conditions, on the other hand, are proximity predicates allowing one to specify imprecisely a desired target value for a certain QoD parameter. The evaluation of a query returns a list of sources that support the specified content description and *satisfy* the strict QoD conditions. The sources are *ranked* according to the degree to which they satisfy the fuzzy conditions. We illustrate the features of this language by the following query:

Query 4 Find the best two sources that maintain information for the temperature in Toronto for the current year. Relevant sources must maintain 60% of all the data and the intervals of samples must be close to 1 hour.

select   **best** 2 s
from   Source s,
          Scqd c **in** $s.scqds$,
          Qod q **in** $c.qods$
where $c.type =$ "Air"
          and $q.soma \geqslant$ {"temperature"}
          and $q.lcd \geqslant$ [(city, {Toronto}), (time, *Current Year*)]
          and $q.completeness > 0.6$
          and $q.granularity$ **close to** "1 hour";

Note that the condition on the *completeness* parameter is a *strict* condition, while that on the *granularity* parameter is a *fuzzy* condition. A *relevant* source for this query is a source that contains an *scqd* that is *greater* than the specified *cd*,[3] and whose completeness is *better* than the cutoff value. Note the overloaded use of the "⩾" operator. In the predicate on *q.soma*, the "⩾" operator means set inclusion. However, in the predicate on *q.lcd*, it means set inclusion of the domains of the corresponding dimension attributes, e.g., `city` and `time`. This query will return an ordered list of sources whose granularity comes closest to 1 hour, i.e., S_1 ($g = 1$ hour), S_3 ($g = 24$ hours).

In order to produce this ordered list, all the sources matching the *lcd* and *completeness* QoD requirements for the granularity value are assigned a score in the interval [0, 1]. The score reflects the degree the source granularity x matches the target granularity value (1 hour). We also need a method of combining the individual scores. Details of how sources are ranked are in [20] and we provide a brief description as follows:

By convention, we choose scoring functions with values in the interval [0, 1] with an exact match represented by a score of 1 and all other approximate matches represented by scores less than 1 (a higher value meaning a better match). In general, given a QoD equality condition of the form *s.x* **close to** v (where x is a dimension and v is a constant value), one possible scoring function is $\theta_v : S \rightarrow [0, 1]$, $\theta_v(s) = 1/(1 + |s.x - v|)$. It is easy to see that this function has the properties mentioned above.

The second problem, that of combining the scores, has been considered in other contexts [23, 24]. For example, in [24], Fagin gives formulas for computing the score for a conjunction of individual conditions. Thus, he examines two cases: first, if the conditions are equally important, he proposes a conservative approach, namely, to take the minimum of all scores. Other strategies have been considered in the literature that use the maximum, the average, etc. The second case is when some conditions are more important than others. As an example, consider we are searching for sources whose completeness is close to 0.5 and whose recency is close to 1 day. We also care twice as much about the recency than about the completeness. In general, if a query consists of n conditions, users can attach to each condition C_i a positive weight w_i such that $\Sigma_{i=1,n} w_i = 1$. Then we combine the individual scores $x_1, ..., x_n$, using the formula [24]:

$$(w_1 - w_2)f(x_1) + 2(w_2 - w_3)f(x_1, x_2) + \cdots + nw_n f(x_1, x_2, ..., x_n),$$

---

[3] Each *cd* is represented by a literal $[(attr_1, dom_1), ..., (attr_k, dom_k)]$ in the query.

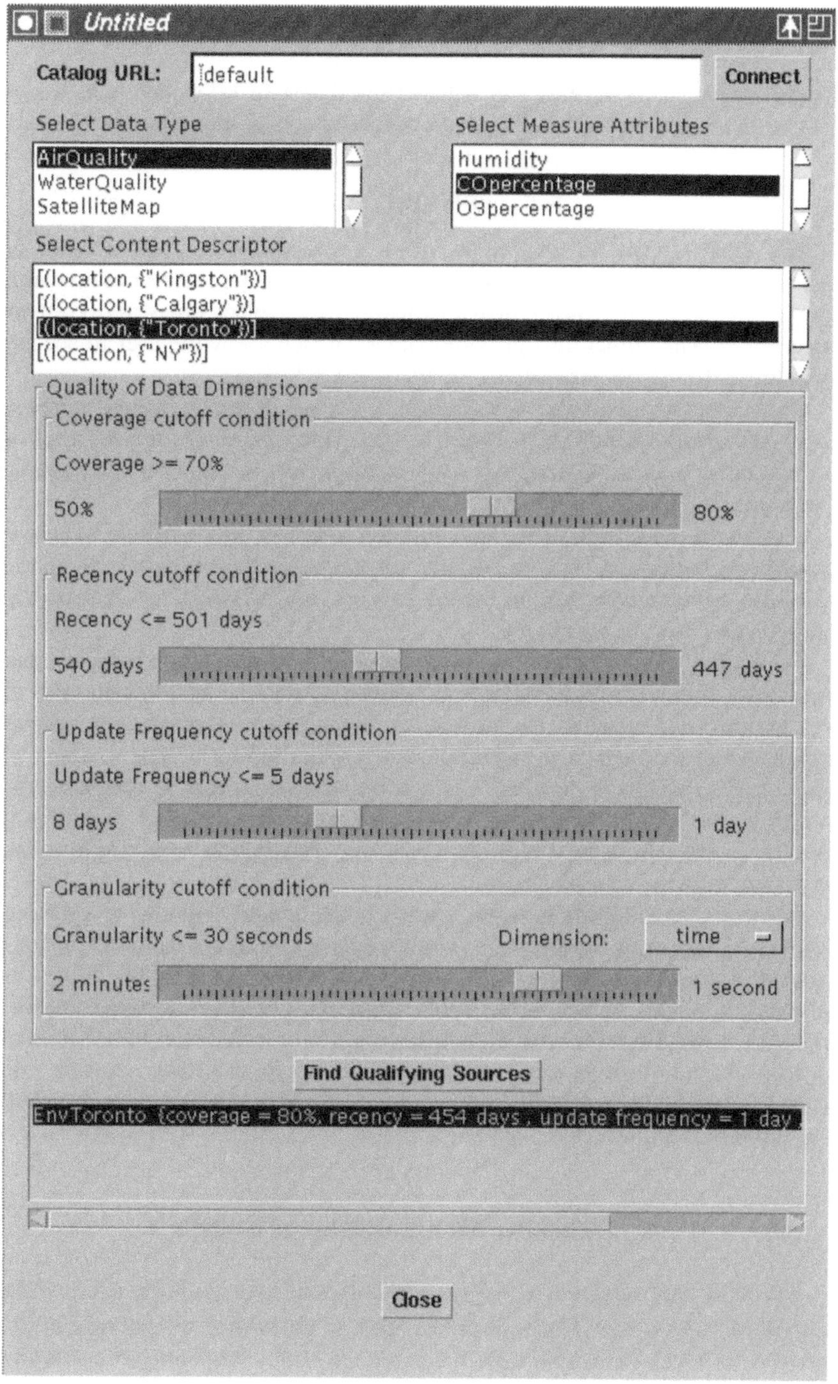

FIG. 6. The QoD applet.

where $w_1 \geqslant w_2 \ldots \geqslant w_n$ and f is a function that can take any number of scores and produce an unweighted combined score, e.g., *min, max, avg.*

5.3 The QoD Applet

The **QoD** applet in Fig. 6 provides a simple and intuitive way of specifying the selection criteria for sources based on their contents and quality of data. The applet provides listboxes to select types and content descriptors. The applet also provides sliders, which allow the user to specify the cutoffs for QoD parameters, in an intuitive fashion.

Upon connection to the WS catalog, a list of all the registered types is displayed in the "Select Data Type" listbox. Once a type is selected, a set of all available content descriptors (*cd*) is displayed in the "Select Content Descriptor" listbox.

It is worth mentioning here that this list contains only "atomic" content descriptors, obtained by individually enumerating the elements of all the attribute domains specified in all the sources, e.g., (location, Toronto) and (location, Kingston).

For each atomic *cd* that is selected, the applet updates the minimum and maximum values for all the sliders, corresponding to the QoD parameters of the sources that support this atomic *cd*. The user can subsequently specify cutoff values for each of the QoD parameters desired in the query. Once all the cutoff values have been set, the qualifying sources can be computed by pressing the "Find Qualifying Sources" button. The system generates a WSQL query capturing these requirements, executes it, and displays the matching sources in rank order.

We note that the **QoD** applet is limited in the queries that can be specified via its interface. For example, it currently only allows users to specify atomic content descriptors. The user may specify the desired *q.lcd* for the query, by selecting multiple atomic descriptors from a (multiple selection) listbox. However, selecting the cutoff parameters for a combination of atomic descriptors is not intuitively supported in the applet interface. Further, the applet currently only allows a query to specify strict matching on the QoD parameters.

6. Efficient Manipulation of Scqd's

The scqd data model is a rich metadata model with multiple (extensible) dimensions. For example, both the number of dimension attributes and the number of QoD parameters can be extended. The complexity of searching scqd's is further increased when a single source cannot answer a query, and we must consider combining scqd's of multiple sources. For these reasons, we must provide efficient access structures to search the scqd's, and to identify the relevant sources.

6.1 Grouping Scqd's Using Partially Ordered Sets

To provide an efficient structure to search the scqd's, we group the scqd's using *lcd*—the content description for some source—and the set of measure attributes *soma*. The scqd's are grouped into *maximal compatibility classes*, where each class is induced by the equality relation applied to the *lcd* (and the *soma*) of the scqd. We refer to each class that is induced as a *bucket*.

Example 6.1 In addition to the scqd's presented in Example 4.1, consider the following:

Air(time, city, temperature, pressure)

S_4 $scqd_{41}$:   (Air, [(city, *CityInCanada*), (time, *YearSince1990*)], $\{qod_{411}\}$)

     qod_{411}:   ([(city, {Toronto}), (time, *CurrentYear*)], 0.9, 5 days, _,
          (time, 2 hours), {temperature, pressure})

S_5 $scqd_{51}$:   (Air, [(city, *CityInCanada*), (time, *CurrentYear*)],
          $\{qod_{511}, qod_{512}\}$)

     qod_{511}:   ([(city, {Kingston}), (time, *CurrentYear*)], 0.7, 7 days, _,
          (time, 4 hours), {temperature})

     qod_{512}:   ([(city, *CityInCanada*), (time, *CurrentYear*)], 0.7, 9 days, _,
          (time, 12 hours), {pressure})

S_6 $scqd_{61}$:   (Air, [(city, *CityInCanada*), (time, *CurrentYear*)],
          $\{qod_{611}, qod_{612}\}$)

     qod_{611}:   ([(city, {Kingston}), (time, *CurrentYear*)], 0.8, 2 days, _,
          (time, 12 hours), {temperature})

     qod_{612}:   ([(city, *CityInCanada*), (time, *CurrentYear*)], 0.7, 9 days, _,
          (time, 12 hours), {pressure})

Table I presents the buckets induced by the relation *equals* on the scqd's. To simplify our example, we do not consider the *soma* at present. The bucket descriptor identifies the relevant scqd metadata (*lcd*) for the bucket. The bucket contents identify the matchings sources and their scqd's.

Consider the following query:

Query 5 Find sources containing Air data for Toronto for the current year.

select   *s*
from   Source *s*,
         Scqd *c* **in** *s.scqds*,
         Qod *q* **in** *c.qods*
where   *c.type* = "Air"
         and   *q.lcd* $\geqslant$ [(city, {Toronto}), (time, *CurrentYear*)];

TABLE I

BUCKETS FOR THE SCQD'S IN EXAMPLES 4.1 AND 6.1

Bucket	Bucket descriptor (lcd descriptor)	Bucket contents
B_{11}	[(city, *CityInCanada*), (time, *YearSince1950*)]	$\{(S_3, scqd_{31})\}$
B_{12}	[(city, {NYC}), (time, *Current Year*)]	$\{(S_2, scqd_{21})\}$
B_{21}	[(city, *CityInCanada*), (time, *Current Year*)]	$\{(S_5, scqd_{51}), (S_6, scqd_{61})\}$
B_{31}	[(city, {Toronto}), (time, *Current Year*)]	$\{(S_1, scqd_{11}), (S_4, scqd_{41})\}$
B_{32}	[(city, {Kingston}), (time, *Current Year*)]	$\{(S_5, scqd_{51}), (S_6, scqd_{61})\}$

The relevant sources for this query will have a local content description *lcd* that is *greater* than [(city, {Toronto}), (time, *Current Year*)]. We can identify the bucket B_{31} (and sources S_1 and S_4), which exactly match the *lcd*. Buckets B_{21} (with sources S_5 and S_6) and B_{11} (source S_3) are also relevant. However, the the quality of data in the corresponding sources (see qod_{311} (S_3), qod_{511} (S_5), and qod_{611} (S_6)) is much worse.

Grouping the scqd's into buckets can reduce the search space of scqd's to find a relevant bucket. However, the number of buckets can still be very large. The number of buckets will typically be dominated by the number of distinct combinations of values for *lcd*, the content descriptions for the sources. With multiple dimension attributes, where each attribute can have a large number of enumerated values in the domain, the number of buckets could become very large. The problem becomes more complicated when we must combine sources to answer queries.

A further reduction in the search space of buckets can be obtained by partially ordering the buckets into a *po-set*.

We consider a relation *includes* on bucket descriptors. We say that bucket descriptor $bd_i = [(Att_{i1}), ..., (Att_{in})]$ *includes* bucket descriptor $bd_j = [(Att_{j1}), ..., (Att_{jn})]$, when the corresponding attributes and their domains, matched by subscripts, are as follows: $Dom_{j1} \subseteq Dom_{i1}, ..., Dom_{jn} \subseteq Dom_{in}$.

For example, the bucket descriptor B_{11} *includes* the bucket descriptor B_{31} in Table I. Using this relation *includes* we can construct the po-set of Fig. 7 for the buckets in Table I. The directed arrow between the bucket B_{11} and B_{21} indicates that the bucket descriptor B_{11} *includes* the bucket descriptor B_{21}. A *superbucket* consists of all the buckets at the same layer of the po-set that cannot be ordered by using the relation *includes*. For example, superbucket SB_1 has buckets B_{11} and B_{12}.

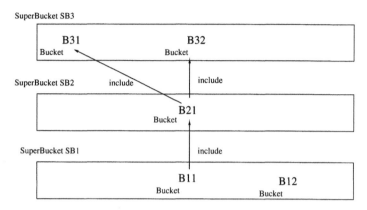

FIG. 7. A po-set for the buckets in Table I.

Formally, $\mathbf{P} = (SB, includes)$ is a partially ordered set on a set of buckets SB under the relation *includes*. Denote by m the height[4] of $\mathbf{P}$. The po-set yields an ordered set $\langle SB_1, ..., SB_m \rangle$ where $SB_1, ..., SB_m$ are named superbuckets, and correspond to a partition of SB. Each superbucket contains a set of incomparable buckets. If a superbucket SB_i succeeds a superbucket SB_j in the sequence, then for each bucket B in SB_i there is a bucket B' in SB_j, *if such a bucket exists in SB*, such that B' includes B. Note that a bucket descriptor bd_i is *more general* than the bucket descriptor bd_j when bd_i *includes* bd_j. The buckets characterized by the **most general** bucket descriptors and the sources that support them are in the first superbucket of the sequence (or bottom-most superbucket in Fig. 7).

Note that bucket B_{12} does not have an *includes* relationship with another bucket in SB, and it can therefore occur in any layer of the po-set. We choose to place it in the bottom-most layer or the most general superbucket.

Using the po-set, we can search the superbuckets to find the relevant buckets and sources for some predicate P, e.g., $q.lcd \geqslant$ [(city, {Toronto}), (time, *CurrentYear*)]. This will be more efficient than searching all the buckets, as before. Starting from the bottom-most superbucket, we find the first superbucket that contains a bucket with a bucket descriptor that *is greater than or exactly equal* to this lcd [(city, {Toronto}), (time, *CurrentYear*)]. This is superbucket SB_1 in Fig. 7. This superbucket corresponds to the *relevant superbucket* for the bucket descriptor [(city, {Toronto}), (time, *CurrentYear*)]. Then the relevant buckets for P

---

[4] The height of a po-set is the cardinality of the largest subset SB' of SB, such that every two buckets in SB' are comparable in $\mathbf{P}$.

are all the buckets in SB_1 with a bucket descriptor that *includes* [(city, {Toronto}), (time, *Current Year*)] and the buckets in the upper superbuckets whose bucket descriptors also *include* the *lcd*. In Fig. 7, the relevant buckets for the predicate P are B_{11}, B_{21}, and B_{31}, in the order (of inclusion) in which they are identified, in the po-set.

We note that several alternate techniques can be used to search the po-sets, e.g., starting from the top-most superbucket, instead of from the bottom-most superbucket. This is discussed in future research.

When searching for relevant buckets, we only used the $\geqslant$ to identify the relevant buckets and sources. Thus, the source *lcd* is more general, compared to the query. In some cases, this comparison is too restrictive. This is particularly true in the case where a single source cannot answer a query, but combining sources will answer a query. We may also have situations where accessing additional sources will improve the quality of the answers provided. In this case, we may wish to consider finding relevant sources using the *intersect* operator, where there is a nonempty intersection between the source *lcd* and the query. This is considered in the next section.

6.2   Computational Issues in Accessing Combination of Scqd's

In the previous section, we discussed how the po-sets can be used to search the superbuckets, in order to find relevant buckets. If a single source cannot be found to be relevant, then the query will fail, and no sources will be selected. However, it is possible that a combination (union) of sources may be relevant to answer the query. We describe a motivating example. We then discuss a naive solution to this problem. We then propose a heuristic that improves on the naive solution.

Consider the following query:

Query 6 Find the best n sources that maintain information for the temperature in Toronto, Kingston, and NYC. Relevant sources must maintain 50% of all the data.

select   **best** n *s*
from   Source *s*,
            Scqd *c* **in** *s.scqds*,
            Qod *q* **in** *c.qods*
where   *c.type* = "Air"
            and *q.lcd* = [(city, {Toronto, Kingston, NYC})]
            and *q.completeness* $\geqslant$ "0.5";

Using the *scqd*'s in Table I, the union of sources $S_1(qod_{111})$, $S_2(qod_{211})$, and $S_6(qod_{611})$, together, can satisfy the query. We note that there are other combinations of sources that will answer the query and they will be identified later. Further, we note that the combinations of sources $S_2(qod_{211})$ and $S_5(qod_{512})$ or $S_2(qod_{211})$ and $S_6(qod_{612})$ or $S_2(qod_{211})$ and $S_3(qod_{311})$ also contain data for the temperature in Toronto, Kingston, and NYC. However, they are not selected because these particular combinations of sources do not maintain at least 50% of the data.

Although a union of the sources S_1, S_2, and S_6 satisfies the query, the po-set of Fig. 7 does not include a relevant bucket for the *lcd* [(city, {Toronto, Kingston, NYC})], and the query will fail.

We first propose a naive solution to the problem of finding combinations of sources. In the first step, we use the po-set to find all buckets that are associated in the *includes* relationship with the *lcd* [(city, {Toronto, Kingston, NYC})] of the query. An alternative would be to find buckets with a nonempty intersect with this *lcd*. Then, in the second step, we generate the power set for these buckets, and determine if any element of the powerset produces a relevant bucket descriptor. We consider the power set since we wish to enumerate all combinations of sources, but we wish to *minimize* the number of sources needed to provide an answer. We note that by choosing the minimum number of relevant sources, there is a possible loss of quality, as will be seen in a later example.

In our example, the buckets B_{31}, B_{32}, and B_{12} are in an *includes* relationship with the *lcd*, and will be identified in the first step. Note that sources in buckets B_{21} and B_{11}, with *lcd* [(city, *CityInCanada*), (time, *CurrentYear*)] and [(city, *CityInCanada*), (time, *YearSince1950*)], respectively, should also be considered. However, they do not satisfy the requirement on completeness. To simplify our example, we do not consider these buckets further.

After generating the power set in the second step, the relevant sources will be the following combinations (union) of sources: $\{S_1, S_2, S_5\}$, $\{S_1, S_2, S_6\}$, $\{S_4, S_2, S_5\}$, and $\{S_4, S_2, S_6\}$.

The disadvantage of the naive solution to the problem is that a large number of descriptors must be derived online. If n buckets are selected, there are 2^n possible relevant combinations of scqd's that must be considered. The number of buckets to be considered is exponential in the cardinality of the domains associated with the attributes in the original *lcd*. Thus, we need a technique to select relevant combinations, without exploring the whole space of combinations.

An alternative solution to this problem is to extend the po-set toward a lattice [25], by including buckets for additional *scqd*'s that can be derived from the combination of some given *scqd*'s. The lattice can be constructed *offline*. We can then use this lattice to identify the relevant buckets *online*.

A (complete) lattice ensures that for any set of the buckets in superbucket i, there is a bucket with a more general bucket descriptor in superbucket $i - 1$ and a bucket with a more specific bucket descriptor in superbucket $i + 1$, if the *scqd*'s and bucket descriptors associated with these buckets exist or they result from the union of existing bucket descriptors.

For example, Fig. 8 is a lattice for the buckets in Fig. 7. Note that bucket B_{21} in Fig. 7 had an *includes* relationship with both buckets B_{31} and B_{32}. Thus, in the lattice, bucket B_{21} will have an *includes* relationship with the bucket obtained from combining $[B_{31} \cup B_{32}]$. Similarly, the bucket from combining $[B_{21} \cup B_{12}]$ will have an *includes* relationship with the bucket combining $[B_{31} \cup B_{32} \cup B_{12}]$. Finally, since bucket B_{11} has an *includes* relationship with bucket B_{21}, the bucket with the most general descriptor in the lattice is the combination of $[B_{11} \cup B_{12}]$.

Thus for the *lcd* {(city, {Toronto, Kingston, NYC})}, we can search the lattice, of Fig. 8, from the bottom-most superbucket, as we did with the po-

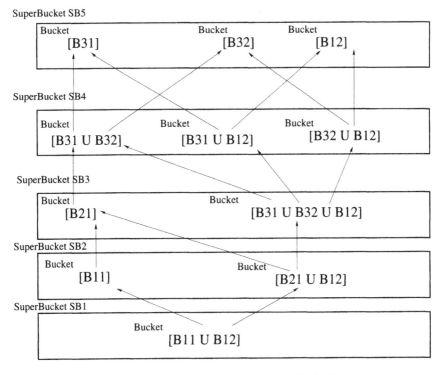

FIG. 8. A complete lattice for the buckets in Fig. 7.

set, and find the relevant buckets, which will be $[B_{11} \cup B_{12}]$, $[B_{21} \cup B_{12}]$ and $[B_{31} \cup B_{32} \cup B_{12}]$, in the order in which they are identified in the lattice.

The *lattice* solution allows us to directly find combinations of sources that are relevant for a query. However, it may also lead to an exponential explosion in the number of buckets in the lattice that must be searched online, to find the relevant bucket. As before, the size of the lattice is dominated by the domain cardinality of the attributes of the *lcd*'s, for all sources.

A final alternative is a *heuristic* that *partially constructs* the (complete) lattice; i.e., it only adds some *select* buckets of the complete lattice to the original po-set of Fig. 7. The heuristic is to add a bucket with a *most general bucket descriptor*, where the most general bucket descriptor includes the bucket descriptors of *all* the *scqd*'s exported by the sources. This partially extended po-set is in Fig. 9. When we compare the extended po-set with the

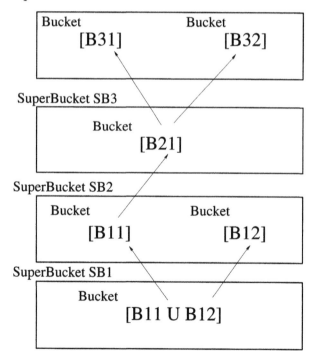

FIG. 9. The partially extended po-set of Fig. 7.

original po-set of Fig. 7 we observe that only one bucket has been added, the combination of $[B_{11} \cup B_{12}]$.

6.3 Finding Best Sources Using the Partially Extended Po-set

The *partially extended* po-set may reduce the complexity of search, when a combination of *scqd*'s is required to answer the query. However, use of this heuristic can lead to problems related to loss of accuracy of the selected scqd's. Consider the following query:

Query 7 Find sources providing temperature data for Toronto and New York City. Relevant sources must be ranked according to their recency.

select	**best** s
from	Source s,
	Scqd c **in** $s.scqds$,
	Qod q **in** $c.qods$,
where	$c.type =$ "Air"
	and $q.soma = \{$"temperature"$\}$
	and $q.lcd \geqslant [($city$, \{$Toronto, NYC$\})]$
	and $q.recency$ **close to** "0 days"

In the partially extended po-set, the relevant bucket for this query will be one formed by $[B_{11} \cup B_{12}]$. This corresponds to the combination of sources $\{S_2, S_3\}$. This combination of sources will have a *combined* recency of 10 days, for this query, if we choose the *weakest* value of the individual recency values, for the combination of sources.

There are other combination of sources, e.g., $\{S_1, S_2\}$ and $\{S_4, S_2\}$, which would have been generated by the naive solution, or would have been found in the lattice. Bucket $[B_{31} \cup B_{12}]$ in the lattice of Fig. 8 would identify these particular combinations. However, this bucket is *not* in the partially extended po-set of Fig. 9. These combinations will have different values for recency. For example, both the combination $\{S_1, S_2\}$ and the combination $\{S_4, S_2\}$, which would have been identified in the lattice, in bucket $[B_{31} \cup B_{12}]$ each has a *combined* recency of 5 days. This is better than the combined recency of 10 days, for the combination of sources $\{S_2, S_3\}$, found in the partially extended po-set.

To summarize, the heuristic for a partially extended po-set can lead to a tradeoff. One alternative is generating the (complete) lattice whose buckets have more accurate scqd metadata. The tradeoff is using a heuristic to partially extend the po-set, and limiting the number of buckets that are generated. The cost of the tradeoff is a loss of accuracy of scqd metadata, when combining multiple scqd's to answer queries.

7. Related Research

The WS architecture and approach is similar to and depends upon work in several areas. Much of this work comes under the theme of the *Semantic Web* proposed by Berners-Lee in [7]. Research in mediation technology has proposed several techniques for describing, integrating, or accessing structured data on the Internet. WS and its extensions to scqd metadata is based on the assumption that wrappers and mediators will support interoperability and provide access to sources. Ongoing research in the information retrieval and digital library community has generated a number of distributed searching protocols and metadata standards in order to facilitate resource discovery for document-like objects and there are some extensions to structured data as well. WS will perform resource discovery for sources with structured data. Finally, various techniques for indexing and querying the Web have been proposed. WS must extend these techniques to WS-XML pages that publish data sources.

We first consider wrapper mediator architectures, as proposed in [26–34]. These systems differ widely in the capabilities of mediators and in the capabilities of wrappers. Wrappers developed for Garlic [28] and the Information Manifold [31] assume the locations of the data sources, types, and wrapper capability are embedded within the wrappers. Wrappers for DISCO [33], TSIMMIS [32], and Web accessible WebSources [30] use declarative languages to export types and query capabilities. Another proposal [12] focuses on CORBA IDL access via WWW protocols, instead of query-based access, to sources. The WS architecture can be extended to include such data sources.

Extending the wrapper and mediator architecture, InfoSleuth [27] proposes information brokering and domain ontologies to describe data sources. We believe that domain ontologies are a promising extension to the catalog server, since they provide a way to structure domain information (types). The Diorama project develops a methodology and toolkits for intelligent integration and access of heterogeneous information sources in enterprise-wide networking environments. The Diorama system consists of several components that extract properties from unstructured data or collect data through other information brokers/mediators, and dynamically convert and assemble gathered information into DIOM objects.

In all these projects, the knowledge of the location of the sources is embedded within the mediators and there is no resource discovery task. Our research is based on the premise that WS-XML documents will be used to publish the location of components (wrappers and data sources).

The importance of the World Wide Web as a repository of information has generated an increasing interest in the research community for the design of high-level, declarative languages for querying it. WebSQL [21] integrates textual retrieval with structure and topology-based queries. Each Web document is associated with a tuple in a virtual Document relation and each hypertext link with a tuple in a virtual Anchor relation. In order to query these virtual tables, one must first define computable subdomains, either using keyword matching or through controlled navigation starting from known URLs. Another Web query language, W3QS [35] includes the specification of syntax and semantics of a SQL-like query language (W3QL) that provides simple access to external Unix programs, advanced display facilities for gathered information, and view maintenance facilities.

An emerging proposal for a standard for exchange of types and structured data, XMLSchema [5, 6] specified in XML, has been gaining wide attention. WS uses XMLSchema to specify the schema and metadata of sources. When query languages for XML are developed, they can be exploited by WS.

The problem of retrieving information from multiple sources has also received considerable attention in the context of bibliographic data. In order to overcome the difficulties generated by the differences in data representation and query mechanisms, the library community has developed the Z39.50 protocol [10, 11], an interoperability standard allowing highly specific searches of distributed data sources. The tasks supported by Z39.50 are resource discovery, query, and retrieval and result presentation. This standard has been extended to accommodate other types of data, in particular, geo-referenced or geo-spatial data. The underlying data model has been extended with GEO objects, and attribute sets have been defined appropriately. We note that different application domains are identified by different attribute sets in Z39.50.

More recently, metadata standards such as the Dublin Core and WebDAV [36, 37] have been proposed in order to facilitate resource discovery for document-like objects. Current efforts are being made for the representation of Dublin Core metadata through metadata standard exchange formats such as RDF [9], which is an extension of XML. WebDAV (Web Distributed Authoring and Versioning) protocol is an Internet standard and defines metadata (called "properties" in the protocol). The WebDAV Working Group is also investigating DASL (DAV Searching and Locating). WS aims to complement these document-centric systems by proposing a metadata-based infrastructure supporting location and access to structured data.

A number of distributed searching protocols for directory information such as LDAP and whois++ [38, 39] have been proposed. The content-based source selection features exhibited by these systems are similar in purpose with those present in WS, although they are supported in different ways. The whois++ system, for example, maintains a hierarchical collection of *centroids* (lists of words extracted from the textual fields in the sources). Our current architecture is based on a centralized store that provides an index into sources that have been discovered and registered in the catalog. This approach to catalog construction using the source discovery language is at the expense of scalability. This issue will be addressed in future work.

Distributed information retrieval systems, for example, the Harvest/ Essence information retrieval-based system [40] are also related to our work. Essence is a customizable information extraction system that is used to extract and structure mostly textual information from documents in Harvest. It exploits the formats of common file types and extracts contents of files. The result is a summary object (a SOIF record) [41]. Collections of SOIF records are indexed and organized into *brokers*, a kind of mediator. Brokers provide information retrieval search on their associated SOIF records. The information stored in SOIF records is similar to the metadata about sources maintained by WS catalogs. One difference is that WS stores connection information for the source, including the location of the source and the type of wrapper. Thus WS can contact discovered sources to obtain metadata, if the source supports a query capability.

To summarize, WS provides the ability to publish the location of sources, and scqd metadata about their structured data contents using the WWW and WS-XML. WS then provides extensions to identify relevant sources using their scqd metadata. While related projects have investigated some of these tasks, WS is the only approach that provides the ability to use WS-XML to publish metadata about the sources, and uses this scqd metadata to select sources.

8. Summary and Future Work

We present the architecture for a system, WebSemantics, which permits publication and discovery of sources containing typed data, using the WWW and XML. WS provides a language for discovering relevant published data sources. The language combines features for searching relevant WS-XML documents that publish data sources with features for searching over the metadata describing these sources.

We extend WebSemantics to support source selection using content and quality metadata. We present a data model for scqd's that are used to express the source metadata. The data model is similar to those used in a data warehousing environment, and is based on a set of dimension attributes, a set of measure attributes, domains, and a set of QoD parameters. We present a query language for the selection and ranking of sources based on their QoD parameters.

We discuss how scqd metadata can be organized in po-sets to support efficient query processing. We consider the situation where a combination of one or more scqd's (or a combination of sources) are needed to answer a query. We discuss how the po-sets can be used to generate combinations of scqd's. We consider a naive solution, where most of the combinations of sources are generated online. We compare with a solution that extends the po-set into a (complete) lattice. We also consider a heuristic solution that partially extends the po-set. We discuss loss of accuracy that results when this heuristic is used.

In future work, we will study efficient techniques to search the lattice and the po-set. Recall that the lattice and po-set could be searched starting from either the top-most or bottom-most superbucket. We will evaluate both techniques to determine when they are more efficient.

We will also consider other techniques to find a *relevant* bucket. Recall that we used the *includes* relation to determine if combinations of buckets could be used to answer the query. In some cases, we may wish to identify combinations of buckets whose descriptor is in an *intersection* relation with the *lcd* of the query. It is also possible that after identifying one or a combination of relevant sources, we could consider additional sources to improve the scqd metadata for the answer.

Finally, we will study the tradeoff between the size of the (complete) lattice and the loss of accuracy of scqd metadata when using the partially extended po-set.

REFERENCES

[1] The global historical climatology network (GHCN). Available at http://www.ncdc.noaa.gov/ol/climate/research/ghcn/ghcn.html.
[2] Global precipitation climatology centre (GPCC). Available at http://www.dwd.de/research/gpcc/.
[3] World data centre for greenhouse gases (WDCGG). Available at http://jcdc.kishou.go.jp/wdcgg.html.
[4] National geophysical data centre (NGDC). Available at http://ngdc.noaa.gov/.
[5] Extensible Markup Language (XML) (1996). Available at http://www.w3.org/XML.
[6] XML Schema (W3C working draft) (2000). Available at http://www.w3.org/TR/xmlschema-0.
[7] Berners-Lee, T. (1998). Semantic Web road map. Available at http://www.w3.org/DesignIssues/Semantic.html.
[8] Meta Content Framework using XML (1997). Available at http://www.w3.org/TR/NOTE-MCF-XML.
[9] Resource Description Framework (RDF) (1999). Available at http://www.w3.org/RDF/.
[10] Lynch, C. A. (1991). "The z39.50 information retrieval protocol: An overview and status report". *Computer Communication Review*, **21**(1), 58–70.
[11] Library of congress maintenance agency page for international standard z39.50. Available at http://lcweb.loc.gov/z3950/agency/agency.html.

[12] Web Interface Definition Language (WIDL) (1997). Available at http://www.webMethods. com.

[13] Huang, K.-T., Lee, Y. W. and Wang, R. Y. (1998). *Quality Information and Knowledge.* Prentice Hall, Englewood Cliffs, NJ.

[14] Mihaila, G., Raschid, L. and Vidal, M. E. (1999). "Querying 'quality of data' metadata". In *Proceedings of the Third IEEE Meta-Data Conference*, Bethesda, MD. Available at http://computer.org/proceedings/meta/1999/.

[15] Anzlic guidelines: Core metadata elements, version 1. Available at http://www.anzlic.org.au/ metaelem.htm.

[16] Directory interchange format (dif) writer's guide, version 7. Available at http:// gcmd.nasa.gov/difguide/difman.html.

[17] Mihaila, G., Raschid, L. and Tomasic, A. (1998). "Equal time for data on the Internet with WebSemantics". In *Proceedings of the 6th International Conference on Extending Database Technology (EDBT)*, Valencia, Spain, pp. 87–101.

[18] Mihaila, G., Raschid, L. and Tomasic, A. (2001). "Locating and accessing data repositories with WebSemantics". *Very Large Data Base Journal*, in press.

[19] Java(tm) Remote Method Invocation (RMI). Available at http://java.sun.com/products/ jdk/rmi/.

[20] Mihaila, G. (2000). *Publishing, Locating, and Querying Networked Information Sources.* Ph.D. thesis, University of Toronto.

[21] Mendelzon, A. O., Mihaila, G. A. and Milo, T. (1997). "Querying the World Wide Web". *Journal of Digital Libraries*, 1(1), 68–88.

[22] Cattell, R. G. G. *et al.* (1996). *The Object Database Standard—ODMG 93, Release 1.2.* Morgan Kaufmann, New York.

[23] Gravano, L. and Garcia-Molina, H. (1997). "Merging ranks from heterogeneous Internet sources". In *Proceedings of the 23rd International Conference on Very Large Data Bases (VLDB)*, Athens, Greece, pp. 196–205.

[24] Fagin, R. (1998). "Fuzzy queries in multimedia database systems". In *Proceedings of the 17th Symposium on Principles of Database Systems (PODS)*, Seattle, WA, pp. 1–10.

[25] Preparata, F. P. and Yeh, R. T. (1973). *Introduction to Discrete Structures.* Addison-Wesley, Reading, MA.

[26] Adali, S., Candan, K. S., Papakonstantinou, Y. and Subrahmaniam, V. S. (1996). "Query caching and optimization in distributed mediator systems". In *Proceedings of the ACM SIGMOD'96*, pp. 137–148.

[27] Bohrer, B. *et al.* (1997). "Infosleuth: Semantic integration of information in open and dynamic environments". In *Proceedings of the ACM International Conference on Management of Data (SIGMOD)*, pp. 195–206.

[28] Haas, L. M., Kossmann, D., Wimmers, E. L. and Yang, J. (1997). "Optimizing queries across diverse data sources". In *Proceedings of VLDB'97*, pp. 276–285.

[29] Gardarin, G. *et al.* (1996). "IRO-DB: A distributed system federating object and relational databases". In *Object-Oriented Multidatabase Systems: A Solution for Advanced Applications* (O. A. Bukhres and A. K. Elmagarmid, Eds.), pp. 684–712. Prentice Hall, Englewood Cliffs, NJ.

[30] Gruser, J.-R., Raschid, L., Vidal, M. E. and Bright, L. (1998). "Wrapper generation for web accessible data sources". In *CoopIS'98*, New York, NY, pp. 14–23.

[31] Kirk, T., Levy, A. Y., Sagiv, Y. and Srivastava, D. (1995). "The information manifold". In *Proc. of the AAAI Spring Symposium on Information Gathering in Distributed Heterogeneous Environments*, Stanford, CA, pp. 85–91.

[32] Papakonstantinou, Y. *et al.* (1996). "Capabilities-based query rewriting in mediator systems". In *Proceedings of PDIS'96*, pp. 170–181.

[33] Tomasic, A., Raschid, L. and Valduriez, P. (1996). "Scaling heterogeneous databases and the design of DISCO". In *Proceedings of ICDCS'96*, pp. 449–457.

[34] Wiederhold, G. (1992). "Mediators in the architecture of future information systems". *Computer*, 25(3), 38–49.

[35] Konopnicki, D. and Shmueli, O. (1995). "W3QS: A query system for the World Wide Web". In *Proceedings of VLDB'95*, pp. 54–65.

[36] Dublin core metadata initiative. Available at http://purl.org/DC.

[37] World Wide Web-distributed authoring and versioning home page. Available at http://www.ics.uci.edu/ejw/authoring/.

[38] Howes, T. A. (1995). The lightweight directory access protocol: X.500 lite. Technical report, University of Michigan.

[39] The NSF Whois++ testbed project (1996). Available at http://www.ucdavis.edu/whoisplus/.

[40] Bowman, C. *et al.* (1995). "The Harvest information discovery and access system". *Computer Networks and ISDN Systems*, 28, 119–125.

[41] The summary object interchange format (soif). Available at http://harvest.transarc.com/Harvest/brokers/soifhelp.html.

Mining Scientific Data[1]

NAREN RAMAKRISHNAN

Department of Computer Science
Virginia Tech
Blacksburg, VA 24061
USA
naren@cs.vt.edu

ANANTH Y. GRAMA

Department of Computer Sciences
Purdue University
West Lafayette, IN 47907
USA
ayg@cs.purdue.edu

Abstract

The past two decades have seen rapid advances in high-performance computing and tools for data acquisition in a variety of scientific domains. Coupled with the availability of massive storage systems and fast networking technology to manage and assimilate data, these have given a significant impetus to data mining in the scientific domain. Data mining is now recognized as a key computational technology, supporting traditional analysis, visualization, and design tasks. Diverse applications in domains such as mineral prospecting, computer-aided design, bioinformatics, and computational steering are now being viewed in the data mining framework. This has led to a very effective cross-fertilization of computational techniques from both continuous and discrete perspectives. In this chapter, we characterize the nature of scientific data mining activities and identify dominant recurring themes. We discuss algorithms, techniques, and methodologies for their effective application and present application studies that summarize the state-of-the-art in this emerging field. We conclude by identifying opportunities for future research in emerging domains.

1. Introduction 120
   1.1 Mining is Induction 121
   1.2 Mining is Compression. 121
   1.3 Mining is Querying 121
   1.4 Mining is Approximation 122

[1] This work was supported in part by National Science Foundation Grants EIA-9974956 and EIA-9984317 to Ramakrishnan and National Science Foundation Grants EIA-9806741, ACI-9875899, and ACI-9872101 to Grama.

2.   Motivating Domains   122
    2.1   Data Mining in Geological and Geophysical Applications   123
    2.2   Data Mining in Astrophysics and Cosmology   126
    2.3   Data Mining in Chemical and Materials Engineering Applications   127
    2.4   Data Mining in Bioinformatics.   131
    2.5   Data Mining in Flows   133
3.   Inductive Mining Techniques   134
    3.1   Underlying Principles   134
    3.2   Best Practices   139
4.   Data Mining as Approximation and Lossy Compression.   143
    4.1   Underlying Principles   144
    4.2   Best Practices   147
5.   Putting It All Together   151
    5.1   Underlying Principles   151
    5.2   Best Practices   153
6.   Future Research Issues   156
    6.1   Mining When Data Is Scarce   156
    6.2   Design of Experiments.   159
    6.3   Mining "On-The-Fly".   159
    6.4   Mining in Distributed and Parallel Environments.   160
7.   Concluding Remarks   161
    References   162

1. Introduction

Computational simulation and data acquisition in scientific and engineering domains have made tremendous progress over the past two decades. A mix of advanced algorithms, exponentially increasing computing power, and accurate sensing and measurement devices have resulted in terabyte-scale data repositories. Advances in networking technology have enabled communication of large volumes of data across geographically distant hosts. This has resulted in an increasing need for tools and techniques for effectively analyzing scientific data sets with the objective of interpreting the underlying physical phenomena. The process of detecting higher-order relationships hidden in large and often noisy data sets is commonly referred to as *data mining.*

The field of data mining has evolved from its roots in databases, statistics, artificial intelligence, information theory, and algorithmics into a core set of techniques that have been successfully applied to a range of problems. These techniques have come to rely heavily on numerical methods, distributed and parallel frameworks, and visualization systems to aid the mining process. In this chapter, we characterize the nature of scientific data mining activities and identify dominant recurring themes. We discuss algorithms, techniques, and methodologies for their effective application, and present application studies that summarize the state-of-the-art in this emerging field.

The diverse and rich background of data mining is reflected in the many distinct views taken by researchers of this evolving discipline. Some of these dominant views are summarized here:

1.1   Mining is Induction

Perhaps the most common view of data mining is one of induction, i.e., proceeding from the specific to the general. This basis finds its roots in the artificial intelligence and machine learning communities and relies on techniques ranging from neural networks [1] to inductive logic programming [2]. Systems such as PROGOL (not PROLOG), FOIL, and Golem view induction as reversing the deduction process in first-order logic inference. Barring any specific constraints on the nature of induced generalizations, one way to generate (mine) them is to systematically explore and analyze a space of possible *patterns*. This idea of "generalization as search" was first proposed by Mitchell [3] and has since resurfaced in various domains, most notably the association-rules mining algorithm of [4] used in commercial market basket analysis. The key idea in this research is to use partial orderings induced by subsumption relations on a concept space to help prune the search for possible hypotheses. Areas that deal most directly with this perspective include Sections 3 and 5.

1.2   Mining is Compression

The process of learning a *concept* from an enumeration of training sets typically leads to a very large space of possible alternatives. Often, the most desirable of these concepts is the one that is most succinct or that is easiest to describe. This principle, known as Occam's Razor, effectively equates learning to compression (where the learned patterns are, in some sense, "smaller to describe" than exhaustively enumerating the original data itself). The emergence of computational learning theory in the 1980's and the effectiveness of models such as MDL (the Minimum Description Length principle) have provided a solid theoretical foundation to this perspective. Several commercial data mining systems employ this aspect to determine the feasibility of the mined patterns. For example, if the description of a defective machine part is longer than an enumeration of possible defective parts, then the learned concept is not very useful.

1.3   Mining is Querying

The view of mining as intelligently querying a data set was first projected in the database systems community. Since most commercial and business data resides in industrial databases and warehouses, mining is often viewed as a sophisticated form of database querying. SQL, the de facto standard for database query languages, currently, does not support queries of the form "find me all machine parts in the database that are defective." The querying aspect allows embedding of mining functions as primitives into standard query languages. As more scientific and engineering data finds its way into databases and XML formats, this form of querying will become more important. It is conceivable that systems might support standard queries of the form "highlight all vortices within specified flow data" in the near future. This perspective is currently most popular in the commercial and economic mining community. Its implications for mining scientific data are discussed in Section 5.

1.4   Mining is Approximation

Mining is often also thought of as a process of systematic approximation. Starting from an exact (lossless) data representation, approximations are introduced in the hope of finding some latent/hidden structure to the data. Such approximations might involve dropping higher-order terms in harmonic approximations, adaptive simplification of geometries, or rank reduction in attribute matrices. A very popular technique that has this flavor is called Latent Semantic Indexing [5–9], an algorithm that introduces approximations using singular-value decompositions of a term-document matrix in information retrieval to find hidden structure. This has parallels in Karhunen–Loeve expansions in signal representation and principal component analysis in statistics. A surview of such *data reduction techniques* appears in [10]. Section 4 most directly deals with this perspective.

2.   Motivating Domains

As the size and complexity of data sets gathered from large-scale simulations and high-resolution observations increases, there is a significant push toward developing tools for interpreting these data sets. Despite its relative infancy, the field of scientific data mining has been applied with significant success in a number of areas. In this section, we outline some key application areas and the data mining tasks within these with a view to motivate the core techniques underlying common data mining tasks. The survey presented is by no means comprehensive. Other applications abound in areas such as computational biology, scientific visualization, robotics, and wireless communications.

2.1   Data Mining in Geological and Geophysical Applications

Data mining applications in geology and geophysics were among the first to be pursued and have achieved significant success in such areas as weather prediction, mineral prospecting, ecological modeling, landuse analysis, and earthquake prediction from satellite maps. An interesting aspect of many of these applications is that they combine spatial and temporal aspects, both in the data and the phenomena being mined.

Data sets in these applications come from both observations and simulation. A prototypical example from weather forecasting relies on data that is typically defined over a grid of observation stations or finite difference simulation models. The underlying variables defined over these discretizations include horizontal velocities, temperature, water vapor and ozone mixing ratio, surface pressure, ground temperature, vertical velocities, precipitation, cloudiness, surface fluxes of sensible and latent heat, surface wind stress, and relative heating. Such data are typically captured at periodic snapshots. For example, in the Atmospheric Global Circulation Model (AGCM), at the lowest grid resolution ($4°$ latitude $\times 5°$ longitude $\times$ 9 atmospheric levels), storing data at periods of 12 h results in over 5 GB of data per year.

Data analysis proceeds with respect to a variety of atmospheric phenomena, such as cyclones, hurricanes, and fronts. The key challenge in analyzing atmospheric data is the imprecise definition of weather phenomena. For example, cyclones are typically defined based on a threshold level of vorticity in quantities such as atmospheric pressure at sea level. Other techniques for detecting cyclones rely on determination of local extrema of the sea level pressure [11]. The outcome of an automated cyclone detection technique is a one-dimensional track in three-dimensional space consisting of two space coordinates and one time coordinate. Other weather-related phenomena such as *blocking features* can also be detected using similar techniques. Blocking features are characterized by well-defined timescales (in the range of weeks) with a westerly flow that is split into two branches. These persistent anomalies are measured by examining the variation of geopotential height from the expected value.

The spatio-temporal nature of most of the analysis tasks makes them extremely challenging. The temporal aspect is typically modeled by characterizing the short- and long-range dependence of processes on various forms of time series analysis. Spatial aspects are modeled using point-process techniques, particularly in weather-related phenomena. For example, storms are viewed as an agglomerate of rain-producing cells distributed over the area within which rain is occurring. These cells are assumed to be stationary and to be distributed in space either independently according to a Poisson process or with clustering according to, say, a Neymann–Scott scheme. In addition, fits to empirical data are achieved by including random variables in the problem formulation to correlate between the durations of cells within a single storm.

The modeling, detection, and prediction of global climate phenomena have received much attention in the high-performance computing community [12]. Such applications involve multiple models at varying levels of fidelity (and often multidisciplinary), parallel computing, and robust methodologies for ensuring that predictions agree with observed behavior. The extreme sensitivity of such phenomena (folklore has that, possibly incorrectly, "a bird flapping its wings in Switzerland can cause thunderstorms in the United States") and interactions between ocean and atmospheric processes make this problem a promising application area for data mining. Effects ranging from warming of the oceans (e.g., El Niño) to the compensatory behavior of monsoons in tropical areas (e.g., the southwest and northeast monsoons in the Indian subcontinent) are important in assessing chances of drought, harsh winters, and flooding, and in the management of water resources.

One of the early successful mining systems for scientific data was CONQUEST (Concurrent Querying in Space and Time) [13]. This system was designed to handle data sets with significant temporal coherence in events and to enable complex multimodal interactive querying and knowledge discovery. Han and colleagues [14] provide a survey of techniques for mining geographical data, with specific emphasis on database perspectives and clustering, including their CLARANS algorithm for spatial mining [15].

Rapid advances in remote sensing have also resulted in large repositories of high-resolution imagery that pose significant challenges for data handling and analysis. One of the analysis tasks that has received some attention is the prediction of the motion of surface faults during an earthquake [16]. QUAKEFINDER [17] is one such system that applies machine learning techniques to the measurement of plate displacements during earthquakes by comparing successive satellite images of a fault-laden area. Similar approaches are being applied to a number of applications relating to monitoring continuous and abrupt tectonic activity, land cover dynamics, and global climate changes.

In addition, data sets from remote sensing are typically characterized by mislabeled or unavailable information (see Fig. 1). While this problem is endemic to many experimental disciplines, it causes particular hardship for applications such as watershed assessment, where landuse distributions and settlement patterns are important drivers of change [18]. They affect surface and groundwater flows, water quality, wildlife habitat, economic value of the land, and infrastructure (directly due to the change itself such as building a

Land Cover for the Watershed Area

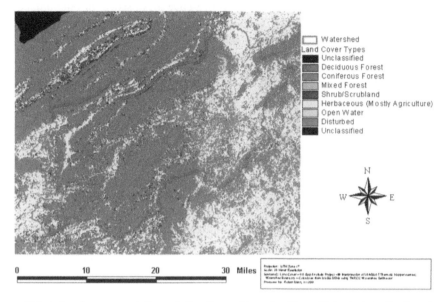

FIG. 1. Landuse segmentation of the Upper Roanoke River Watershed in Southwest Virginia, USA. Areas marked "Unclassified" and "Mixed Forest" pose difficulties for evaluating the effect of settlement patterns. Data mining can help identify mislabeled areas and correlate unlabeled regions with known land cover features. Figure courtesy of R. Dymond (Virginia Tech). Reproduced in colour between pages 142 and 143.

housing development, and indirectly due to the effects of the change, such as increased flooding), and cause economic effects on municipalities (taxes raised versus services provided). Modeling such effects in a system requires the accurate and effective determination of land-use classifications; however, out-of-date field measurements and lack of knowledge of precise commercial and vegetation boundaries often result in mislabeled training data [19], thus posing bottlenecks in data mining. The more broader task of map analysis using geographical information system (GIS) data is important in identifying clusters of wild life behavior in forests [20], modeling population dynamics in ecosystems [21], and modeling socio-economics [22].

An important application of data mining in geophysics relates to the detection of subsurface mineral deposits, oil reservoirs, and other artifacts. Typical data sets in these applications are collected from excitation and observation stations in borewells. For example, an agent is injected into one of the borewells and measurements are made at nearby observation bores. Such measurements are typically taken at regular intervals (and thus the temporal nature of data) over prespecified observation points. Carefully examining this data for artifacts reveals presence (or absence) of phenomena being studied. An approach to mining porosity of prospect regions by automatically deriving analytic formulas is described in [23]. Such applications are characterized by great economic importance, and the accompanying need to ensure privacy and confidentiality in data mining. Other computational aspects of Earth systems science can be found in the May–June 2000 Special Issue of IEEE/AIP *Computing in Science and Engineering* (*CiSE*) on this topic [24].

2.2 Data Mining in Astrophysics and Cosmology

The recent past has seen an explosion in the amount of data available to astrophysicists for analyzing a wide variety of phenomena. These data hold the key to such fundamental questions as the origins of the universe, its evolution, the structures that lie deep within, and the presence of extraterrestrial lifeforms. A number of researchers are actively working on various high-profile projects relating to analysis of astrophysical data.

The main source of astrophysical data is in the form of surveys of the sky in different segments of the electromagnetic spectrum. We are rapidly getting to the point where surveys are generating more data than can be assimilated by semi-automated means. SKICAT (Sky Image Classification and Archiving Tool) was one of the early systems that recognized the need for automated analysis of large-scale sky surveys [25, 26]. SKICAT was also instrumental in popularizing data mining in the scientific community. The goal was to provide an automated means for analyzing data from the Palomar Observatory Sky Survey (POSS-II), which consists of approximately 107 galaxies and 10^8 stars. The magnitude of this amount of data clearly precludes manual analysis. The SKICAT system attempted to address the basic question of determining which of the objects in the survey belong to various classes of galaxies and stars. The system extracts a variety of features derived from image-processing techniques and uses a tree classifier to classify celestial objects into one of several known classes. More recently the Sloan Digital Sky Survey [27], on the order of terabytes, is expected to become the benchmark reference for knowledge discovery in computational cosmology. See [27] and other articles in the March–April 1999 special issue of IEEE/AIP *CiSE* [28] for more information on such projects.

One of the key sources of data relating to the origin of the universe is believed to be cosmic background radiation (CMB). This radiation provides an excellent measure of the inhomogeneities in the distribution of matter in the universe over a period of billions of years. Fluctuations in photon intensity indicate the variations in density and velocity of radiation at a point when the universe was highly ionized. They also provide information about the amount of gravitational clustering during different epochs in the universe's history through which the photons pass [29]. Telescopes such as Hubble and Keck have made visible galaxies that are at much earlier stages of their evolution than the Milky Way. This will potentially enable us to chart our own evolution if we can effectively analyze radiation data. Large-scale CMB data are available from a variety of astrophysical experiments such as COBE [30, 31], BOOMERANG [32], MAXIMA [33], and Planck [34]. A complete analysis of CMB requires large-scale simulation and analysis of full-sky maps at very high resolutions.

Recently, a project by the name SETI@home (Search for Extraterrestrial Intelligence [35]) gained prominence due, in large part, to its ingenious approach to harnessing the large computational resources of the Internet. This project analyzes data collected from the Arecibo Radio Telescope in Puerto Rico to search for patterns and anomalies indicating extraterrestrial intelligence. The data are parceled into packets of 330 KB and sent off to participating clients (to date, there have been more than two million client machines running the SETI analysis software). These clients look for interesting artifacts in the data and report back potential anomalies to the server. "Interesting artifacts" in this context correspond to strong and steady signals in a narrow frequency band, pulsed signals, and continuous tones, among other features.

In addition to addressing the issue of analyzing data from various parts of the electromagnetic spectrum, research has also focused on supporting tools and techniques. These tools include compression techniques, improved information storage and retrieval structures, distributed frameworks, and data fusion. Data fusion can play an important role in astrophysical applications since emissions in different ranges of the spectrum may correlate to manifest interesting artifacts in data [36–38].

2.3 Data Mining in Chemical and Materials Engineering Applications

Data mining challenges in chemical and materials engineering can be broadly classified into the following categories: structure classification and prediction of properties, structure–activity relationships, and materials design.

The problem of predicting the behavior of materials under various physical conditions has been studied using regression analysis [39, 40]. Extensive experimental and simulation data have been used to compute such higher-order relationships as "thermal conductivity and Young's modulus of silicon nitride scale with the density as $\rho^{1.5}$ and $\rho^{3.6}$" and that "pores appear in silicon nitride as density reduces to 2.6 g/cc." [41]. Physical processes such as crack propagation and fracture surface characteristics have also been investigated (Fig. 2). Data handling and compression frameworks to support discovery of such relationships have been developed [41, 42].

The goal of designing materials with specified properties is a more complex one considering the fact that the forward problem of predicting material properties is itself not completely understood. Furthermore, applications involving life-expectancy-based design require that all or most

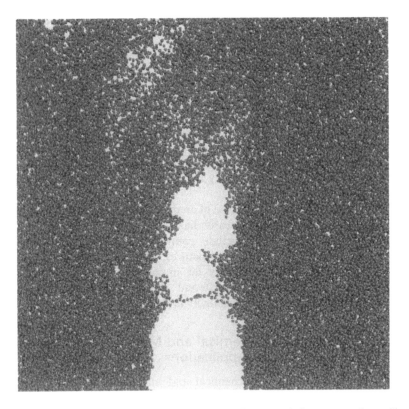

FIG. 2. Molecular dynamics simulation demonstrating a crack in an amorphous silicon nitride film. Slow intramicrocrack propagation produces smooth surfaces, while coalescence of microcracks leads to rapid propagation and produces rough surfaces. The nature of crack surfaces is important in many applications. The problem of extracting a crack surface dynamically from large-scale molecular dynamics simulation data is an important analysis task. Figure courtesy of A. Nakano (Louisiana State University). Reproduced in colour between pages 142 and 143.

parts of a structural component fail simultaneously. For this reason, heuristics and machine learning approaches have a very important role to play in this area. Industrial applications of materials design include composites and blends, agricultural chemicals, refrigerants, and solvents. With increased environmental awareness and concerns, greater emphasis is being placed on the design of novel materials.

Traditional approaches to the design of materials have relied on a trial-and-error paradigm. The complexity of this paradigm lies both in the large dimensionality of the search space and the need to guide the search process with appropriate heuristics. Computer-aided materials design (CAMD) has thus gained prominence over the recent past. CAMD fundamentally poses an inverse problem in which the structure must be inferred from function (or properties). A number of traditional approaches ranging from neural networks and genetic algorithms to tree classifiers have been explored by researchers. One such system—GENESYS [43, 44]—has been found to be useful in the design of several novel materials.

Crack propagation studies and failure analysis are now becoming increasingly sophisticated with the advent of parallel molecular dynamics [45], nanoscale simulations [41], and problem-solving environments (PSEs) [46]. Understanding how and why materials fail and fracture constitutes one of the grand challenge problems in computational materials science. Figure 3 describes a materials analysis scenario

FIG. 3. Wireframe model of a wood-based composite showing failed layers (gray) and active layers (black), and the orientation of fibers in each layer. In this figure, the second layer has failed. The horizontal protrusions are proportional in length to the magnitude of forces being applied to the layers at the time of failure. Data mining can help characterize failure criteria, by taking into account fatigue data and domain-specific background knowledge. Figure courtesy of C. A. Shaffer (Virginia Tech).

involving wood-based composites [46]. The failure of one or more layers upon simulation of various forces, as shown, helps in assessing the strength properties of reinforced materials. Data mining in this context can help characterize interface phenomena from typical data sets, which, in turn, can be utilized in adaptive control and dynamic analysis. In addition, technologies such as Micro-Electro Mechanical Systems (MEMS) open up the possibility of designing smart and intelligent structures [47], embedded Internet devices, and programmable vector fields for micromanipulators [48]. Such devices currently lack powerful programming abstractions and languages that can support distributed intelligence and large-scale autonomy.

At a broader level, multidisciplinary analysis and design (MAD) of complex devices such as gas turbine engines require knowledge and computational models from multiple disciplines. For example, the analysis of an engine involves the domains of *thermodynamics* (specifies heat flow throughout the engine), *reactive fluid dynamics* (specifies the behavior of the gases in the combustor), *mechanics* (specifies the kinematic and dynamic behaviors of pistons, links, cranks, etc.), *structures* (specifies the stresses and strains on the parts), and *geometry* (specifies the shape of the components and the structural constraints). The design of the engine requires that these different domain-specific analyses interact in order to find the final solution. While these different domains might share common parameters and interfaces, each of them is governed by its own constraints and limitations. There are now thousands of well-defined software modules for modeling various parts and behaviors or for supporting the simulation process. For most design aspects, there are multiple software modules to choose from. These embody different numerical methods (iterative or direct solvers), numerical models (standard finite differences, collocation with cubic elements, Galerkin with linear elements, rectangular grids, triangular meshes), and physical models (cylindrical symmetry, steady state, rigid body mechanics, full 3D time-dependent physics). Data mining can reveal the most appropriate models and algorithms to choose in a particular situation, by mining benchmark studies involving batteries of standardized problems and domains [49]. Furthermore, such complex devices typically have tens of thousands of parts, many of which experience extreme operating conditions. Important physical phenomena take place at spatial scales from tens of micrometers (combustion, turbulence, material failure) to meters (gas flow, rotating structures) and at temporal scales from microseconds to months. Modeling such complex phenomena can benefit from techniques such as qualitative computing [50] and order-of-magnitude reasoning [51, 52]. An excellent survey of computational techniques in mechanics appears in [53].

2.4   Data Mining in Bioinformatics

Bioinformatics constitutes perhaps one of the most exciting and challenging application areas for data mining. This information-centric view of biology has ushered in a veritable revolution in genomics involving technologies such as DNA sequencing and linkage analysis. A compelling frontier is the design of software tools that can harness and mine the continuing amount of data generated by such research efforts. Recently, Celera Genomics, Inc. (Maryland, USA), and the federally funded multinational Human Genome Project have announced the creation of a rough map of the entire human genome. These studies attempt to discover all of the approximately 35 000–100 000 human genes and make them accessible for further biological study and to determine the complete sequences of the three-billion DNA subunits. Determining the structure of complex organic molecules, correlating the structure and function of the molecule, and engineering a molecule with a desired function present key challenges in bioinformatics. The size and complexity of the molecules renders these tasks extremely difficult and computation-intensive.

Extensive research has been done on computational techniques for correlating structure and function of the gene. These techniques span the areas of machine learning (clustering, classification), algorithmics (sequence alignments, pattern matching), and statistics (Bayesian learning, model fitting). An example of structure–function correlation is illustrated in the case of tumor protein $p53$ (TP_{53}). The human gene TP_{53} belongs to the family $p53$ of proteins. This family is responsible for suppressing the growth of tumors ("preventing cancerous mutiny" [54]). Through extensive data analysis, it has been found that $p53$ is frequently mutated or inactivated in about 60% of cancers. Also, it has been found that $p53$ interacts with cancer-associated HPV ($e6$) viral proteins, causing the degradation of $p53$. This requires an additional factor $e6-ap$, which stably associates with $p53$ in the presence of HPV viral proteins.

In contrast to TP_{53} about which a fair deal is known, there are other proteins about which very little is known. For example, it is known that $BRC1\_HUMAN$ (breast cancer type 1 susceptibility protein) is known to have high incidences of mutations in breast and ovarian cancer families (45% of inherited breast cancers). However, the precise function of this protein is not known, and is suspected to be responsible for regulating gene expression. Relatively little is known about the other proteins in this family. Clearly, the usefulness of this information is tremendous.

The rapid emergence of microarray technologies contributes another major opportunity for data mining. Microarrays provide an experimental approach for measuring levels of gene expression changes at a system-wide scale, as subject to growth, stress, and other conditions. Levels of gene expression are measured by cohybridization (of nucleic acid samples) and determination of the ratio of signal expression by laser scanners. The intensity values (or ratios) thus determined are used to create an image file (see Fig. 4) that serves as the starting point for data mining. This domain is characterized by imperfections in the experimental process, lack of repeatability, and the high cost of obtaining experimental data. In addition, the sources and causes of experimental variability are not well understood. The detection of such gene expression changes (for varying levels of stress, say) coupled with modeling time and/or position effects is an area of active research in the bioinformatics community. Clustering of gene expression levels should take into account a priori background knowledge for hypothesizing gene regulatory networks. Standardization of data formats and experiment management support are also important for effective and seamless applications of data mining.

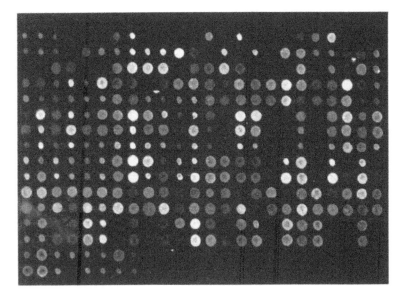

FIG. 4. Biological variation of gene expression in Loblolly pine clones by microarray analysis. Data mining is used to identify clusters of genes that are coexpressed under similar stress/drought conditions, helping to hypothesize and/or update gene regulatory networks. The microarray is printed in four 24 × 16 subquadrants, one of which is shown here. Figure courtesy of Y.-H. Sun (NCSU). Reproduced in colour between pages 142 and 143.

2.5 Data Mining in Flows

Finite element formulations of a variety of flow simulations and structures have been among the most compute-intensive applications of large-scale supercomputers. These techniques have been used to understand and design machine parts, airframes and projectiles, and noninvasive medical procedures for cauterizing tumors among other things. The underlying problems range from "how to stir vegetable soup in a pot so that each serving contains the same composition of ingredients" to "how to design stealth airframes to minimize scattering signatures and detection by enemy radar."

Analyzing fluid flows, especially turbulent flows, remains an extremely difficult and challenging problem. Minimizing turbulence is at the heart of reducing drag on airfoils and automobiles, improving performance of jet engines, and maximizing convective cooling. At the same time, maximizing turbulence is important, for example, in complete mixing of charge in engine cylinders and the distance a dimpled golf ball travels on a drive. Emerging medical applications of flows rely on focused electromagnetic fields that generate eddy currents within specific regions of the body to cauterize tumors. Particulate flows are being investigated for understanding blockages in arteries and vascular athresclerosis.

Simulations and observations in this domain address the forward problem of predicting flow behavior and its impact, and the inverse problem of designing features that optimize desired flow behavior. For example, the presence of longitudinal grooves, also known as riblets, placed a few tens of microns apart on airframes can reduce viscous drag by as much as 6%. Similarly, active surfaces composed of MEMS sensors and actuators can be controlled to minimize drag on airframes.

The input data for analysis of flows typically come from large-scale simulations. Scalar and vector fields such as pressure, potential, and velocity are defined over a finite element or a finite difference grid. Typical grids from large simulations can be in the range of 10^7 elements with over 100 bytes of data defined at each grid point per time step [55]. This corresponds to roughly a gigabyte of data at each time step. The simplest analysis tasks correspond to extraction of artifacts such as vortices and saddle points from simulation data [56–60]. This corresponds to a spatio-temporal mining process that detects, for instance, singularities in the flow field. More complex tasks in analyzing flows correspond to correlating flow structure with function, for example, predicting drag coefficient of airfoils. Ultimately, the goal is to develop structures that exhibit more desirable properties. In the case of airframes, this could be stability characteristics (or instability/maneuverability) and drag. Research efforts [61–63] have relied on neural networks and genetic programming to optimize the design process for airfoils.

More recently, fluid flow simulations have been used to study the formation of blockages in arteries. It has been noted that when a vein graft is incorporated to bypass a blockage, new blockages start to form almost immediately. The onset and rate of growth of these blockages depends on a variety of factors—the adhesiveness of graft walls, the pressure of particulate fluid flowing through the graft, and the concentration and nature of particulates [64, 65]. Simulations are being used to design materials with low adhesiveness that can be used for vein grafts. It has been observed that the formation of blockages can be impeded by increasing the fluid pressure within the graft. In experiments, this is achieved by pinching the artery. Machine learning techniques are being explored for determining both the physical composition and the structure of the artificial graft.

3. Inductive Mining Techniques

We start our discussion of data mining techniques by examining some key approaches that have been successfully applied to various scientific domains. The most commonly held view of data mining is one of induction—proceeding from the specific to the general. Techniques in this family differ in the nature of the induced representations (decision trees/rules/correlations/deviations/trends/associations, etc.), the form of the data they operate on (continuous/time-series/discrete/labeled/nominal, etc.), and the domains motivating their application (financial/economic/scientific/engineering/computational, etc.). The patterns, in turn, can be characterized based on aspects such as accuracy, precision, expressiveness, interpretability, "surprisingness/interestingness," and actionability (by the scientific enterprise). For example, a pattern that can translate into sound scientific decisions is better than one that is accurate, interesting, but provides no tangible benefit. A good example is reflected in the pattern "People who are good at knitting tend not to have the Y chromosome" [54]!

3.1 Underlying Principles

3.1.1 Clustering

An area where tremendous progress has been made in inductive learning is *clustering*—a fundamental procedure in pattern recognition that looks for regularities in training exemplars. By revealing associations between individuals of a population, it can be used to provide a compact representation of the input problem domain (see Fig. 5). The basic goal of clustering is to obtain a c-partition of the input data that exhibits categorically homogeneous subsets, where n is the number of training exemplars and $2 \leqslant c \leqslant n$ [67]. Different clustering methods have been proposed that represent clusters in different ways—for example, using a representative exemplar of a cluster, a probability distribution over a space of attribute values, necessary and sufficient conditions for cluster membership, etc. To represent a cluster by a collection of training exemplars and to "assign" new samples to existing clusters, some form of a utility measure is used. This is normally based on some mathematical property, such as distance, angle, curvature, symmetry, and intensity, exhibited by the members of the cluster. Various techniques have been proposed to reveal such associations; the most prevalent model pattern recognition as a form of either density estimation (unsupervised) or classification (supervised). Complexity control can then be achieved by regularization methods that operate within the structural risk minimization framework [68]. It has been recognized [69] that *no* universal clustering criterion can exist and that selection of any such criterion is subjective and depends on the domain of application under question. Clustering serves key applications in sky survey cataloging [70], bioinformatics [71], spatial data mining [15], geographical mining [72], dynamical systems analysis [73], and various other domains. See [74] for an excellent survey on clustering algorithms as proposed in the database community.

3.1.2 Scientific function-finding

From a heuristics point of view, the "empirical discovery" research of Langley, Simon, and Bradshaw in the 1980's [75] constitutes arguably one

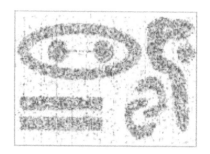

FIG. 5. (left) Typical unlabeled input data to a clustering algorithm. (right) Clusters mined by the CHAMELEON algorithm based on similarity and proximity metrics [66]. Figure courtesy of G. Karypis (University of Minnesota). Reproduced in colour between pages 142 and 143.

of the earliest systematic studies of data mining in scientific domains. The BACON system presented in [75] attempts scientific function-finding and uses a set of heuristics to explore the space of possible functional forms between columns in a numerical table. For example, if two columns of a table correspond to quantitative measurements of the force and the distance between atomic particles, BACON would use the monotonically decreasing relationship between the two columns to identify their product as a potential (new) column (of values) for further exploration, eventually leading to the inverse square relationship between the two variables. BACON has been shown to rediscover relationships such as Kepler's laws, Dalton's equations in chemistry, and other patterns in thermodynamics, optics, and electricity. In addition, it has been shown to form internal representations of "intrinsic concepts" that are later used in expressing the laws. We will return to this issue in our discussion on constructive induction (see later). While the original goal of BACON was to study the use of heuristic search as a mechanism for data-driven discovery, its main drawback was the inability to handle noise and uncertainty in physical data measurements. Detection of such higher-order relationships now constitutes a major activity in computational science (see the earlier section on data mining applications in materials engineering). Note that function-finding is broader than curve fitting since the functional form and/or structure of the relationship is not known beforehand.

3.1.3 Universal function approximators

More general forms of functional relationships can be modeled by neural networks [76], which are shown to approximate any function to any required level of accuracy (perhaps with exponential increase in complexity) [77]. Neural networks use one or more layers of intermediate functional elements to model the dependence of an output signal(s) on given input parameters. It is shown in [77] that two layers of in-between elements are sufficient to model any continuous function. The task of learning in this scenario is thus to determine the interconnection strengths and threshold biases (weights) that will result in acceptable approximation. While the general problem of determining weights has been shown to be NP-complete [78], neural networks have emerged as a valuable tool for engineers and scientists in pattern recognition, signal processing, and function approximation. Such applications utilize some form of gradient-descent or other local optimization techniques to "train" neural networks. Since neural networks function effectively as "black-boxes," their use in enabling knowledge discovery is limited. Their results are notorious for being inscrutable and it is typically very difficult to reverse-engineer a set of logical rules that capture their decision-making. Limited successes have been achieved in mining "M-of-N rules" that model patterns of the form "If three of these five features are present, the patient has coronary heart disease" [1]. Neural networks also suffer from other drawbacks, such as the capacity to incorporate prior knowledge in only a limited form [79] and excessive dependence on the original network topology [80]. For an excellent introduction, we refer the reader to [76].

3.1.4 Logical representations

While neural networks are attribute-value based techniques, more expressive schemes can be obtained by harnessing the representational power of logic (specifically, first-order logic). In this formalism, facts and measurements are represented as logical facts and data mining corresponds to forming an intensional rule that uses relational representations to model the dependence of a "goal" predicate on certain input predicates (relations). This "inductive logic programming" (ILP) approach [81] can be used to find patterns such as

```
patient(X,'diabetes') :- symptom(X,'S1'), symptom(X,'S2').
```

Which indicates that a patient (X) suffers from diabetes if he/she demonstrates symptoms S1 and S2. Note the easy comprehensibility of the rule, which could be later used in diagnostics and what-if analyses. In addition, such rules can also be recursive, a feature that makes ILP amenable to automated program synthesis [81] and discovery of complex relationships such as protein secondary structure [2]. In addition, ILP allows the incorporation of a priori background knowledge, a necessary prerequisite for mining in complex structured domains. ILP systems typically take a database of positive examples, negative examples, and background knowledge and attempt to construct a predicate logic formula (such as patient(X,Y)) so that all (most) positive examples can be logically derived from the background knowledge and no (few) negative examples can be logically derived. ILP has strong parallels in deductive database technology, as demonstrated in [82]. Figure 6 describes the results of correlating the mutagenicity of chemical compounds with their structure [83]. As shown, the expressiveness of ILP [81] makes it a highly desirable tool in structured domains where comprehension and interpretation of patterns is important.

In the most general setting of first-order logic, relational induction as described above is undecidable. A first restriction to function-free horn clauses results in decidability (this is the form of programs used in the

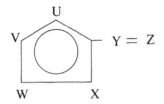
Y = Z

A chemical is highly mutagenic if it contains a double bond conjugated to a 5-membered aromatic ring via a carbon atom.

FIG. 6. Two representations of a construct mined by ILP in a chemical setting. The input consists of positive and negative examples of mutagenic compounds, detailing their bonding structure. The background knowledge consists of commonly known rules in chemistry and bond theory. The output is represented in two forms: (left) graphical depiction and (right) English statement of the pattern. Figure courtesy of A. Srinivasan (Oxford University).

programming language PROLOG). Decidability here is with respect to induction; for deduction, first-order logic is semi-decidable. However, ILP is often prohibitively expensive and the standard practice is to restrict the hypothesis space to a proper subset of first-order logic (the popularity of association rules [4] can be attributed to a further restriction of the hypothesis space that permits certain optimizations). Some commercial systems (like Golem [84]) further require that background knowledge be ground, meaning that only base facts can be provided as opposed to intensional information (rules). This renders the overall complexity polynomial in the space of the database but pseudo-polynomial (and sometimes exponential) in the space of the modifiable parameters (such as the rule length, clause depth, compression factor, and rule cover). In addition, the ability to process, represent, and mine predicates involving numeric attributes is limited. Nevertheless, ILP has witnessed successful applications in bio-informatics, finite-element mesh design, chemical structure prediction, water quality prediction, and biological structure discovery. See [2] for an excellent survey of ILP applications.

3.1.5 Constructive induction

This compelling research frontier refers to the "invention" of new features for subsequent use in data mining. An excellent example of human-performed constructive induction can be had from Francis Crick's experiences in unraveling the language of DNA. We use the fascinating account of Matt Ridley in [54] to illustrate the basic idea. Crick was attempting to determine how sequences comprising four bases (A, adenine; C, cytosine; G, guanine; T, thymine) coded for twenty amino acids. The goal was to determine the right level of in-between representation (codons) that aided in this transcription process. Crick's reasoning was that two bases for each amino acid is too few (16) while three bases provide an ample starting point for fine tuning the analysis. To prevent Nature from making translation errors, he reasoned that base sequences that could be misread should be eliminated. This removed sequences such as AAA, etc., leading to 60 sequences, which can be clustered into 20 groups of sequences whose members are equivalent under rotational transformations (ACG, CGA, GAC, etc.). While this idea turned out to be close but not perfect—three bases were right, but not the encoding—it provides an excellent example of the benefits of constructive induction in data mining. Ridley reports that this has been called the "greatest wrong theory in history." From a computational perspective, Craven and Shavlik [85] showed that the problem of finding the right codon representation is notoriously difficult with traditional machine learning techniques. As the mass of data generated under the Human Genome Project gets assimilated, the role of (semi-automated) constructive induction will only become paramount.

3.1.6 Integrated approaches

While ILP provides a logic-based representation for scientific background knowledge, other approaches to mining in scientific domains utilize various forms of theory-driven reasoning to augment, direct, and support empirical analyses. For example, the MECHEM program [86] uses domain-specific constraints on chemical reaction pathways to direct the search for plausible molecular reaction steps. MECHEM has found applications in areas such as urea synthesis and propane oxidation. Similar systems have been reported in graph theory, link analyses, and componential analyses. A survey of such systems that credits their success to systematic and comprehensive search in large spaces and good paradigms of human–computer interaction [88] is provided in [87]. It thus cannot be overemphasized that data mining processes are fundamentally iterative and interactive [89]. Systems that enable such interaction and perform integrated exploration and mining [90] can thus improve performance in the long run, while sacrificing some exploration time in the short term.

3.2 Best Practices

One of the key issues to be addressed prior to data mining is the decision on the right mechanism for representation. For example, while a simple structure might exist, the feature coordinate system might not reflect the simplicity properly. Consider the case when a particular feature system imposes the following pattern involving disease symptoms and medical treatments [91]:

$$\text{Treatment 1 is best if } x^2 + y^2 \leqslant 1$$

$$\text{Treatment 2 is best otherwise.}$$

If we now choose new coordinates (x', y') such that

$$\begin{pmatrix} x' \\ y' \end{pmatrix} = \begin{pmatrix} 1 & 1.0001 \\ 1 & 1.0000 \end{pmatrix} \begin{pmatrix} x \\ y \end{pmatrix},$$

then Treatment 1 is best in a very long, very thin area (in (x', y') coordinates). If the following features are now chosen,

$$f1 = x'$$

$$f2 = y'$$

$$f3 = x' + y' \sin x' + z1$$

$$f4 = x' - y' + 1/x' + e^{x'} + z2,$$

where $z1$ and $z2$ are irrelevant, or random, it will then take a lot of data and effort to recover the original simple pattern. Thus, the pattern mined might depend in an unstable manner on the features actually used $(f1, f2, f3, f4)$ and no reasonable amount of brute force computing can provide a robust selection methodology in such a situation. In addition, the algorithms/techniques used should be able to isolate as many irrelevant features as possible from the induced generalization. We identify various issues that are pertinent in mining scientific data.

3.2.1 Determining high-level structures

The past decades have witnessed the maturing of clustering algorithms, primarily with the advent of statistical pattern recognition and database systems. It is beyond the scope of this chapter to summarize these developments. As identified in [92], it is important to caution, however, that the indiscriminate application of clustering algorithms is not recommended and every application domain merits serious study and preprocessing before attempting clustering and/or interpreting the results of clustering. Such preprocessing techniques involve principal component analysis, feature handcrafting, data filtering, and visualization procedures such as Sammon's mapping, which produces class-preserving projections. Most clustering algorithms assume a prior on the structure of the induced clusters (e.g., some parametric approaches), thresholds on observed features, or nonparametric ideas such as valley-seeking [93]. An interesting approach to clustering is provided by the Chameleon system [66], which induces a graph (based on a neighborhood metric), and then views clustering as a form of graph partitioning. This approach allows the incorporation of both interconnectivity and closeness constraints on the induced clusters (background knowledge in a limited form). As shown in Fig. 5, it is flexible enough to handle clusters of widely varying sizes, shapes, densities, and orientations. An alternative to clustering numerical data based on such measures of similarity constitutes clustering based on co-occurrence and categorical information [94, 95], which helps prevent information loss due to discretization.

A more holistic approach to determining high-level structures is demonstrated in the SAL system [96], which provides the imagistic paradigm of spatial aggregation [97], ontologies for scientific data abstractions (fields, graphs, etc.), and a compositional modeling framework for structure discovery in data-rich domains. Various important mining operations can be realized by applying primitives in a programmatic manner to neighborhood graphs, such as aggregation and classification. Figure 7 describes a snapshot of the SAL system that uses the graph-theoretic primitives to find thermal hills in the flow obtained by aggregating classes of temperature values. The SAL framework has been used in many applications, including weather data analysis [11], and optimization and qualitative analysis of other physical systems [97]. The role played by such frameworks in integrated control and system design is elaborated upon later in the chapter.

3.2.2 Controlling the complexity of induction

Various mechanisms have been proposed to address the complexities of techniques such as inductive logic programming to form high-level representations. Three main approaches can be identified. At a basic level, domain-specific restrictions are being increasingly incorporated into the mining process. For example, both syntactic and semantic restrictions help curtail the search. A syntactic restriction refers to constraints posed on the nature of predicates that can appear in the antecedent and consequent parts of a rule and the nature of variable interactions allowed in the predicates. Semantic restrictions model consistency constraints and provide various means of *sanity checks*. Such constraints can also enable optimizations that *push* costly mining operations deeper into the computational pipeline [98]. Second, generality orderings are used to guide the induction of rules. Such orderings are used to prune the search

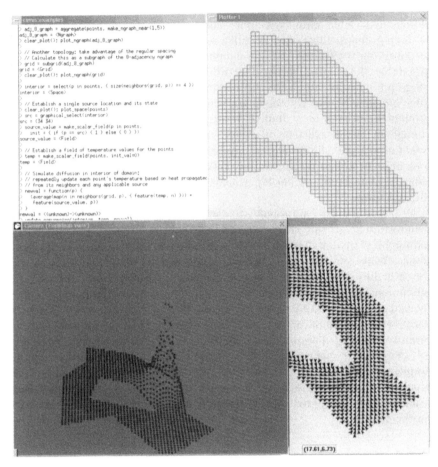

FIG. 7. An instance of the SAL interpreter: window showing typical user interaction (top left), the finite difference discretization (top right), resulting heat flows (bottom left), and the thermal hill from a single source (bottom right). Figure courtesy of C. Bailey-Kellogg (Dartmouth College). Reproduced in colour between pages 142 and 143.

space for generating plausible hypotheses and to aid in abduction (which is the process of constructing a rule that needs to be justified further). Finally, the software architectures of data mining systems are typically augmented with natural database query interfaces [99], so this aspect can be utilized to provide meta-patterns for rule generation ("Find me a pattern that connects something about patients' athletic activities to the dates of occurrence of some symptoms") [100].

Land Cover for the Watershed Area

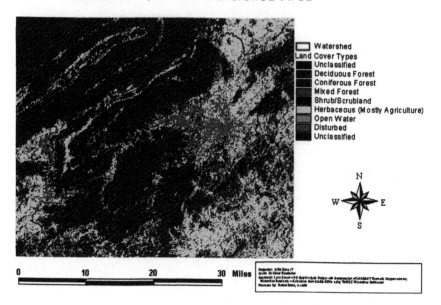

FIG. 1. Landuse segmentation of the Upper Roanoke River Watershed in Southwest Virginia, USA. Areas marked "Unclassified" and "Mixed Forest" pose difficulties for evaluating the effect of settlement patterns. Data mining can help identify mislabeled areas and correlate unlabeled regions with known land cover features. Figure courtesy of R. Dymond (Virginia Tech).

FIG. 2. Molecular dynamics simulation demonstrating a crack in an amorphous silicon nitride film. Slow intramicrocrack propagation produces smooth surfaces, while coalescence of microcracks leads to rapid propagation and produces rough surfaces. The nature of crack surfaces is important in many applications. The problem of extracting a crack surface dynamically from large-scale molecular dynamics simulation data is an important analysis task. Figure courtesy of A. Nakano (Louisiana State University).

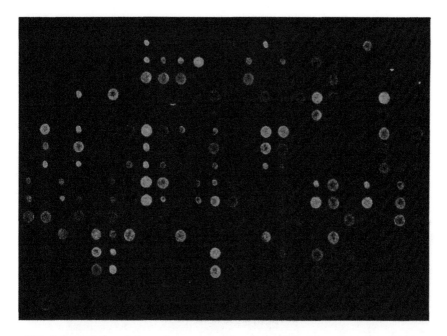

FIG. 4. Biological variation of gene expression in Loblolly pine clones by microarray analysis. Data mining is used to identify clusters of genes that are coexpressed under similar stress/drought conditions, helping to hypothesize and/or update gene regulatory networks. The microarray is printed in four 24 × 16 subquadrants, one of which is shown here. Figure courtesy of Y.-H. Sun (NCSU).

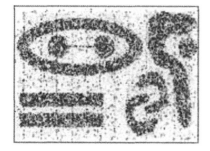 

FIG. 5. (left) Typical unlabeled input data to a clustering algorithm. (right) Clusters mined by the CHAMELEON algorithm based on similarity and proximity metrics [66]. Figure courtesy of G. Karypis (University of Minnesota).

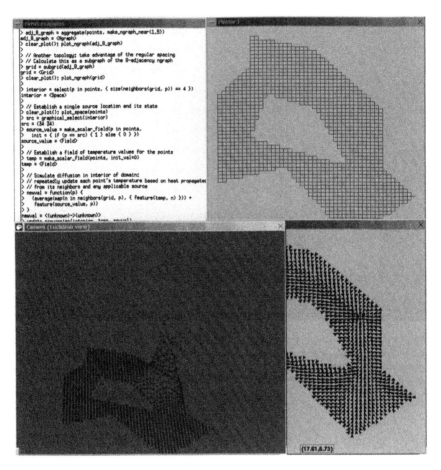

FIG. 7. An instance of the SAL interpreter: window showing typical user interaction (top left), the finite difference discretization (top right), resulting heat flows (bottom left), and the thermal hill from a single source (bottom right). Figure courtesy of C. Bailey-Kellogg (Dartmouth College).

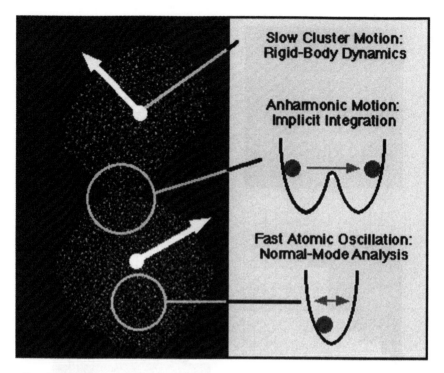

FIG. 8. Illustration of difference between global conformational changes and localized atomic displacements. While the localized displacements across all particles display no coherent behavior, global conformational displacements exhibit coherence within the two clusters. The white arrows indicate movement of clusters (coherent behavior) over time scales much larger than those of atomic vibrations. Such analysis is useful for detecting phenomena such as crack propagation and formation of pores. Figure courtesy of A. Nakano (Louisiana State University; http://www.cclms.lsu.edu/cclms/group/Faculty/nakano.html).

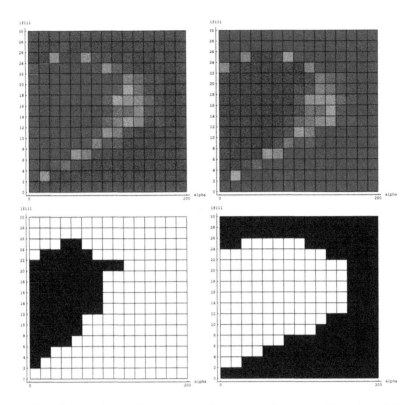

FIG. 14. Mining and visualizing recommendation spaces for gmres (top left) and direct solve (top right) on nearly singular PDE problems. The intensity in the colormap reflects the number of problem instances in a bucket for which the given algorithm was superior; 90% confidence regions mined automatically for gmres (bottom left) and direct solve (bottom right), for droptol = 0, by the method described in [129] are also shown. For these regions, the given methods were superior for at least 90% of the problem instances.

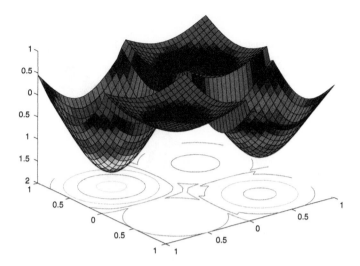

FIG. 15. A 2D pocket function. Note the global minimum in the $[-1, 0] \times [0, 1]$ quadrant. Data mining can help reveal the locations of the pockets; one structure-exploiting approach, based on learning evaluation functions for further optimization, is to correlate the magnitude of local minima with the starting point for descent algorithms [134].

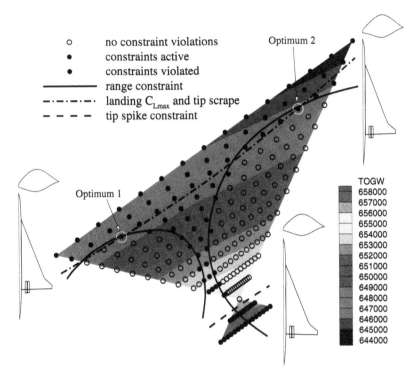

FIG. 16. A slice of an aircraft design space through three design points [124]. Note the nonconvexity of the feasible design space induced by the various constraints. Figure courtesy of Layne T. Watson (Virginia Tech).

3.2.3 Handling uncertainty and noise in measurements

As mentioned earlier, typical data sets are characterized by mislabeled or unavailable data, and lack of repeatability or accuracy in measurements (see the examples on microarray data and land-use segmentation described earlier). A promising approach that is found to be effective in such domains is described in [101], where various forms of data relationships underlying the domain are explicitly modeled as qualitative correlations, which are then used to determine inaccurate data. An application to infrared spectrum identification is also described in [101]. A matrix-theoretic approach to this problem is provided by the singular-value decomposition (SVD), introduced in Section 4. SVD can help perform subset selection on either the variables or the data points, thus aiding noise reduction and/or removal of redundancy.

3.2.4 Inventing new features

Research into constructive induction has provided various solutions to this problem, although the larger fundamental question still remains. In an attribute-value setting, statistical software such as SAS/STAT contain various forms of regression tools that incrementally postulate and add terms to form functional relations. In relational settings, description logics (sometimes called terminological logics) have been proposed as an extension to first-order logic [102] where all but one of the variables are quantified. This allows the expression of predicates such as "at least two," or "at most three," which can be viewed as operating upon the individual original user-supplied predicates. Such systems have been used for research into correlating patient symptoms with diseases, and have been shown to excel ILP in their representational basis [103]. In addition, [103] shows that such representations form one of the largest subsets of first-order logic that is tractable under inductive inference. It has also been shown that ILP (with its logical representation language) is well suited for constructive induction [104] by introducing features consisting of connected sequences of predicates.

4. Data Mining as Approximation and Lossy Compression

The approach of "stepping back to get a bigger picture" is often used (sometimes inadvertently) for analyzing large data sets. We discuss this family of techniques as mining by approximation or lossy compression.

4.1   Underlying Principles

In many applications of scientific data mining, the problem of identifying artifacts of interest in data is similar, if not identical, to the task of lossy data compression. The objective of lossy compression is one of reducing effective storage while retaining as much of the information content as possible. This correspondence between data compression and mining has roots in information theory (mutual information), numerical methods (rank reduction, eigenvalue analysis), algorithmics (geometric simplifications), and applications (latent semantic indexing, etc.).

4.1.1   Compressing data defined over geometry and topologies

An important class of problems in scientific computing relies on mesh-based and mesh-free bases for solving integral and differential equations. This class spans particle dynamics, finite element/difference techniques, and boundary element methods. Many of these problems have a time dependency and generate extremely large data sets over typical application runs. The rich set of tools in this domain has prompted the formulation of problems in other domains (such as information retrieval and market basket analysis) as problems defined over point sets using a vector-space model. The issue of compressing these data sets has received considerable attention, although the correspondence between compression and mining has been tenuous. Compression and analysis of large scientific data sets takes on two major forms: detection of features that span several spatio-temporal scales and detection of artifacts at a specified scale. We discuss these in the context of a variety of applications.

4.1.2   Detecting and coding multiresolution phenomena

Large-scale simulations in molecular dynamics, astrophysics, and materials processing result in time-dependent data, with each time step comprising a set of points (typically in 3D space) and attributes associated with each of these points. Attributes range from scalar fields such as potential and pressure to vector fields such as velocity and electrostatic/-gravitational fields. These applications present considerable challenges for simulation and modeling due to the highly multiresolution nature of the associated physical phenomena and the dense nature of node interactions—specifically that in many of these applications, each particle is impacted by every other particle. This issue of all-to-all interaction complexity is addressed by fast methods such as the fast multipole method (FMM) [105] and Barnes–Hut [106]. These methods introduce systematic approximations that reduce computational complexity while causing bounded errors.

Consider the problem of analyzing data from a particle dynamics simulation in materials processing. In these simulations, the smallest time step must often match the frequency of atomic vibrations, i.e., in the range of femtoseconds. However, global conformational changes take several orders of magnitude longer than this time scale. Moreover, these global displacements are often indistinguishable from localized atomic displacements, necessitating the use of innovative algorithms and analysis techniques. This is illustrated in Fig. 8, in which a heuristic clustering technique is applied to identify aggregates of particles displaying coherent displacements over large timescales. This large aggregate displacement is indicated by white arrows. The particles within the clusters themselves display localized displacements.

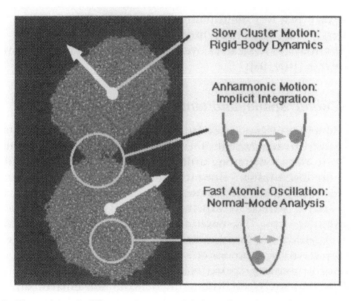

FIG. 8. Illustration of difference between global conformational changes and localized atomic displacements. While the localized displacements across all particles display no coherent behavior, global conformational displacements exhibit coherence within the two clusters. The white arrows indicate movement of clusters (coherent behavior) over time scales much larger than those of atomic vibrations. Such analysis is useful for detecting phenomena such as crack propagation and formation of pores. Figure courtesy of A. Nakano (Louisiana State University; http://www.cclms.lsu.edu/cclms/group/Faculty/nakano.html). Reproduced in colour between pages 142 and 143.

There are several approaches to detecting such aggregate particle behavior. These approaches range from clustering (see Section 3) to rank-reduction techniques. In the case of identifying aggregate displacements, clustering techniques use velocity fields (or differences of positions) over several time steps to identify particles belonging to the same aggregate. Note that clustering here is not based on physical proximity, rather on the attribute associated with the behavior being examined. Nakano [107] uses this approach to examine aggregate behavior in particle systems. This technique uses a membership function $p(i, c)$, which describes the degree of association between atom i and cluster c. The principle of maximum entropy is used to determine $p(i, c)$. In addition to using this as an analysis technique, it is also possible to reduce computational cost of the simulation using clustering. This approach relies on a hierarchy of subdynamics for computing particle trajectories. Atoms are first grouped together into clusters. Dynamics at the cluster level are modeled by rigid-body motion using a large time step. The fast oscillatory motion of atoms around the local minima in potential is then computed and superimposed. It has been demonstrated that for simulations of sintering of two silicon nitride nanoclusters, the fuzzy-body/implicit-integration/normal-mode (FIN) scheme described above achieves over an order-of-magnitude improvement in performance [107, 108].

4.1.3 Coding spatial and temporal coherence

In addition to problems associated with multiresolution phenomena, it is often necessary to examine data at a single resolution level (both spatial and temporal) to detect interesting artifacts. In typical domains, neighboring particles (or discretization elements) exhibit spatial as well as temporal coherence—i.e., spatially proximate particles are expected to exhibit similar behavior and a particle is expected to exhibit coherent behavior over consecutive time steps. The onset of such physical artifacts as cracks and fissures is signaled by a loss in coherence. Such artifacts are of interest and must be preserved by compression schemes.

The task of encoding spatial coherence (or the lack thereof) can be achieved by recursively subdividing the domain and differentially coding with respect to the expected value for the subdomain. This process fits in well with the hierarchical approximations used in many fast simulation techniques (multipole methods, multigrid solvers). Approximations introduced by fast methods also introduce a distortion radii around computed parameters. These parameters can be quantized to any point within the distortion radii without additional loss in accuracy. This process is illustrated in Yang et al. [42].

In addition to analyzing high-dimensional geometry (continuous attribute sets), in many applications, it is necessary to compress functions implicitly defined over meshes (as opposed to point sets). This involves the additional task of simplifying the topology in addition to the geometry. A number of schemes have been developed for lossless as well as lossy compression of meshes. Lossless compression techniques for specifying connectivity rely on node orderings for unrolling surface meshes into rings or concentric layers [109–111]. Lossy compression of topology relies on schemes for merging discretization elements based on the error introduced by the simplification. Simple metrics for minimizing this error rely on gradients (merge elements where gradient is minimum) or explicit integration of error in function between simplified and original discretizations. A careful choice of weights for attributes and error metric results in a very effective analysis tool based on mesh simplifications.

4.2   Best Practices

4.2.1   Compressing continuous attribute sets

The key to effective quantization of high-dimensional geometry is to identify regions of high and low density and distortion radii. A uniform quantization scheme must rely on a discretization resolution equal to the smallest distortion radii for any attribute. This can result in a significant overhead with respect to compression ratios. Consequently, a multi-dimensional adaptive quantization scheme is needed for arbitrary distributions of attribute values.

One such scheme [42] constructs a hierarchical decomposition of the attribute space from a given set of attribute values and distortion radii. This process is illustrated for a two-dimensional problem in Fig. 9. The domain is recursively subdivided into quads until each quad contains one entity and the center of the quad is within the distortion radius of the entity contained within. Once such a hierarchical structure has been constructed, entities are assigned to leaf nodes that lie within distortion radii. The problem of representing entity attributes now reduces to the problem of representing populated leaf-level nodes in the tree. This is done by encoding the path from the root to the leaf node. By associating a predefined ordering of children in the tree, we can associate d bits per level in the tree for a d-dimensional attribute set. We illustrate this process for a 2D problem in Fig. 9. In the example, entity a is at level three in the tree and according to the predefined node ordering for children of a node, it is represented as 00 00 11. This provides the basic quantization mechanism.

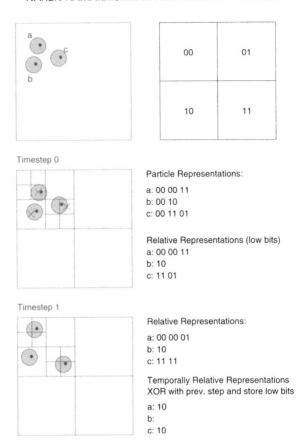

FIG. 9. Illustration of compression of particle position data using a distortion sphere, and spatial and temporal coherence.

This compression and analysis framework can be improved using a number of optimizations. Entities (nodes) that are spatially proximate (in physical space and not attribute space) are likely to share large prefixes in the path from root to leaf. This implies that if the entities are sorted in a proximity preserving order (such as Morton or Hilbert curves), then we can represent entity attributes relative to the previous attributes. The use of spatial coherence for improving compression ratios is illustrated in Fig. 9, Timestep 0 in the context of a particle system. The quantized representations for particles a, b, and c are given by 00 00 11, 00 10, and 00 11 01 respectively. Assuming that these particles are sorted in the order a, b, and then c, it is easy to see that particles b and c share the prefix 00 with particle a. Consequently, the prefix does not need to be stored for these and the representations for b and c are simply 10 and 11 01. While this may not seem to be a significant improvement in this example, in typical trees, the depth can be high. For example, with a normalized domain of unit size in each dimension, a distortion radius of 10^{-3} would require up to 10 levels in the oct tree. In such cases with higher particle densities, significant improvements result from the use of spatial coherence.

4.2.2 Violations of spatial coherence

The above framework can be very effective for both compression and analysis. Consider the problem of identifying subdomains that violate the spatial coherence condition. This may occur, for instance, during the formation of cracks or fissures in materials. Here, neighboring particles will exhibit significantly different velocities at the onset of a crack. In this case, a differentially coded, spatially ordered representation of particle velocities would require a large number of bits. The number of bits required to store the position is a good estimation of the spatial coherence. Similar methods can be used to analyze other quantities relating to temporal coherence as well. For example, consider a compression scheme in which difference in particle positions over time steps are coded in the hierarchical framework. Here, the number of bits is a reflection on the energy of the particles. A similar approach can be used to identify high-potential regions in the domain.

4.2.3 Rank reduction

In each of the above cases, the basic compression technique relies on a distortion radius in a high-dimensional space and quantizes the space adaptively to points within the distortion radius. There are other techniques that are more computationally expensive but are amenable to higher-level analysis functions. One such technique relies on rank-reduction of the attributes associated with each point.

Consider, once again, a given point set with an attribute vector at each of the points. The set of all attribute vectors can be viewed as a matrix. A simple rank-one approximation to the matrix is such that each nonzero entry in the column vector can be thought of as having a weighted representation of the corresponding row vector. Using this approach, each point can be mapped to one or more of the singular vectors computed from a SVD of the attribute vector set matrix. Compression is achieved by simply storing the singular vectors and indexing into this set of singular vectors at points instead of complete attribute vectors.

This technique is powerful from the point of view of data analysis as well. Multiple points mapped to the same set of singular vectors can be viewed as exhibiting approximately identical behavior (in terms of their attribute vectors). This process is illustrated in Fig. 10. The set of singular vectors can be viewed as the dominant cluster behavior and can be used to further characterize system behavior. Techniques similar to this have been explored for identifying principal components for visualizing data with very high dimensionality and for compressing discrete transaction data using semi-discrete transforms (SDD) [112–114].

A critical aspect of using lossy compression techniques for data analysis is the selection of appropriate functions over which simplification metrics can be defined. Consider the analysis of a fluid flow simulation with a view to identifying vortices. On a simply connected domain, the velocity flow field consists of two parts—a pure gradient component (with zero curl) and a

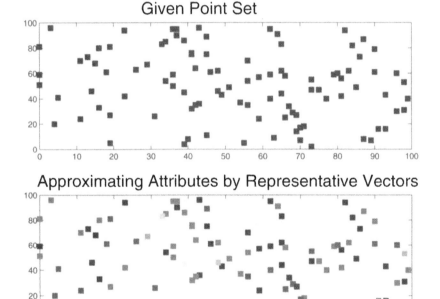

FIG. 10. Using rank-reduction techniques for analyzing the behavior associated with point sets. Each of the points with the same color is mapped to the same singular vector; i.e., their attributes are within some bounded distance from the representative singular vector. Please see [113, 114] for more details.

pure curl component (with zero div). Given an arbitrary vector field V associated with a fluid, vorticity is defined as the curl of V. The process of lossy compression must preserve error with respect to the curl of V while deemphasizing other parameters. Similar considerations arise in almost all applications. A unified framework relying on a weighted set of attribute vectors (with all appropriate features) can handle such applications well.

5. Putting It All Together

5.1 Underlying Principles

The operational strength of techniques such as those presented earlier relies on an integration of methodologies for storage, retrieval, and post-processing in data mining. The importance of support for such data-intensive operations is increasingly underscored in scientific circles [115–118]. In this section, we outline various aspects of data mining in larger scientific contexts with illustrative examples.

5.1.1 Recommender systems

One of the emerging areas of research in computational science and engineering is the design of powerful programming abstractions for application support systems [119–121]. For example, the LSA system [119] can compose a linear system analyzer by using a plug-and-play paradigm to chain together individual components. This compositional modeling framework requires the knowledge-based selection of solution components for individual application domains—in this case, linear algebra. Such *recommender systems* can help in the natural process of a scientist/engineer making selections among various choices of algorithms/software. They are typically designed offline by organizing a battery of benchmark problems and algorithm executions [122], and mining it to obtain high-level rules that can form the basis of a recommendation. Data mining thus plays a major role in providing decision support in large-scale simulations.

5.1.2 Interactive visualization

Concomitant with such tools, visualization of recommendation spaces, and providing mechanisms for incremental exploration of data becomes paramount. Figure 11 describes the interface to VizCraft—a PSE for conceptual design of aircraft [123]. The goal of this PSE is to minimize the take-off gross weight (TOGW) for a 250-passenger high-speed civil

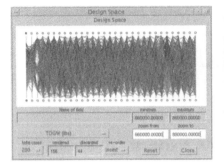 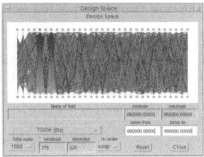

FIG. 11. (left) Visualizing 156 aircraft design points in 29 dimensions [123]. (right) A rearrangement of variables with corresponding color driver change reveals an interesting association. Figure courtesy of C. A. Shaffer (Virginia Tech).

transport (HSCT) [124]. There are 29 design variables with 68 constraints in a highly nonconvex design space. The scenario in Fig. 11 describes a collection of data points over the 29 dimensions superimposed on each other. As can be seen, a rearrangement of the "driving variable" reveals an interesting association between two aspects of aircraft design. Coupled with virtual reality devices, interactive visualization also plays a major role in applications such as molecular docking, determining protein secondary structure, working in hazardous environments, and telemedicine.

An important aspect of scientific data mining relates to inlined mining and simulation tasks. It can be argued that if one can identify specific processes (and/or subdomains) that are interesting, then computational resources could be steered toward these processes, while supporting other simulation tasks only in so far as to maintain the fidelity of the interesting phenomena. This concept of *computational steering* [125] plays an important role in reducing the computation associated with large-scale simulations. For example, applications such as eukaryotic cell cycle modeling involve tens to hundreds of parameters that must be dynamically modified, tracked, and tuned to achieve desired metabolic processes. Integration of computation, interaction, and post-processing is the target of many commercial software ventures.

5.1.3 Data and experiment management

The realization of the above two goals relies on efficient data modeling that supports the data generation, data analysis, automatic knowledge acquisition, and inference processes in computational science. One of the main requirements of data modeling involves providing storage for problem populations in a structured way, and enabling management of the execution environment by keeping track of the constraints implied by the physical characteristics of the application. In addition, the quantity of information generated for computational steering and manipulated by recommender systems requires a powerful and adaptable database management system (DBMS) with an open architecture. However, traditional relational and OO models are inadequate because fully extensible functionality is required for an environment that keeps changing not only in the size of the data but also in the schema. For example, bioinformatics applications require specialized data structures and customized tables for each new experimental technique introduced [126]. Such frequent changes to source schema are not well addressed by current systems.

5.1.4 Information integration

With the rapid emergence of data formats and applications such as bioinformatics supporting a veritable cottage industry of databases, information integration becomes paramount to support holistic scenarios. For example, the query "Find all information pertaining to human chromosome 22" was considered an impossible query under the Human Genome Project until just a few years back [126]. Information integration is typically addressed by remapping queries to originating sources, introducing a transparency layer of middleware in between data sources, or using other mediator-based schemes. This is thus one of the main issues underlying applications such as health care management [127] and digital libraries [117, 128].

5.2   Best Practices

5.2.1 Data modeling and representation

Significant advances have been made in database support for PSEs and computational steering. We present concepts from the PYTHIA framework [122] that aids in the rapid prototyping of recommender systems for computational science. In order to facilitate the storage and execution of experiments, the input specification of a problem (e.g., ODEs, PDEs) is decomposed into a set of database tables in PYTHIA. There is a one-to-one mapping between the components of the problem specification and the basic entities in PYTHIA's schema. Features of problem components are also modeled by other tables, and tables representing relations are used for designating the constraints in associating features with basic entities.

Figure 12 provides a schema for the definition of a PDE feature that can be instantiated along with associated connections to other records. Experiments are also managed by yet another table, in that each experiment record holds all the necessary information for executing a collection of problems in a specific system. PYTHIA communicates with the host PSE via devices such as I/O files and software buses. In order to avoid redundancy in the implementation, an experiment record uses foreign keys for representing the logical connections with the basic records. Tables that store performance data are used for saving selected parts from the output files produced by running these experiments. Atomic entities will be domain-specific since they represent the problem definition objects of a targeted domain, but the performance- and knowledge-related data schema extend easily to other problem domains. Such a representation for performance information is depicted in Fig. 13. The performance analysis of algorithms proceeds with respect to user-specified criteria, such as the total time taken for solving the linear system that arises from the discretization of a PDE. Generalization of such performance rankings produces recommendation spaces and regions (via, say, inductive logic programming) that can help in selecting algorithms for newly presented problems. Figure 14 describes a comparison between an iterative solver (gmres) and a direct solver by mining 45 000 PDE solves on nearly singular problems. The shape of the induced recommendation spaces provides insight into the relative efficacies of the methods. For example, Fig. 14 shows that when the droptol parameter for the linear solver is zero, the lfill parameter must fall within a relatively narrow interval in order for the iterative method to be the preferred choice. For more details, we refer the reader to [129].

The SAL system presented in Fig. 7 achieves a similar objective by combining the interpretation of structures in physical fields with physical knowledge such as locality and linear superposability, thus allowing control

```
-- table no 1
create table FEATURE (
  name      text,     -- record name (primary key)
  nfeatures integer,  -- no. of attributes identifying this featur
  features  text[],   -- numeric/symbolic/textual identification
  forfile   text      -- file-based feature information
);
```

FIG. 12. Example schema for the feature record.

```
Field           | Value
name            | pde54 dom02 fd-itpack-rscg SP2-17
system          | pellpack
comp_db         | linearalgebra
composite_id    | pde54 domain 02 fd-itpack-rscg
perfind_set     | pellpack-std-par-grd
pid             | 1432
sequence_no     | 17
eqparms         | pde #54 parameter set 5
solverseq       | 950x950 proc 4 reduced system cg
rundata         | IBM SP2 with 18 compute nodes
. . . .
nerror          | 3
errornames      | {"max abs error","L1 error","L2 error"}
errorvals       | {"0.0022063","0.00011032","0.00022281"}
```

FIG. 13. An (incomplete) instance of performance data from the PDE benchmark.

placement and parameters to be designed in an *explainable* manner [130]. In other words, data mining constitutes a fundamental methodology in control design.

5.2.2 Integrating numeric, symbolic, and geometric information

Qualitative analysis of dynamical systems originated from the MaC Project at MIT [131]; the approach taken is to support intelligent simulation by representations and mechanisms that autonomously design and monitor complex physical systems through appropriate mixtures of numerical and symbolic computing and knowledge-based methods. Programs developed in this manner have been shown to automatically prepare numerical experiments from high-level descriptions, and exploit techniques like imagistic reasoning (see discussion on the SAL system in Section 3) and computer vision to identify promising areas for future experiments. Mining qualitative models using the QSIM representation is undertaken in [132]; this work resembles incorporating tighter constraints on induction techniques like ILP. Such integration of multimodal reasoning will only become more important with increased emphasis on computational science and the replacement of many wet-lab procedures by simulation.

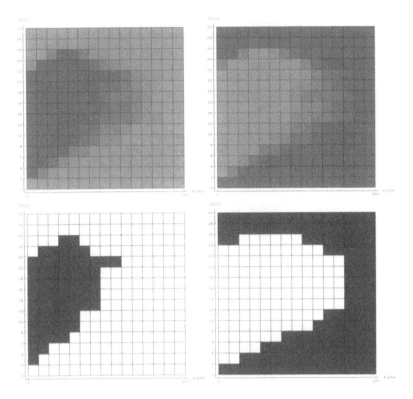

FIG. 14. Mining and visualizing recommendation spaces for gmres (top left) and direct solve (top right) on nearly singular PDE problems. The intensity in the colormap reflects the number of problem instances in a bucket for which the given algorithm was superior; 90% confidence regions mined automatically for gmres (bottom left) and direct solve (bottom right), for droptol = 0, by the method described in [129] are also shown. For these regions, the given methods were superior for at least 90% of the problem instances. Reproduced in colour between pages 142 and 143.

6. Future Research Issues

6.1 Mining When Data Is Scarce

While massive databases catalog and provide access to petabytes of archived field data or measurements (e.g., sky surveys [70], and the Human Genome Project [54]), much scientific data are gathered from sophisticated mathematical models, codes, and simulations. For domains such as gas turbine dynamics simulation and aircraft design, such complex simulations require days, weeks, or even years on petaflops class computing systems.

From a data mining point of view, this raises interesting issues not present in many other commercial (and even scientific) domains. First, these applications are characterized not by an abundance of data, but rather by a scarcity of data (owing to the cost and time involved in conducting simulations).

6.1.1 de Boor's function

Visualize the n-dimensional hypercube defined by $x_i \in [-1, 1]$, $i = 1 \ldots n$, with the n-sphere of radius 1 centered at the origin ($\Sigma x_i^2 \leqslant 1$) embedded inside it. Note that the ratio of the volume of the cube (2^n) to that of the sphere ($\pi^{n/2}/(n/2)!$) grows unboundedly with n. In other words, the volume of a high-dimensional cube is concentrated in its corners (a counterintuitive notion at first). Carl de Boor exploited this property to design a difficult-to-optimize function that assumes a *pocket* in each corner of the cube (Fig. 15), that is, just outside the sphere [133]. It is easily seen that the function has 2^n local minima and the goal of mining in this scenario is to be able to (i) identify the locations of the pockets and (ii) obtain some indication of where the "biggest dip" is located. In real-world scientific domains, n is large (say, 30, which means it will take more than a half-million points to just

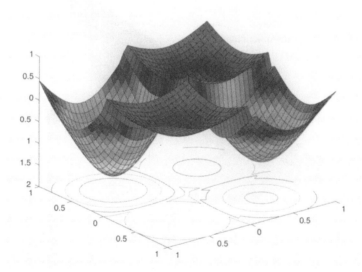

FIG. 15. A 2D pocket function. Note the global minimum in the $[-1, 0] \times [0, 1]$ quadrant. Data mining can help reveal the locations of the pockets; one structure-exploiting approach, based on learning evaluation functions for further optimization, is to correlate the magnitude of local minima with the starting point for descent algorithms [134]. Reproduced in colour between pages 142 and 143.

represent the corners of the *n*-cube!) and global optimization algorithms require that the pocket function be evaluated at a large number of points. Arguably, the task is simplified considerably if one has a symbolic form of the pocket function to analyze, but such information amenable to a priori analyses is typically not available.

6.1.2 Aircraft design

This problem is exacerbated in domains such as aircraft design (see Fig. 11). Figure 16 shows a cross section of the design space for the representative problem described earlier in Section 5.1.2. Frequently, the designer will change some aspect of a nominal design point, and run a simulation to see how the change affects the objective function and various constraints dealing with aircraft geometry and performance/aerodynamics.

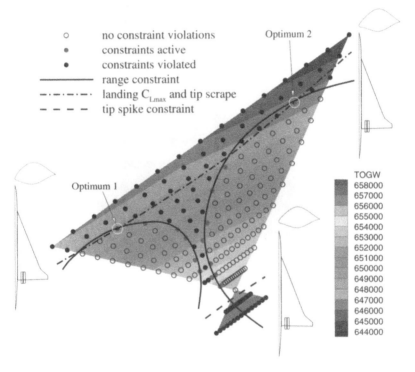

FIG. 16. A slice of an aircraft design space through three design points [124]. Note the nonconvexity of the feasible design space induced by the various constraints. Figure courtesy of Layne T. Watson (Virginia Tech). Reproduced in colour between pages 142 and 143.

Such a simple approach will be infeasible in the foreseeable future, because months, often years, are required to explore a high-dimensional design space, even at low fidelity. As new designs evolve and mature to fit new uses, the need to quickly explore many design and parameter choices becomes increasingly important. Ideally, the design engineer would like a high-level mining system to identify the pockets that contain good designs and that merit further consideration; traditional tools from optimization and approximation theory can then be applied to fine-tune such preliminary analyses.

6.2 Design of Experiments

More importantly, in contrast to business domains, the computational scientist has complete control over the data acquisition process (regions of the design space where data can be collected). A cheap surrogate model can then be constructed that can serve as an alternative starting point for data mining. This methodology, known quite simply as "Design and Analysis of Computer Experiments (DACE)," is prevalent in the statistical design literature [135] but hasn't received much attention in the data mining community. The goal is to extract useful patterns from the surrogate models, rather than the original, costly codes (or field data, which cannot be controlled). Considerable attention has been devoted to the use of sampling for mining very structured patterns, such as association rules [136] (this work, however, does not address the issue of "where to sample"). Similar aspects are currently being addressed in a project relating to designing experiments for biological molecule crystallization [137, 138].

6.3 Mining "On-The-Fly"

Inducing control policies that capture patterns on a dynamic scale can help in run-time recommendation of algorithms, algorithm switching, and large-scale application composition. The goal here is to integrate the data collection and data mining stages in computational science by incremental refinement techniques such as reinforcement learning [139]. For example, consider the Van der Pol relaxed system of dimension 2 [140]:

$$x'' - \mu(1 - x^2)x' + x = 0$$

graphed in Fig. 17 that has a limit cycle whenever $\mu > 0$. For this ODE, the value of x increases for small values and decreases for large values. This problem is complicated because it alternates between being stiff and nonstiff several times in the region of interest, causing difficulties for traditional

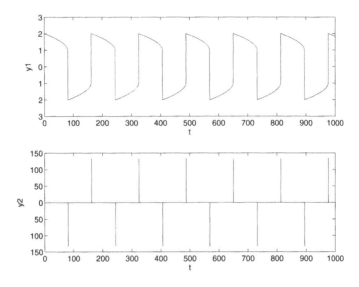

FIG. 17. A contour plot of the Van der Pol oscillator of dimension 2 used to model radio circuits, heart beats, and pulsating stars. Note that the two components of the solution evolve on multiple time scales. Solving this ODE requires switching between stiff and nonstiff methods many times during the domain of integration. Data mining can help mine switching policies to prevent *thrashing* between the two families of algorithms.

ODE software. By modeling it as a nondeterministic, stationary system, and learning the utility of taking certain actions (e.g., "switch algorithm") in various states, control policies can be induced that help automate the "type-insensitivity" of mathematical software.

6.4 Mining in Distributed and Parallel Environments

Distributed and parallel platforms form an integral part of most data collection and analysis frameworks. Data mining has several important roles to play in such frameworks. In addition to mining with a view to understanding the scientific and engineering processes, mining can play a critical role in rendering many problems tractable. It is impossible to communicate large repositories of geographically distributed data to a client for analysis. Distributed mining can analyze local data and progressively communicate information as required by the client. This view of distributed data mining is consistent with ideas of progressive compression and transmission.

Experiments such as SETI present an interesting computing paradigm for large-scale data analysis. Extensions of this paradigm relying on mobile code for analysis present significant untapped potential for scientific data mining. This motivates a truly asynchronous framework—one in which analysis tasks are farmed off and results incorporated into a collective mined information set, if and when they become available. A similar approach to incorporating data as it becomes available to refine a hypothesis follows from the paradigm of dynamic data mining.

7. Concluding Remarks

The field of scientific data mining is still in its infancy. As scientists address various problems associated with large-scale simulation and data collection, the associated data handling and analysis problems will become more acute. We envision a balance between, and tight integration of, inlined analysis and computing tasks. A consolidation of various approaches from statistical analysis, information theory, and numerical methods will result in a theoretically sound set of tools for a range of common analysis tasks. While data analysis has already seen some success in understanding scientific and engineering processes, we envision a much greater impact in the near future in domains such as bioinformatics, astrophysics, and materials processing.

One of the major impending developments in computing will be the ubiquitous use of embedded systems (see, for instance, [141]). It is estimated that within the next decade, over 98% of all computing devices will be embedded in physical environments. Such sensing and actuation environments will require a new class of techniques capable of dynamic data analysis in faulty, distributed frameworks. Widespread use of MEMS devices will pose formidable data analysis and handling problems. Examples of such applications include active structures and surfaces. Active structures are capable of sensing environmental changes to adapt themselves. Experiments with active structures involve adaptive chassis for automobiles and earthquake-tolerant buildings. Active surfaces are used on aircraft wings to minimize drag by controlling turbulence in the surface. Such devices are based on very fine grain processing and communication elements with hard deadlines for analysis and actuation. The notion of *anytime* analysis, where the analysis task can be stopped at any point of time (real time constraints) and results up to best current estimates are made available, will be critical.

Finally, we expect the dichotomy between commercial and scientific data analysis to blur. Instead, a classification along dimensions of discrete and continuous data based on an underlying generating model will be more suitable. This will result in a rich set of tools for analyzing data from a varied set of sources.

REFERENCES

[1] Fu, L. (1999). "Knowledge discovery based on neural networks". *Communications of the ACM*, **42**(11), 47–50.

[2] Muggleton, S. (1999). "Scientific knowledge discovery using inductive logic programming". *Communications of the ACM*, **42**(11), 42–46.

[3] Mitchell, T. (1982). "Generalization as search". *Artificial Intelligence*, **18**(2), 203–226.

[4] Agrawal, R., Imielinski, T. and Swami, A. (1993). "Mining associations between sets of items in large databases". In *Proceedings of the ACM SIGMOD International Conference on Management of Data*, pp. 207–216. ACM Press, New York.

[5] Berry, M., Drmac, Z. and Jessup, E. (1999). "Matrices, vector spaces, and information retrieval". *SIAM Review*, **41**(2), 335–362.

[6] Berry, M., Dumais, S. and O'Brien, G. (1995). "Using linear algebra for intelligent information retrieval". *SIAM Review*, **37**(4), 573–595.

[7] Berry, M. and Fierro, R. (1996). "Low-rank orthogonal decompositions for information retrieval applications". *Numerical Linear Algebra with Applications*, **3**(4), 301–328.

[8] Jiang, J., Berry, M., Donato, J. and Ostrouchov, G. (1999). "Mining consumer product data via latent semantic indexing". *Intelligent Data Analysis*, **3**(5), 377–398.

[9] Letsche, T. and Berry, M. (1997). "Large-scale information retrieval with latent semantic indexing". *Information Sciences—Applications*, **100**, 105–137.

[10] Barbara, D., DuMouchel, W., Faloutsos, C., Haas, P., Hellerstein, J., Ioannidis, Y., Jagadish, H., Johnson, T., Ng, R., Poosala, V., Ross, K. and Sevcik, K. (1997). "The New Jersey data reduction report". *Bulletin of the IEEE Technical Committee on Data Engineering*, **20**(4), 3–45.

[11] Huang, X. and Zhao, F. (1998). Finding structures in weather maps. Technical Report OSU-CISRC-3/98-TR11, Department of Computer and Information Science, Ohio State University.

[12] Semtner, A. (2000). "Ocean and climate modeling". *Communications of the ACM*, **43**(4), 80–89.

[13] Stolorz, P., Mesrobian, E., Muntz, R., Santos, J., Shek, E., Yi, J., Mechoso, C. and Farrara, J. (1995). "Fast spatio-temporal data mining from large geophysical datasets". In *Proceedings of the First International Conference on Knowledge Discovery and Data Mining*, Montreal, Quebec, Canada, pp. 300–305.

[14] Koperski, K., Han, J. and Adhikary, J. (2001). "Mining knowledge in geographical data". *IEEE Computer*, in press.

[15] Ng, R. and Han, J. (1994). "Efficient and effective clustering methods for spatial data mining". In *Proceedings of the Twentieth International Conference on Very Large Databases*, Santiago de Chile, Chile, pp. 144–155.

[16] Preston, E., SaMartins, J., Rundle, J., Anghel, M. and Klein, W. (2000). "Models of earthquake faults with long-range stress transfer". *Computing in Science and Engineering (Special Issue on Computational Earth System Science)*, **2**(3), 34–41.

[17] Stolorz, P., Blom, R., Crippen, R. and Dean, C. (2000). QUAKEFINDER: Photographing earthquakes from space. Technical report, Machine Learning Systems Group, Jet Propulsion Laboratory, California Institute of Technology, Pasadena, CA. Available at http://www-aig.jpl.nasa.gov/public/mls/quakefinder/.

[18] Rubin, E., Dietz, R., Lingam, S., Chanat, J., Speir, C., Dymond, R., Lohani, V., Kibler, D., Bosch, D., Shaffer, C., Ramakrishnan, N. and Watson, L. (2000). "From landscapes to waterscapes: A PSE for landuse change analysis". In *Proceedings of the 16th IMACS World Congress*, Lausanne, Switzerland (R. Owens, Ed.).

[19] Brodley, C. and Friedl, M. (1999). "Identifying mislabeled training data". *Journal of Artificial Intelligence Research*, **11**, 131–167.

[20] Berry, M., Comiskey, J. and Minser, K. (1994). "Parallel analysis of clusters in landscape ecology". *IEEE Computational Science and Engineering*, **1**(2), 24–38.

[21] Abbott, C., Berry, M., Comiskey, J., Gross, L. and Luh, H.-K. (1997). "Parallel individual-based modeling of everglades deer ecology". *IEEE Computational Science and Engineering*, **4**(4), 60–78.

[22] Berry, M., Flamm, R., Hazen, B. and MacIntyre, R. (1996). "LUCAS: A system for modeling land-use change". *IEEE Computational Science and Engineering*, **3**(1), 24–35.

[23] Li, C. and Biswas, G. (1995). "Knowledge-based scientific discovery in geological databases". In *Proceedings of the First International Conference on Knowledge Discovery and Data Mining (KDD-95)*, pp. 204–209. ACM Press, New York.

[24] Rundle, J. (2000). "Computational earth system science". *Computing in Science and Engineering*, **2**(3), 20–21.

[25] Fayyad, U., Weir, N. and Djorgovski, S. (1993). "Automated cataloging and analysis of ski survey image databases: The SKICAT system". In *Proc. of the Second Int. Conf. on Information and Knowledge Management*, pp. 527–536. Washington, DC.

[26] Weir, N., Fayyad, U., Djorgovski, S. and Roden, J. (1995). "The SKICAT System for Processing and Analyzing Digital Imaging Sky Surveys". *Publications of the Astronomy Society of the Pacific*, **107**, 1243–1254.

[27] Szalay, A. (1999). "The Sloan Digital Sky Survey". *Computing in Science and Engineering*, **1**(2), 54–62.

[28] Tohline, J. and Bryan, G. (1999). "Cosmology and computation". *Computing in Science and Engineering*, **1**(2), 17–18.

[29] Hu, W. (1996). An introduction to the cosmic microwave background. Technical report, Institute for Advanced Study, School of Natural Sciences, Olden Lane, Princeton, NJ 08540. Available at http://www.sns.ias.edu/~whu/beginners/introduction.html.

[30] Bennett, C., Banday, A., Gorski, K., Hinshaw, G., Jackson, P., Keegstra, P., Kogut, A., Smoot, G., Wilkinson, D. and Wright, E. (1996). "4-Year COBE DMR cosmic microwave background observations: Maps and basic results". *Astrophysical Journal*, **464**, L1.

[31] Leisawitz, D. (1999). COBE analysis software, Version 4.1. Technical report, Astrophysics Data Facility, NASA Goddard Space Flight Center, Greenbelt, MD 20771, USA. Available at http://space.gsfc.nasa.gov/astro/cobe/cgis.html.

[32] de Bernardis, P., Ade, P. A. R., Bock, J. J. *et al.* (2000). "A flat universe from high-resolution maps of the cosmic microwave background radiation". *Nature*, **404**, 955–959. Available at http://www.physics.ucsb.edu/~boomerang/papers.html.

[33] Lee, A., Ade, P. A. R., Balbi, A. *et al.* (1998). *MAXIMA:* "An experiment to measure temperature anisotropy in the cosmic microwave background". In *Proceedings from 3K Cosmology from Space*, Rome, Italy. [CD-ROM]

[34] Bersanelli, B., Bouchet, F. R., Efstathiou, G. *et al.* (1996). The PLANCK phase A study report. Technical Report D/SCI(96)3, ESA. Available at http://astro.estec.esa.nl/SA-general/Projects/Planck/report/report.html.

[35] Anderson, D., Korpela, E., Werthimer, D. *et al.* (1999). SETI@home: The search for extraterrestrial intelligence. Technical report, Space Sciences Laboratory, University of California at Berkeley. Available at http://setiathome.ssl.berkeley.edu/.

[36] Korn, F., Jagadish, H. and Faloutsos, C. (May 1997). "Efficiently supporting ad hoc queries in large datasets of time sequences". In *ACM SIGMOD*, Tucson, AZ, pp. 289–300. Available at ftp://olympos.cs.umd.edu/pub/TechReports/sigmod97.ps.

[37] Moore, A. (1998). Very fast EM-based mixture model clustering using multiresolution kd-trees. Technical report, Carnegie Mellon University. Available at http://ranger. phys.cmu.edu/users/nichol/KDI/refs.html.

[38] Moore, A. and Lee, M. (1998). "Cached sufficient statistics for efficient machine learning with large datasets". *Journal of Artificial Intelligence Research*, **8**, 67–91.

[39] Vashishta, P., Kalia, R., Nakano, A. and Jin, W. (1996). "Silica under very large positive and negative pressures: Molecular dynamics simulation on parallel computers". *International Journal of Thermophysics*, **17**(1), 169–178.

[40] Vashishta, P., Nakano, A., Kalia, R. and Ebbsjo, I. (1996). "Crack propagation and fracture in ceramic films million atom molecular dynamics simulation on parallel computers". *Materials Science and Engineering B*, **37**, 56–71.

[41] Nakano, A., Kalia, R. and Vashishta, P. (1995). "Dynamics and morphology of brittle cracks: A molecular-dynamics study of silicon nitride". *Physical Review Letters*, **75**, 3138–3141.

[42] Yang, D.-Y., Grama, A. and Sarin, V. (1999). "Error-bounded compression of particle data for hierarchical approximation techniques". In *Proceedings of the Supercomputing Conference*. Portland, Oregon, USA.

[43] Venkatasubramanian, V., Chan, K. and Caruthers, J. (1994). "Computer-aided molecular design using genetic algorithms". *Computers and Chemical Engineering*, **18**(9), 833–844.

[44] Venkatasubramanian, V., Chan, K. and Caruthers, J. (1995). "Evolutionary large scale molecular design using genetic algorithms". *Journal of Chemical Information and Computer Science*, **35**, 188–195.

[45] Nakano, A., Kalia, R. and Vashishta, P. (1999). "Scalable molecular-dynamics, visualization, and data-management algorithms for material simulations". *Computing in Science and Engineering*, **1**(5), 39–47.

[46] Goel, A., Phanouriou, C., Kamke, F., Ribbens, C., Shaffer, C. and Watson, L. (1999). "WBCSim: A prototype problem solving environment for wood-based composites simulations". *Engineering with Computers*, **15**(2), 198–210.

[47] Berlin, A. and Gabriel, K. (1997). "Distributed MEMS: New challenges for computation". *IEEE Computational Science and Engineering*, **4**(1), 12–16.

[48] Böhringer, K., Donald, B., MacDonald, N., Kovacs, G. and Suh, J. (1997). "Computational methods for design and control of MEMS micromanipulator arrays". *IEEE Computational Science and Engineering*, **4**(1), 17–29.

[49] Drashansky, T., Houstis, E., Ramakrishnan, N. and Rice, J. R. (1999). "Networked agents for scientific computing". *Communications of the ACM*, **42**(3), 48–54.

[50] Forbus, K. (1997). "Qualitative reasoning". In *The Computer Science and Engineering Handbook* (A. Tucker, Ed.), pp. 715–730. CRC Press, Boca Raton, FL.

[51] Murthy, S. (1998). "Qualitative reasoning at multiple resolutions". In *Proceedings of the Seventh National Conference on Artificial Intelligence*, pp. 296–300. American Association for Artificial Intelligence, Madison, Wisconsin, USA.

[52] Nayak, P. (1992). "Order of magnitude reasoning using logarithms". In *Proceedings of KR-92*, Cambridge, Massachusetts, USA. pp. 201–210.

[53] Noor, A. (1997). "Computational structural mechanics". In *The Computer Science and Engineering Handbook* (A. Tucker, Ed.), pp. 847–866. CRC Press, Boca Raton, FL.

[54] Ridley, M. (2000). *Genome: The Autobiography of a Species in 23 Chapters*. HarperCollins, New York.

[55] Sarin, V. and Sameh, A. (1998). "An efficient iterative method for the generalized Stokes problem". *SIAM Journal on Scientific Computing*, **19**(1), 206–226.

[56] Peikert, R. and Roth, M. (1999). "The 'parallel vectors' operator—A vector field visualization primitive". In *IEEE Visualization '99 Conference*, San Francisco, CA, pp. 263–270.

[57] Sadarjoen, I. and Post, F. (1999). *Geometric methods for vortex extraction*. In "Joint EUROGRAPHICS—IEEE TCVG Symposium on Visualization", Vienna, Austria.

[58] Soria, J. and Cantwell, B. (1992). *Identification and classification of topological structures in free shear flows*. In "Eddy Structure Identification in Free Turbulent Shear Flows", Poitiers, France" (J. P. Bonnet and M. N. Glauser, Eds.), pp. 121–125. Kluwer Academic, Dordrecht, MA.

[59] Tanaka, M. and Kida, S. (1993). "Characterization of vortex tubes and sheets". *Physics of Fluids A*, **5**(9), 2079–2082.

[60] Yates, L. and Chapman, G. (1990). Streamlines, vorticity lines, and vortices. Technical Report AIAA-91-9731, American Inst. of Aeronautics and Astronautics.

[61] Gage, P., Kroo, I. and Sobieski, I. (1995). "A variable-complexity genetic algorithm for topological design". *AIAA Journal*, **33**(11), 2212–2217.

[62] Gallman, J. and Kroo, I. (1996). "Structural optimization for joined wing synthesis". *Journal of Aircraft*, **33**(1), 214–223.

[63] Nguyen, T. and Huang, T. (1994). "Evolvable 3D modeling for model-based object recognition systems". In *Advances in Genetic Programming* (K. E. Kinnear, Jr., Ed.), Chap. 22, pp. 459–475. MIT Press, Cambridge, MA.

[64] Lei, M., Kleinstreuer, L. and Archie, J. (1997). "Hemodynamic simulations and computer-aided designs of graft-artery junctions". *Journal of Biomechanical Engineering*, **119**, 343–348.

[65] Liu, S. (1996). "Vein graft engineering". *Advances in Bioengineering*, **33**, 473–474.

[66] Karypis, G., Han, E.-H. and Kumar, V. (1999). "Chameleon: Hierarchical clustering using dynamic modeling". *IEEE Computer*, **32**(8), 68–75.

[67] Bezdek, J. (1981). *Pattern Recognition with Fuzzy Objective Function Algorithms*. Plenum Press, New York.

[68] Vapnik, V. (1995). *The Nature of Statistical Learning Theory*. Springer-Verlag, New York.

[69] Ruspini, E. (1969). "A new approach to clustering". *Information and Control*, **15**, 22–32.

[70] Fayyad, U., Haussler, D. and Stolorz, P. (1996). "Mining scientific data". *Communications of the ACM*, **39**(11), 51–57.

[71] Schulze-Kremer, S. (1999). "Discovery in the Human Genome Project". *Communications of the ACM*, **42**(11), 62–64.

[72] Knorr, E. and Ng, R. (1996). "Finding aggregate proximity relationships and commonalities in spatial data mining". *IEEE Transactions on Knowledge and Data Engineering*, **8**, 884–897.

[73] Zhao, F. (1994). "Extracting and representing qualitative behaviors of complex systems in phase spaces". *Artificial Intelligence*, **69**(1–2), 51–92.

[74] Ganti, V., Gehrke, J. and Ramakrishnan, R. (1999). "Mining very large databases". *IEEE Computer*, **32**(8), 38–45.

[75] Langley, P., Simon, H. and Bradshaw, G. (1990). "Heuristics for empirical discovery". In *Readings in Machine Learning* (J. Shavlik and T. Dietterich, Eds.), pp. 356–372. Morgan Kaufmann, New York.

[76] Jordan, M. and Bishop, C. (1997). "Neural networks". In *The Computer Science and Engineering Handbook* (A. Tucker, Ed.), pp. 536–556. CRC Press, Boca Raton, FL.

[77] Cybenko, G. (1989). "Approximation by superpositions of a sigmoidal function". *Mathematics of Controls, Signals, and Systems*, **2**, 303–314.

[78] Blum, A. and Rivest, R. (1992). "Training a 3-node neural network is NP-Complete". *Neural Networks*, **5**(1), 117–127.

[79] Towell, G. and Shavlik, J. (1994). "Knowledge-based artificial neural networks". *Artificial Intelligence*, **70**, 119–165.

[80] Opitz, D. and Shavlik, J. (1997). "Connectionist theory refinement: Genetically searching the space of network topologies". *Journal of Artificial Intelligence Research*, **6**, 177–209.

[81] Bratko, I. and Muggleton, S. (1995). "Applications of inductive logic programming". *Communications of the ACM*, **38**(11), 65–70.

[82] Dzeroski, S. (1996). "Inductive logic programming and knowledge discovery in databases". In *Advances in Knowledge Discovery and Data Mining* (U. Fayyad, G. Piatetsky-Shapiro, P. Smyth, and R. Uthurusamy, Eds.), pp. 117–152. AAAI/MIT Press, Cambridge, MA.

[83] Srinivasan, A. and King, R. (1999). "Using inductive logic programming to construct structure-activity relationships". In *Predictive Toxicology of Chemicals: Experiences and Impact of AI Tools (Papers from the 1999 AAAI Spring Symposium)* (G. Gini and A. Katrizsky, Eds.), pp. 64–73. AAAI Press, Menlo Park, CA.

[84] Muggleton, S. and Feng, C. (1990). "Efficient induction of logic programs". In *Proceedings of the First International Conference on Algorithmic Learning Theory* (S. Arikawa, S. Goto, S. Ohsuga, and T. Yokomori, Eds.), pp. 368–381. Japanese Society for Artificial Intelligence, Tokyo.

[85] Craven, M. and Shavlik, J. (1993). "Learning to represent codons: A challenge problem for constructive induction". In *Proceedings of the Thirteenth International Joint Conference on Artificial Intelligence*, Chambery, France, pp. 1319–1324.

[86] Valdés-Pérez, R. (1994). "Conjecturing hidden entities via simplicity and conservation laws: Machine discovery in chemistry". *Artificial Intelligence*, **65**(2), 247–280.

[87] Valdés-Pérez, R. (1999). "Discovery tools for scientific applications". *Communications of the ACM*, **42**(11), 37–41.

[88] Valdés-Pérez, R. (1999). "Principles of human computer collaboration for knowledge discovery in science". *Artificial Intelligence*, **107**(2), 335–346.

[89] Hellerstein, J., Avnur, R., Chou, A., Hidber, C., Olston, C., Raman, V., Roth, T. and Haas, P. J. (1999). "Interactive data analysis: The control project". *IEEE Computer*, **32**(8), 51–59.

[90] Ramakrishnan, N. and Grama, A. (1999). "Data mining: From serendipity to science (Guest Editors' Introduction to the Special Issue on Data Mining)". *IEEE Computer*, **32**(8), 34–37.

[91] Rice, J. (1995). Potential PYTHIA development/research thrusts. Internal Memo, Pellpack Research Group, Department of Computer Sciences, Purdue University.

[92] Cheeseman, P. and Stutz, J. (1996). "Bayesian classification (AutoClass): Theory and practice". In *Advances in Knowledge Discovery and Data Mining* (U. Fayyad, G. Piatetsky-Shapiro, P. Smyth, and R. Uthurusamy, Eds.), pp. 153–180. AAAI/MIT Press, Cambridge, MA.

[93] Fukunaga, K. (1990). *Introduction to Statistical Pattern Recognition*. Academic Press, San Diego.

[94] Gibson, D., Kleinberg, J. and Raghavan, P. (1998). "Clustering categorical data: an approach based on dynamical systems". In *Proc. 24th Int. Conf. on Very Large Databases*, New York, USA. pp. 311–322.

[95] Ganti, V., Gehrke, J. and Ramakrishnan, R. (1999). "CACTUS: Clustering categorical data using summaries". In *Proc. Fifth ACM SIGKDD International Conference on Knowledge Discovery and Data Mining*, San Diego, California, USA. pp. 73–83.

[96] Zhao, F., Bailey-Kellogg, C., Huang, X. and Ordonez, I. (1999). "Intelligent simulation for mining large scientific datasets". *New Generation Computing*, **17**(4), 333–347.

[97] Yip, K. and Zhao, F. (1996). "Spatial aggregation: Theory and applications". *Journal of Artificial Intelligence Research*, **5**, 1–26.

[98] Han, J., Lakshmanan, L. and Ng, R. T. (1999). "Constraint-based, multidimensional data mining". *IEEE Computer*, **32**(8), 46–50.

[99] Imielinski, T. and Mannila, H. (1996). "A database perspective on knowledge discovery". *Communications of the ACM*, **39**(11), 58–64.

[100] Shen, W.-M., Ong, K., Mitbander, B. and Zaniolo, C. (1996). "Metaqueries for data mining". In *Advances in Knowledge Discovery and Data Mining* (U. Fayyad, G. Piatetsky-Shapiro, P. Smyth, and R. Uthurusamy, Eds.), pp. 375–398. AAAI/MIT Press, Cambridge, MA.

[101] Zhao, Q. and Nishida, T. (1995). "Using qualitative hypotheses to identify inaccurate data". *Journal of Artificial Intelligence Research*, **3**, 119–145.

[102] Frazier, M. and Pitt, L. (1996). "Classic learning". *Machine Learning*, **25**(2–3), 151–193.

[103] Kietz, J.-U. and Morik, K. (1994). "A polynomial approach to the constructive induction of structured knowledge". *Machine Learning*, **14**(1), 193–217.

[104] Srinivasan, A. and King, R. (1999). "Feature construction with inductive logic programming: A study of quantitative predictions of biological activity aided by structural attributes". *Data Mining and Knowledge Discovery*, **3**(1), 37–57.

[105] Board, J. and Schulten, K. (2000). "The fast multipole algorithm". *Computing in Science and Engineering*, **2**(1), 76–79.

[106] Barnes, J. and Hut, P. (1986). "A hierarchical $O(n \log n)$ force calculation algorithm". *Nature*, **324**, 446–449.

[107] Nakano, A. (1997). "Fuzzy clustering approach to hierarchical molecular dynamics simulation of multiscale materials phenomena". *Computer Physics Communications*, **105**, 139–150.

[108] Nakano, A. (1999). "A rigid-body based multiple time-scale molecular dynamics simulation of nanophase materials". *International Journal of High Performance Computer Applications*, **13**(2), 154–162.

[109] Bajaj, C., Pascucci, V. and Zhuang, G. (1999). "Single resolution compression of arbitrary triangular meshes with properties". *Computational Geometry: Theory and Applications*, **14**, 167–186.

[110] Rossignac, J. (1999). "Edgebreaker: Connectivity compression for triangle meshes". *IEEE Transactions on Visualization and Computer Graphics*, **5**(1), 47–61.

[111] Taubin, G. and Rossignac, J. (1996). "Geometric compression through topological surgery". *ACM Transactions on Graphics*, **17**(2), 84–115.

[112] Kolda, T. and O'Leary, D. (1998). "A semidiscrete matrix decomposition for latent semantic indexing in information retrieval". *ACM Transactions on Information Systems*, **16**(4), 322–346.

[113] Ruth, P., Grama, A., Ramakrishnan, N. and Kumar, V. (2000). Compression of and pattern extraction from large sets of attribute vectors. Technical report, Department of Computer Sciences, Purdue University, W. Lafayette, IN 47907.

[114] Yang, D.-Y., Johar, A., Szpankowski, W. and Grama, A. (2000). "Summary structures for frequency queries on large transaction sets". In *Data Compression Conference*, Snowbird, UT, pp. 238–247.

[115] Chandy, K., Bramley, R., Char, B. and Reynders, J. (1998). Report of the NSF Workshop on Problem Solving Environments and Scientific IDEs for Knowledge, Information and Computing (SIDEKIC'98). Technical report, Los Alamos National Laboratory.

[116] Moore, R., Baru, C., Marciano, R., Rajasekar, A. and Wan, M. (1998). "Data-intensive computing". In *The Grid: Blueprint for a New Computing Infrastructure* (C. Kesselman and I. Foster, Eds.). Morgan Kaufmann, New York, Chapter 5, pp. 107–129.

[117] Moore, R., Prince, T. and Ellisman, M. (1998). "Data-intensive computing and digital libraries". *Communications of the ACM*, **41**(11), 56–62.

[118] Rice, J. and Boisvert, R. (1996). "From scientific software libraries to problem-solving environments". *IEEE Computational Science and Engineering*, **3**(3), 44–53.

[119] Gannon, D., Bramley, B., Stuckey, T., Villacis, J., Balasubramanian, J., Akman, E., Breg, F., Diwan, S. and Govindaraju, M. (1998). "Component architectures for distributed scientific problem solving". *IEEE Computational Science and Engineering*, **5**(2), 50–63.

[120] Grosse, E. (1996). "Network programming and CSE". *IEEE Computational Science and Engineering*, **3**(2), 40–41.

[121] Saltz, J., Sussman, A., Graham, S., Demmel, J., Baden, S. and Dongarra, J. (1998). "Programming tools and environments". *Communications of the ACM*, **41**(11), 64–73.

[122] Houstis, E., Verykios, V., Catlin, A., Ramakrishnan, N. and Rice, J. (2000). "PYTHIA II: A knowledge/database system for managing performance data and recommending scientific software". *ACM Transactions on Mathematical Software*, **26**(2), 227–253.

[123] Goel, A., Baker, C., Shaffer, C., Grossman, B., Haftka, R., Mason, W. and Watson, L. (2001). "VizCraft: A problem solving environment for aircraft configuration design". *Computing in Science and Engineering*, **3**(1), 56–66.

[124] Knill, D., Giunta, A., Baker, C., Grossman, B., Mason, W., Haftka, R. and Watson, L. (1999). "Response surface models combining linear and euler aerodynamics for supersonic transport design". *Journal of Aircraft*, **36**(1), 75–86.

[125] Parker, S., Johnson, C. and Beazley, D. (1997). *Computational steering software systems and strategies.* In "IEEE Computational Science and Engineering", 4 (4), pp. 50–59.

[126] Buneman, P., Davidson, S., Hart, K., Overton, C. and Wong, L. (1995). "A data transformation system for biological data sources". In *Proceedings of the VLDB Conference*, pp. 158–169.

[127] Grimson, J., Grimson, W. and Hasselbring, W. (2000). "The SI challenge in health care". *Communications of the ACM*, **43**(6), 48–55.

[128] Adam, N., Atluri, V. and Adiwijaya, I. (2000). "SI in digital libraries". *Communications of the ACM*, **43**(6), 64–72.

[129] Ramakrishnan, N. and Ribbens, C. (2000). "Mining and visualizing recommendation spaces for elliptic PDEs with continuous attributes". *ACM Transactions on Mathematical Software*, **26**(2), 254–273.

[130] Bailey-Kellogg, C. and Zhao, F. (1999). "Influence-based model decomposition". In *Proc. of the National Conference on Artificial Intelligence (AAAI'99)*, Orlando, Florida, USA, pp. 402–409.

[131] Abelson, H., Eisenberg, M., Halfant, M., Katzenelson, J., Sacks, E., Sussman, G., Wisdom, J. and Yip, K. (1989). "Intelligence in scientific computing". *Communications of the ACM*, **32**, 546–562.

[132] Hau, D. and Coiera, E. (1997). "Learning qualitative models of dynamic systems". *Machine Learning*, **26**(2–3), 177–211.

[133] Rice, J. (1992). "Learning, teaching, optimization and approximation". In *Expert Systems for Scientific Computing* (E. Houstis, J. Rice, and R. Vichnevetsky, Eds.), pp. 89–123. North-Holland, Amsterdam.

[134] Boyan, J. and Moore, A. (2000). "Learning evaluation functions to improve optimization by local search". *Journal of Machine Learning Research*, **1**, 77–112.

[135] Sacks, J., Welch, W., Mitchell, T. and Wynn, H. (1989). "Design and analysis of computer experiments". *Statistical Science*, **4**(4), 409–435.

[136] Kivinen, J. and Mannila, H. (1994). "The power of sampling in knowledge discovery". In *Proceedings of PODS' 1994*, Minneapolis, Minnesota, USA, pp. 77–85.

[137] Hennessy, D., Gopalakrishnan, V., Buchanan, B., Rosenberg, J. and Subramanian, D. (1994). "Induction of rules for biological macromolecule crystallization". In *Proceedings of the 2nd International Conference on Intelligent Systems for Molecular Biology*, Stanford, California, USA, pp. 179–187.

[138] Hennessy, D., Gopalakrishnan, V., Buchanan, B. and Subramanian, D. (1994). "The crystallographer's assistant". In *Proceedings of AAAI'94*, Seattle, Washington, USA. p. 1451.

[139] Kaelbling, L., Littman, M. and Moore, A. (1996). "Reinforcement learning: A survey". *Journal of Artificial Intelligence Research*, **4**, 237–285.

[140] Zwillinger, D. (1992). *Handbook of Ordinary Differential Equations*. Academic Press, San Diego.

[141] Estrin, D., Govindan, R. and Heidemann, J. (2000). "Embedding the Internet: Introduction". *Communications of the ACM*, **43**(5), 38–42.

History and Contributions of Theoretical Computer Science

JOHN E. SAVAGE

Department of Computer Science
Brown University
Providence, RI 02912
USA
savage@cs.brown.edu

ALAN L. SELMAN

Department of Computer Science and Engineering
University at Buffalo
226 Bell Hall
Buffalo, NY 14260–2000
USA
selman@cse.buffalo.edu

CARL SMITH

Department of Computer Science
University of Maryland
College Park, MD 20741
USA
smith@cs.umd.edu

Abstract

We briefly review some of the major accomplishments of theoretical computer science. Results from theoretical computer science have had enormous impact on the development of programming languages and other areas of computer science. The impact of research in theoretical computer science is now being felt in the areas of cryptography, communication networks, multimedia and graphical systems, parallel computation, VLSI, and learning and programming languages and software. Theoretical computer science has also influenced biology, mathematics, manufacturing, and astronomy.

1. Introduction 172
2. A Brief History 173
   2.1 Historical Highlights 173
   2.2 Prospects for the Future 174

ADVANCES IN COMPUTERS, VOL. 55
ISBN 0-12-012155-7

171

3. Theory in the Practice of Computing 174
   3.1 Cryptography and Secure Computation 175
   3.2 Communication Networks 175
   3.3 Computational Geometry 175
   3.4 Parallel Computer Architecture 176
   3.5 Software Systems 176
   3.6 Programming Languages. 176
   3.7 VLSI Design. 177
   3.8 Learning Theory. 177
4. Contributions to Other Disciplines 178
   4.1 Biology 178
   4.2 Mathematics. 178
   4.3 Manufacturing. 179
   4.4 Astronomy 179
5. Foundational Research 179
   5.1 Computational Complexity 180
   5.2 Design and Analysis of Algorithms. 181
   5.3 New Theories of Algorithms and Heuristics 182
6. Summary 182
   Acknowledgements 183
   References 183

1. Introduction

For more than 50 years, as computing systems have diminished in size and grown in complexity, theoretical computer scientists have built the foundations of their discipline by developing models of computation and related methods of analysis. After the early recognition of the relevance of the theory of formal languages to the practice of compiler construction, theoretical computer science became a cornerstone of virtually every computer science undergraduate degree program.

In the early days of computer science a great deal of time and energy was devoted to the development of basic concepts, design of fundamental algorithms, identification and development of major subdisciplines, and the classification of problems by their difficulty, activities that actively engaged many theoretical computer scientists. Today the emphasis is primarily on the design and implementation of very large computer systems. The role of theoretical computer scientists today is to examine fundamental problems of the field through modeling, analysis, and experimentation. General computer science research has also changed very significantly as well. Because modern computer systems are often too large to be studied solely through experimentation, even "practical" computer scientists find themselves using models and analysis, the tools of theoretical computer science, to study these systems.

Below we provide a brief history of theoretical computer science followed by a review of its contributions to the practice of computer science and other scientific and engineering disciplines.

2. A Brief History

Theoretical computer science is a cornerstone for computer science. It "underlies many aspects of the construction, explanation, and understanding of computers. Many ... theoretical concepts from different sources have now become so embedded in computing and communications that they pervade the thinking of all computer scientists" [1].

What is theoretical computer science? "Theoretical computer scientists seek to understand computational phenomena, the expressibility of languages, the design and performance of algorithms, and general limits on computation. Thus, they ask what is computation, what can be computed, how it can be done, and at what cost. In this quest, they use formal models, methods of analysis, and some experimentation. They learn from and contribute to practice. Finally, they seek to expand the core activities of the field to better address hard computational problems" [2].

2.1 Historical Highlights

Theoretical concepts can take decades to be assimilated into the mainstream of computing, but when they are assimilated they can have a profound practical impact. The stored-program computer, a concept central to computer science, owes its origins to Alan Turing, who studied the fundamental nature of computation in the 1930's. The practice of programming computers was significantly advanced by the development of the theory of automata and languages by Chomsky and others in the 1950's. Building on the foundations of context free grammars, Knuth and others introduced algorithms and data structures for the efficient and practical parsing of high-level languages, leading to tools such as YACC, thereby enabling the software revolution of the 1960's. In the 1970's theoreticians, exploring the intrinsic complexity of computational problems, identified the large class of NP-complete problems, everyday problems that appear to be so difficult to solve that no foreseeable increase in computing power would enable their exact solution. Theoreticians interested in studying computational complexity were led to the discovery of hard problems that serve as the underpinnings for modern computer-security systems, notably the RSA public-key cryptosystem. Also, they have demonstrated the utility of mathematical logic and automata theory to the verification of complex computer systems; for example model-checking technology is now widely used by hardware vendors.

Research innovations in the past 10 to 15 years have resulted in new formulations and results that promise a big impact in the future. We now have fast (polynomial-time) algorithms that provide approximate answers, with fixed performance bounds, to many NP-complete problems. We now use randomized algorithms that provide fast solutions to hard problems with high probability. We also employ interactive proof systems (the goal is to convince one player of the truth of a statement known to a second player) to verify electronic exchanges. These are but a few examples of recent and current successes.

The explanatory value of theoretical computer science is illustrated by the modern Web browser (originally developed at CERN and the National Center for Supercomputing Applications at Illinois scientific computing centers). It embodies the concept of the abstract machine developed in the 1970's. When a user follows a link to data, a browser invokes the appropriate interpreter (an abstract machine) to process the data, for example, to view an image or run a Java program.

2.2 Prospects for the Future

In concert with the PITAC committee [3], we believe that future computer systems will be large and complex, exhibiting complex interactions. Understanding such systems will be an enormous intellectual challenge that requires the efforts of both theoretical and experimental computer scientists. We must develop scalable hardware and software system models capable of handling the high emergent complexity of such systems and subject them to analysis before making large investments in their implementation. Emphasizing these challenges, George Strawn, of the office of the Assistant Director for CISE, said "we don't understand at a scientific level many of the things that we are building" [4].

To summarize, "We need more basic research—the kind of groundbreaking, high-risk/high-return research that will provide the ideas and methods for new disciplinary paradigms a decade or more in the future. We must make wise investments that will bear fruit over the next 40 years" [3].

3. Theory in the Practice of Computing

We now give some examples that demonstrate the important role that theoretical computer science has played in understanding practical computer science problems.

3.1 Cryptography and Secure Computation

The field of cryptography continues to flourish, with contributions to both theory and practice. New techniques for cryptanalysis (differential and linear cryptanalysis) have greatly enhanced our ability to assess the strength of conventional cryptosystems, while the development of factorization and discrete logarithm techniques based on the number field sieve provides a deeper understanding of the foundations of public-key cryptography. New protocols have been devised for applications such as electronic cash and key escrow that may impact the practice of electronic commerce. Relationships between cryptography and other fields, such as machine learning and approximation, have been greatly expanded. Techniques for proving security of cryptographic primitives and protocols have been significantly improved.

3.2 Communication Networks

On-line algorithms and multicommodity flow algorithms have proven useful for admission control and for routing of virtual circuits in asynchronous transfer mode (ATM) networks. Theoretically optimal algorithms led to the development of a new, practical admission control and routing algorithm. Extensive simulation of this algorithm showed that it significantly outperforms the standard approaches. Variants of this algorithm will be implemented in ATM switches manufactured by AT&T. Research in load balancing and Web caching by theoretical computer scientists led to the creation of Akamai, a highly visible new Web-caching company.

3.3 Computational Geometry

Techniques from computational geometry have been used in a wide variety of other areas of computing. For example, algorithms for generating Delaunay triangulations and triangulations with various local properties have been applied to mesh generation in computational fluid dynamics. Voronoi diagrams and data structures for nearest-neighbor searching are used in clustering algorithms, which in turn are central to the speech and image compression required for multimedia systems to run on personal computers. Techniques developed in computational geometry for computing triangulations, line segment intersections, and terrain visibility are used in geographic information systems. Visibility graphs and the visibility complex have been used in systems for computer vision and computer graphics. Graph-drawing algorithms are used in advanced graphic user interfaces and visualization systems.

3.4   Parallel Computer Architecture

Algorithm development and the analysis of parallel architectural models such as mesh-connected processors, hypercubes, cube-connected cycles, and butterfly networks have informed and shaped the design of many parallel multiple-processor machines in use today. Research on algorithms for routing in networks, including (multiphase) randomized routing, has also influenced parallel machine design.

3.5   Software Systems

Many software systems have incorporated ideas and algorithms first developed in a theoretical framework. For example, evolving algebras have been used to specify languages (e.g., C, Prolog, and VHDL), to define real and virtual architectures (e.g., APE, PVM, and Transputer), to validate standard language implementations (e.g. Prolog and Occam), and to validate distributed protocols. Versions of epistemic logic are widely used for the design and analysis of existing and new authentication protocols. Interactive theorem provers like ProofPower, a commercial prover based on an academic prototype (HOL), are used to verify properties of critical systems. Coordinating Communicating Systems (CCS) has been found to be an invaluable aid in the modeling, analysis, and design of safety-critical systems. Components of real systems involved in land and air transport, process control, and computer operating systems have been analyzed using CCS. Process calculi and related modal logics have also been used, for example, to formally specify and analyze a cache coherence protocol for a multiprocessor architecture currently under development; to prove the correctness of a leader election protocol for a point-to-point network; and to design and analyze a rendezvous-based scheduler to be used in an embedded software system.

3.6   Programming Languages

The methods of structured operational semantics, which derived input both from the lambda calculus and its model theory, reached a point in the 1980's where full-scale languages could be defined in such a way that properties of the language (e.g., determinacy of evaluation and the lack of dangling pointers) could be rigorously proven. Simultaneously, semantic and syntactic theories of types have been deployed to yield language designs that are provably "type-sound," leading both to a significant increase in the reliability of a language and to greater efficiency in implementation (since type-information need not be present at run-time in a type-sound language).

Standard ML (meta language) is an industrial-strength language whose formal definition (in 1990) exploited these advances.

Standard ML serves as a vehicle for many research projects, particularly those concerned with mechanized reasoning, program analysis, and compiler construction. Standard ML also serves as the subject of study for many investigations in programming language design.

Monads were introduced in the late 1980's to computer science as a way of structuring denotational semantics, increasing our understanding of programming languages. Many different language features, including nontermination, state, exceptions, continuations, and interaction, can be viewed as monads. More recently, they have been widely used as a programming technique in pure functional programming languages such as Haskell. Monads are used externally to extend the capabilities provided by the Glasgow Haskell compiler. They are used to provide input–output and interaction with C and updateable arrays and references.

3.7 VLSI Design

The theory of VLSI algorithms and architecture has guided the development of VLSI design. Theory has confirmed the quality of designs for special problems such as matrix multiplication and convolution and has influenced the development of layout algorithms for unstructured problems.

Computer-aided design of digital systems (including VLSI design) depends heavily upon the results and techniques of the theoretical algorithms community. One example of this is in the layout of VLSI circuits. Automated layout uses both fundamental results in graph algorithms and specialized application of methods developed in the theoretical community. Many layout algorithms rely on minimum spanning tree and shortest-path algorithms; improvements in these algorithms and related data structures are directly usable by layout applications. The models and algorithms developed for single-layer routing are a successful application of theoretical techniques. Heuristics for NP-complete layout problems draw heavily on foundations for more basic problems such as graph partitioning and graph coloring.

3.8 Learning Theory

Algorithms have been developed within the computational learning theory community that learn subclasses of finite probabilistic automata. They have already been applied successfully in systems that perform handwriting recognition, speech recognition, part-of-speech-tagging, DNA sequence modeling, and text correction. Experimental evidence comparing these new systems with previously existing systems has been favorable. Learning algorithms and techniques for deterministic automata have been applied to reinforcement learning, which is a promising new paradigm for machine learning. Finally, learning algorithms for automata have also been applied to robot motion planning. Finding algorithms with better performance for these and other applications motivates the search for new, more general subclasses of automata that have efficient learning algorithms.

4. Contributions to Other Disciplines

In this section we give examples of contributions that theoretical computer scientists have made to various science and engineering disciplines.

4.1 Biology

A central algorithmic operation in computational biology is the comparison of two very long DNA sequences to establish a relationship between them. Most sequence comparison programs use dynamic programming techniques. As the lengths of the sequences grow, however, such programs become very slow. To speed them up, heuristics were proposed in the 1980's. In 1990, those heuristics were cast into an algorithmic framework, called sparse dynamic programming. That framework, its techniques, and other new ideas from the algorithms community are a foundation for new sequence alignment software.

4.2 Mathematics

Theoretical computer science has also found applications in mathematics. In particular, domain theory has developed in the past 25 years as a mathematical foundation for the semantics of programming languages. Recently, domain theory has been applied in several branches of mathematics, including dynamical systems, measure and integration theory, and fractals. Domain theory has been used in finite-state discrete stochastic processes, iterated function systems, fractal image compression, neural nets, and the Ising model in statistical physics. A new, fast algorithm for polynomial decomposition is included in AXIOM, the symbolic computation language developed by IBM.

4.3 Manufacturing

A program *qhull* for computing convex hulls has been used in the implementation of an algorithm to compute support structures for objects produced through layered manufacturing, a process in which material is deposited and later removed by a laser. During the construction of an object in this fashion, it might be necessary to build external supports either to prevent the object from toppling or to support floating components and overhanging material. The support structures, if necessary, must be built simultaneously with the object, and hence must be accounted for in the path planning of the laser beam or the deposition nozzle. The use of *qhull* reduced run-times from minutes to seconds to compute possible bases for the object to rest on, and to test if the center of mass of the object is directly above the convex hull of the object's base.

4.4 Astronomy

Network flow techniques have been used to determine telescope settings as part of the Sloan Digital Sky Survey, an astrophysics grand challenge problem. The goal of the survey is to determine the relative locations and velocities of approximately five million of the visible galaxies. The desired information can be computed from spectral (light frequency) data for each galaxy. A rough estimate of the time and money needed for data collection is around five years and five million U.S. dollars. The cost of data collection is proportional to the number of times the telescope must be retargeted. A heuristic based on the network flow theory is currently used to target the telescope.

5. Foundational Research

Recent successes strongly indicate that we can expect a continued flow of important results from theoretical work for the foreseeable future—results that can transform the course of computer science research and, ultimately, the way technology is used. In many cases, these results emerge in unpredictable ways from apparently unrelated investigations of fundamental problems.

While many of the deep theoretical problems that are attracting the best minds in our field are rooted in, or inspired by, overarching challenges, it is often difficult for researchers to properly tackle such problems in the context of an application-driven research environment. One reason for this is the long time period needed for work on fundamental problems to come to full fruition. In addition, solutions to such problems draw on diverse mathematical and computational methods, and so the interaction of a broad community of theoretical researchers is essential.

Moreover, the best theoretical results typically influence the course of research in application areas, so it is extremely useful to maintain an identifiable corpus of theoretical knowledge that is accessible to the computer science community and to the scientific research community at large.

A third reason for the importance of foundational research is that it targets high-risk and speculative problems whose solutions often have surprising or unpredictable consequences. Such research often provides the seed corn for major innovations.

For all of these reasons, unfettered research in foundational theoretical areas is vital; it provides a better understanding of the capabilities and limitations of computers and ensures future innovations in science and technology.

5.1 Computational Complexity

Fundamental questions remain on the relationships among models of computation, information representation, and manipulation, and on good ways to express algorithms. The P versus NP question is perhaps the most famous of these, the refinement of which has led to many other important questions in complexity theory. P is the collection of all problems that can be solved in polynomial time and includes all the problems that can be solved efficiently by computers. The class NP (nondetermistic polynomial time) includes literally thousands of problems from operations research that crop up routinely in manufacturing and networking applications. The fastest known algorithms for problems in this class can only handle very small data sets. Unless P equals NP, we will never be able to obtain exact solutions for realistically sized versions of these problems. Progress on complexity-theoretic problems, even when of the "negative" type (such as providing evidence for the intractability of certain problems), can completely change computer scientists' approaches to practical problems in surprising ways. For one thing, researchers no longer waste time seeking efficient solutions to intractable problems. Instead, they invent and learn techniques for coping with intractability. The computational hardness of certain problems has been exploited for cryptography. Currently, computational hardness of certain problems is being harnessed to obtain efficient deterministic (error-free) algorithms for problems where random (and thus error-prone) algorithms previously seemed necessary.

The theory-of-computing community continues to produce wonderful fundamental ideas, and, over time, these influence practice in important ways. The interplay among concepts such as pseudorandom number generation, interactive proofs, and secure cryptographic protocols is beautiful and deep, and has significant potential to impact the practice of cryptography. The introduction of interactive proof systems and probabilistically checkable proofs has broadened and enriched our understanding of the concept of proof. Probabilistically checkable proofs have turned out to be a fundamental tool for studying the limits of polynomial-time approximation algorithms.

Foundational questions will require a concerted effort in the areas of classical Turing machine-like models and variants (such as randomized or quantum models), models of learning, formal methods and program inference, models of nonsymbolic reasoning, logical characterization of complexity classes, lower bounds, models of online computation, models for communication of information, models for inferring information from incomplete data, models for data storage and retrieval in a multimedia context, and parallel and distributed models. Study of connections between models and results in more than one of these areas can be particularly fruitful. For example, online algorithms, common in key frameworks such as operating systems, financial control, and real-time systems, have generated fundamental concepts that are important for distributed systems design, in particular where information flow is more complex than traditional input/output.

5.2 Design and Analysis of Algorithms

Foundational work on algorithms design has the goal of breaking long-standing barriers in performance. There are many situations where complicated algorithms, such as Strassen and Schönhage's multiplication algorithm, were deemed inferior for years. With steady increases in problem sizes such algorithms now are preferred on appropriate high-performance computing platforms.

In other cases (such as linear programming), initial breakthroughs in reducing asymptotic running time, while not practical in and of themselves, serve to stimulate new research that eventually leads to practical algorithms. What tends to happen is that once a barrier, such as the existence of a polynomial-time algorithm for a problem, is broken, there is strong justification and real motivation for researchers to revisit a problem that previously appeared impenetrable. Very often, painstaking refinement of the seminal breakthrough technique leads to a truly practical algorithm. Ultimately, this type of research has long-lasting impact on the practice of computing. Tantalizing open questions remain, such as whether there is a polynomial-time algorithm for graph isomorphism, or whether one can efficiently learn Boolean formulas that are in disjunctive normal form from random examples.

5.3 New Theories of Algorithms and Heuristics

While theoretical work on models of computation and methods for analyzing algorithms has had enormous payoffs, we are not done. In many situations, simple algorithms do well. Take for example the Simplex algorithm for linear programming, or the success of simulated annealing on certain supposedly "intractable" problems. We don't understand why! It is apparent that worst-case analysis does not provide useful insights on the performance of many algorithms on real data. Our methods for measuring the performance of algorithms and heuristics and our models of computation need to be further developed and refined. Theoreticians are investing increasingly in careful experimental work leading to the identification of important new questions in the algorithms area. Developing means for predicting the performance of algorithms and heuristics on real data and on real computers is a grand challenge in algorithms.

On numerous occasions, theory of computing research has provided the insights that explain why popular, important heuristic algorithms work. Significantly, these insights have suggested major improvements to the heuristics. One example of this scenario was the study by Turner in the 1980's that explained why the decades-old Cuthill–McKee heuristic for minimizing the bandwidth of sparse linear systems works well in practice; this understanding allowed Turner to devise an improved heuristic. A second example, also from the 1980's, explained why the Kernighan–Lin graph bisection heuristic, which is important in the field of circuit layout, works well in practice.

6. Summary

Results from theoretical computer science have been regularly applied to the field of computer science and to other disciplines. In this paper we have highlighted recent contributions to communication networks, parallel computer architecture, software systems, VLSI design, learning theory, biology, mathematics, manufacturing, and astronomy. We can expect similar contributions in the future.

ACKNOWLEDGEMENTS

Parts of this paper were prepared by the SIGACT Long Range Planning Committee (Amihood Amir, Manuel Blum, Michael Loui, Christos Papadimitriou, John Savage, and Carl Smith) [5]. Other portions are drawn from a report funded by the National Science Foundation and coauthored by Anne Condon, Herbert Edelsbrunner, E. Allen Emerson, Lance Fortnow, Stuart Haber, Richard Karp, Daniel Leivant, Richard Lipton, Nancy Lynch, Ian Parberry, Christos Papadimitriou, Michael Rabin, Arnold Rosenberg, James S. Royer, John Savage, Alan L. Selman, Carl Smith, Eva Tardos, and Jeffrey Scott Vitter [6].

REFERENCES

[1] Committee on Innovations in Computing and Communications: Lessons from History (1999). *Funding a Revolution: Government Support for Computing Research.* National Research Council. 1999.
[2] Condon, A., Fich, F., Frederickson, G. N., Goldberg, A., Johnson, D. S., Loui, M. C., Mahaney, S., Raghavan, P., Savage, J. E., Selman, A., and Shmoys, D. B. (1996). "Strategic directions in research in theory of computing". *ACM Computing Surveys*, **28**, 575–590.
[3] Joy, B. and Kennedy, K. (1999). *Information Technology Research: Investing in Our Future.* President's Information Technology Advisory Committee, Report to the President.
[4] Strawn, G. (1999). *Science News*, **155**.
[5] Amir, A., Blum, M., Loui, M., Papadimitriou, C., Savage, J. and Smith, C. (1996). "Contributions of theoretical computer science to practice". *SIGACT*, unpublished. [See http://sigact.csci.unt.edu/sigact/longrange/contributions.html.]
[6] Condon, A., Edelsbrunner, H., Emerson, E. A., Fortnow, L., Haber, S., Karp, R., Leivant, D., Lipton, R., Lynch, N., Parberry, I., Papadimitriou, C., Rabin, M., Rosenberg, A., Royer, J., Savage, J., Selman, A., Smith, C., Tardos, E., and Vitter, J. (1999). "Challenges for theory of computing: Report of an NSF-Sponsored workshop on research in theoretical computer science". *SIGACT News*, **30**(2), 62–76. [See http://www.cse.buffalo.edu/selman/report.]

Security Policies

ROSS ANDERSON

Computer Laboratory
University of Cambridge
Cambridge
UK
ross.anderson@cl.cam.ac.uk

FRANK STAJANO

Computer Laboratory
University of Cambridge
Cambridge
UK
frank.stajano@cl.cam.ac.uk
AT&T Laboratories
Cambridge
UK
fms@att.com

JONG-HYEON LEE

Filonet
Korea
jhlee@filonet.com

Abstract

A security policy is a high-level specification of the security properties that a given system should possess. It is a means for designers, domain experts and implementers to communicate with each other, and a blueprint that drives a project from design through implementation and validation.

We offer a survey of the most significant security policy models in the literature, showing how "security" may mean very different things in different contexts, and we review some of the mechanisms typically used to implement a given security policy.

1. What is a Security Policy?. 186
  1.1 Definition 188
  1.2 Origins 189

ADVANCES IN COMPUTERS, VOL. 55
ISBN 0-12-012155-7

185

2. The Bell-LaPadula Policy Model 190
   2.1 Classifications and Clearances 191
   2.2 Automatic Enforcement of Information Flow Control 193
   2.3 Formalising the Policy 194
   2.4 Tranquility 196
   2.5 Alternative Formulations 197
3. Examples of Multilevel Secure Systems 199
   3.1 SCOMP 200
   3.2 Blacker 200
   3.3 MLS Unix, CMWs and Trusted Windowing 201
   3.4 The NRL Pump 202
   3.5 Logistics Systems 203
   3.6 Purple Penelope 203
   3.7 Future MLS Systems 204
   3.8 What Goes Wrong 204
4. The Biba Integrity Model 207
5. The Clark-Wilson Model 209
6. The Chinese Wall Model 211
7. The BMA Policy 212
8. Jikzi 214
9. The Resurrecting Duckling 216
10. Access Control 219
   10.1 ACLs 219
   10.2 Capabilities 220
   10.3 Roles 221
   10.4 Security State 221
11. Beyond Access Control 222
   11.1 Key Management Policies 223
   11.2 Corporate Email 226
12. Automated Compliance Verification 227
13. A Methodological Note 228
14. Conclusions 230
   Acknowledgements 230
   References 231

1. What is a Security Policy?

Security engineering is about building systems to remain dependable in the face of malice as well as error and mischance. As a discipline, it focuses on the tools, processes and methods needed to design, implement and test complete systems, and to adapt existing systems as their environment evolves.

In most engineering disciplines, it is useful to clarify the requirements carefully before embarking on a project. Such a comment may sound so obvious as to border on the useless, but it is of special relevance to computer security. First, because it is all too often ignored [9]: diving straight into the design of crypto protocols is more fascinating for the technically minded. Second, because security is a holistic property—a quality of the system taken as a whole—which modular decomposition is not sufficient to guarantee. (We shall see in Section 3.8.1 below that connecting secure components together does not necessarily yield a secure system.) It is thus important to understand clearly the security properties that a system should possess, and state them explicitly at the start of its development. As with other aspects of the specification, this will be useful at all stages of the project, from design and development through to testing, validation and maintenance.

A top down representation of the protection of a computer system might consist of the three layers shown in figure 1.

- At the highest level of abstraction, the whole system is represented by a concise and formalised set of goals and requirements: the **policy**.
- At the bottom level, the system is composed of **mechanisms** such as the computing hardware, the cryptographic primitives, tamper resistant enclosures and seals as well as procedural items such as biometric scanning of individuals (iris, fingerprint, voiceprint...) for purposes of authentication.
- Between those two extremes there will be some **middleware** that connects together the available mechanisms in order to build the system that conforms to the policy. This may include access control structures—whether or not enforced by the operating system—and cryptographic protocols.

The security policy is a set of high-level documents that state precisely what goals the protection mechanisms are to achieve. It is driven by our understanding of threats, and in turn drives our system design. Typical statements in a policy describe which subjects (e.g. users or processes) may

Fig. 1. Layers of protection in a computer system

access which objects (e.g. files or peripheral devices) and under which circumstances. It plays the same role in specifying the system's protection properties, and in evaluating whether they have been met, as the system specification does for general functionality. Indeed, a security policy may be part of a system specification, and like the specification its primary function is to communicate.

1.1 Definition

Many organisations use the phrase *security policy* to mean a collection of content-free statements. Here is a simple example:

Megacorp Inc security policy

1. This policy is approved by Management.
2. All staff shall obey this security policy.
3. Data shall be available only to those with a "need-to-know".
4. All breaches of this policy shall be reported at once to Security.

This sort of thing is common but is of little value to the engineer.

1. It dodges the central issue, namely "Who determines 'need-to-know' and how?"
2. It mixes statements at a number of different levels. Organizational approval of a policy should logically not be part of the policy itself (or the resulting self-reference makes it hard to express it formally).
3. The protection mechanism is implied rather than explicit: "staff shall obey"—but what does this mean they actually have to do? Must the obedience be enforced by the system, or are users "on their honour"?
4. It's unclear on how breaches are to be detected and on who has a duty to report them.

Because the term "security policy" is so widely abused to mean a collection of platitudes, there are three more precise terms that have come into use to describe the specification of a system's protection requirements.

A **security policy model** is a succinct statement of the protection properties that a system, or generic type of system, must have. Its key points can typically be written down in a page or less. It is the document in which the protection goals of the system are agreed with an entire community, or with the top management of a customer. It may also be the basis of formal mathematical analysis.

A **security target** is a more detailed description of the protection mechanism that a specific implementation provides, and of how they relate to a list of control objectives (some but not all of which are typically derived from the policy model).

A **protection profile** is like a security target but expressed in an implementation-independent way to enable comparable evaluations across products and versions. This can involve the use of a semi-formal language, or at least of suitable security jargon. It is a requirement for products that are to be evaluated under the *Common Criteria* [61] (a framework used by many governments to facilitate security evaluations of defence information systems, and which we'll discuss below). The protection profile forms the basis for testing and evaluation of a product.

When we don't have to be so precise, we may use the phrase *security policy* to refer to any or all of the above. We will never use the term to refer to a collection of platitudes. We will also avoid a third meaning of the phrase—a list of specific configuration settings for some protection product. We will refer to that as *configuration management* in what follows.

1.2   Origins

Sometimes we are confronted with a completely new application and have to design a security policy model from scratch. More commonly, there already exists a model; we just have to choose the right one, and develop it into a protection profile and/or a security target. Neither of these tasks is easy. Indeed one of the main purposes of this chapter is to provide a number of security policy models, describe them in the context of real systems, and examine the engineering mechanisms (and associated constraints) that a security target can use to meet them. Let us then introduce, in chronological order, the three major waves of security policy models that have been presented in the open literature. We shall review them individually in greater detail in subsequent sections.

Historically, the concept of a security policy model came from the military sector. The first one to appear, **Bell-LaPadula** [14], was introduced in 1973 in response to US Air Force concerns over the confidentiality of data in time-sharing mainframe systems. This simple yet influential model is based on restricting information flow between labelled clearance levels such as "Confidential" and "Top Secret". Its conceptual framework also forms the basis of other derived models such as **Biba** [17], which deals with integrity instead of confidentiality.

A second wave of policy models emerged in the 1980's from formalising well-established practices in the business sector. An abstraction of the double entry bookkeeping systems used in accounting and banking gave rise in 1987 to the **Clark-Wilson** security policy model [24]. Then Brewer and Nash, in 1989, introduced the **Chinese Wall** model [21] to represent the internal confidentiality constraints of a professional firm whose partners may be serving competing customers, and must avoid conflicts of interest.

A third wave came from the development of policy models for applications in various other fields—an activity that our group at Cambridge has pursued extensively in recent years. Case studies include the **BMA** (British Medical Association) security policy model [10], concerned with the confidentiality and accessibility of a patient's medical records; **Jikzi** [11] which describes the requirements of electronic publishing; and the **Resurrecting Duckling** [68], for secure transient association among, for example, wireless devices.

The lesson that can be drawn by observing such a wide spectrum of policy models is that security means radically different things in different applications. But whether we develop the system's security target using an established policy model or draw up a new model from scratch, a thorough understanding of the application environment and of established work patterns is essential, both to decide on a suitable model and to check that no threats have been overlooked. Consultation with domain experts is highly advisable. The wisdom provided by experience has few worthy substitutes and a careful study of the history of past attacks on similar systems is the best way to turn the ingenuity of yesterday's crooks to the advantage of today's designers [9].

2. The Bell-LaPadula Policy Model

By the early 1970's, people had realised that the protection offered by commercial operating systems was poor, and was not getting any better. As soon as one operating system bug was fixed, some other vulnerability would be discovered. Even unskilled users would discover loopholes and use them opportunistically.

A study by James Anderson led the US government to conclude that a secure system should do one or two things well, and that these protection properties should be enforced by mechanisms that were simple enough to verify and that would change only rarely [2]. It introduced the concept of a *reference monitor*—a component of the operating system that would mediate access control decisions and be small enough to be subject to analysis and tests, the completeness of which could be assured. In modern parlance, such components—together with their associated operating procedures—make up the *Trusted Computing Base* (TCB). More formally, the TCB is defined as the set of components (hardware, software, human, etc.) whose correct functioning is sufficient to ensure that the security policy is enforced—or, more vividly, whose failure could cause a breach of the security policy. The goal was to make the security policy so simple that the TCB could be amenable to careful verification.

But what are these core security properties that should be enforced above all others?

2.1 Classifications and Clearances

The Second World War, and the Cold War that followed, led NATO governments to move to a common protective marking scheme for labelling the sensitivity of documents. *Classifications* are labels such as *Unclassified, Confidential, Secret* and *Top Secret* (see Fig. 2). The original idea was that information whose compromise could cost lives was marked "Secret" while information whose compromise could cost many lives was "Top Secret". Government employees have *clearances* depending on the care with which they've been vetted. The details change from time to time but a "Secret" clearance may involve checking fingerprint files, while "Top Secret" can also involve background checks for the previous five to fifteen years' employment [71].

The access control policy was simple: an official could read a document only if his clearance was at least as high as the document's classification. So an official cleared to "Top Secret" could read a "Secret" document, but not vice versa. The effect is that information may only flow upwards, from confidential to secret to top secret, but it may never flow downwards unless an authorized person (known as a *trusted subject*) takes a deliberate decision to declassify it.

There are also document handling rules; thus a "Confidential" document might be kept in a locked filing cabinet in an ordinary government office, while higher levels may require safes of an approved type, guarded rooms with control over photocopiers, and so on. (The NSA security manual [58] gives a summary of the procedures used with "Top Secret" intelligence data.)

The system rapidly became more complicated. The damage criteria for classifying documents were expanded from possible military consequences

TOP SECRET
SECRET
CONFIDENTIAL
OPEN

FIG. 2. A classification hierarchy.

to economic harm and political embarrassment. The UK has an extra level, "Restricted", between "Unclassified" and "Confidential"; the USA used to have this too but abolished it after the Freedom of Information Act was introduced. America now has two more specific markings: "For Official Use only" (FOUO) refers to unclassified data that can't be released under FOIA, while "Unclassified but Sensitive" includes FOUO plus material that might be released in response to a FOIA request. In the UK, "Restricted" information is in practice shared freely, but marking low-grade government documents "Restricted" allows journalists and others involved in leaks to be prosecuted. (Its other main practical effect is that when an unclassified US document is sent across the Atlantic, it automatically becomes "Restricted" in the UK and then "Confidential" when shipped back to the USA. American military system people complain that the UK policy breaks the US classification scheme; Brits complain about an incompatible US refinement of the agreed system.)

There is also a system of codewords whereby information, especially at Secret and above, can be further restricted. For example, information which might reveal intelligence sources or methods—such as the identities of agents or decrypts of foreign government traffic—is typically classified "Top Secret Special Compartmented Intelligence" or TS/SCI, which means that so-called *need to know* restrictions are imposed as well, with one or more codewords attached to a file. Some of the codewords relate to a particular military operation or intelligence source and are available only to a group of named users. To read a document, a user must have all the codewords that are attached to it. A classification level, plus a set of codewords, makes up a *security label* or (if there's at least one codeword) a *compartment*. Section 2.3 below offers a slightly more formal description, while a more detailed explanation can be found in [8].

Allowing upward only flow of information also models wiretapping. In the old days, tapping someone's telephone meant adding a physical tap to the wire. Nowadays, it's all done in the telephone exchange software and the effect is somewhat like making the target calls into conference calls with an extra participant. The usual security requirement is that the target of investigation should not know he is being wiretapped. What's more, a phone can be tapped by multiple principals at different levels of clearance. If the FBI is investigating a complaint that a local police force conducted an unlawful wiretap on a politician in order to blackmail him, they will also tap the line and should be able to see the police tap (if any) without the police detecting their presence.

Now that wiretaps are implemented as conference calls with a silent third party, care has to be taken to ensure that the extra charge for the conference call facility goes to the wiretapper, not to the target. (The addition of ever new features in switching software makes the invisible implementation of wiretapping ever more complex.) Thus wiretapping requires almost exactly the same information flow policy as does traditional classified data: High can see Low data, but Low can't tell whether High is reading any and if so what.

2.2   Automatic Enforcement of Information Flow Control

The next problem was how to enforce this information flow policy in a computer system. The seminal work here was the Bell-LaPadula (BLP) model of computer security, formulated in 1973 [14]. It is also known as **multilevel security**, and systems that implement it are often called *multilevel secure* or *MLS* systems. Their principal feature is that information can never flow downwards.

The Bell-LaPadula model enforces two properties:

- The *simple security property*: no process may read data at a higher level. This is also known as *no read up (NRU)*;
- The **-property*: no process may write data to a lower level. This is also known as *no write down (NWD)*.

The *-property was Bell and LaPadula's critical innovation. It was driven by the fear of attacks using malicious code. An uncleared user might write a Trojan and leave it around where a system administrator cleared to "Secret" might execute it; it could then copy itself into the "Secret" part of the system and write secret data into unclassified objects that the attacker would later retrieve. It's also quite possible that an enemy agent could get a job at a commercial software house and embed some code in a product which would look for secret documents to copy. If it could then write them down to where its creator could read it, the security policy would have been violated. Information might also be leaked as a result of a bug, if applications could write down.

Vulnerabilities such as malicious and buggy code are assumed to be given. It is therefore necessary for the system to enforce the security policy independently of user actions (and by extension, of the actions taken by programs run by users). So we must prevent programs running at "Secret" from writing to files at "Unclassified", or more generally prevent any process at High from signalling to any object at Low. In general, when systems are built to enforce a security policy independently of user actions, they are described as having *mandatory access control*, as opposed to the *discretionary access control* in systems like Unix where users can take their own access decisions about their files. (We won't use these phrases much as they traditionally refer only to BLP-type policies and don't include many other policies whose rules are just as mandatory).

It should also be noted that another significant contribution of the work of Bell and LaPadula is not at the level of the security policy model itself but at the meta-level of talking about security policies in a formal way. Their presentation is based on a simple mathematical formalism that captures the security properties of interest and allows one to derive proofs about the security, or insecurity, of a given system.

2.3 Formalising the Policy

Each subject and object in the system is assigned a *security label* or *protective marking* which consists of a number of *sub-markings* of which the most important is a *classification level* (e.g. Top Secret, Confidential etc) and a set of further sub-markings (*categories*) which means labels or compartments. A binary relation called "*dominates*" is then defined between any two security labels *a* and *b* in the following way.

$$\forall a, b \in labels:$$

$$a \ dominates \ b$$

$$\Updownarrow$$

$$level(a) \geqslant level(b) \land categories(a) \supseteq categories(b)$$

This relation is a partial order, since it is antisymmetric and transitive. Given an appropriate set of security labels over which the two auxiliary functions *join*() and *meet*() can be defined, it forms a mathematical structure known as a lattice[1] [27], an example of which is shown in figure 3. Someone with a "Top Secret" clearance isn't allowed to read a document marked (*Secret*, {*Crypto*}), despite it being at a lower level; he also needs a "Crypto" clearance, which will place him at (*Top Secret*, {*Crypto*}), and this dominates the document's classification.

(Note that, to reduce clutter on such diagrams, it is customary to omit any arrows that can be deduced by transitivity.)

A predicate (i.e. a boolean-valued function) called "*allow*()", taking as arguments a subject, an object and an action, may then be defined in this

---

[1] The operators *join*() and *meet*() each take two elements from the set of labels and return another one, the least upper bound or the greatest lower bound respectively. Note that not all sets of labels give rise to a lattice under *dominates*: there may be sets of labels where one pair of elements does not have a least upper bound (or a greatest lower bound). For an example, remove the node (*Top Secret*, {*Crypto, Foreign*}) from figure 3.

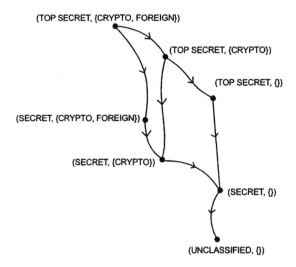

FIG. 3. The "dominates" relation on a lattice of security labels.

framework. Stating a particular security policy is then equivalent to defining this function, which is in fact a complete formal specification for the behaviour of the reference monitor. The two rules of the BLP model can then be expressed as follows.

1. No read up (simple security property):

$$\forall s \in subjects, \ o \in objects:$$

$$allow(s, o, read) \Leftrightarrow label(s) \ dominates \ label(o)$$

2. No write down (star property):

$$\forall s \in subjects, \ o \in objects:$$

$$allow(s, o, write) \Leftrightarrow label(o) \ dominates \ label(s)$$

A state machine abstraction makes it relatively straightforward to verify claims about the protection provided by a design. Starting from a secure state, and performing only state transitions allowed by the rules of the chosen policy model, one is guaranteed to visit only secure states for the system. This is true independently of the particular policy, as long as the policy itself is not inconsistent. As we said, this idea of how to model a security policy formally was almost as important as the introduction of the BLP policy model itself.

This simple formal description omits some elaborations such as *trusted subjects*—principals who are allowed to declassify files. We'll discuss alternative formulations, and engineering issues, below.

2.4 Tranquility

The introduction of BLP caused some excitement: here was a straightforward security policy that appeared to be clear to the intuitive understanding yet still allowed people to prove theorems. But McLean [54] showed that the BLP rules were not in themselves enough. He introduced the conceptual construction of *System Z*, a system that suffered from blatant disclosure problems even though it officially complied with the letter of the BLP model. In System Z, a user can ask the system administrator to temporarily declassify any file from High to Low. So Low users can legitimately read any High file.

Bell's argument was that System Z cheats by doing something the model doesn't allow (changing labels isn't a valid operation on the state), and McLean's argument was that BLP didn't explicitly tell him so. The issue is dealt with by introducing a *tranquility property*. The strong tranquility property says that security labels never change during system operation, while the weak tranquility property says that labels never change in such a way as to violate a defined security policy.

The motivation for the weak property is that in a real system we often want to observe the principle of least privilege and start off a process at the uncleared level, even if the owner of the process were cleared to "Top Secret". If she then accesses a confidential email, her session is automatically upgraded to "Confidential"; and in general, her process is upgraded each time it accesses data at a higher level (this is known as the *high water mark* principle). Such upgrades would not normally break a sensible security policy.

The practical implication of this is that a process acquires the security label or labels of every file that it reads, and these become the default label set of every file that it writes. So a process that has read files at "Secret" and "Crypto" will thereafter create files marked (at least) "Secret Crypto". This will include temporary copies made of other files. If it then reads a file at "Top Secret Daffodil" then all files it creates after that will be labelled "Top Secret Crypto Daffodil", and it will not be able to write to any temporary files at "Secret Crypto". The effect this has on applications is that most application software needs to be rewritten (or at least significantly modified) to run on MLS platforms.

Finally it's worth noting that even with this refinement, BLP still doesn't deal with the creation or destruction of subjects or objects, which is one of the hard problems of building a real MLS system.

2.5 Alternative Formulations

System Z was one of several criticisms questioning the adequacy of the BLP model: this prompted research into other ways to describe multilevel secure systems and by now there are a number of competing models, some of which have been used to build real systems. We will now take a brief tour of the evolution of multilevel models, and without loss of generality we shall limit the discussion to two security levels, High and Low.

The first multilevel security policy was a version of high water mark written in 1967–8 for the **ADEPT-50**, a mandatory access control system developed for the IBM S/360 mainframe [75]. This used triples of level, compartment and group, with the groups being files, users, terminals and jobs. As programs (rather than processes) were subjects, it was vulnerable to Trojan horse compromises, and it was more complex than need be. Nonetheless, it laid the foundation for BLP, and also led to the current IBM S/390 mainframe hardware security architecture.

The second was the **lattice model** that we mentioned above. A primitive version of this was incorporated into the the Pentagon's World Wide Military Command and Control System (WWMCCS) in the late 1960s, but this did not have the star-property. The realization that a fielded, critical, system handling Top Secret data was vulnerable to attack by Trojans caused some consternation [66]. Three improved lattice models were produced in the early 1970s: by Schell, Downey and Popek of the US Air Force in 1972 [67]; a Cambridge PhD thesis by Fenton, which managed labels using a matrix, in 1973 [36]; and by Walter, Ogden, Rounds, Bradshaw, Ames and Shumway of Case Western University who also worked out a lot of the problems with file and directory attributes [73, 74], which they fed to Bell and LaPadula.[2] Finally, the lattice model was systematized and popularized by Denning from 1976 [28].

Noninterference was introduced by Goguen and Meseguer in 1982 [41]. In a system with this property, High's actions have no effect on what Low can see. **Nondeducibility** is less restrictive and was introduced by Sutherland in 1986 [70]. Here the idea is to try to prove that Low cannot deduce anything with 100% certainty about High's input. Low users can see High actions, just not understand them; a more formal definition is that any legal string of high level inputs is compatible with every string of low level events. So for every trace Low can see, there is a similar trace that didn't involve High input. But different low-level event streams may require

---

[2] Walter and his colleagues deserve more credit than history has given them. They had the main results first [73] but Bell and LaPadula had their work heavily promoted by the US Air Force. Fenton has also been largely ignored, not being an American.

changes to high-level outputs or reordering of high-level/low-level event sequences.

The motive for nondeducibility is to find a model that can deal with applications such as a LAN on which there are machines at both Low and High, with the High machines encrypting their LAN traffic. (Quite a lot else is needed to do this right, from padding the High traffic with nulls so that Low users can't do traffic analysis, and even ensuring that the packets are the same size—see [65] for an early example of such a system.)

Nondeducibility has historical importance since it was the first nondeterministic version of Goguen and Messeguer's ideas. But it is hopelessly weak. There is nothing to stop Low making deductions about High input with 99% certainty. There are also many problems when we are trying to prove results about databases, and have to take into account any information that can be inferred from data structures (such as from partial views of data with redundancy) as well as considering the traces of executing programs.

Improved models include **Generalized Noninterference** and **Restrictiveness**. The former is the requirement that if one alters a high level input event in a legal sequence of system events, the resulting sequence can be made legal by, at most, altering subsequent high-level output events. The latter adds a further restriction on the part of the trace where the alteration of the high-level outputs can take place. This is needed for technical reasons to ensure that two systems satisfying the restrictiveness property can be composed into a third which also does. See [53] which explains these issues.

The **Harrison-Ruzzo-Ullman** model [43] tackles the problem of how to deal with the creation and deletion of files, an issue on which BLP is silent. It operates on access matrices and verifies whether there is a sequence of instructions that causes an access right to leak to somewhere it was initially not present. This is more expressive than BLP, but more complex and thus less tractable as an aid to verification.

Woodward proposed a **Compartmented Mode Workstation** (CMW) policy, which attempted to model the classification of information using floating labels, as opposed to the fixed labels associated with BLP [42, 78]. It was ultimately unsuccessful, because information labels tend to float up too far too fast (if the implementation is done correctly), or they float up more slowly (but don't block all the opportunities for unapproved information flow). However, CMW ideas have led to real products—albeit products that provide separation more than information sharing.

The **type enforcement** model, due to Boebert and Kain [20] and later extended by Badger and others [13], assigns each subject to a *domain* and each object to a *type*. There is a *domain definition table* (DDT) which acts as an access control matrix between domains and types. This is a natural model in the Unix setting as types can often be mapped to directory structures. It is more general than policies such as BLP, as it starts to deal with integrity as well as confidentiality concerns.

Finally, the policy model getting the most attention at present from researchers is **role-based access control** (RBAC), introduced by Ferraiolo and Kuhn [37]. This sets out to provide a more general framework for mandatory access control than BLP in which access decisions don't depend on users' names but on the functions which they are currently performing within the organisation. Transactions which may be performed by holders of a given role are specified, then mechanisms for granting membership of a role (including delegation). Roles, or groups, had for years been the mechanism used in practice in organisations such as banks to manage access control; the RBAC model starts to formalise this. It can deal with integrity issues as well as confidentiality, by allowing role membership (and thus access rights) to be revised when certain programs are invoked. Thus, for example, a process that calls untrusted software (which has, for example, been downloaded from the Net) might lose the role membership required to write to sensitive system files. We'll discuss this kind of engineering problem further below.

We won't go into the details of how to express all these properties formally. We will remark though that they differ in a number of important ways. Some are more expressive than others, and some are better at handling properties such as *composability*—whether a system built out of two components that are secure under some model is itself secure. We shall discuss this in section 3.8.1 below; for now, we will merely remark that two nondeducibility secure systems can compose into one that is not [52]. Even the more restrictive noninterference can be shown not to compose.

3. Examples of Multilevel Secure Systems

The enormous influence of BLP and its concept of multilevel security is perhaps best conveyed by a more detailed look at the variety of actual systems that have been built according to its principles.

Following some research products in the late 1970's (such as KSOS [16], a kernelised secure version of Unix), products that implemented multilevel security policies started arriving in dribs and drabs in the early 1980's. By about 1988, a number of companies started implementing MLS versions of their operating systems. MLS concepts were extended to all sorts of products.

3.1   SCOMP

One of the most important products was the *secure communications processor* (SCOMP), a Honeywell derivative of Multics launched in 1983 [39]. This was a no-expense-spared implementation of what the U.S. Department of Defense believed it wanted: it had formally verified hardware and software, with a minimal kernel and four rings of protection (rather than Multics' seven) to keep things simple. Its operating system, STOP, used these rings to maintain up to 32 separate compartments, and to allow appropriate one-way information flows between them.

SCOMP was used in applications such as military *mail guards*. These are specialised firewalls that allowed mail to pass from Low to High but not vice versa [29]. (In general, a device that does this is known as a *data diode*.) SCOMP's successor, XTS-300, supports C2G, the Command and Control Guard. This is used in a Pentagon system whose function is to plan U.S. troop movements and associated logistics. Overall military plans are developed at a high classification level, and then distributed at the appropriate times as orders to lower levels for implementation. (The issue of how high information is deliberately downgraded raises a number of issues. In this case, the guard examines the content of each record before deciding whether to release it.)

SCOMP has had wide influence—for example, in the four rings of protection used in the Intel main processor line—but its most significant contribution to the security community was to serve as a model for the U.S. Trusted Computer Systems Evaluation Criteria (the *Orange Book*) [72]. This was the first systematic set of standards for secure computer systems, being introduced in 1985 and finally retired in December 2000. Although it has since been replaced by the Common Criteria, the Orange Book was enormously influential, and not just in America. Countries such as Britain, Germany, and Canada based their own national standards on it, and these national standards were finally subsumed into the Common Criteria [61].

The Orange Book allowed systems to be evaluated at a number of levels with A1 being the highest, and moving downwards through B3, B2, B1 and C2 to C1. SCOMP was the first system to be rated A1. It was also extensively documented in the open literature. Being first, and being fairly public, it set the standard for the next generation of military systems. This standard has rarely been met since; in fact, the XTS-300 is only evaluated to B3 (the formal proofs of correctness required for an A1 evaluation were dropped).

3.2   Blacker

Blacker was a series of encryption devices designed to incorporate MLS technology [15]. Previously, encryption devices were built with separate processors for the ciphertext, or *Black* end and the cleartext or *Red* end. There are various possible failures that can be prevented if one can coordinate the Red and Black processing. One can also provide greater operational flexibility as the device is not limited to separating two logical networks, but can provide encryption and integrity assurance selectively, and interact in useful ways with routers. However, a high level of assurance is required that the Red data won't leak out via the Black. (For an actual example of such a leak, see [79].)

Blacker entered service in 1989, and the main lesson learned from it was the extreme difficulty of accommodating administrative traffic within a model of classification levels [76]. As late as 1994, it was the only communications security device with an A1 evaluation. So like SCOMP it influenced later systems. It was not widely used though, and its successor (the Motorola Network Encryption System) which is still in use, has only a B2 evaluation.

3.3 MLS Unix, CMWs and Trusted Windowing

Most of the available MLS systems are modified versions of Unix, and they started to appear in the late 1980's. An example is AT&T's System V/MLS [1]. This added security levels and labels, initially by using some of the bits in the group id record and later by using this to point to a more elaborate structure. This enabled MLS properties to be introduced with minimal changes to the system kernel. Other products of this kind included SecureWare (and its derivatives, such as SCO and HP VirtualVault), and Addamax.

Compartmented Mode Workstations (CMWs) allow data at different levels to be viewed and modified at the same time by a human operator, and ensure that labels attached to the information are updated appropriately. The initial demand came from the intelligence community, whose analysts may have access to "Top Secret" data, such as decrypts and agent reports, and produce reports at the "Secret" level for users such as political leaders and officers in the field. As these reports are vulnerable to capture, they must not contain any information that would compromise intelligence sources and methods.

CMWs allow an analyst to view the "Top Secret" data in one window, compose a report in another, and have mechanisms to prevent the accidental copying of the former into the latter (so cut-and-paste operations work from "Secret" to "Top Secret" but not vice versa). CMWs have proved useful in operations, logistics and drug enforcement as well [44].

For the engineering issues involved in doing mandatory access control in windowing systems, see [33, 34] which describe a prototype for Trusted X, a system implementing MLS but not information labelling. It runs one instance of X Windows per sensitivity level, and has a small amount of trusted code that allows users to cut and paste from a lower level to a higher one. For the specific architectural issues with Sun's CMW product, see [35].

3.4   The NRL Pump

It was soon realised that simple mail guards and crypto boxes were too restrictive, as many more internet services were developed besides mail. Traditional MLS mechanisms (such as blind write-ups and periodic read-downs) are inefficient for real-time services.

The US Naval Research Laboratory therefore developed the *Pump*—a one-way data transfer device using buffering and randomization to allow one-way information flow while limiting backward leakage [45, 47] (see Fig. 4). The attraction of this approach is that one can build MLS systems by using pumps to connect separate systems at different security levels. As these systems don't process data at more than one level, they can be built from cheap commercial-off-the-shelf (COTS) components [46]. As the cost of hardware falls, this becomes the preferred option where it's possible.

The Australian government has developed a product called *Starlight*, which uses pump-type technology married with a keyboard switch to provide an MLS-type windowing system (albeit without any visible labels) using trusted hardware to connect the keyboard and mouse with High and Low systems [3]. There is no trusted software. It has been integrated with the NRL Pump [46]. A number of semi-commercial data diode products have also been introduced.

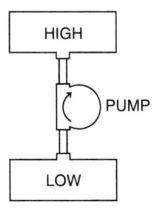

FIG. 4. The pump.

3.5 Logistics Systems

Military stores, like government documents, can have different classification levels. Some signals intelligence equipment is "Top Secret", while things like jet fuel and bootlaces are not; but even such simple commodities may become "Secret" when their quantities or movements might leak information about tactical intentions. There are also some peculiarities: for example, an inertial navigation system classified "Confidential" in the peacetime inventory might contain a laser gyro platform classified "Secret".

The systems needed to manage all this seem to be hard to build, as MLS logistics projects in both the USA and UK have been expensive disasters. In the UK, the Royal Air Force's Logistics Information Technology System (LITS) was a 10 year (1989–99), £500m project to provide a single stores management system for the RAF's 80 bases [57]. It was designed to operate on two levels: "Restricted" for the jet fuel and boot polish, and "Secret" for special stores such as nuclear bombs. It was initially implemented as two separate database systems connected by a pump to enforce the MLS property. The project became a classic tale of escalating costs driven by creeping requirements changes. One of these changes was the easing of classification rules with the end of the Cold War. As a result, it was found that almost all the "Secret" information was now static (e.g., operating manuals for air-drop nuclear bombs that are now kept in strategic stockpiles rather than at airbases). In order to save money, the "Secret" information is now kept on a CD and locked up in a safe.

Logistics systems often have application security features too. The classic example is that ordnance control systems alert users who are about to breach safety rules by putting explosives and detonators in the same truck or magazine [56].

3.6 Purple Penelope

In recent years, the government infosec community has been unable to resist user demands to run standard applications (such as MS Office) that are not available for multilevel secure platforms. One response is "Purple Penelope". This software, from a UK government agency, puts an MLS wrapper round a Windows NT workstation. This implements the high water mark version of BLP, displaying in the background the current security level of the device and upgrading it when necessary as more sensitive resources are read. It ensures that the resulting work product is labelled correctly.

Rather than preventing users from downgrading, as a classical BLP system might do, it allows them to assign any security label they like to their output. However, if this involves a downgrade, it requires the user to confirm the release of the data using a trusted path interface, thus ensuring no Trojan Horse or virus can release anything completely unnoticed. Of course, a really clever malicious program can piggy-back classified material on stuff that the user does wish to release, so there are other tricks to make that harder. There is also an audit trail to provide a record of all downgrades, so that errors and attacks (whether by users, or by malicious code) can be traced after the fact [63].

3.7   Future MLS Systems

The MLS industry sees an opportunity in using its products as platforms for firewalls, Web servers and other systems that are likely to come under attack. Thanks to the considerable effort that has often gone into finding and removing security vulnerabilities in MLS platforms, they can give more assurance than commodity operating systems can that even if the firewall or Web server software is hacked, the underlying operating system is unlikely to be.

The usual idea is to use the MLS platform to separate trusted from untrusted networks, then introduce simple code to bypass the separation in a controlled way. In fact, one of the leading firewall vendors (TIS) was until recently a developer of MLS operating systems, while Secure Computing Corporation, Cyberguard and Hewlett-Packard have all offered MLS based firewall products. The long tradition of using MLS systems as pumps and mail guards means that firewall issues are relatively well understood in the MLS community. A typical design is described in [22].

3.8   What Goes Wrong

In computer security, as in most branches of engineering, we learn more from the systems that fail than from those that succeed. MLS systems have been an effective teacher in this regard; the large effort expended in building systems to follow a simple policy with a high level of assurance has led to the elucidation of many second- and third-order consequences of information flow controls.

3.8.1   Technical issues

One of the most intractable technical issues is *composability*. It is easy to design two systems that are each secure in themselves but which are completely insecure when connected together. For example, consider a simple device (figure 5) that accepts two High inputs H_1 and H_2; multiplexes them; encrypts them by xor'ing them with a one-time pad (i.e., a random

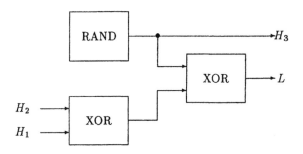

FIG. 5. Insecure composition of secure systems with feedback.

generator); outputs the other copy of the pad on H_3; and outputs the ciphertext. Being encrypted with a cipher system giving perfect secrecy, this is considered to be Low (output L).

In isolation this device is provably secure. However, if feedback is permitted, then the output from H_3 can be fed back into H_2, with the result that the High input H_1 now appears at the Low output L.

This trivial example highlighted problems in connecting two devices of the same type, but things become significantly more difficult when dealing with heterogeneous systems. If the systems to be composed obey different policies, it is a hard problem in itself even to establish whether the policies can be made to be compatible at all! Lomas [50], for example, describes the difficulty of reconciling the conflicting security policies of different national branches of the same investment bank. In fact, establishing the conditions under which security policies compose is a long standing area of research.

There are many other technical problems. We will summarise them here briefly; for a fuller account, the reader should consult Anderson [8].

Covert channels arise when a high process can signal to a low process by affecting some shared resource. For example, it could position the disk head at the outside of the drive at time t_i to signal that the i-th bit in a Top Secret file was a 1, and position it at the inside to signal that the bit was a 0. A typical modern operating system has many such channels, which provide a means for a virus that has migrated up to "High" to signal back down to "Low".

Polyinstantiation refers to the problem of maintaining data consistency when users at different clearance levels work with different versions of the data. Some systems conceal the existence of High data by inventing cover stories, and problems can arise if Low users then rely on these: it is easy to end up with multiple inconsistent copies of a database.

Aggregation refers to the fact that a collection of Low facts may enable an attacker to deduce a High one. For example, we might be happy to declassify any single satellite photo, but declassifying the whole collection would reveal our surveillance capability and the history of our intelligence priorities.

Overclassification is common. Because processes are automatically upgraded as they see new labels, the files they use have to be too. New files default to the highest label belonging to any possible input. The result of all this is a chronic tendency for objects to migrate towards the highest level of classification in the system.

Downgrading is a huge problem. An intelligence analyst might need to take a satellite photo classified at TS/SCI, and paste it into a "Secret" assessment for field commanders. This contravenes the BLP model, and so has to be handled by a trusted subject (that is, trusted code). But often the most difficult parts of the problem have to be solved by this code, and so the MLS mechanisms add little. They can provide very high quality data separation, but the real problems are more likely to lie in the controlled sharing of data.

Application incompatibility is often the worst problem of all; in many cases it is the show-stopper. For example, a process that reads a High file and is upgraded will automatically lose the ability to write to a Low file, and many applications simply cannot cope with files suddenly vanishing. The knock-on effects can be widespread. For example, if an application uses a license server and is upgraded, then the license server must be too, so it vanishes from the ken of other copies of the application running at Low, whose users get locked out.

These technical problems are discussed at greater length in Anderson [8]. They are important not just to builders of multilevel secure systems but because variants of them surface again and again in other systems with mandatory access control policies.

3.8.2   Political and economic issues

The most telling argument against MLS systems is economic. They are built in small volumes, and often to high standards of physical robustness, using elaborate documentation, testing and other quality control measures driven by military purchasing bureaucracies. Administration tools and procedures are usually idiosyncratic, which adds to the cost; and many applications have to be rewritten to cope with the MLS functionality.

One must never lose sight of the human motivations that drive a system design, and the indirect costs that it imposes. Moynihan provides a critical study of the real purposes and huge costs of obsessive secrecy in US foreign and military affairs [55]. Following a Senate enquiry, he discovered that President Truman was never told of the Venona decrypts because the material was considered "Army Property"—despite its being the main motive for the prosecution of Alger Hiss. As his book puts it, "Departments and agencies hoard information, and the government becomes a kind of market. Secrets become organizational assets, never to be shared save in exchange for another organization's assets." He reports, for example, that in 1996 the number of original classification authorities decreased by 959 to 4,420 (following post-Cold-War budget cuts) but the total of all classification actions reported increased by 62 percent to 5,789,625. Yet despite the huge increase in secrecy, the quality of intelligence made available to the political leadership appears to have degraded over time. Effectiveness is undermined by inter-agency feuding and refusal to share information, and by the lack of effective external critique. So a case can be made that MLS systems, by making the classification process easier and controlled sharing harder, actually impair operational effectiveness.

4. The Biba Integrity Model

The usual formal definition of mandatory access control is that information flow restrictions are enforced independently of user actions. Although this is often taken to mean BLP, the majority of fielded systems that enforce such controls do so to protect integrity properties. The typical example comes from an electricity utility, where the main operational systems such as power dispatching and metering can feed information into the customer billing system, but not vice versa. Similar one-way information flows are found in banks, railroads, hospitals and a wide range of other commercial and government systems.

The first security policy model to deal with such integrity protection was due to Biba [17] and is often referred to as "Bell-LaPadula upside down". Its key observation is that confidentiality and integrity are in some sense dual concepts—confidentiality is a constraint on who can read a message, while integrity is a constraint on who may have written or altered it.

In BLP, information cannot flow down towards levels of lower confidentiality, since this would cause a leak. In Biba, conversely, information cannot flow up towards levels of higher integrity, or the "impure" data from the lower-integrity levels would contaminate the "pure" data held in the higher levels. This may be formulated in terms of a No Read Down and a No Write Up property that are the exact dual of the corresponding ones in BLP.

Further applications in which Biba is often applied (without the system builders being even aware of its existence) include the following.

- An electronic medical device such as an ECG may have two separate modes: calibration and use. The calibration data must be protected from being corrupted by normal users, who will therefore be able to read it but not write to it. When a normal user resets the device, it will lose its current user state (i.e., any patient data in memory) but the calibration will remain unchanged.

● In computer supported cooperative work, some of the authors may be very careful in noting all the precise details of their bibliographic citations from first hand references, while others may content themselves with less complete records, perhaps only cross-checked on the Web rather than on the actual articles. In such a case, the more meticulous authors will probably refrain from copying citations from their colleagues' files (No Read Down) and not grant their colleagues permission to modify their own bibliography files (No Write Up).

The duality between Biba and BLP means that the System Z objections apply here too, and the introduction of tranquility properties becomes necessary. The obvious interpretation is a *low water mark* policy in which the integrity label of an object defaults to the lowest label read by the process that created it.

An example of implementation is LOMAC, an extension to Linux with a low water mark policy [40]. This is designed to deal with the problem of malicious code arriving over the Net. The system provides two levels — high and low integrity — with system files at High and the network at Low. As soon as a program (such as a demon) receives traffic from the network, it is automatically downgraded to Low. Thus even if the traffic contains an attack that succeeds in forking a root shell, this shell won't have the ability to write to the password file, for example, as a normal root shell would. As one might expect, a number of system tasks (such as logging) become tricky and require trusted code. However, these mechanisms still cannot stop a virus that has infected Low from replicating and sending copies of itself out over the network.

As mentioned above, integrity concerns can also be dealt with by the type enforcement and RBAC models. However, in their usual forms, they revise a principal's privilege when an object is invoked, while low watermark revises it when an object is read. The latter policy is more prudent where we are concerned with attacks exploiting code that is not formally invoked but simply read (examples include buffer overflow attacks conducted by "data" read from the Internet, and "documents" that actually contain macros — currently the most popular medium for virus propagation).

An interesting problem is that of combining the apparently contradictory requirements of Biba and BLP, as would be needed in a system for which both confidentiality and integrity were equally important goals. The trivial approach based on a single set of security labels for both confidentiality and integrity leads to an extremely restrictive system in which information cannot flow either up or down, but only sideways, among items at the same security level; this does comply with both policies simultaneously, but probably does not yield a very useful system.

A more intriguing solution is to assign different labels for confidentiality and integrity, and in particular to make high integrity correspond to low confidentiality and vice versa. Depending on the context, this may not be as absurd as it may sound at first. Consider for example that systems software needs extremely high integrity, but very low confidentiality; whereas this may be reversed for data items such as user preferences. This approach has the advantage that both policy models end up dictating information flow in the same direction [1]. Researchers are now starting to build more complex models that accommodate both confidentiality and integrity to observe their interaction [48].

5. The Clark-Wilson Model

Most mandatory integrity policies used in real systems are somewhat more complex than Biba, and the most influential of them is Clark-Wilson (CW). This model distills a security policy out of the centuries-old practice of double-entry bookkeeping (arguably one of the most significant ideas in finance after the invention of money). Its main goal is to ensure the integrity of a bank's accounting system and to improve its robustness against insider fraud.

The idea behind double-entry bookkeeping is, like most hugely influential ideas, extremely simple. Each transaction is posted to two separate books, as a credit in one and a debit in the other. For example, when a firm is paid $100 by a creditor, the amount is entered as a debit in the accounts receivable (the firm is now owed $100 less) and as a credit in the cash account (the firm now has $100 more cash). At the end of the day, the books should *balance*, that is, add up to zero; the assets and the liabilities should be equal. (If the firm has made some profit, then this is a liability the firm has to the shareholders.) In all but the smallest firms, the books will be kept by different clerks, and have to balance at the end of every month (at banks, every day). By suitable design of the ledger system, we can see to it that each shop, or branch, can be balanced separately. Thus most frauds will need the collusion of two or more members of staff; and this principle of split responsibility is complemented by audit.

Similar schemes had been in use since the Middle Ages, and had been fielded in computer systems since the 1960's; but a proper model of their security policy was only introduced in 1987, by Clark and Wilson [24]. In their model, some data items are constrained so that they can only be acted on by a certain set of transactions known as transformation procedures.

More formally, there are special procedures whereby data can be input— turned from an *unconstrained data item*, or UDI, into a *constrained data item*, or CDI; *integrity verification procedures* (IVP's) to check the validity of any CDI (e.g., that the books balance); and *transformation procedures* (TPs), which may be thought of in the banking case as transactions that preserve balance. In the general formulation, they maintain the integrity of CDIs; they also write enough information to an append-only CDI (the audit trail) for transactions to be reconstructed. Access control is by means of triples (subject, TP, CDI), which are so structured that a dual control policy is enforced. Here is the formulation found in [1].

1. The system will have an IVP for validating the integrity of any CDI.
2. Application of a TP to any CDI must maintain its integrity.
3. A CDI can only be changed by a TP.
4. Subjects can only initiate certain TPs on certain CDIs.
5. CW-triples must enforce an appropriate separation of duty policy on subjects.
6. Certain special TPs on UDIs can produce CDIs as output.
7. Each application of a TP must cause enough information to reconstruct it to be written to a special append-only CDI.
8. The system must authenticate subjects attempting to initiate a TP.
9. The system must let only special subjects (i.e., security officers) make changes to authorisation-related lists.

One of the historical merits of Clark and Wilson is that they introduced a style of security policy that was not a direct derivative of BLP. In particular, it involves the maintenance of application-level security state—firstly, in the audit log, and secondly to track the shared control mechanisms. These can be quite diverse. They can operate in parallel (as when two bank managers are needed to approve a transaction over a certain amount) or in series (as when different people in a company are responsible for raising an order, accepting delivery, paying an invoice and balancing a departmental budget). Although the details can be highly application specific, this new approach provided an overall framework for reasoning about such systems, and fuelled research into security policies that were not based on label-based classification.

Despite being very different from the rules of the BLP model, the Clark-Wilson rules still fall into the general pattern of first defining a subset of the states of the system as "secure", and then defining transition rules that, when applied to secure states, are guaranteed to lead into further secure states, thus preserving the fundamental invariant of the system. Insofar as a security policy is an abstract description of the desired behaviour of the Trusted Computing Base, the above pattern captures fairly well the concept of "security policy" as we defined it in the introduction.

6. The Chinese Wall Model

The Chinese Wall security policy, introduced by Brewer and Nash in 1989 [21], models the constraints of a firm of professionals—such as computer consultants, advertising agents or investment bankers—whose partners need to avoid situations where *conflicts of interest* or *insider dealing* might become possible.

Suppose the firm consults for a variety of companies, for example three oil companies, four banks and two computer companies. Any partner consulting for a company of a given type, say "oil company", would face a conflict of interest if she were also to consult for any other company of that type. But nothing should stop her from simultaneously consulting for a company of another type, such as a bank. As long as the consultant has not yet interacted with companies of a given type, she is free to choose any company of that type for a new assignment. However, as soon as she consults for one of them, a closed "Chinese Wall" is erected around her, with that company inside and all the other companies of the same type outside. So the consultant's personal Chinese Wall changes whenever she consults for a company of a new type.

The authors explicitly compare their policy with BLP and describe it using a similar formalism based on a simple security property and a star property. These two rules are somewhat more complicated than their BLP equivalents.

Given a data object o, for example the payroll file of Shell, $y(o)$ indicates the company to which o refers, namely Shell, and $x(o)$ denotes the type of company, in this case "oil company", which may also be seen as the set of companies among which there is a conflict of interests from the point of view of an analyst who accesses o.

The critical difference from BLP is that the Chinese Wall model needs to retain *state* in order to keep track of the objects (and therefore companies) with which analysts have been "contaminated". The state is kept in a two-dimensional matrix of Boolean values, N, indexed by subject and object: $N_{s,o}$ is true if and only if subject s has previously accessed object o.

The simple security property says that each subject can access objects from at most one company of any given type. In particular, subject s can access object o only if one of the two following circumstances is verified.

Either s has never dealt with a company of type $x(o)$, i.e., there is no object p such that $N_{s,p}$ is true and $x(p) = x(o)$; or s is already committed to the specific company $y(o)$, i.e., for each object p such that $N_{s,p}$ is true and $x(p) = x(o)$ we also have that $y(p) = y(o)$.

This still leaves scope for information leaks through indirect routes. Analyst Alice might be consulting for oil company Shell and bank Citicorp, while analyst Bob might be consulting for Exxon and Citicorp. Nothing as yet prevents Alice from writing Shell-related financial information in a Citicorp object that Bob might later read, thus causing a conflict with Bob's allegiance to Exxon.

The star property covers this case. Subject s is only allowed to write to object o if the simple property is satisfied and if, for every object p that s has previously read, either $y(p) = y(o)$ or p is a "sanitised" object. To sanitise an object o is to transform it in such a way that no conflict of interest will occur if the sanitised object is disclosed to companies belonging to $x(o)$. This may be achieved through a trusted subject applying appropriate de-identification or other data laundering mechanisms. Sanitised objects can be elegantly included in the model by introducing an artificial company type "sanitised" containing only one company. Since the cardinality of the type is 1, such objects may be accessed by all analysts without any conflict of interests.

The Chinese Wall model made a seminal contribution to the theory of access control. It also sparked a debate about the extent to which it is consistent with the MLS tranquility properties, and some work on the formal semantics of such systems (see, for example, Foley [38] on the relationship with non-interference).

There are also some interesting new questions about covert channels. For example, could an oil company find out whether a competitor that used the same consultancy firm was planning a bid for a third oil company, by asking which specialists were available for consultation and noticing that their number had dropped suddenly?

7. The BMA Policy

The healthcare sector offers another interesting scenario in which confidentiality requirements are paramount, but radically different from those in the military context. Medical privacy is a legal right in many countries, and frequently a subject of controversy. As the information systems in hospitals and medical practices are joined together by networks, potentially large numbers of people have access to personal health information, and this has led to some abuses. The problem is likely to get worse as genetic data become widely available. In Iceland a project to build a national medical database that will incorporate not just medical records but also genetic and genealogical data, so that inherited diseases can be tracked across generations, has caused an uproar [7, 6].

The protection of medical information is also a model for protecting personal information of other kinds, such as the information held on individual customers by banks, insurance companies and government agencies. In EU countries, citizens have rights to *data protection*. In broad terms, this means that they must be notified of how their personal data may be used, and in the case of especially sensitive data (affecting health, sexual behaviour and preferences, political and trade union activity and religious belief) they either must give consent to information sharing or have a right of veto. This raises the issue of how one can construct a security policy in which the access control decisions are taken not by a central authority (as in Bell-LaPadula) or by the system's users (as in discretionary access control) but by the data subjects.

In a 1996 project for which one of us was responsible, the British Medical Association developed a security policy for clinical information systems [10]. This model focuses on access control, patient privacy and confidentiality management. It has a horizontal structure of access control rather than a vertical hierarchy as used in the BLP model, although its confidentiality properties bear some relation to BLP as applied to compartments.

The goals of the BMA security policy were to enforce the principle of patient consent, and to prevent too many people getting access to too large databases of identifiable records. It did not try to do anything new, but merely to codify existing best practice. It also sought to express other security features of medical record management such as safety and accountability.

The policy consists of nine principles:

1. (Access control) Each identifiable clinical record shall be marked with an access control list naming the people or groups of people who may read it and append data to it. The system shall prevent anyone not on the access control list from accessing the record in any way.
2. (Record opening) A clinician may open a record with herself and the patient on the access control list. Where a patient has been referred, she may open a record with herself, the patient and the referring clinician(s) on the access control list.
3. (Control) One of the clinicians on the access control list must be marked as being responsible. Only she may alter the access control list, and she may only add other health care professionals to it.
4. (Consent and notification) The responsible clinician must notify the patient of the names on his record's access control list when it is

opened, of all subsequent additions, and whenever responsibility is transferred. His consent must also be obtained, except in emergency or in the case of statutory exemptions.

5. (Persistence) No-one shall have the ability to delete clinical information until the appropriate time period has expired.

6. (Attribution) All accesses to clinical records shall be marked on the record with the subject's name, as well as the date and time. An audit trail must also be kept of all deletions.

7. (Information flow) Information derived from record A may be appended to record B if and only if B's access control list is contained in A's.

8. (Aggregation control) There shall be effective measures to prevent the aggregation of personal health information. In particular, patients must receive special notification if any person whom it is proposed to add to their access control list already has access to personal health information on a large number of people.

9. (Trusted computing base) Computer systems that handle personal health information shall have a subsystem that enforces the above principles in an effective way. Its effectiveness shall be subject to evaluation by independent experts.

This policy is strictly more expressive than Bell-LaPadula (it contains a BLP-type information flow control mechanism in principle 7, but also contains state). A fuller discussion from the point of view of access control, aimed at a technical audience, can be found at [4].

The fundamental innovation of the BMA model is not at first sight obvious. Previous models had tried to produce a security policy for the "electronic patient record"—a phrase that has come to mean the entirety of a person's health information, from conception through autopsy. This turned out to be an intractable problem, because of the different groups of people who had access to different subsets of the record. So the solution adopted by the BMA model was to define the record as the maximal set of health information about a person that shared the same access control list.

A system now deployed in a number of British hospitals, which works along these lines and broadly complies with the BMA policy, is described in [26].

8. Jikzi

In the last decade of the twentieth century the World Wide Web staked a plausible claim to be the most significant event in publishing since the invention of the printing press. Anyone can now access, from anywhere in the world, a vast multifaceted and continuously updated hypertextual network of documents.

The problem with this new medium, compared with the established world of paper-based publishing, is its ephemeral nature. There is no guarantee that the interesting and useful Web page we are consulting now will be there tomorrow—or, more subtly, that it won't have been edited to deny something that it today asserts. There are few guarantees about the identity of the author of a page and any text can be repudiated at any time by withdrawing or modifying it.

These properties make the new medium questionable for applications that need better guarantees of integrity, such as drugs databases, company business records and newspaper archives[3].

To address the requirements of secure publishing, we implemented a system based on the idea of retaining all versions of the relevant documents forever, without ever deleting any of them. We called it Jikzi, after the first ever book published using a movable type printing press (this is a Buddhist text printed in Korea in 1377, some 63 years before Gutenberg).

The security policy model of the Jikzi system is as follows. As a foundation, we assume the domain D of published documents to be partitioned into two sets: the controlled documents, CD, whose integrity and authenticity are guaranteed by the system, and the uncontrolled documents, UD, on which no constraints are placed. The policy proper is stated as six principles:

1. Neither deletion nor replacement is allowed within CD.
2. The creator of a document defines its revision access condition and only authorised principals with respect to the condition are allowed to revise it; all revisions in CD must be stored and browsable.
3. Authenticity validation procedures must be available for validating the authenticity of CD members.
4. Any action to CD members must maintain the authenticity of the document.
5. Authentication of a member of CD can be performed by any user.
6. Transformation from UD to CD must be one-way and the principal who transformed a document becomes the creator of the document in CD.

The policy protects controlled documents by preventing any destructive modifications to them. If we need to modify a controlled document, we may

---

[3] George Orwell's famous novel *1984* depicts a world in which even paper-based newspaper archives were retroactively changed so that history would suit the current government.

produce a revised copy of it, but all the previous versions will stay archived for the lifetime of the system.

Principle 6 assumes a transformation from an uncontrolled document to its controlled version. The one-wayness of the transform means that a document, once controlled, cannot become uncontrolled, since Principle 1 does not allow deletions from *CD*. It is of course possible to take an uncontrolled copy of a controlled document, and from then on the life of the copy will no longer be controlled; but the previous history of the document in *CD* remains unchanged.

In the paper-based commercial world, write-once documents have existed for a long time (e.g. business ledgers). One of us is using the above policy to build an online data repository service.

Conversely, sometimes our data will not require persistence, but rather volatility. As we shall discuss in section 11.2, there are plausible scenarios in which we may wish all controlled documents to *disappear* after a fixed delay since their creation.

9. The Resurrecting Duckling

Authentication of principals in a distributed system is a well studied problem with established solutions. The traditional solutions, however, rely on the existence of an online server, either for the distribution of "tickets", as in Kerberos[4], or to check whether a public key has been revoked, as in the various public key infrastructures[5]. Where such a server is not available, a new strategy must be found.

The problem becomes apparent in the example of a universal remote control that needs to be configured so as to control a new DVD player that its owner just bought. We want the DVD player to obey this remote control but not any other, so as to prevent accidental (or malicious) activation by our neighbour's remote control. We also want to be able to rescind this association, so that we may resell or give away the player once a better model comes out; but this facility should be restricted, to prevent a thief who steals the player from using it. The goal may be summarised as "secure

---

[4] Kerberos [60] is an online authentication protocol based on Needham-Schroeder [59] and developed at MIT for the Athena project in the late 1980s. The general idea is as follows. Client *A* wishes to access resource server *B*, and therefore needs to authenticate itself to *B* as a valid user. *A* and *B* don't know each other, but they each know (i.e. share a secret with) the authentication server *S*. So *A* contacts *S* and receives from it a time-limited "ticket" that it can show to *B* to prove its identity. A variant of Kerberos is used in Windows 2000.

[5] See section 11.1.

transient association", and the abstract problem has much wider applicability than just consumer electronics: one may conceive further instances as diverse as the temporary binding of an e-wallet to an ATM (nobody should be able to interfere while I am performing my transaction, but the ATM should be ready to bind to another customer's e-wallet as soon as I go away) and the temporary binding of a hospital thermometer to a doctor's PDA.

A metaphor inspired by biology will help us describe the security policy model we developed to implement secure transient association [68].

As Konrad Lorenz beautifully narrates [51], a duckling emerging from its egg will recognise as its mother the first moving object it sees that makes a sound, regardless of what it looks like: this phenomenon is called imprinting. Similarly, our device (whose egg is the shrink-wrapped box that encloses it as it comes out of the factory) will recognise as its owner the first entity that sends it a secret key through an electrical contact. As soon as this "imprint key" is received, the device is no longer a newborn and will stay faithful to its owner for the rest of its life. If several entities are present at the device's birth, then the first one that sends it a key becomes the owner: to use another biological metaphor, only the first sperm gets to fertilise the egg.

We can view the hardware of the device as the body, and the software (and particularly its state) as the soul. As long as the soul stays in the body, the duckling remains alive and bound to the same mother to which it was imprinted. But this bond is broken by death: thereupon, the soul dissolves and the body returns in its pre-birth state, with the resurrecting duckling ready for another imprinting that will start a new life with another soul. Death is the only event that returns a live device to the pre-birth state in which it will accept an imprinting. We call this process *reverse metempsychosis*. Metempsychosis refers to the transmigration of souls as proposed in a number of religions; our policy is the reverse of this as, rather than a single soul inhabiting a succession of bodies, we have a single body inhabited by a succession of souls.

With some devices, death can be designed to follow an identifiable transaction. A hospital thermometer can be designed to die (lose its memory of the previous key and patient) when returned to the bowl of disinfectant at the nursing station. With others, we can arrange a simple timeout, so that the duckling dies of old age. With other devices (and particularly those liable to be stolen) we will arrange for the duckling to die only when instructed by its mother: thus only the currently authorised user may transfer control of the device. In order to enforce this, some level of tamper resistance will be required: assassinating the duckling without damaging its body should be made suitably difficult and expensive. (Of course, there will be applications in which one wishes to protect against accidental death of the mother duck—such as if the remote control breaks. In such cases, we can make a "backup mother" duck by squirrelling away a copy of the imprinting key.)

Some systems, such as Bluetooth, grant control to whoever has the ability to manipulate the device: if you can touch it, you can control it. The Duckling policy is different, because it specifies an element of tamper resistance to protect the crucial state transition of re-imprinting; that is, *resurrection control*. It follows that a passer-by cannot take ownership of an unattended duckling. So an imprinted car stereo is useless to a thief.

After a narrative illustration of the policy, we now list its four principles for reference.

1. (Two States) The entity that the policy protects, called the duckling, can be in one of two states: imprintable or imprinted (see figure 6). In the imprintable state, anyone can take it over. In the imprinted state, it only obeys another entity called its mother duck.
2. (Imprinting) The transition from imprintable to imprinted, known as imprinting, happens when the mother duck sends an imprinting key to the duckling. This may be done using physical contact, or by some other channel whose confidentiality and integrity are protected adequately.
3. (Death) The transition from imprinted to imprintable is known as death. It may only occur under a specified circumstance, such as death by order of the mother duck (default), death by old age (after a predefined time interval), or death on completion of a specific transaction.
4. (Assassination) The duckling must be uneconomical for an attacker to assassinate (which means to cause its death in circumstances other than as prescribed by the Death principle of the policy).

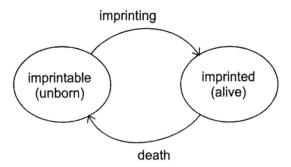

FIG. 6. A state diagram for the Resurrecting Duckling.

10.   Access Control

As we have seen, security policies started primarily as coherent sets of constraints describing who could access what, and when. Even if our last few examples have shown more general scenarios, controlling access to resources tends to be the primary goal of many security policy models.

In the general case, given the set S of all the subjects in the system, and the set O of all the objects, we may build a classical two-dimensional access matrix with a row for each subject and a column for each object and where each cell of the matrix contains a Boolean value specifying whether that subject is allowed to access that object. In practice there will also be a third dimension to this matrix, indexed by the type of access (create, read, write, execute, browse, delete, etc.).

10.1   ACLs

Centralised administration of such a vast collection of individually significant security bits is difficult; to make the task more manageable, the matrix is usually split by columns or by rows.

When it is split by columns, to each object is associated a list of the subjects that are allowed to access it. This, appropriately enough, is called an Access Control List, or ACL (pronounced "ackle"). An example of this is given by the string of permission bits that Unix associates with each file. The sequence "rwxrwxrwx" represents three sets of "read, write, execute" permission bits, the sets respectively mapping to "user" (the owner of the file), "group" (any subject in a designated group that has been associated with the file) and "other" (any other subject). If the permission is granted, the corresponding bit is set and is represented by its letter in the string; otherwise, the bit is reset and is represented by a hyphen instead of the letter.

It is important to note that these permission bits may be set by the owner of the file at her own discretion—hence the term "discretionary access control" to denote this situation as opposed to the "mandatory access control" of BLP and related multilevel secure systems in which no user can override the stated rules about information flow between clearance levels.

In general, mandatory access control makes it easier to guarantee that a stated security policy will be enforced. Central administration of a complex access matrix in constant flux as files and directories are created and destroyed is a very hard task, so mandatory access control usually implies a simplified view of the world, as in the BLP model, where users cannot specify all the individual access bits independently. Where finer control is necessary, discretionary access control is a manageable way to achieve greater flexibility. The two strategies may even be combined, as in Unix

System V/MLS, where a base layer of mandatory access control is complemented by discretionary access control to further regulate accesses that are not constrained by the multilevel security rules.

10.2 Capabilities

If the access matrix is instead split by rows, we obtain for each subject a list of the objects to which she has access. The elements of such a list are called *capabilities*, meaning that if an object *o* is in the list for subject *s*, then *s* is capable of accessing *o*. In some systems, such as Windows 2000, there is also the concept of a "negative capability", to explicitly indicate that the given subject is not allowed to access the given object. There may be hierarchies of users, groups and directories through which a subject obtains both positive and negative capabilities for the same object and there will be rules that state which ones override the others.

To compare the interplay between the different approaches, observe the case of the BMA policy (section 7). Although it was naturally expressed in terms of access control lists, when it came to implementing it in a hospital the most natural expression was in capabilities or certificates. The majority of access control rules could be expressed in statements of the form "a nurse may read, and append to, the records of all patients who have been in her ward during the previous 90 days".

It should be noted that the concept of capability as a row of the access matrix is subtly different from the original one of a capability as "a bit string that you either know or don't know", as introduced by the Cambridge CAP machine [77] which implemented capabilities in hardware. There, each object was associated with an unguessable bit string (the capability) generated by the creator of the object; any subject wishing to access the object had to prove that it knew the capability[6]. Any subject with the right to access a given object could extend this right to another subject simply by telling it the capability. Even more interesting constructions were possible with the introduction of proxies (intermediate objects, acting as a layer of indirection, that among other things make revocation possible): instead of giving subject *s* the capability *c*(*o*) of object *o*, the creator of *o* makes a proxy object *p* and gives *c*(*o*) to *p*; it then gives *s* the capability *c*(*p*) of the proxy, through which *s* can indirectly access *o* without knowing *c*(*o*). The twist is

---

[6] To clarify the difference between this idea of capability and the previous one, note that in this context a negative capability can't work. A negative capability would have to be a bit string that, if known, denies access to a resource (instead of granting it). Since it is up to the client to exhibit the capabilities he knows in order to be granted access, anyone given a negative capability might obviously find it convenient to just "forget" it!

that now the creator of o can revoke s's right to access o by simply deleting the proxy object—all without affecting the workings of any other subjects that might have been legitimately accessing o at the time. Capabilities fell into disuse in the 1980s and early 1990s, and were used only in a small number of systems, such as the IBM AS/400 series. They are now making a comeback in the form of public key certificates, which act as credentials for access to a set of resources. We'll discuss certificates below.

10.3   Roles

We also mentioned *role based access control*. Instead of assigning access rights (or, more generally, "privileges") to individual subjects such as Joe and Barbara, we assign them to roles such as "receptionist" and "personnel manager", and then give one or more roles to each subject. This is a very powerful organisational tool, in that it is much more meaningful to express a security target in terms of roles, which can be made to have well-defined and relatively stable semantics within the company, rather than in terms of individuals, whose functions (and employment status) may change over time.

To obtain the full benefits of such a scheme it is essential to maintain the distinction between subjects and roles, particularly when it comes to auditing. As an example of detrimental blurring of the two, consider the common case of the Unix "root" account on multiuser system with several administrators. Conceptually, "root" is a role, with which several subjects (the system administrators, who by the way have individual user accounts as well) are endowed. At the operating system level, however, "root" is only another subject, or user account, albeit a privileged one. This means that when, by malice or incompetence, one of the system administrators moves a dangerous file to an inappropriate place, the record of ownership and permissions will only say that this was done by "root", not by "Joe acting as root". Oracle in essence reimplements an entire user management and access control system on top of that provided by the underlying operating system, and seems to have got this right, with a clear separation between roles and users.

10.4   Security State

It must be noted that pure access control is not the best mechanism when the policy requires state to be retained. A subtle example of this comes from Clark-Wilson models that specify dual control, i.e., the fact that certain data items must be approved by two principals from different groups (say a yellow manager and a blue one) before becoming valid. Due to workflow constraints it is impractical to impose atomicity on the validation, since this would force the yellow and blue managers always to look at the transactions slips together. What is done instead is that the transaction slip is placed in the inbox of the yellow manager, gets approved by her at some point, then it moves to the inbox of the blue manager, obtains its second approval and finally becomes valid. The system must therefore keep track of additional state for each Unconstrained Data Item to represent the approvals so far collected on the way to become a Constrained Data Item. Implementing a solution using only pure access control mechanisms (e.g. by creative use of intermediate files and directories with carefully chosen permissions and groups) is theoretically possible, but convoluted and error-prone. For example one has to prevent the blue manager from moving into the "valid" directory a transaction that was never approved by yellow.

The problem is even more evident in the Chinese Wall case, where there is explicit mention of a Boolean matrix of state bits to indicate whether a consultant has ever interacted with any companies of a given type. Here too it is theoretically possible to pervert the file system's access control mechanisms into some means of artificially retaining the required state, such as by giving a consultant a positive capability for a company he decides to work for and simultaneously a negative capability for all the other companies in its conflict-of-interest class.

The cleaner alternative to these programming tricks is to keep the security state in a data structure explicitly devoted to that purpose. But where will such a data structure reside? Since it no longer implements a general purpose facility, like the permission bits of the file system, it is likely to migrate from the operating system into the application. The problem of *encapsulating* this data structure (in the object oriented sense) then arises: no other program must be able to modify the security state, except by using the methods provided by the application that is enforcing the policy. This is not always trivial to ensure.

11. Beyond Access Control

So not all security policies are elaborate sets of rules about access control. There are many contexts in which the aspect of greatest interest in the system is not access control but authentication, or delegation, or availability—or perhaps a combination of those and other properties. Biba and Jikzi are examples where integrity matters more than access control. These are not just a matter of controlling write access to files, as they bring in all sorts of other issues such as reliability, concurrency control and resistance to denial-of-service attacks.

On a more general level, we may speak of "security policy" whenever a consistent and unambiguous specification is drawn, stating the required behaviour of the system with respect to some specific security properties. Although we have presented a gallery of policy models and we have insisted on their strengths and general applicability, it is not necessary for a policy target to be derived as a specialisation of a model.

To clarify these points, let's examine a couple of examples of policies that are neither devoted to access control nor derived from established models.

11.1 Key Management Policies

Public key cryptography, as readers will know, is the technique introduced by Diffie and Hellman [30] whereby each principal is endowed with a pair of keys, one public and one private, whose associated cryptographic transformations are the inverse of each other. The public key is widely disseminated while the private key is kept secret. This can be used for encryption or for digital signature. By publishing an encryption key and keeping the corresponding decryption key private, anyone can, using the public key, encrypt messages that only the holder of the private key will be able to decrypt. By publishing a signature verification key and keeping the corresponding signature creation key private, a principal can generate signatures that anybody can verify using the public key but which no other principal could have produced.

For such a system to work on a large scale, a way to manage and distribute public keys must be deployed. In particular, one must avoid the "man in the middle" attacks that become possible if malicious principals can convince their unsuspecting victims to accept forged public keys as those of their intended correspondents.

The CCITT X.509 recommendation [23], published in 1988, was the first serious attempt at such an infrastructure. It was part of the grander plan of X.500, a global distributed directory intended to assign a unique name to every principal (person, computer, peripheral, etc.) in the world—so called *Distinguished Names*. In this context, X.509 used *certificates* (i.e., signed statements) that bound unique names to public keys. Originally this was meant to control which principals had the right to modify which subtrees of X.500, but soon its use as an identity instrument became prevalent and it is used today to certify the public keys used with SSL, the protocol used for secure access to Web sites. Web sites wishing to accept credit card transactions typically have an encryption key certified by a company such as Verisign whose public key is well known; customers entering credit card numbers or other sensitive data can check the certificate to ensure that the public key with which the data will be encrypted is certified by Verisign to belong to the intended destination. X.509 is thus an example of a hierarchical public key infrastructure with a small number of global *roots*—master certification authorities on which all name certificates ultimately depend.

However the software that did most to bring public key cryptography into the mainstream was Zimmermann's *Pretty Good Privacy*—better known as simply PGP [80]—which has become the de facto standard for email encryption. One of PGP's conceptual innovations was the rejection of this hierarchical infrastructure of certification authorities in favour of a decentralised "web of trust" in which all the users, as peers, mutually certify the validity of the keys of their interlocutors. Users may thus obtain uncertified keys over insecure channels, as long as they can build "chains of trust" starting from people they know and leading to those keys.

There have been at least two attempts to get the best of both worlds. Ellison's Simple Public Key Infrastructure (SPKI), later to join forces with Rivest and Lampson's Simple Distributed Security Infrastructure (SDSI) [31, 32, 64], also rejected the concept of a single global certification authority. They bind keys directly to capabilities rather than via names. One of the core concepts is that of *local names*—identifiers that do not have to be globally unique as long as they are unique in the context in which they are used. Global names can be reintroduced as needed by placing a local name in the relevant context. So "Microsoft's public key" becomes "DNS's .com's Microsoft's public key", with DNS being a privileged context.

Without a single root, a user of the system must repeatedly make decisions on the validity of arbitrary keys and may at times be requested to express a formal opinion on the validity of the key of another principal (by "signing" it). For consistency it is desirable that these actions be governed by a policy. Let us examine some examples—we shall refer to PGP for concreteness, since this is the most widely deployed system among end users.

The "signature of Alice on Bob's key" is actually a signature on the combination of Bob's public key and Bob's name. It means: "I, Alice, solemnly certify that, to the best of my knowledge, this key and this name do match". To Charlie, who must decide on the validity of Bob's key, this statement is only worth as much as Alice's reputation as an honest and competent introducer; in fact, PGP lets you assign a rating (denoted as "trust level") to each introducer, as well as a global confidence threshold that must be reached (by adding up the ratings of all the introducers) before a key can be considered as valid. For example you may request two signatures from marginally trusted introducers, or just one from a fully trusted one; but someone with a higher paranoia level might choose five and two respectively.

Such a rule would amount to a policy stating which keys to accept as valid. But the interesting aspects, as usual, come up in the details. A fundamental but easily neglected element of this policy would be a precise operational definition of when to classify an introducer as untrusted, marginally trusted or fully trusted.

The dual problem, equally interesting and probably just as neglected by individual users of PGP, is that of establishing a policy to govern one's signing of other people's keys. This is important if one wishes to be considered as a trustworthy introducer by others. One possible such policy might say:

1. I shall only certify a key if I have received or checked it in a face-to-face meeting with its owner.
2. I shall only certify a key if I have personally verified the passport of its owner.
3. Whenever I sign a key, I shall record date, key id and fingerprint in a signed log that I keep on my Web page.

Such a policy is known as a *certification practice statement*, and can offer some procedural guarantees about the quality of the certifications that one has performed. It gives an independent observer a chance to assess the relative quality of the certification offered by different introducers (assuming that their claims about compliance can be believed).

An observer could for example remark that the policy above, while apparently very strict, does not actually ascertain whether the named principal controls the private key corresponding to the public key being signed. Alice might follow the above policy and still sign a public key that Bob presents as his, but which he instead just copied off Charlie's Web page. This would not allow Bob to read Alice's (or anybody's) correspondence to Charlie, but it would enable him to damage Alice's reputation as a trustworthy introducer ("Look, she signed that this key belongs to Bob, but it's not true! She's too gullible to be an introducer!").

We might try to fix this hole by adding a challenge-response step to the policy: Alice shall only sign Bob's key if Bob is able to sign a random number chosen by Alice.

One lesson from all this is that policies, like ideas, tend to only become clear once we write them down in detail. It will be much harder to spot a methodological flaw if the de facto policy has never been explicitly stated. This even applies to the above "fix": without a more explicit description of how to perform the challenge-response, it is impossible to say whether the proposed exchange is safe or still vulnerable to a "middleperson" attack. For example, Bob might offer to certify Charlie's key and simultaneously present it to Alice as his own for her to certify. She gives him a random challenge, he passes it to Charlie and Charlie provides the required signature. Bob now sends this signature to Alice who mistakenly certifies the key as Bob's.

Certification practice statements are even more important when we are dealing with a commercial or government certification authority rather than with private individuals using PGP. Such statements typically also set out the precise circumstances in which certificates will be revoked, and what liability (if any) will be borne for errors.

11.2 Corporate Email

Another scenario calling for a policy unrelated to access control and not derived from one of the classical models is offered by corporate email. As the Microsoft trial demonstrated, a company can easily make the case against itself through the informal (but often revealing) messages that its executives exchange via email while discussing the campaign against their competitors.

A company aware of this precedent, and concerned that its off-the-record internal messages could be used against it, might decide to get rid of them at the first sign of trouble. But this could be very risky for a company already under investigation, as a court could punish it for contempt or obstruction.

So a company may establish a policy to delete all email messages older than, say, one year. If the company has information in its archives, a court might force its disclosure; if the company deletes the information once the investigation has started, it is at risk; but if the company has an explicit established policy of not archiving old email, then it cannot be faulted for not being able to produce old correspondence.

Another example comes from our university. Examiners are required to destroy exam papers, working notes and other documents after four months. If they were kept too long, students could acquire the right to see them under data protection law, and this would violate our confidentiality policy; but destroying them too soon might prejudice appeals.

A policy of timely destruction has to address a number of practical issues (such as system backups and data on local discs), which makes its implementation nontrivial. A simple technique might involve encrypting all messages before storing them using a company-wide limited-lifetime key held in a tamper resistant box that deletes it after the specified time interval. Efficient purging of unreadable messages is left as a garbage collection task for the system administrator.

Of course none of this stops people from taking copies of messages while they are still readable, but:

1. If we wanted to stop that, we would need further and more complicated mechanisms to implement the policy.

2. It would never be possible to implement such a policy in a completely watertight manner: after all, a determined employee could always print out the mail or, if even that were forbidden, photograph the screen.

3. We probably don't want that anyway: it would be wrong to see the legitimate user reading email as the potential enemy when the real one is his carelessness. Taking a permanent copy of an important message should be allowed, as long as this exceptional action requires explicit confirmation and is audited.

At any rate, apart from the implementation details, the point we want to emphasise here is the use of a policy as a legal defence. The security property of interest in this case is not access control but **plausible deniability**. (It's not really a matter of "no-one may read X after time T" but "even the system administrator will not be able to create a user who can".)

12. Automated Compliance Verification

Once policy is refined from a general model to a specific target, there is interest in a system that would automatically verify whether any given proposed action is acceptable.

Blaze, Feigenbaum and Lacy introduced the concept of trust management [19]: a unified approach to specifying security policies and credentials and to verifying compliance. The system they proposed and built, PolicyMaker, includes an application-independent engine whose inputs are policy assertions, security credentials (i.e., "certificates") and the proposed action, and whose output is a series of "acceptance records" that say which assertions, if any, authorise the action. The idea is for this generic engine to be configured by an appropriate application-specific policy. Requests for security-critical actions must be accompanied by appropriate credentials in order to satisfy the system that the principal issuing the request has the authority to do so.

Related work includes SPKI and SDSI, which address not only authorisation but also naming, i.e. the association of identities to public keys. PolicyMaker explicitly refuses to deal with the problem of naming; its authors argue that it is orthogonal to authorisation and therefore irrelevant to the issue of compliance checking.

The successor to PolicyMaker, called KeyNote, is now RFC 2704 [18]. PolicyMaker was designed for generality as a framework in which to explore trust management concepts, perhaps at the expense of efficiency. For example the assertions could be arbitrary programs. KeyNote is rather designed for simplicity, competitiveness and efficiency, with the aim of being fielded in real applications. Popular open source projects including the Apache-SSL Web server and the OpenBSD operating system already use KeyNote.

13.   A Methodological Note

As a final exhibit in this gallery of examples it is worth mentioning our study of the security requirements for a computer-based National Lottery system [5]. More than the security policy model in itself, what is most instructive in this case is methodology employed for deriving it.

Experienced software engineers know that perhaps 30% of the cost of a software product goes into specifying it, 10% into coding, and the remaining 60% on maintenance.

Specification is not only the second most expensive item in the system development life cycle, but is also where the most expensive things go wrong. The seminal study by Curtis, Krasner and Iscoe of large software project disasters found that failure to understand the requirements was mostly to blame [25]: a thin spread of application domain knowledge typically led to fluctuating and conflicting requirements, which in turn caused a breakdown in communication. They suggested that the solution was to find an "exceptional designer" with a deep understanding of the problem who would assume overall responsibility.

But there are many cases where an established expert is not available, such as when designing a new application from scratch or when building a competitor to a closed, proprietary system whose behaviour can only be observed at a distance. It therefore seemed worthwhile to see if a high quality security specification could be designed in a highly parallel way, by getting a lot of different people to contribute drafts in the hope that most of the possible attacks would be considered in at least one of them.

We carried out such an experiment in 1999 by recruiting volunteers from a captive audience of final year undergraduates in computer science at the University of Cambridge: we set one of their exam questions to be the definition of a suitable security policy for a company planning to bid for the licence to the British National Lottery.

The model answer had a primary threat model that attackers, possibly in cahoots with insiders, would try to place bets once the result of the draw was known, whether by altering bet records or forging tickets. The secondary threats were that bets would be placed that had not been paid for, and that attackers might operate bogus vending stations that would pay small claims but disappear if a client won a big prize.

The security policy that follows logically from this is that bets should be registered online with a server that is secured prior to the draw, both against tampering and against the extraction of sufficient information to forge a winning ticket; that there should be credit limits for genuine vendors; and that there should be ways of identifying bogus vendors. Once the security policy has been developed in enough detail, designing enforcement mechanisms should not be too hard for someone skilled in the computer security art.

Valuable and original contributions from the students came at a number of levels, including policy goal statements, discussions of particular attacks, and arguments about the merits of particular protection mechanisms.

At the level of goals, for example, one candidate assumed that the customer's rights must have precedence: "All winning tickets must be redeemable! So failures must not allow unregistered tickets to be printed." Another candidate assumed the contrary, and thus the "worst outcome should be that the jackpot gets paid to the wrong person, never twice." Such goal conflicts are harder to identify when the policy goals are written by a single person.

As for attacks, some candidates suggested using the broadcast radio clock signal as an authentication input to the vending terminals; but one candidate correctly pointed out that this signal could be jammed without much difficulty. This caused some consternation to the auditor of a different online gaming system, which appears to be vulnerable to time signal spoofing.

There was a lot of discussion not just on how to prevent fraud but how to assure the public that the results were trustworthy, by using techniques such as third party logging or digital signatures. The candidates' observations on protection mechanisms also amounted to a very complete checklist. Items such as "tickets must be associated with a particular draw" might seem obvious, but a protocol design that used a purchase date, ticket serial number and server-supplied random challenge as input to a MAC computation might appear plausible to a superficial inspection. The evaluator might not check to see whether a shopkeeper could manufacture tickets that could be used in more than one draw. Experienced designers appreciate the value of such checklists.

The lesson drawn from this case study was that requirements engineering, like software testing and unlike software development, is susceptible to parallelisation. When developing the threat analysis, security requirements and policy model for a new system, rather than paying a single consultant to think about a problem for twenty days, it will often be more efficient to pay fifteen consultants to think about it for a day each and then have an editor spend a week hammering their ideas into a single coherent document.

14. Conclusions

A security policy is a specification of the protection goals of a system. Many expensive failures are due to a failure to understand what the system security policy should have been. Technological protection mechanisms such as cryptography and smartcards may be more glamorous for the implementer, but technology-driven designs have a nasty habit of protecting the wrong things.

At the highest level of abstraction, a security policy model has little if any reference to the mechanisms that will be used to implement it. At the next level down, a protection profile sets out what a given type of system or component should protect, without going into implementation detail, and relates the protection mechanisms to threats and evironmental assumptions. A security target gives a precise statement of what a given system or component will protect and how. Especially at the highest levels the policy functions as a means of communication. Like any specification, it is a contract between the implementer and the client—something that both understand and by which both agree to be bound.

Our historical perspective has shown how security policies were first formally modelled in the 1970s to manage disclosure threats in military systems. They were then extended to issues other than confidentiality and to problems other than access control. We have also seen a spectrum of different formulations, from the more mathematically oriented models that allow one to prove theorems to informal models expressed in natural language. All have their place. Often the less formal policies will acquire more structure once they have been developed into protection profiles or security targets and the second- and third-order consequences of the original protection goals have been discovered.

We now have a sufficiently large gallery of examples, worked out in varying levels of detail, that when faced with a project to design a new system, the security engineer should first of all assess whether she can avoid reinventing the wheel by adopting one of them. If this is not possible, familiarity with previous solutions is always helpful in coming up with an appropriate new idea. Finally, the methodological issues should not be underestimated: security always benefits from peer review and many heads are better than one.

ACKNOWLEDGEMENTS

The authors are grateful to Jeremy Epstein, Virgil Gligor, Paul Karger, Ira Moskowitz, Marv Schaefer, Rick Smith, Karen Spärck Jones and Simon Wiseman for helpful discussions.

Portions of this chapter will appear in Ross Anderson's book *Security Engineering* [8], to which the reader should refer for more detail. Other portions have appeared in Jong-Hyeon

Lee's PhD dissertation [49] and in other publications by the authors that were cited in the relevant sections [10, 11, 12, 68, 69, 5].

REFERENCES

[1] Edward Amoroso. *Fundamentals of Computer Security Technology*. Prentice-Hall, Englewood Cliffs, New Jersey, 1994. ISBN 0-13-305541-8.

[2] J. Anderson. "Computer Security Technology Planning Study". Tech. Rep. ESD-TR-73-51, AFSC, Hanscom AFB, Bedford, MA, Oct 1972. AD-758 206, ESD/AFSC.

[3] M. Anderson, C. North, J. Griffin, R. Milner, J. Yesberg and K. Yiu. "Starlight: Interactive Link". In "12th Annual Computer Security Applications Conference", pp. 55–63. IEEE, 1996. ISBN 0-8186-7606-X.

[4] Ross Anderson. "A Security Policy Model for Clinical Information Systems". In "Proceedings of the IEEE Symposium on Research in Security and Privacy", Research in Security and Privacy, pp. 30–43. IEEE Computer Society, Technical Committee on Security and Privacy, IEEE Computer Society Press, Oakland, CA, May 1996.

[5] Ross Anderson. "How to Cheat at the Lottery (or, Massively Parallel Requirements Engineering)". In "Proceedings of the Annual Computer Security Applications Conference 1999", Phoenix, AZ, USA, 1999. URL http://www.cl.cam.ac.uk/~rja14/lottery/lottery.html.

[6] Ross J. Anderson. "The DeCODE Proposal for an Icelandic Health Database". *Læknabladhidh (The Icelandic Medical Journal)*, **84**(11):874–875, Nov 1998. URL http://www.cl.cam.ac.uk/users/rja14/iceland/iceland.html. The printed article is an excerpt from a document produced for the Icelandic Medical Association. The full text of the latter is available online.

[7] Ross J. Anderson. "Comments on the Security Targets for the Icelandic Health Database", 1999. URL http://www.ftp.cl.cam.ac.uk/ftp/users/rja14/iceland-admiral.pdf.

[8] Ross J. Anderson. *Security Engineering: A Guide to Building Dependable Distributed Systems*. Wiley, 2001. ISBN 0-471-38922-6.

[9] Ross John Anderson. "Why Cryptosystems Fail". *Communications of the ACM*, **37**(11):32–40, 1994.

[10] Ross John Anderson. "Security in Clinical Information Systems". British Medical Association, Jan 1996. ISBN 0-7279-1048-5.

[11] Ross John Anderson and Jong-Hyeon Lee. "Jikzi: A New Framework for Secure Publishing". In "Proceedings of Security Protocols Workshop '99", Cambridge, Apr 1999.

[12] Ross John Anderson and Jong-Hyeon Lee. "Jikzi—A New Framework for Security Policy, Trusted Publishing and Electronic Commerce". *Computer Communications*, to appear.

[13] L. Badger, D. F. Sterne, D. L. Sherman, K. M. Walker and S. A. Haghighat. "Practical Domain and Type Enforcement for UNIX". In "Proceedings of the 5th USENIX UNIX Security Symposium", pp. 66–77. Oakland, CA, May 1995.

[14] D. Elliot Bell and Leonard J. LaPadula. "Secure Computer Systems: Mathematical Foundations". Mitre Report ESD-TR-73-278 (Vol. I–III), Mitre Corporation, Bedford, MA, Apr 1974.

[15] T. Benkart and D. Bitzer. "BFE Applicability to LAN Environments". In "Seventeenth National Computer Security Conference", pp. 227–236. NIST, Baltimore, Maryland, 11–14 Oct 1994.

[16] T. Berson and G. Barksdale. "KSOS-Development Methodology for a Secure Operating System". In "Proc. NCC", pp. 365–371. AFIPS, AFIPS Press, Montvale, NJ, Jun 1979. Vol. 48.

[17] Ken Biba. "Integrity Considerations for Secure Computing Systems". Mitre Report MTR-3153, Mitre Corporation, Bedford, MA, 1975.

[18] Matt Blaze, Joan Feigenbaum, John Ioannidis and A. Keromytis. "The KeyNote Trust-Management System Version 2". IETF RFC 2704, Internet Engineering Task Force, Sep 1999. URL http://www.cis.ohio-state.edu/htbin/rfc/rfc2704.html.

[19] Matt Blaze, Joan Feigenbaum and Jack Lacy. "Decentralized Trust Management". In "Proceedings of the IEEE Symposium on Research in Security and Privacy", Research in Security and Privacy. IEEE Computer Society,Technical Committee on Security and Privacy, IEEE Computer Society Press, Oakland, CA, May 1996.

[20] W. E. Boebert and R. Y. Kain. "A Practical Alternative to Hierarchical Integrity Policies". In "Proceedings of the 8th National Computer Security Conference", pp. 18–27. NIST, 1985.

[21] David F. C. Brewer and Michael J. Nash. "The Chinese Wall Security Policy". In "1989 IEEE Symposium on Security and Privacy", pp. 206–214. Oakland, CA, 1989.

[22] C. Cant and S. Wiseman. "Simple Assured Bastion Hosts". In "13th Annual Computer Security Application Conference", pp. 24–33. IEEE Computer Society, 1997. ISBN 0-8186-8274-4.

[23] CCITT. "Data Communications Networks Directory". Tech. Rep. 8, CCITT, Melbourne, Nov 1988. Recommendations X.500-X.521, IXth Plenary Assembly.

[24] David D. Clark and David R. Wilson. "A Comparison of Commercial and Military Computer Security Policies". In "1987 IEEE Symposium on Security and Privacy", pp. 184–194. Oakland, CA, 1987.

[25] Bill Curtis, Herb Krasner and Neil Iscoe. "A Field Study of the Software Design Process for Large Systems". *Communications of the ACM*, **31**(11):1268–1287, Nov 1988.

[26] I. Denley and S. Weston-Smith. "Privacy in clinical information systems in secondary care". *British Medical Journal*, **318**:1328–1331, May 1999.

[27] Dorothy E. Denning. "A Lattice Model of Secure Information Flow". *Communications of the ACM*, **19**(5):236–243, May 1976. ISSN 0001-0782. Papers from the Fifth ACM Symposium on Operating Systems Principles (Univ. Texas, Austin, Tex., 1975).

[28] Dorothy E. Denning. "A Lattice Model of Secure Information Flow". *Communications of the ACM*, **19**(5):236–243, May 1976. ISSN 0001-0782.

[29] Dorothy E. R. Denning. *Cryptography and Data Security.* Addison-Wesley, Reading, 1982. ISBN 0-201-10150-5.

[30] Whitfield Diffie and Martin E. Hellman. "New directions in cryptography". *IEEE Transactions on Information Theory*, **IT-22**(6):644–654, 1976.

[31] Carl Ellison. "The nature of a useable PKI". *Computer Networks*, **31**(8):823–830, May 1999.

[32] Carl M. Ellison, Bill Frantz, Butler Lampson, Ron Rivest, Brian M. Thomas and Tatu Ylonen. "SPKI Certificate Theory". IETF RFC 2693, Internet Engineering Task Force, Sep 1999. URL http://www.cis.ohio-state.edu/htbin/rfc/rfc2693.html.

[33] J. Epstein, H. Orman, J. McHugh, R. Pascale, M. Branstad and A. Marmor-Squires. "A High Assurance Window System Prototype". *Journal of Computer Security*, **2**(2–3):159–190, 1993.

[34] J. Epstein and R. Pascale. "User Interface for a High Assurance Windowing System". In "Ninth Annual Computer Security Applications Conference", pp. 256–264. IEEE, Orlando, Florida, USA, 6–10 Dec 1993. ISBN 0-8186-4330-7.

[35] Glenn Faden. "Reconciling CMW Requirements with Those of X11 Applications". In "Proceedings of the 14th Annual National Computer Security Conference", Washington, DC, USA, Oct 1991. Architecture of the windowing portion of Sun's CMW.

[36] J. S. Fenton. *Information Protection Systems.* PhD dissertation, Cambridge University, 1973.

[37] D. Ferraiolo and R. Kuhn. "Role-Based Access Controls". In "15th NIST-NCSC National Computer Security Conference", pp. 554–563. Oct 1992.

[38] Simon N. Foley. "Aggregation and separation as noninterference properties". *Journal of Computer Security*, 1(2):158–188, 1992.

[39] L. J. Fraim. "SCOMP: A Solution to the Multilevel Security Problem". *Computer*, 16(7):26–34, Jul 1983.

[40] T. Fraser. "LOMAC: Low Water-Mark Integrity Protection for COTS Environments". In "Proceedings of the 2000 IEEE Symposium on Security and Privacy", pp. 230–245. IEEE Computer Society Press, 2000.

[41] J. A. Goguen and J. Meseguer. "Security Policies and Security Models". In "Proceedings of the 1982 Symposium on Security and Privacy (SSP '82)", pp. 11–20. IEEE Computer Society Press, Los Alamitos, CA., USA, Apr 1990.

[42] R. D. Graubart, J. L. Berger and J. P. L. Woodward. "Compartmented Mode, Workstation Evaluation Criteria, Version 1". Tech. Rep. MTR 10953 (also published by the Defense Intelligence Agency as document DDS-2600-6243-91), The MITRE Corporation, Bedford, MA, USA, Jun 1991. Revised requirements for the CMW, including a description of what they expect for Trusted X.

[43] Michael A. Harrison, Walter L. Ruzzo and Jeffrey D. Ullman. "Protection in Operating Systems". *Communications of the ACM*, 19(8):461–471, Aug 1976. ISSN 0001-0782.

[44] G. Huber. "CMW Introduction". *ACM SIGSAC*, 12(4):6–10, Oct 1994.

[45] M. H. Kang and I. S. Moskowitz. "A Pump for Rapid, Reliable, Secure Communications". In ACM (ed.), "Fairfax 93: 1st ACM Conference on Computer and Communications Security, 3–5 November 1993, Fairfax, Virginia", pp. 118–129. ACM Press, New York, NY 10036, USA, 1993. ISBN 0-89791-629-8.

[46] M. H. Kang, J. N. Froscher and I. S. Moskowitz. "An Architecture for Multilevel Secure Interoperability". In "13th Annual Computer Security Applications Conference", pp. 194–204. IEEE Computer Society, San Diego, CA, USA, 8–12 Dec 1997. ISBN 0-8186-8274-4.

[47] M. H. Kang, I. S. Moskowitz, B. Montrose and J. Parsonese. "A Case Study of Two NRL Pump Prototypes". In "12th Annual Computer Security Applications Conference", pp. 32–43. IEEE, San Diego CA, USA, 9–13 Dec 1996. ISBN 0-8186-7606-X.

[48] P. A. Karger, V. A. Austell and D. C. Toll. "A New Mandatory Security Policy Combining Secrecy and Integrity". Tech. Rep. RC 21717 (97406), IBM, Mar 2000.

[49] Jong-Hyeon Lee. "Designing a reliable publishing framework". Tech. Rep. 489, University of Cambridge Computer Laboratory, Apr 2000.

[50] Mark Lomas. "Auditing against Multiple Policies (Transcript of Discussion)". In "Proceedings of Security Protocols Workshop 1999", No. 1796 in Lecture Notes in Computer Science, pp. 15–20. Springer-Verlag, Apr 1999.

[51] Konrad Lorenz. *Er redete mit dem Vieh, den Vögeln und den Fischen (King Solomon's ring)*. Borotha-Schoeler, Wien, 1949.

[52] Daryl McCullough. "A Hookup Theorem for Multilevel Security". *IEEE Transactions on Software Engineering*, 16(6):563–568, Jun 1990. ISSN 0098-5589. Special Section on Security and Privacy.

[53] J. McLean. "Security Models". In "Encyclopedia of Software Engineering", John Wiley & Sons, 1994.

[54] John McLean. "A comment on the 'basic security theorem' of Bell and LaPadula". *Information Processing Letters*, 20(2):67–70, Feb 1985. ISSN 0020-0190.

[55] D. P. Moynihan. *Secrecy—The American Experience*. Yale University Press, 1999. ISBN 0-300-08079-4.

[56] Paul Mukherjee and Victoria Stavridou. "The Formal Specification of Safety Requirements for Storing Explosives". *Formal Aspects of Computing*, 5(4):299–336, 1993.

[57] M. Nash and R. Kennett. "Implementing Security Policy in a Large Defence Procurement". In "12th Annual Computer Security Applications Conference", pp. 15–23. IEEE, San Diego, CA, USA, 9–13 Dec 1996. ISBN 0-8186-7606-X.

[58] National Security Agency. "The NSA Security Manual". Tech. rep., NSA. URL http://www.cl.cam.ac.uk/ftp/users/rja14/nsaman.tex.gz. (Leaked copy.).

[59] Roger Michael Needham and Michael Schroeder. "Using Encryption for Authentication in Large Networks of Computers". *Communications of the ACM*, **21**(12):993–999, 1978.

[60] B. Clifford Neuman and John T. Kohl. "The Kerberos Network Authentication Service (V5)". IETF RFC 1510, Internet Engineering Task Force, Sep 1993.

[61] NIST. "Common Criteria for Information Technology Security, Version 2.1". Tech. Rep. ISO IS 15408, National Institute of Standards and Technology, Jan 2000. URL http://csrc.nist.gov/cc/.

[62] Public Record Office. "Functional Requirements for Electronic Record Management Systems", Nov 1999. URL http://www.pro.gov.uk/recordsmanagement/eros/invest/reference.pdf.

[63] B. Pomeroy and S. Wiseman. "Private Desktops and Shared Store". In "Computer Security Applications Conference", pp. 190–200. IEEE, Phoenix, AZ, USA, 1998. ISBN 0-8186-8789-4.

[64] Ronald L. Rivest and Butler W. Lampson. *SDSI—A Simple Distributed Security Infrastructure*, Apr 1996. URL http://theory.lcs.mit.edu/~cis/sdsi.html. V1.0 presented at USENIX 96 and Crypto 96.

[65] J. Rushby and B. Randell. "A Distributed Secure System". In "IEEE Computer", pp. 55–67. IEEE, Jul 1983.

[66] RR Schell. "Computer Security: The Achilles' Heel of the Electronic Air Force?" *Air University Review*, **30**(2):16–33, Jan–Feb 1979.

[67] RR Schell, PJ Downey and GJ Popek. "Preliminary notes on the design of secure military computer systems". Tech. Rep. MCI-73-1, Electronic Systems Division, Air Force Systems Command, 1 Jan 1973. URL http://seclab.cs.ucdavis.edu/projects/history/papers/sche73.pdf.

[68] Frank Stajano and Ross Anderson. "The Resurrecting Duckling: Security Issues in Ad-Hoc Wireless Networks". In Bruce Christianson, Bruno Crispo and Mike Roe (eds.), "Security Protocols, 7th International Workshop Proceedings", Lecture Notes in Computer Science. Springer-Verlag, 1999. URL http://www.cl.cam.ac.uk/~fms27/duckling/. Also available as AT&T Laboratories Cambridge Technical Report 1999.2.

[69] Frank Stajano and Ross Anderson. "The Resurrecting Duckling: Security Issues in Ad-Hoc Wireless Networks". In "Proceedings of 3rd AT&T Software Symposium", Middletown, New Jersey, USA, Oct 1999. URL http://www.cl.cam.ac.uk/~fms27/duckling/. Abridged and revised version of the Security Protocols article by the same name. Also available as AT&T Laboratories Cambridge Technical Report 1999.2b.

[70] David Sutherland. "A Model of Information". In "Proc. 9th National Security Conference", pp. 175–183. Gaithersburg, Md., 1986.

[71] US Department of Defense. "Technical Rationale behind CSC-STD-003-85: computer security requirements". Tech. Rep. CSC-STD-004-85, US Department of Defense, 1985.

[72] US Department of Defense. "Trusted Computer System Evaluation Criteria". Tech. Rep. 5200.28, US Department of Defense, 1985.

[73] KG Walter, WF Ogden, WC Rounds, FT Bradshaw, SR Ames and DG Shumway. "Models for Secure Computer Systems". Tech. Rep. 1137, Case Western Reserve University, 31 Jul 1973. Revised 21 Nov 1973.

[74] K. G. Walter, W. F. Ogden, W. C. Rounds, F. T. Bradshaw, S. R. Ames and D. G. Shumway. "Primitive Models for Computer Security". Tech. Rep. ESD-TR-74-117, Case Western Reserve University, 23 Jan 1974. URL http://www.dtic.mil.

[75] Clark Weissman. "Security Controls in the ADEPT-50 Time-Sharing System". In "Proc. Fall Joint Computer Conference, AFIPS", vol. 35, pp. 119–133. 1969.

[76] Clark Weissman. "BLACKER: Security for the DDN, Examples of A1 Security Engineering Trades". In "Proceedings of the 1992 IEEE Computer Society Symposium on Security and Privacy (SSP '92)", pp. 286–292. IEEE, May 1992. ISBN 0-8186-2825-1.

[77] M. V. Wilkes and R. M. Needham (eds.). *The Cambridge Cap Computer and its Operating System*. North-Holland, New York, 1979. ISBN 0-444-00357-6.

[78] J. P. L. Woodward. "Security Requirements for System High and Compartmented Mode Workstations". Tech. Rep. MTR 9992, Revision 1 (also published by the Defense Intelligence Agency as document DDS-2600-5502-87), The MITRE Corporation, Bedford, MA, USA, Nov 1987. The original requirements for the CMW, including a description of what they expect for Trusted X.

[79] P. Wright. *Spycatcher—The Candid Autobiography of a Senior Intelligence Officer*. William Heinemann Australia, 1987. ISBN 0-85561-098-0.

[80] Philip R. Zimmermann. *The Official PGP User's Guide*. MIT Press, Cambridge, MA, 1995. ISBN 0-262-74017-6.

Transistors and IC Design

YUAN TAUR

IBM T. J. Watson Research Center
Yorktown Heights
New York
USA

Abstract

This chapter focuses on the basic building blocks of today's computer chips: CMOS transistors and their design principles. Section 1 briefly reviews the history of the evolution of CMOS transistors and why they now have become the prevailing IC technology in the microelectronics industry. The elementary guidelines of CMOS scaling—the more a transistor is scaled, the higher becomes its packing density, the higher its circuit speed, and the lower its power dissipation—are covered in depth in Section 2. Section 3 examines several key nonscaling issues that have become prominent below 0.25-µm design rules. These factors arise from the fundamental principles of quantum mechanics and thermodynamics and will ultimately impose a limit to continued CMOS scaling. A 25-nm CMOS design, likely to be near the limit of scaling, is described in Section 4. Finally, Section 5 discusses interconnect scaling and addresses the question whether future microprocessor performance will be limited by transistors or by wires.

1.	Introduction to CMOS VLSI	238
2.	MOSFET Scaling Theory	242
	2.1 Constant-Field Scaling	242
	2.2 Constant-Voltage Scaling	245
	2.3 2-D Scale Length Theory	246
3.	CMOS Device Issues Below 0.25 µm	251
	3.1 Power Supply and Threshold Voltage	251
	3.2 Gate Oxide	256
	3.3 Gate Electrode	258
	3.4 Channel Profile Design	260
	3.5 Source–Drain Doping Requirements	263
	3.6 Dopant Number Fluctuations	264
4.	25-nm CMOS Design	266
	4.1 Short-Channel Device Design	266
	4.2 Source–Drain Doping Requirements	268
	4.3 Polysilicon-Gate Depletion Effects	271
	4.4 Monte Carlo Simulations of 25-nm CMOS	272
5.	Interconnect Issues	273
	5.1 Interconnect Scaling	273
	5.2 Global Wires	276
	References	278

ADVANCES IN COMPUTERS, VOL. 55
ISBN 0-12-012155-7

237

1. Introduction to CMOS VLSI

The invention of the transistor in 1947 marked the birth of the semiconductor electronics industry that has had an enormous impact on the way people work and live. Over the past two decades, the steady down-scaling of transistor dimensions has been the main stimulus to the growth of silicon integrated circuits (ICs) and the computer industry. The more an IC is scaled, the higher becomes its packing density, the higher its circuit speed, and the lower its power dissipation. These have been key in the evolutionary progress leading to today's computers and communication systems that offer superior performance, dramatically reduced cost per function, and much reduced physical size, over their predecessors.

In the evolution of silicon ICs, the bipolar transistor technology was developed early on and was applied to the first integrated-circuit memory in mainframe computers in the 1960's. Bipolar transistors have been used all along where raw circuit speed is most important, for bipolar circuits remain the fastest at the individual circuit level. However, the large power dissipation of bipolar circuits has severely limited their integration level, to about 10^4 circuits per chip. This integration level is quite low by today's *very-large-scale-integration* (VLSI) standard.

The idea of modulating the surface conductance of a semiconductor by the application of an electric field was first invented in 1930. However, early attempts to fabricate a surface field-controlled device were not successful because of the presence of large densities of surface states, which effectively shielded the surface potential from the influence of an external field. The first *metal-oxide-semiconductor field-effect transistor* (MOSFET) on a silicon substrate using SiO_2 as the gate insulator was fabricated in 1960 [1]. During the 1960's and 1970's, n-channel or p-channel MOSFETs were widely used, along with bipolar transistors, for implementing circuit functions on a silicon chip. Although the MOSFET devices were slow compared to the bipolar devices, they had a higher layout density and were relatively simple to fabricate; the simplest MOSFET chip could be made using only four masks and a single doping step! However, just like bipolar circuits, single-polarity MOSFET circuits also suffered from relatively large standby power dissipation, and hence were limited in the level of integration on a chip.

The major breakthrough in the level of integration came in 1963 with the invention of CMOS (*complementary MOS*) [2] in which both n-channel and p-channel MOSFETs are constructed simultaneously on the same substrate. A schematic cross section of modern CMOS transistors, consisting of an n-channel MOSFET and a p-channel MOSFET integrated on the same chip, is shown in Fig. 1. The key physical features of the modern CMOS

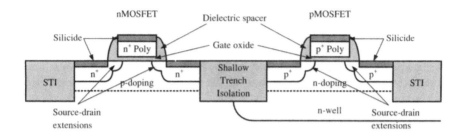

FIG. 1. Schematic device cross section for an advanced CMOS technology.

technology, as illustrated in Fig. 1, include a p-type polysilicon gate for the p-channel MOSFET and an n-type polysilicon gate for the n-channel MOSFET, source and drain extensions, refractory metal silicide on the polysilicon gate as well as on the source and drain diffusion regions, and shallow-trench oxide isolation (STI).

The most basic building block of digital CMOS circuits is a CMOS inverter. A CMOS inverter consists of an nMOSFET and a pMOSFET, as shown in Fig. 2 [3]. The source terminal of the nMOSFET is connected to

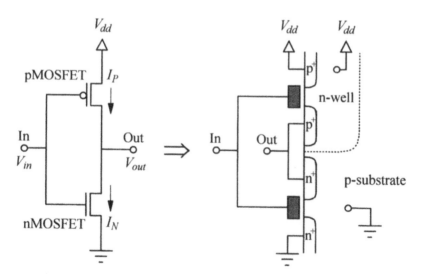

FIG. 2. Circuit diagram and schematic cross section of a CMOS inverter.

the ground, while the source of the pMOSFET is connected to V_{dd}. The gates of the two MOSFETs are tied together as the input node. The two drains are tied together as the output node. In such an arrangement, the complementary nature of n- and pMOSFETs allows one and only one transistor to be conducting in one of the two stable states. For example, when the input voltage is high or when $V_{in} = V_{dd}$, the gate-to-source voltage of the nMOSFET equals V_{dd}, which turns it on. At the same time, the gate-to-source voltage of the pMOSFET is zero, so the pMOSFET is off. The output node is then pulled down to the ground potential by currents through the conducting nMOSFET. On the other hand, when the input voltage is low or when $V_{in} = 0$, the nMOSFET is off since its gate-to-source voltage is zero. The gate-to-source voltage of the pMOSFET, however, is $-V_{dd}$, which turns it on (a negative gate voltage turns on a pMOSFET). The output node is now pulled up to V_{dd} by the conducting pMOSFET. Since the output voltage is always opposite to the input voltage (V_{out} is high when V_{in} is low and vice versa), this circuit is called an inverter. Note that since only one of transistors is on in the steady state, there is no static current or static power dissipation. Power dissipation occurs only during switching transients when a current is flowing through the circuit. By cleverly designing the "switch activities" of the circuits on a chip to minimize active power dissipation, engineers have been able to integrate hundreds of millions of CMOS transistors on a single chip and still have the chip readily air-coolable. Until recently, the integration level of CMOS has not been limited by chip-level power dissipation, but by chip fabrication technology. Another advantage of CMOS circuits comes from the ratioless, full rail-to-rail logic swing, which improves the noise margin and makes a CMOS chip easier to design.

As linear dimensions reached the 0.5-μm level in the early 1990's, the performance advantage of bipolar transistors was outweighed by the significantly greater circuit density of CMOS devices. The system performance benefit of integrated functionality superseded that of raw transistor performance and practically all the VLSI chips in production today are based on CMOS technology. Bipolar transistors are used only where raw circuit speed makes an important difference. Consequently, bipolar transistors are usually used in small-size bipolar-only chips, or in so-called BiCMOS chips where most of the functions are implemented using CMOS transistors and only a relatively small number of circuits are implemented using bipolar transistors.

Advances in lithography and etching technologies have enabled the industry to scale down transistors in physical dimensions, and to pack more transistors in the same chip area. Such progress, combined with a steady growth in chip size, resulted in an exponential growth in the number of transistors and memory bits per chip. The recent trends and future projections in these areas are illustrated in Fig. 3. Dynamic random access memories (DRAMs) have characteristically contained the highest component count of any IC chips. This has been so because of the small size of the one-transistor memory cell, and because of the large and often insatiable demand for more memory in computing systems.

One remarkable feature of silicon devices that fuels the rapid growth of the information technology industry is that their speed increases and their cost decreases as their size is reduced. The transistors manufactured today are 20 times faster and occupy less than 1% of the area of those built 20 years ago. This is illustrated in the trend of microprocessor units (MPUs) in Fig. 3. The increase in the clock frequency of microprocessors is the result of a combination of improvements in microprocessor architecture and improvements in transistor speed.

This article reviews the state-of-the-art CMOS device principles and design issues that lie at the heart of modern computer technology. Section 2 starts with the basic MOSFET scaling theory and discusses the fundamental nonscaling factors that have had a profound impact on CMOS evolution. Section 3 examines the key device issues facing today's sub-0.25-μm CMOS generations. Section 4 describes a feasible design for 25-nm CMOS, likely to

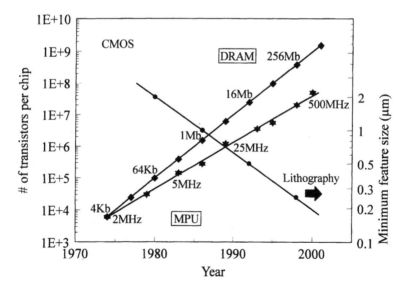

FIG. 3. Trends in lithographic feature size, number of transistors per chip for DRAM and microprocessor chips.

be near the limit of CMOS scaling. Section 5 addresses the interconnect issues and discusses the strategies where wire delays will not limit the performance of a CMOS VLSI chip.

2. MOSFET Scaling Theory

CMOS technology evolution in the past 20 years has followed the path of device scaling for achieving density, speed, and power improvements. Elementary theory [4] tells us that MOSFET transconductance per device width increases with shorter channel lengths, i.e., with reduced source-to-drain spacing. The intrinsic capacitance of a short-channel MOSFET is also lower, making it easier to switch. However, for a given process, channel length cannot be arbitrarily reduced even if allowed by lithography because of the short-channel effect. For digital applications, the most undesirable short-channel effect is a reduction in the gate threshold voltage at which the device turns on, especially at high drain voltages. Full realization of the benefits of the new high-resolution lithographic techniques therefore requires the development of new device designs, technologies, and structures that can be optimized to keep short-channel effects under control at very small dimensions.

2.1   Constant-Field Scaling

In constant field scaling [5], it was proposed that one can keep short-channel effect under control by scaling down the vertical dimensions, e.g., gate insulator thickness and junction depth, along with the horizontal dimensions, while also proportionally decreasing the applied voltages and increasing the substrate-doping concentration (decreasing the depletion width). This is shown schematically in Fig. 4. The principle of constant-field scaling lies in scaling the device voltages and the device dimensions (both horizontal and vertical) by the same factor, κ (>1), such that the electric field (**E**) remains unchanged. This assures that the reliability of the scaled device is not worse than the original device.

2.1.1   Rules for constant-field scaling

Table I shows the scaling rules for various device parameters and circuit performance factors. Doping concentration N_a must be increased by the scaling factor, κ, in order to keep Poisson's equation, $\nabla \cdot \mathbf{E} = -q N_a / \varepsilon_{si}$,

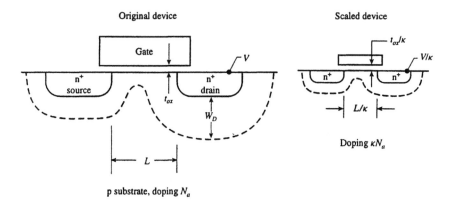

FIG. 4. Principles of MOSFET constant-electric-field scaling.

TABLE I

SCALING OF MOSFET DEVICE AND CIRCUIT PARAMETERS

	MOSFET device and circuit parameters	Multiplicative factor ($\kappa > 1$)
Scaling assumptions	Device dimensions (t_{ox}, L, W, x_j)	$1/\kappa$
	Doping concentration (N_a, N_d)	κ
	Voltage (V)	$1/\kappa$
Derived scaling behavior of device parameters	Electric field (E)	1
	Carrier velocity v	1
	Depletion layer width (W_d)	$1/\kappa$
	Capacitance ($C = \varepsilon A/t$)	$1/\kappa$
	Inversion layer charge density (Q_i)	1
	Current, drift (I)	$1/\kappa$
	Channel resistance (R_{ch})	1
Derived scaling behavior of circuit parameters	Circuit delay time ($\tau \sim CV/I$)	$1/\kappa$
	Power dissipation per circuit ($P \sim VI$)	$1/\kappa^2$
	Power-delay product per circuit ($P \times \tau$)	$1/\kappa^3$
	Circuit density ($\propto 1/A$)	κ^2
	Power density (P/A)	1

invariant with respect to scaling. Here ε_{si} is the permittivity of silicon and q is the electronic charge. The maximum drain depletion width,

$$W_D = \sqrt{\frac{2\varepsilon_{si}(\psi_{bi} + V_{dd})}{qN_a}}, \tag{1}$$

scales down approximately by κ provided that the power supply voltage, V_{dd}, is much greater than the built-in potential, ψ_{bi}. All capacitances (including wiring load) scale down by κ since they are proportional to area and inversely proportional to thickness. Charge per device ($\sim C \times V$) scales down by κ^2 while the inversion-layer charge density (per unit gate area), Q_i, remains unchanged after scaling. Since the electric field at any given point is unchanged, the carrier velocity ($v = \mu \times E$) at any given point is also unchanged (mobility μ is the same for the same vertical field). Therefore, any velocity saturation effects will be similar in both the original and the scaled devices.

The drift current per MOSFET width,

$$\frac{I_{drift}}{W} = Q_i v = Q_i \mu E, \tag{2}$$

is unchanged with respect to scaling. This means that the drift current scales down by κ, consistent with the behavior of both the linear and the saturation MOSFET currents. A key implicit assumption is that the threshold voltage also scales down by κ. Note that the velocity-saturated current also scales the same way since the saturation velocity is a constant, independent of scaling. However, the diffusion current per MOSFET width,

$$\frac{I_{diff}}{W} = D_n \frac{dQ_i}{dx} = \mu_n \frac{kT}{q} \frac{dQ_i}{dx}, \tag{3}$$

where D_n is the diffusivity and kT the thermal energy, scales up by κ since dQ_i/dx is inversely proportional to channel length. Therefore, the diffusion current does not scale down the same way as the drift current. This has significant implications in the nonscaling of MOSFET subthreshold currents as will be discussed further in Section 3.1.

2.1.2 Effect of scaling on circuit parameters

With both the voltage and the current scaled down by the same factor, it follows that the active channel resistance of the scaled-down device remains unchanged. It is further assumed that parasitic resistance is either negligible or unchanged in scaling. The circuit delay, which is proportional to $R \times C$ or $C \times V/I$, then scales down by κ. This is the most important conclusion of constant-field scaling: once the device dimensions and the power supply voltage are scaled down, the circuit speeds up by the same factor. Moreover, power dissipation per circuit, which is proportional to $V \times I$, is reduced by κ^2. Since the circuit density has increased by κ^2, the power density, i.e., the active power per chip area, remains unchanged in the scaled-down device. This has important technological implications in that, in contrast to bipolar devices, packaging of the scaled CMOS devices does not require more elaborate heat sinking. The power-delay product of the scaled CMOS circuit shows a dramatic improvement by a factor of κ^3 (Table I).

2.2 Constant-Voltage Scaling

Although constant-field scaling provides a basic framework for shrinking CMOS devices to gain higher density and speed without degrading reliability and power, there are several factors that scale neither with the physical dimension nor with the operating voltage. The primary reason for the nonscaling effects is that neither the thermal voltage kT/q nor the silicon bandgap E_g changes with scaling. The former leads to subthreshold nonscaling; i.e., threshold voltage cannot be scaled down like other parameters. The latter leads to nonscalability of built-in potential, depletion layer width, and short-channel effect.

The only mathematically consistent way to keep Poisson's equation and all the boundary conditions invariant is constant-voltage scaling [4]. Under constant-voltage scaling, the electric field scales up by κ and the doping concentration N_a scales up by κ^2. The maximum drain depletion width, Eq. (1), then scales down by κ. Both the power supply voltage and the threshold voltage for a uniformly doped (N_a) MOSFET,

$$V_t = V_{fb} + 2\psi_B + \frac{\sqrt{2\varepsilon_{si}qN_a(2\psi_B + V_{bs})}}{C_{ox}} \tag{4}$$

remain unchanged. Here V_{fb} is the flatband voltage determined by the work function of the gate electrode, $C_{ox} = \varepsilon_{ox}/t_{ox}$ is the gate oxide capacitance per unit area, $2\psi_B$ is the surface potential or band bending at the onset of strong inversion, and V_{bs} is the reverse bias voltage applied to the substrate.

Although constant-voltage scaling leaves the solution of electrostatic potential to 2-D Poisson's equation unchanged except for a constant multiplicative factor of the electric field, it cannot be practiced without limit since the power density increases by a factor of κ^2 to κ^3. Higher fields also cause hot electron and oxide reliability problems. In reality, CMOS

TABLE II

CMOS VLSI TECHNOLOGY GENERATIONS

Feature size (μm)	Power supply voltage (V)	Gate oxide thickness (Å)	Oxide field (MV/cm)
2	5	350	1.4
1.2	5	250	2.0
0.8	5	180·	2.8
0.5	3.3	120	2.8
0.35	3.3	100	3.3
0.25	2.5	70	3.6

technology evolution has followed mixed steps of constant-voltage and constant-field scaling as is evident in Table II, where the supply voltage and device parameters of several generations of CMOS VLSI technology are listed. It is clear that the oxide field has been increasing over the generations rather than staying constant.

2.3   2-D Scale Length Theory

Apart from power and performance factors, the most important aspect of MOSFET scaling is to keep short-channel effects under control. Figure 5 shows the essential 2-D characteristics of a short-channel MOSFET. A key parameter is the gate depletion width, W_d, within which the mobile carriers (holes in the case of nMOSFETs) are swept away by the applied gate field. The gate depletion width reaches a maximum, W_{dm}, at the onset of strong inversion (threshold voltage) when the surface potential or band bending is such that the electron concentration at the surface equals the hole concentration in the bulk substrate ($2\psi_B$ condition). For uniformly doped substrates,

$$W_{dm} = \sqrt{\frac{4\varepsilon_{si}kT \ln(N_a/n_i)}{q^2 N_a}}, \tag{5}$$

where n_i is the intrinsic carrier concentration. A rectangle is formed by the boundary of the gate depletion region, the gate electrode, and the source and drain regions, as depicted in Fig. 5 [6]. Two-dimensional effects can be characterized by the aspect ratio of this rectangle. When the horizontal dimension, i.e., the channel length, is at least twice as long as the vertical dimension, the device behaves like a long-channel

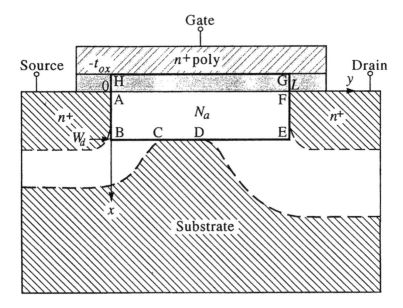

FIG. 5. Simplified geometry for analyzing 2-D effects in a short-channel MOSFET. The white area represents depletion regions where mobile carriers are swept away by the built-in field.

MOSFET with good short-channel behavior. For channel lengths shorter than that, the 2-D effect kicks in and the minimum surface potential that determines the threshold voltage is controlled more by the drain than by the gate.

The rectangular box consists of a silicon region of thickness W_{dm} and an oxide region of thickness t_{ox}. At the interface, the vertical fields (E_x) obey the boundary condition, $\varepsilon_{si}E_{x,si} = \varepsilon_{ox}E_{x,ox}$, where ε_{si}, ε_{ox} are the permittivities of silicon and oxide, respectively. As far as the vertical field is concerned, the oxide region can be replaced by a silicon region with an equivalent thickness of $(\varepsilon_{si}/\varepsilon_{ox})t_{ox}$ [6]. Therefore, for thin gate insulators such as the case with SiO_2, the vertical height of the rectangular box can be approximated by $W_{dm} + (\varepsilon_{si}/\varepsilon_{ox})t_{ox}$, where $\varepsilon_{si}/\varepsilon_{ox} \approx 3$ is the ratio between the dielectric constants of silicon and oxide. This means that the minimum channel length is $L_{min} \approx 2(W_{dm} + 3t_{ox})$ [4]. To scale MOSFETs to shorter channel lengths, it is necessary to scale both W_{dm} and t_{ox} proportionally.

W_{dm} is calculated from Eq. (5) and plotted versus N_a in Fig. 6. To avoid excessive short-channel effects, the substrate (or well) doping concentration

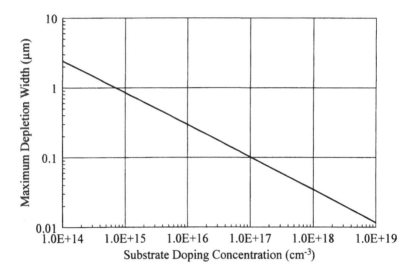

FIG. 6. Depletion region width at $2\psi_B$ threshold condition versus doping concentration for uniformly doped substrates.

in a CMOS device design should be chosen such that the minimum channel length, L_{min}, is about 2–3 times W_{dm}. This is similar to the well-known criterion that the minimum channel length should be greater than the sum of the source and the drain depletion widths. Further details on channel profile and threshold design are discussed in Section 3.4.

The above approximation assumes that the vertical field is the dominant component at the interface between the silicon and the gate insulator. This may not be the case for thick oxides or for high-κ (high dielectric constant) gate insulators that may be needed when the tunneling current through thin oxides becomes prohibitively high (Section 3.2). In principle, high-κ gate insulators can be physically thicker, thus alleviating the tunneling problem, while still delivering the same field effect or gate capacitance measured by the ratio ε_i/t_i, where ε_i and t_i are the permittivity and the thickness of the insulator film. The above 1-D boundary condition for vertical fields is sufficient for describing a long-channel device. In short-channel devices, however, 2-D effects are important and one must take both the lateral and the vertical fields into account.

For lateral fields (E_y) tangential to the interface, the boundary condition is $E_{y,si} = E_{y,ox}$, independent of the dielectric constants. By properly matching the boundary conditions of both components of electric fields at the silicon–insulator interface, one can derive a scale length λ that is a solution to the equation [7]

$$\varepsilon_{si} \tan(\pi t_i/\lambda) + \varepsilon_i \tan(\pi W_{dm}/\lambda) = 0, \tag{6}$$

where W_{dm} again is the depth of the depletion region in silicon. λ also goes into the length-dependent term of the maximum potential barrier in a MOSFET of channel length L: $\propto \exp(-\pi L/2\lambda)$ [6]. The ratio L/λ is a good measure of how strong the 2-D effect is. For the short-channel V_t rolloff and the drain-induced barrier lowering (DIBL) to be acceptable, the above exponential factor must be much less than 1, which means the minimum useful channel length is about 1.5–2.0 times λ.

Equation (6) must be solved numerically for λ. The results for Si–SiO$_2$, i.e., $\varepsilon_{si}/\varepsilon_i = 3$, is shown as constant λ contours in a t_i–W_{dm} plane in Fig. 7. For the large depletion depth regime, $t_i/\lambda \ll 1$ applies and Eq. (6) can be approximately solved as $\lambda \approx W_{dm} + (\varepsilon_{si}/\varepsilon_i)t_i$, which is the result based on 1-D vertical fields discussed before. This corresponds well to the $\lambda = 75$ nm case in Fig. 7, but note that the slope of the contours increases dramatically for shorter scale lengths, $\lambda < 30$ nm, indicating a significant departure from the simple case. This increased slope may be beneficial to highly scaled MOSFETs, since it implies that the penalty for using insufficiently scaled

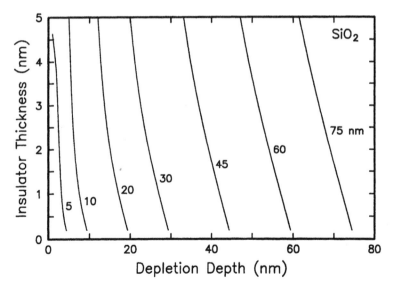

FIG. 7. Plot of constant λ contours in a t_i–W_{dm} plane for $\varepsilon_{si}/\varepsilon_i = 3$, i.e., $\varepsilon_i = 3.9$. Each curve is labeled by its λ value.

oxide thickness is less than might have been expected, although it also corresponds to the degraded subthreshold slope. Equation (6) can also be approximated in the opposite extreme, when $W_{dm}/\lambda \ll 1$, in which case $\lambda \approx t_i + (\varepsilon_i/\varepsilon_{si})W_{dm}$. This regime is beginning to appear in the upper left corner of Fig. 7.

The dependence of the scale length λ on the dielectric constant of the gate insulator is shown in Fig. 8 [7]. The curve is calculated for $W_{dm} = 15$ nm and for a constant ε_i/t_i, i.e., for the same $t_{ox}^{eq} \equiv (\varepsilon_{ox}/\varepsilon_i)t_i$ (= 1 nm). When $\varepsilon_i < \varepsilon_{si}$ ($= 11.7\varepsilon_0$) and $t_i \ll W_{dm}$, an approximate solution is, again, $\lambda \approx W_{dm} + (\varepsilon_{si}/\varepsilon_i)t_i$, dominated by W_{dm}. When $\varepsilon_i \gg \varepsilon_{si}$, however, λ starts to increase for a given t_{ox}^{eq}, indicating that the lateral field is becoming important. This suggests that it is undesirable from the scale length point of view to develop very-high-permittivity insulators for MOSFETs unless the equivalent oxide thicknesses are very thin. Thicker, high-permittivity layers almost always result in increased minimum channel length for MOSFETs, especially for those with the most aggressively scaled depletion depth. On the other hand, an insulator with $\varepsilon_i/\varepsilon_0 \approx 10$ appears quite ideal. In the extreme limit of very high ε_i and t_i, $\lambda \approx t_i + (\varepsilon_i/\varepsilon_{si})W_{dm}$, limited by the physical thickness of the gate insulator, regardless of its dielectric constant. This shows that even for ultra-high-κ gate insulators, the physical film thickness must be kept to less than half of the channel length to be useful.

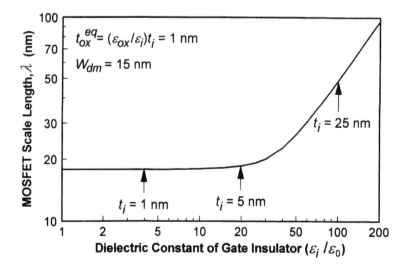

FIG. 8. Plot of scale length λ versus dielectric constant $(\varepsilon_i/\varepsilon_0)$ for an equivalent oxide thickness $(\varepsilon_{ox}/\varepsilon_i)t_i$ of 1 nm and a silicon depletion depth W_{dm} of 15 nm, where ε_0 is the permittivity of free space, and ε_{ox} is that of SiO_2.

3.   CMOS Device Issues Below 0.25 μm

When the CMOS channel length scales to below 0.25 μm, the nonscaling factors discussed in Section 2.2 start to have a major effect on device design. It becomes necessary to trade off between performance and power. The choice of device parameters is dependent on the application and product needs. For microprocessor technologies, performance gain is usually the overriding factor, in contrast to power and density factors for memory chips.

3.1   Power Supply and Threshold Voltage

Because of subthreshold (diffusion) current nonscaling and reluctance to depart from the standardized voltage levels of the previous generation, the power supply voltage was seldom scaled in proportion to channel length. In fact, the field has been gradually rising over the generations rather than staying constant. This trend can be clearly seen in Table II and Fig. 9 where power supply voltage (V_{dd}), threshold voltage (V_t), and gate oxide thickness (t_{ox}) are plotted as a function of MOSFET channel length [8]. High electric field can lead to a number of deleterious effects, such as hot-carrier injection into gate oxide and electromigration resulting from the increased current density, that could impact chip reliability. More importantly, a higher-than-scaled voltage level drives up the active power of a CMOS chip, which is given by (crossover currents are usually negligible)

$$P_{ac} = C_{sw} V_{dd}^2 f, \tag{7}$$

where C_{sw} is the total node capacitance being charged and discharged in a clock cycle, and f is the clock frequency. As CMOS technology advances, clock frequency goes up. The total switching capacitance is likely to increase as well, as one tries to integrate more circuits into the same or even larger chip area. The active power of today's high-performance microprocessors is already in the 50-W range. Besides power management systems with architectural innovation, the most effective way to curb the growth of active power is to reduce the power supply voltage.

3.1.1   Threshold voltage nonscaling

Threshold voltage deviates from the ideal scaling behavior even farther than the power supply voltage, as seen in Fig. 9. MOSFET threshold voltage is defined as the gate voltage at which significant current starts to flow from the source to the drain (Fig. 10). Below the threshold voltage,

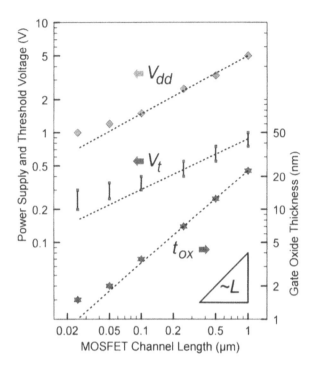

FIG. 9. History and trends of power supply voltage (V_{dd}), threshold voltage (V_t), and gate-oxide thickness (t_{ox}) versus channel length for CMOS logic technologies.

the current does not drop immediately to 0. Rather, it decreases exponentially with a slope on the logarithmic scale inversely proportional to the thermal energy kT. This is because some of the thermally distributed electrons at the source of the transistor have high enough energy to overcome the potential barrier controlled by the gate voltage and flow to the drain (Fig. 10, inset). Such a subthreshold behavior follows directly from fundamental thermodynamics and is independent of power supply voltage and channel length.

The standby power of a CMOS chip is given by [4]

$$P_{off} = W_{tot} V_{dd} I_{off} = W_{tot} V_{dd} I_0 \exp\left(-\frac{qV_t}{mkT}\right), \qquad (8)$$

where W_{tot} is the total turned-off device width with V_{dd} across it, I_{off} is the average off-current per device width at 100°C (worst-case temperature), I_0

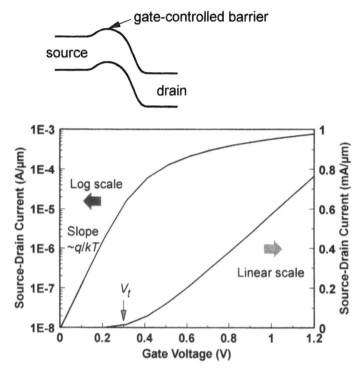

FIG. 10. MOSFET current in both logarithmic (left) and linear (right) scales versus gate voltage. Inset shows the band diagram of an nMOSFET.

is the extrapolated current per width at threshold voltage (on the order of $1-10$ $\mu A/\mu m$ for 0.1-μm devices), m is a dimensionless body-effect coefficient typically ≈ 1.2, and V_t is the threshold voltage at $100°C$. Even if V_t is kept constant, the leakage current of turned-off devices would increase in proportion to $1/t_{ox}$ and (W_{tot}/L) because the current at threshold condition I_0 is proportional to the inversion charge density at threshold, $Q_i \sim (1-2)(kT/q)C_{ox}$. The off-state leakage current would further increase by about $10\times$ for every 0.1-V reduction of V_t. Fortunately, the leakage current and therefore the standby power is quite low in today's CMOS chips. This allows some room for a slightly downward trend of V_t as shown in Fig. 9. For a chip with an integration level of 100 million transistors, the average leakage current of turned-off devices should not exceed a few times 10^{-8} A. This constraint bounds the threshold voltage to a minimum of about ~ 0.2 V at the operating temperature ($100°C$ worst case).

3.1.2 Power vs performance tradeoff

The increasing V_t/V_{dd} ratio in Fig. 9 means a loss of gate overdrive that degrades CMOS circuit performance gained from scaling. Figure 11 plots the relative CMOS performance ($\propto 1/\text{delay}$) as a function of V_t/V_{dd}. The dependence can be fitted by a function, $0.7 - V_t/V_{dd}$, which is stronger than that of the on current ($\propto 1 - V_t/V_{dd}$) because of the finite rise time of the driving stage [4]. Since V_t cannot be reduced below 0.2 V and since CMOS performance is a sensitive function of the V_t/V_{dd} ratio, there is very little performance to gain by scaling the power supply voltage to significantly below 1 V.

The above considerations can be represented in general as tradeoffs between power and performance in a power supply voltage–threshold voltage design plane (Fig. 12). Performance is gained at the expense of higher active power or higher standby power or both. For high-performance CMOS, power supply voltage will be decreased more slowly than the historical trend (Fig. 9), leading to higher chip power and more aggressive device designs at higher electric fields. For low-power applications, like in handheld wireless units, threshold voltage will not be reduced as aggressively and the supply voltage can be further scaled

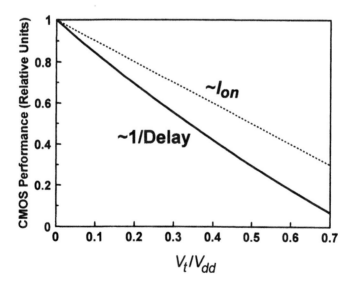

FIG. 11. Relative CMOS performance ($\propto 1/\text{delay}$) as a function of V_t/V_{dd}. The dependence can be fitted by a function, $0.7 - V_t/V_{dd}$, which is stronger than that of the on current ($\propto 1 - V_t/V_{dd}$).

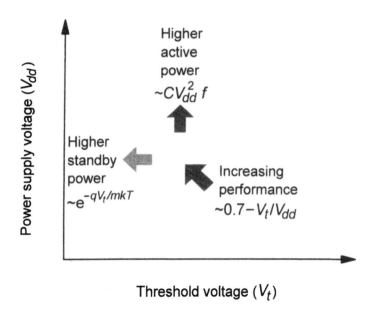

FIG. 12. Relative trends of CMOS performance, active power, and standby power in a V_{dd}–V_t design plane.

down with significant savings in the power-delay product. This is demonstrated in Fig. 13 where the power per device of a 0.1-μm CMOS ring oscillator is plotted versus the gate delay by varying the power supply voltage [9]. Near the high-performance design point ($V_{dd} = 1.5$ V) discussed above, a 10% lower performance can bring in 30–40% savings in active power.

There are other schemes for meeting leakage power requirements. For example, one can fabricate multiple-threshold-voltage devices on a chip. Low-threshold devices could be used in critical logic paths for speed, while high-threshold devices would be used everywhere else, including memory arrays, for low standby power. One can also sense the circuit activity and cut off the power supply to logic blocks that are not switching—an approach known as sleep mode. Other possibilities include dynamic-threshold devices for which the threshold voltage is controlled by a backgate bias voltage in either bulk or silicon-on-insulator device structures. Yet another option is low-temperature CMOS. Low-temperature operation not only steepens the subthreshold slope and improves mobility, but also reduces wire resistance. However, all of these solutions will generally carry a cost in density and complexity.

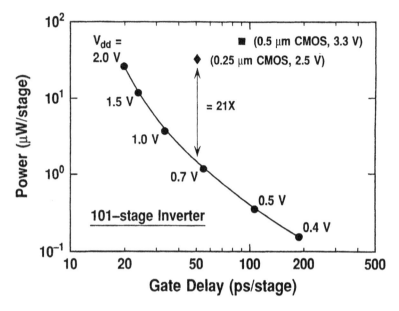

FIG. 13. Measured power per stage versus gate delay of a 0.1-μm CMOS ring oscillator with V_{dd} as a variable. The device widths are $W_n = 3$ μm, $W_p = 4$ μm.

3.2   Gate Oxide

To keep adverse 2-D electrostatic effects on threshold voltage (short-channel effect) under control, gate oxide thickness is reduced nearly in proportion to channel length as shown in Fig. 9. This is necessary in order for the gate to retain more control over the channel than the drain. A simple rule is that gate-oxide thickness needs to be about 1/50 to 1/25 of channel length [4]. For CMOS devices with channel lengths of 100 nm or shorter, an oxide thickness of < 3 nm is needed. This thickness consists of only a few layers of atoms and is approaching fundamental limits. While it is amazing that SiO_2 can carry us this far without being limited by extrinsic factors such as defect density, surface roughness, or large-scale thickness and uniformity control, oxide films this thin are subject to quantum mechanical tunneling, giving rise to a gate leakage current that increases exponentially as the oxide thickness is scaled down. Tunneling currents for oxide thicknesses ranging from 3.6 to 1.0 nm are plotted versus gate voltage in Fig. 14 [10]. In the direct tunneling regime, the current is rather insensitive to the applied voltage or field across the oxide, so a reduced voltage operation will not offer much relief. Although the gate leakage current may be at a level negligible compared with the on-state current of a device, it will first have an

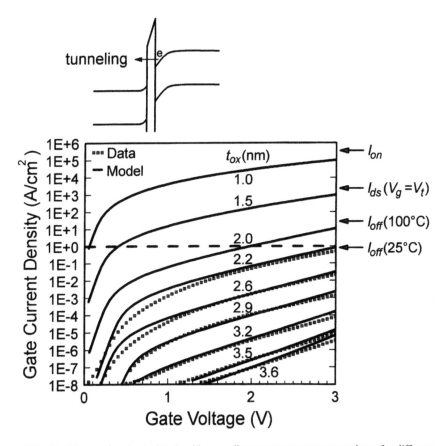

FIG. 14. Measured and calculated oxide tunneling currents versus gate voltage for different oxide thicknesses. Inset shows the band diagram for tunneling in a turned-on nMOSFET.

effect on the chip standby power. Note that the leakage power will be dominated by turned-on nMOSFETs in which electrons tunnel from the silicon inversion layer to the positively biased gate (Fig. 14, inset). Edge tunneling in the gate-to-drain overlap region of turned-off devices should not be a fundamental issue as one can always build up the corner oxide thickness by additional oxidation of polysilicon after gate patterning. pMOSFETs have a much lower leakage than nMOSFETs because there are very few electrons in the p^+ poly gate available for tunneling to the substrate and hole tunneling has a much lower probability. If one assumes that the total active gate area per chip is on the order of 0.1 cm^2, the maximum tolerable gate leakage current would be on the order of 1–10 A/cm^2. This sets a lower limit of about 1.5 nm for the gate oxide thickness. Dynamic memory devices have a more stringent leakage requirement and therefore a thicker limit on gate oxide.

Another quantum phenomenon that becomes prominent for such a thin oxide and high surface vertical field is the inversion layer quantization effect depicted in Fig. 15. With the inversion electrons confined to a thin layer of 1–2 nm thick, the allowed energy states consist of subbands displaced upward from the bottom of the conduction band [11]. This has a twofold effect on MOSFET characteristics. First, it takes more band bending and therefore a higher gate voltage to populate the lowest subband with inversion electrons. Second, the center of mass of the inversion charge distribution is farther away from the surface than that of the classical model (Fig. 15, inset). This means less inversion charge induced per gate voltage swing, in other words, lower gate capacitance, and therefore lower transconductance. The effect is equivalent to adding about 0.4 nm to the gate oxide thickness when the MOSFET is on. Even though it has been present in previous technologies, the effect is more acute when the physical oxide thickness is scaled to below 3–4 nm. Note that the inversion layer quantization effect has no bearing in the subthreshold region when the MOSFET is off and the gate capacitance is dominated by the depletion charge.

3.3 Gate Electrode

To achieve low-threshold voltages for both nMOS and pMOS devices in a CMOS chip, dual n^+ and p^+ polysilicon gates are still required (Fig. 1), despite their shortcomings in conductivity and depletion effects. This is because threshold voltages are dictated by the gate work functions, as seen in Eq. (4). A midgap work function metal gate, while free of depletion effects, would either result in threshold magnitudes too high for both devices or require compensating doping of the channel, leading to buried channel operation with poor short-channel characteristics.

A frequently raised concern with doped poly gates is the effect of poly depletion on CMOS performance. Depletion effects occur in polysilicon in the form of a thin space charge layer near the gate oxide interface, which acts to reduce the gate capacitance and inversion charge density for a given gate drive [12]. The percentage of gate capacitance attenuation becomes more significant as the oxide thickness is scaled down. Since the width of the poly depletion layer is not a constant, but depends on both the gate voltage and the potential along the channel, treating it as an equivalent oxide layer will substantially overestimate its effect. It is misleading to lump both the poly depletion effect and the inversion layer quantization

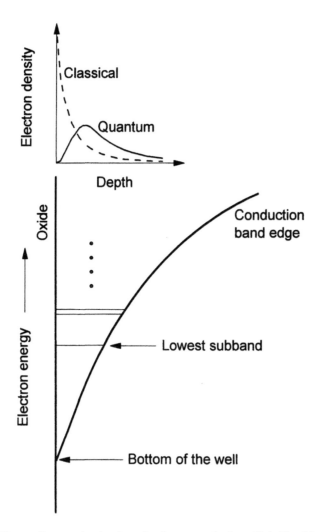

FIG. 15. Energy diagram showing inversion layer quantization effect. The thin horizontal lines indicate the bottom of the allowed subbands for electrons confined in the potential well. Top inset compares the electron distribution between the classical and quantum mechanical models.

effect into a single parameter (t_{inv}). The net performance loss due to polysilicon depletion effects is actually much less severe than that suggested by the small signal MOS capacitance measurements. In fact, the delay of intrinsic, unloaded circuits is hardly affected, because while poly depletion degrades the drive current, it is nearly offset by the fact that the charge needed for the next stage is also reduced. A careful analysis of the performance loss due to the poly depletion effect is presented in Section 4.

3.4   Channel Profile Design

3.4.1   Retrograde doping

Various vertically nonuniform doping profiles, such as high–low and low–high, have been employed in previous CMOS generations to tailor both the gate depletion depth and the threshold magnitude simultaneously (Fig. 16) [13]. As discussed in Section 2.3, to scale down MOSFET channel length without excessive short-channel effect, both the oxide thickness and the gate-controlled depletion width in silicon (W_{dm}, Eq. (5)) must be reduced in proportion to L. The latter requires increased doping concentration, which, for a uniformly doped channel, leads to a higher depletion charge and electric field at the silicon surface. These in turn cause the potential across the oxide and therefore the threshold voltage, Eq. (4), to go up. To reduce the gate-controlled depletion width while fulfilling the V_t-reduction trend depicted in Fig. 9, a retrograde, i.e., low–high, channel doping is needed below the 0.25-μm channel length [4]. Figure 17 shows a schematic band-bending diagram at the threshold condition for a uniformly doped and an extreme retrograde profile with an undoped surface layer of thickness x_s. For the same gate depletion width (W_{dm}), the surface electric field and the total depletion charge of an extreme retrograde channel is one-half of that of a uniformly doped channel. This reduces the threshold voltage and improves mobility.

Retrograde channel doping represents a vertically nonuniform profile that allows the threshold voltage to decouple from the gate-controlled depletion width (W_{dm}, Eq. (5)). However, the body-effect coefficient, $m = 1 + (\varepsilon_{si}/W_{dm})/(\varepsilon_{ox}/t_{ox}) \approx 1 + (3t_{ox}/W_{dm})$, and with it the inverse subthreshold slope, $(\ln 10)(mkT/q)$, are still coupled to the gate depletion width W_{dm}. The sensitivity of threshold voltage to substrate bias, measured by $m - 1$, is usually referred to as the body effect. Body effect tends to degrade MOSFET currents when the source-to-substrate junction is reverse-biased. For a given t_{ox}, reduction in W_{dm} improves the short-channel effect (measured by $L_{min} \approx 2(W_{dm} + 3t_{ox})$), but compromises substrate sensitivity and subthreshold slope. Since both the inverse subthreshold slope, $2.3mkT/q$, and the substrate sensitivity, $dV_t/dV_{bs} = m - 1$, degrade with higher m, m should be kept close to 1. A larger m also results in a lower saturation current in nonvelocity-saturated devices [4]. Another issue is that

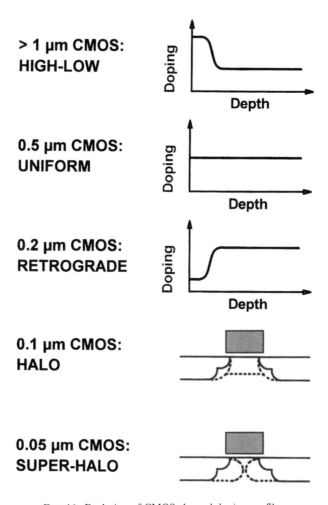

> 1 µm CMOS:
HIGH-LOW

0.5 µm CMOS:
UNIFORM

0.2 µm CMOS:
RETROGRADE

0.1 µm CMOS:
HALO

0.05 µm CMOS:
SUPER-HALO

FIG. 16. Evolution of CMOS channel doping profiles.

once the extreme retrograde limit (Fig. 17) is reached, further reduction of W_{dm} may drive V_t up to unacceptable values (unless some extraordinarily sharp counterdoping can be realized). Typically, one requires $m < 1.5$, or $3t_{ox}/W_{dm} < 1/2$. The above design considerations are illustrated in Fig. 18 [4]. The lower limit of t_{ox} is imposed by technology constraints to V_{dd}/E_{ox}^{max}, where E_{ox}^{max} is the maximum oxide field. For a given L and V_{dd}, the allowable parameter space in a $t_{ox} - W_{dm}$ design plane is a triangular area bounded by SCE, the oxide field, and the subthreshold slope (also substrate sensitivity) requirements.

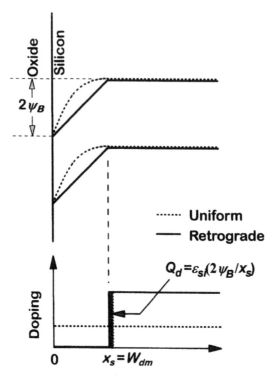

FIG. 17. Band diagrams at the threshold condition for a uniformly doped and an extreme retrograde-doped channel (profiles shown below).

3.4.2 Halo doping

Halo doping or nonuniform channel profile in the lateral direction was introduced below 0.2 μm to provide yet another degree of freedom that can be tailored to further minimize V_t tolerances due to short-channel effects (Fig. 16). Such a profile can be realized by angled ion implantation self-aligned to the gate with a very restricted amount of diffusion. The highly nonuniform profile sets up a higher effective doping concentration toward shorter devices, which counteracts short-channel effects. This results in off-currents insensitive to channel length variations and allows CMOS scaling to the shortest channel length possible. Because of the flat V_t dependence on channel length, superhalo permits a nominal device to operate at a lower threshold voltage, thereby gaining significant performance benefit. The halo doping level is ultimately limited by band-to-band tunneling currents in the high-field region near the drain.

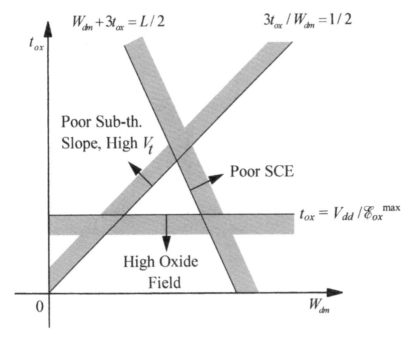

FIG. 18. A $t_{ox}-W_{dm}$ design plane. Some tradeoff among the various factors can be made within the parameter space bounded by SCE, subthreshold slope, and oxide field considerations.

3.5   Source–Drain Doping Requirements

As the CMOS channel length is scaled down, the lateral doping profile of source and drain junctions should also sharpen in step and be kept abrupt on the scale of a fraction of the channel length. Otherwise, short-channel effects degrade rapidly. This is because channel length is largely set by the points of current injection from the surface inversion layer into the bulk, as illustrated in the simple 1-D current model in Fig. 19 [4]. When the gate voltage is high enough to turn on the nMOSFET channel, an n^+ surface accumulation layer is also formed in the gate-to-source or -drain overlap region [14]. Current flow out of the inversion channel stays in the accumulation layer near the surface until the local source–drain doping becomes high enough that the bulk conductance exceeds that of the accumulation layer. The region where the current flows predominantly in the accumulation layer is considered as a part of the effective channel length. The injection points occur inside the source and drain regions at a doping concentration on the order of 10^{19} cm^{-3} [15]. Any source–drain doping that extends beyond this point into the channel tends

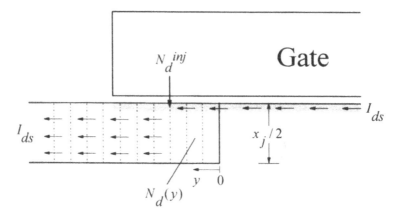

FIG. 19. Schematic diagram of a simple 1-D model for current injection from the surface into the bulk. As far as the resistance is concerned, the source or drain region is modeled as uniform stripes of doping concentration $N_d(y)$ and width $x_j/2$.

to compensate or counterdope the channel region and aggravate the short-channel effect.

This has significant implications on the short-channel V_t rolloff, as illustrated in Fig. 20 where the net doping concentration $(N_d - N_a)$ at the surface is plotted along the channel length direction for various source–drain profiles [15]. For a given L_{eff} or L_{inj} ($= 0.1\ \mu\mathrm{m}$), the distance between the points where the doping concentration falls to N_d^{inj} ($= 8 \times 10^{18}\ \mathrm{cm}^{-3}$ in this case) is fixed. It is clear that the more graded the source–drain profile is, the deeper the n-type doping tail penetrates into the channel and compensates or reverses the p-type doping inside the channel. This is detrimental to the short-channel effect as the edge regions become more easily depleted and inverted by the source and drain fields (opposite to the *halo* effect). It is therefore essential to reduce the lateral width of the graded source–drain region as the channel length is scaled down [16].

3.6   Dopant Number Fluctuations

As CMOS devices are scaled down, the number of dopant atoms in the depletion region of a minimum geometry device decreases. Due to the discreteness of atoms, there is a statistical random fluctuation of the number of dopants within a given volume around its average value. For example, in a uniformly doped $W = L = 100$ nm nMOSFET, if $N_a = 10^{18}\ \mathrm{cm}^{-3}$ and $W_{\mathrm{dm}} = 35$ nm, the average number of acceptor atoms in the depletion region is $N = N_a L W W_{\mathrm{dm}} = 350$. The actual number fluctuates from device to

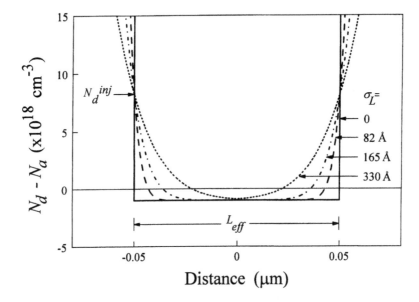

FIG. 20. Net n-type concentration along the surface of a 0.1-μm (L_{eff}) nMOSFET versus lateral distance from the source to the drain. The injection points (N_d^{inj}) are kept the same for all four cases of different lateral doping gradients.

device with a standard deviation $\sigma_N = \langle (\Delta N)^2 \rangle^{1/2} = N^{1/2} = 18.7$, which is a significant fraction of the average number N. Since the threshold voltage of a MOSFET depends on the charge of ionized dopants in the depletion region (last term in Eq. (4)), this translates into a threshold voltage fluctuation that could impact the operation of VLSI circuits.

The effects of discrete random dopants become more important as the channel length and width are scaled down. The uncertainty due to discrete random dopants for a uniform channel doping N_a can be shown analytically to be [4]

$$\sigma_{Vt} = \frac{q}{C_{\mathrm{ox}}} \sqrt{\frac{N_a W_{\mathrm{dm}}}{3LW}}. \tag{9}$$

In the above 100-nm example, $\sigma_{Vt} = 17.5$ mV if $t_{\mathrm{ox}} = 3.5$ nm. This is small compared with the typical threshold voltage uncertainty due to short-channel effects, but could be significant in minimum geometry devices, for example, in an SRAM cell.

Threshold voltage fluctuations due to discrete dopants are greatly reduced in a retrograde-doped channel. Consider the extreme retrograde-doped channel in Fig. 17 where $W_{dm} = x_s$, the width of the undoped region. All of the depletion charge is located at the edge of the heavily doped region with a magnitude $Q_d = \varepsilon_{si}(2\psi_B/x_s)$, independent of the doping concentration of that region (once it is high enough) [17]. This essentially eliminates the effect of dopant number fluctuations on the threshold voltage. Of course, the technological challenge is then on controlling the tolerance of the undoped layer thickness x_s so that it does not introduce a different kind of threshold voltage variation.

4. 25-nm CMOS Design

From the discussions in Section 3, CMOS design options below 0.1 μm are severely constrained by fundamental issues of oxide tunneling and voltage nonscaling. In this section, the limit of CMOS scaling is explored and a feasible design is presented for 25-nm (channel length) bulk CMOS [18], without continued scaling of oxide thickness and power supply voltage. Key issues, such as gate work function, channel and source–drain doping requirements, poly depletion effect, dopant fluctuations, and nonequilibrium carrier transport in 25-nm CMOS, are addressed.

4.1   Short-Channel Device Design

While straight 2-D scaling calls for a gate oxide thinner than 1 nm for 25-nm MOSFETs, direct tunneling leakage in oxide/nitride gate insulators will limit the equivalent gate oxide thickness to 1.5 nm [10]. To maintain adequate off-currents for an integration level of 10^8–10^9 devices per chip, the threshold voltage must be kept at a minimum value of 0.2 V under the worst-case conditions. A suitable choice of the power supply voltage is 1.0 V, as a reasonable tradeoff among active power, device performance, and high-field effects. With the nonscaled gate oxide and supply voltage, an optimized, vertically and laterally nonuniform doping profile, called the *superhalo* [17], is needed to control the short-channel effect. Figure 21 shows such a doping profile, along with simulated potential contours for a 25-nm MOSFET [18]. The highly nonuniform profile tends to offset short-channel effects, yielding I_{off} independent of channel length variations between 20 and 30 nm (Fig. 22). The superior short-channel effect obtained with the superhalo is shown in Fig. 23, compared with a nonhalo retrograde profile. It is possible to adjust the retrograde profile, with only vertical nonuniformity, to yield similar I_{off} and I_{on} at the minimum channel length of 20 nm as the superhalo profile. However, at the nominal channel length of 25 nm, the threshold voltage for

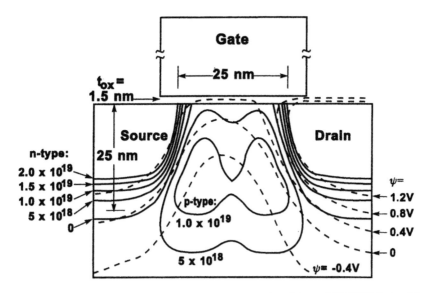

FIG. 21. Source, drain, and superhalo doping contours in a 25-nm nMOSFET design. The channel length is defined by the points where the source–drain doping concentration falls to 2×10^{19} cm^{-3}. The dashed lines show the potential contours for zero gate voltage and a drain bias of 1.0 V. $\psi = 0$ refers to the midgap energy level of the substrate.

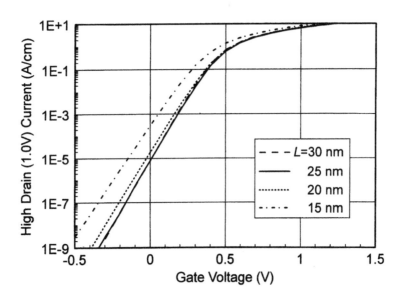

FIG. 22. Simulated subthreshold currents for channel lengths from 30 to 15 nm with a superhalo profile. $I_{off} = 10^{-5}$ A/cm (1 nA/μm) for 20-, 25-, and 30-nm devices. $t_{ox} = 1.5$ nm is assumed.

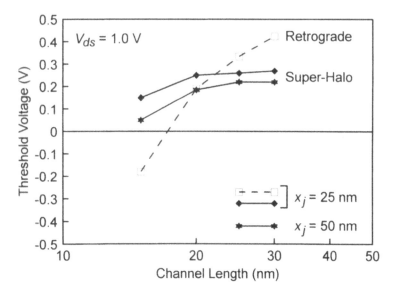

FIG. 23. Short-channel threshold rolloff for superhalo and retrograde (nonhalo) doping profiles. Threshold voltage is defined as the gate voltage where $I_{ds} = 1\ \mu A/\mu m$.

the retrograde profile quickly goes up, degrading CMOS delays as prescribed in Fig. 11. In contrast, the superhalo allows the nominal device to operate at a lower threshold voltage, thereby gaining significant performance benefit: 30–40% over nonhalo devices as shown in Fig. 24. Note that CMOS delay is largely a function of the high-drain threshold voltage. Drain-induced barrier lowering—the difference between the low-drain and high-drain threshold voltages—while still present in superhalo devices, has only a minor effect on the delay performance.

4.2   Source–Drain Doping Requirements

Figure 23 also shows that the V_t rolloff in the superhalo case is rather insensitive to the vertical junction depth, with only a slight change when the junction depth is doubled from 25 to 50 nm for the same halo profile. This points to a way out of the high-resistance problem associated with very shallow extensions [19]. The lateral source–drain gradient, however, is much more critical, as can be seen in Fig. 25, which shows that short-channel effect degrades rapidly once the profile is more graded than 4–5 nm/decade. This can be understood from the discussions in Section 3.5 and Figs. 19 and 20. The abruptness requirements of both the source–drain

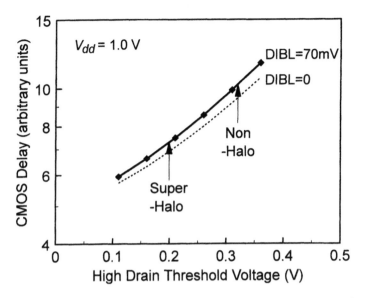

FIG. 24. CMOS delay (relative) versus high-drain threshold voltage. Nonhalo devices must operate at a higher V_t to ensure low I_{off} of the worst-case device.

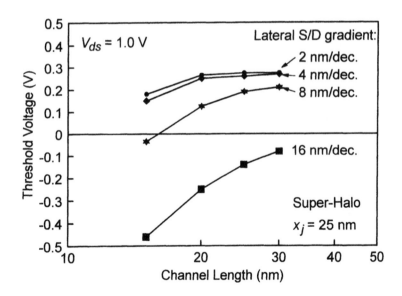

FIG. 25. Effect of lateral source–drain doping gradient on short-channel effect.

and the halo doping profiles dictate absolutely minimum thermal cycles after the implants. Note that a raised source–drain structure may help making contacts, but does not by itself satisfy the abruptness requirement discussed here.

One of the concerns with the high p-type doping level and narrow depletion regions in Fig. 21 is the band-to-band tunneling through the high-field region between the p-type halo and the drain. Figure 26 plots the calculated tunneling current density as a function of the electric field, along with published data on the reverse leakage current of n^{++}/p^+ diodes [20, 21]. For the peak field intensity at high drain and zero gate biases shown in Fig. 21, the tunneling current density is on the order of 1 A/cm². This should not constitute a major component of the device leakage current, given the narrow width of the high-field region. If necessary, the peak field can be further reduced by trading off with a more graded source–drain profile, and/or by applying a forward bias to the p-type substrate to lower the potential difference across the drain junction.

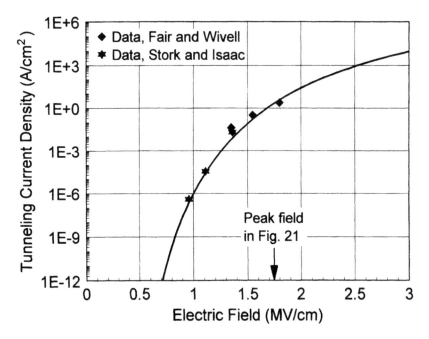

FIG. 26. Band-to-band tunneling current density (normalized to a junction voltage of 1 V) versus electric field. The arrow indicates the maximum field strength under the off condition in Fig. 21.

4.3   Polysilicon-Gate Depletion Effects

The threshold design in Fig. 23 assumes dual n^+/p^+ Si work function gates for nMOS/pMOS, respectively. A midgap work function metal gate would clearly result in threshold voltage magnitudes far too high for both devices [4]. However, with doped poly gates, one must address the effect of poly depletion on CMOS performance. A time-dependent (mixed mode) 2-D device model is used to simulate CMOS inverter delays with and without poly depletion [4]. Figure 27 compares the simulated on-currents between a poly-gated and a metal-gated device with the same channel doping profile. The threshold voltage is adjusted so that both devices have the same off-current. While typical C-V data of 1.5-nm oxides show about 40% less capacitance at inversion than that of the physical oxide, the currents are degraded by only 10–20%. One of the reasons is that part of the capacitance loss comes from quantum mechanical effect in the inversion layer, which is present regardless of the gate material [10]. Another factor is that not all of the poly depletion charge is located at the far edge of the poly depletion layer that enters the small-signal C-V measurement. Current loss is mainly determined by the distance from the centroid of the poly depletion charge to the oxide interface, which is about half of the depletion layer width. A third

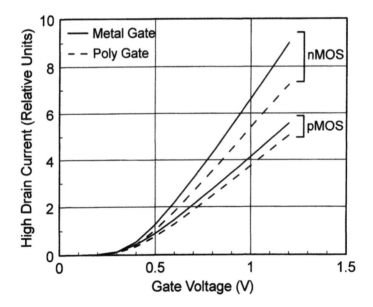

FIG. 27. n/pMOS currents with and without poly depletion effect. Poly doping concentrations assumed are 8×10^{19} cm^{-3}.

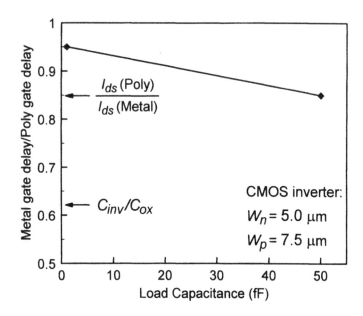

FIG. 28. CMOS delay degradation due to poly depletion effect as a function of load capacitance.

factor, more applicable to the less velocity-saturated pMOS in Fig. 27, is that while the inversion charge density is higher in metal-gate devices, carrier mobilities are lower because of the higher vertical field (like having a thinner oxide).

The simulated delay degradation as a function of the load capacitance is shown in Fig. 28. The intrinsic, unloaded inverter delay is only slightly degraded ($\approx 5\%$) because although poly depletion causes a loss in the drive current, it also decreases the charge needed for the next stage. These two effects tend to cancel each other. For the heavily loaded case in which the devices drive a large fixed capacitance, the delay degradation approaches those of the on-currents in Fig. 27 ($\approx 15\%$). This can be compensated to some extent by using wider devices. On the average, the performance loss due to poly depletion effect is about 10% for partially loaded 25-nm CMOS circuits with a 1.5-nm thick oxide.

4.4 Monte Carlo Simulations of 25-nm CMOS

Extensive 3-D statistical simulations were carried out on the effects of dopant fluctuations on threshold voltage in 25-nm CMOS. For the doping profile in Fig. 21, dopant number fluctuations cause a $10/\sqrt{W}$ mV-μm$^{1/2}$

(1σ) uncertainty in the threshold voltage [22], where W is the device width. This should be tolerable for logic circuits, but is a design consideration in minimum width devices in SRAM cells.

To evaluate the potential on-state performance of 25-nm CMOS, detailed Monte Carlo simulations were performed using the simulator DAMO-CLES [23]. Both n- and p-channel MOSFETs have been simulated, yielding low-output conductance, high-performance I-V characteristics for both device types. The transconductance exceeds 1500 mS/mm for this nFET, with an estimated f_T higher than 250 GHz. Transient Monte Carlo simulations were also done for a 3-stage chain of 25-nm CMOS inverters. The projected delay time is 4–4.5 ps, about three times faster than 100-nm CMOS (1.5 V).

The 25-nm design point is likely to be near the limit of CMOS scaling in view of both the oxide and the band-to-band tunneling currents. It should be noted that other alternative device structures, such as ultra-thin SOI or double-gate MOSFETs, are also subject to similar limitations around 25 nm [24].

5. Interconnect Issues

It has been postulated that microprocessor performance could be limited by interconnect RC delays before running into CMOS device limits. In general, interconnect capacitance and resistance have negligible effects on the delay of local circuits such as CMOS inverters or NAND gates. However, they play a major role in VLSI system performance, especially in standard-cell designs where wire capacitance dominates circuit delay. While interconnect RC issues cannot be separated from circuit and system design methodology, this section summarizes the scaling principles of wire delay and describes a wiring hierarchy scheme for global wire management.

5.1 Interconnect Scaling

A straightforward strategy on interconnect scaling similar to that of MOSFET scaling is shown schematically in Fig. 29 [5]. All linear dimensions—wire length, width, thickness, spacing, and insulator thickness—are scaled down by the same factor, κ, as the device scaling factor. Wire lengths (L_w) are reduced by κ since the linear dimension of the devices and circuits that they connect to is reduced by κ. Both the wire and the insulator thicknesses are scaled down along with the lateral dimension for otherwise the fringe capacitance and wire-to-wire coupling (crosstalk) would increase disproportionately. Table III summarizes the rules for interconnect scaling.

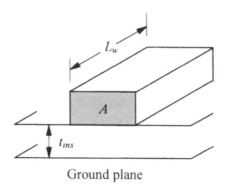

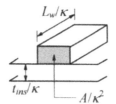

FIG. 29. Scaling of interconnect lines and insulator thicknesses.

TABLE III

SCALING OF LOCAL INTERCONNECT PARAMETERS

	Interconnect parameters	Scaling factor ($\kappa > 1$)
Scaling assumptions	Interconnect dimensions (t_w, L_w, W_w, t_{ins}, W_{sp})	$1/\kappa$
	Resistivity of conductor (ρ_w)	1
	Insulator permittivity (ε_{ins})	1
Derived wire scaling behavior	Wire capacitance per unit length (C_w)	1
	Wire resistance per unit length (R_w)	κ^2
	Wire RC delay (τ_w)	1
	Wire current density ($I/W_w t_w$)	κ

All material parameters, such as the metal resistivity ρ_w and the dielectric constant ε_{ins}, are assumed to remain the same. Wire capacitance then scales down by κ the same way as the device capacitance (Table I), while wire capacitance per unit length, C_w, remains unchanged (approximately 2 pF/cm for silicon-dioxide insulation). Wire resistance, on the other hand, scales up by κ, in contrast to the device resistance, which does not change with scaling (Table I). Wire resistance per unit length, R_w, then scales up by κ^2, as indicated in Table III. It is also noted that the current density of interconnects increases with κ, which implies that reliability issues such as electromigration may become more serious as the wire dimension is scaled down. Fortunately, a few material and process advances in metallurgy have taken place over the generations to keep electromigration in check in VLSI technologies.

5.1.1 Interconnect resistance

Interconnect RC delay (τ_w) of an interconnect line with resistance per unit length R_w, capacitance per unit length C_w, and length L_w is given by [4]

$$\tau_w = \tfrac{1}{2} R_w C_w L_w^2. \tag{10}$$

Using $R_w = \rho_w / W_w t_w$ and $C_w \approx 2\pi\varepsilon_{ins}$ (approximated by concentric cylinders with a radii ratio of $\approx e$), one can express Eq. (10) as

$$\tau_w \approx \pi\varepsilon_{ins}\rho_w \frac{L_w^2}{W_w t_w}, \tag{11}$$

where W_w and t_w are the wire width and thickness, respectively. One of the key conclusions of interconnect scaling is that the wire RC delay τ_w does not change as the device dimension and intrinsic delay are scaled down. Eventually, this will impose a limit on VLSI performance. Fortunately, for conventional aluminum metallurgy with silicon-dioxide insulation, $\rho_w \approx 3 \times 10^{-6}$ Ω-cm and

$$\tau_w \approx (3 \times 10^{-18} \text{ s}) \frac{L_w^2}{W_w t_w}. \tag{12}$$

It is easy to see that the RC delay of local wires is negligible as long as $L_w^2 / W_w t_w < 3 \times 10^5$. For example, a 0.25 μm × 0.25 μm size wire 100 μm long has an RC delay of 0.5 ps, which is quite negligible even when compared with the intrinsic delay (≈ 20 ps) of a 0.1-μm CMOS inverter [25]. Therefore, a local circuit macro can be scaled down with all W_w, t_w, and L_w reduced by the same factor without running into serious RC problems.

5.2   Global Wires

Based on the above discussion, RC delay of local wires will not limit circuit speed even though it cannot be reduced through scaling. The RC delay of global wires, on the other hand, is an entirely different matter. Unlike local wires, the length of global wires, on the order of the chip dimension, does not scale down since chip size actually increases slightly for advanced technologies with better yield/defect density to accommodate a much higher number of circuit counts. Even if we assume chip size does not change, the RC delay of global wires scales up by κ^2 from Eq. (12). It is clear that one quickly runs into trouble if the cross-sectional area of global wires is scaled down the same way as the local wires. For example, for a 0.5 μm CMOS technology, $L_w^2/W_w t_w \sim 10^8 - 10^9$, and $\tau_w \sim 1$ ns, severely impacting system performance. The use of copper wires instead of aluminum would reduce the numerical factor in Eq. (12) by a factor of about 1.5 and provide some relief. A number of solutions have been proposed to deal with the problem. The most obvious one is to minimize the number of cross-chip global interconnects in the critical paths as much as possible through custom layout/design and use of sophisticated design tools. One can also use repeaters to reduce the dependence of RC delay on wire length from a quadratic one to a linear one [26]. A more fundamental solution is to increase or not to scale the cross-sectional area of global wires. However, just increasing the width and thickness of global wires is not enough since wire capacitance will then increase significantly, which degrades both performance and power. Intermetal dielectric thickness must be increased in proportion to keep the wire capacitance per unit length constant. Of course, there is a technology price to pay to build such low-RC global wires. It also means more levels of interconnects since one still needs several levels of thin, dense local wires to make the chip "wirable".

The best strategy for interconnect scaling is then to scale down the size and spacing of lower levels in step with device scaling for local wiring, and to use unscaled or even scaled-up levels on top for global wiring, as shown schematically in Fig. 30 [27]. Unscaled wires allow the global RC delay to remain essentially unchanged as seen from Eq. (12). Scaled-up (together with the insulator thickness) wires allow the global RC delay to scale down together with the device delay. This is even more necessary if chip size increases with every generation. Ultimately, the scaled-up global wires would approach the transmission-line limit when the inductive effect becomes more important than the resistive effect. This happens when the signal rise time is shorter than the time of flight over the length of the line. Signal propagation is then limited by the speed of electromagnetic wave, $c/(\varepsilon_{ins}/\varepsilon_0)^{1/2}$, instead of by RC delay. Here $c = 3 \times 10^{10}$ cm/s is the velocity

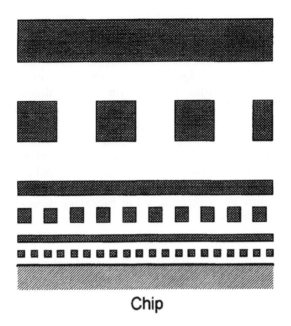

Chip

FIG. 30. Schematic cross section of wiring hierarchy that addresses both the density and the global RC delay in a high-performance CMOS processor.

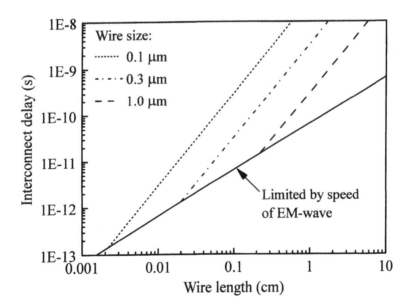

FIG. 31. RC delay versus wire length for three different wire sizes (assuming square wire cross sections). Wires become electromagnetic-wave-propagation limited when the RC delay equals the time of flight over the line length. An oxide insulator is assumed here.

of light in vacuum. For oxide insulators, $(\varepsilon_{ins}/\varepsilon_0)^{1/2} \approx 2$, the time of flight is approximately 70 ps/cm. Figure 31 shows the interconnect delay versus wire length calculated from Eq. (12) for three different wire cross sections [17]. The RC delays (dotted, dashed, and chained lines) exhibit a slope of 2 versus L_w in the log–log scale. The solid line, representing the speed-of-light limit $(\varepsilon_{ins}/\varepsilon_0)^{1/2} L_w/c$, has a slope of 1. For a given wire size, the delay becomes RC limited above a certain wire length proportional to the cross-sectional area. In other words, for a longer global wire to reach the speed-of-light limit, a larger wire cross section is needed. The transmission-line situation is more often encountered in packaging wires [26].

REFERENCES

[1] Kahng, D. and Atalla, M. M. (1960). "Silicon dioxide field surface devices". Presented at *Device Research Conference, Pittsburgh*.

[2] Wanlass, F. and Sah, C. T. (1963). "Nanowatt logic using field-effect metal-oxide-semiconductor triodes". In *Technical Digest of the 1963 International Solid-State Circuit Conference*, pp. 32–33.

[3] Burns, J. R. (1964). "Switching response of complementary-symmetry MOS transistor logic circuits". *RCA Review*, **25**, 627.

[4] Taur, Y. and Ning, T. H. (1998). *Fundamentals of Modern VLSI Devices*, Cambridge Univ. Press, New York.

[5] Dennard, R. H., Gaensslen, F. H., Yu, H. N., Rideout, V. L., Bassous, E. and LeBlanc, A. R. (1974). "Design of Ion-Implanted MOSFETs with Very Small Physical Dimensions". *IEEE Journal of Solid-State Circuits*, **9**, 256.

[6] Nguyen, T. N. (1984). "Small-geometry MOS transistors: Physics and modeling of surface- and buried-channel MOSFETs". *Ph.D. Thesis*, Stanford University.

[7] Frank, D. J., Taur, Y. and Wong, H.-S. (1998). "Generalized scale length for two-dimensional effects in MOSFETs". *IEEE Electron Device Letters*, **19**, 385.

[8] Taur, Y. Buchanan, D. A., Wei Chen, *et al.* (1997). *CMOS scaling into the nanometer regime*. In "IEEE Proceedings", p. 486.

[9] Mii, Y., Wind, S., Taur, Y., Lii, Y., Klaus, D. and Bucchignano, J. (1994). "An ultra-low power 0.1 μm CMOS". In *1994 VLSI Technology Symp. Technical Digest*, pp. 9–10.

[10] Lo, S.-H., Buchanan, D. A., Taur, Y. and Wang, W. (1997). "Quantum-mechanical modeling of electron tunneling current from the inversion layer of ultra-thin-oxide nMOSFETs". *IEEE Electron Device Letters*, **18**, 209–211.

[11] Stern, F. (1972). "Self-consistent results for *n*-type Si inversion layers". *Physical Review B*, **5**(12), 4891–4899.

[12] Wong, C. Y., Sun, J. Y.-C., Taur, Y., Oh, C. S., Angelucci, R. and Davari, B. (1988). "Doping of n⁺ and p⁺ polysilicon in a dual-gate CMOS process". In *1988 IEDM Technical Digest*, pp. 238–241.

[13] Taur, Y. (1999). "The incredible shrinking transistor". *IEEE Spectrum*, 25.

[14] Ng, K. K. and Lynch, W. T. (1986). "Analysis of the gate-voltage dependent series resistance of MOSFETs". *IEEE Trans. Electron Devices*, **33**, 965.

[15] Taur, Y. (2000). "MOSFET channel length: Extraction and interpretation". *IEEE Trans. Electron Devices*, **47**, 160–170.

[16] Taur, Y., Mii, Y. J., Logan, R. and Wong, H. S. (1995). "On effective channel length in 0.1 μm MOSFETs". *IEEE Electron Device Letters*, **16**, 136.

[17] Taur, Y. and Nowak, E. J. (1997). "CMOS devices below 0.1 μm: How high will performance go?" In *1997 IEDM Technical Digest*, p. 215.

[18] Taur, Y., Wann, C. H. and Frank, D. J. (1998). "25 nm CMOS design considerations". In *1998 IEDM Technical Digest*, p. 789.

[19] Thompson, S., Packan, P., Ghani, T. *et al.* (1998). "Source-drain extension scaling for 0.1 μm and below channel length MOSFETs". In *1998 VLSI Tech. Symp.*, p. 132.

[20] Fair, R. B. and Wivell, H. W. (1976). "Zener and avalanche breakdown in as-implanted low-voltage silicon N-P junctions". *IEEE Trans. Electron Devices*, **23**, 512.

[21] Stork, J. M. C. and Isaac, R. D. (1983). "Tunneling in base-emitter junctions". *IEEE Trans. Electron Devices*, **30**, 1527.

[22] Frank, D. J., Taur, Y., Ieona, M. and Wong, H.-S. (1999). "Monte Carlo modeling of threshold variation due to dopant fluctuations". In *VLSI Technology Symposium*, Kyoto, Japan, June, pp. 169–170.

[23] Laux, S. E., Fischetti, M. V. and Frank, D. J. (1990). "Monte Carlo analysis of semiconductor devices: The DAMOCLES program". *IBM Journal of Research and Development*, **34**, 466.

[24] Wong, H.-S. P., Frank, D. J. and Solomon, P. M. (1998). "Device design considerations for double-gate, ground-plane, and single-gate ultra-thin SOI MOSFETs at the 25 nm gate length generation". In *1998 IEDM Technical Digest*, p. 407.

[25] Taur, Y., Wind, S., Mii, Y. *et al.* (1993). "High performance 0.1 μm CMOS devices with 1.5 V power supply". In *1993 IEDM Technical Digest*, p. 127.

[26] Bakoglu, H. B. (1990). *Circuits, Interconnections, and Packaging for VLSI*. Addison-Wesley, Reading, MA.

[27] Sai-Halasz, G. A. (1995). "Performance trends in high-end processors". *Proceedings of the IEEE*, **83**, 20–36.

Author Index

A

Abbatel, J., 57, *83*
Abbott, C., 125, *163*
Ableson, H., 155, *168*
Adali, S., 113, *117*
Adam, N., 153, *168*
Adhikary, J., 124, *162*
Adiwijaya, I., 153, *168*
Agrawal, R., 121, 138, *162*
Akman, E., 151, *168*
Ames, S.R., 197, *234, 235*
Amir, A., 183, *183*
Amoroso, E., 201, 209, 210, *231*
Anderson, D., 127, *163*
Anderson, J., 190, *231*
Anderson, M., 202, *231*
Anderson, R.J., 186, 190, 192, 205, 206, 213, 214, 217, 228, 231, *231, 234*
Anderson, S., 6, *46*
Angelucci, R., 273, *279*
Anghel, M., 124, *162*
Archie, J., 134, *165*
Atalla, M.M., 238, *278*
Atluri, V., 153, *168*
Austell, V.A., 209, *233*
Avnur, R., 139, *166*

B

Bacsich, P., 11, *47*
Baden, S., 151, *168*
Badger, L., 198, *231*
Bailey-Kellogg, C., 141, 154, *166, 168*
Bajaj, C., 147, *167*
Baker, C., 151, 152, *168*
Bakoglu, H.B., 276, 278, *279*
Balabanian, N., 76, *85*
Balasubramanian, J., 151, *168*
Banday, A., 127, *163*

Bane, P.W., 54, *82*
Barbara, D., 122, 135, *162*
Barksdale, G., 199, *231*
Barlow, J.P., 77, *85*
Barnes, J., 145, *167*
Baru, C., 151, *167*
Bassous, E., 242, 247, 273, *278*
Beazley, D., 152, 153, *168*
Bell, D.E., 189, 193, *231*
Benkart, T., *231*
Bennett, B., 6, *46*
Bennett, C., 127, *163*
Berdichevsky, D., 78, *85*
Berger, J.L., 198, *233*
Berghel, H., 68, 72, *83, 84*
Berlin, A., 130, *164*
Berners-Lee, T., 89, 113, *116*
Berry, M., 122, 125, *162, 163*
Bersanelli, B., 127, *163*
Berson, T., 199, *231*
Bezdek, J., 135, *165*
Biba, K., 189, 207, *232*
Bishop, C., 136, 137, *165*
Biswas, G., 125, *163*
Bitzer, D., *231*
Blank, D., 72, *84*
Blaze, M., 227, *232*
Blom, R., 124, *162*
Blum, A., 136, *165*
Blum, M., 183, *183*
Board, J., 145, *167*
Boebert, W.E., 227, *232*
Bohrer, B., *et al.*, 113, *117*
Böhringer, K., 130, *164*
Boisvert, R., 151, *168*
Bolt, D.B., 73, *84*
Boothby, N.G., 75, *84*
Bosak, J., 70, *84*
Bosch, D., 124, *162*
Bouton, C., 6, *46*
Bowman, C., 114, *118*

Boyan, J., 157, *168*
Bradley, S.P., 54, *82*
Bradshaw, F.T., 197, *234, 235*
Bradshaw, G., 135, 136, *165*
Bradsher, M., 6, *46*
Bramley, B., 151, *168*
Bramley, R., 151, *167*
Branstad, M., 201, *232*
Bratko, I., 137, *166*
Bray, T., 70, *84*
Breg, F., 151, *168*
Brewer, D.F.C., 190, 211, *232*
Brewington, B.E., 69, *84*
Bright, L., 113, *117*
Brodley, C., 125, *163*
Brodley, C.E., 71, *84*
Bruffee, K.A., 28, 29, 31, *47*
Bryan, G., 125, *163*
Brynjolfsson, E., 68, *84*
Bucchignano, J., 255, *278*
Buchanan, B., 159, *168, 169*
Buchanan, D.A., 256, 271, *278*
Buneman, P., 153, *168*
Burns, J.R., 239, *278*
Busnel, R.G., 54, *82*

C

Candan, K.S., 113, *117*
Cant, C., 204, *232*
Cantwell, B., 133, *165*
Carroll, B., 54, *83*
Caruthers, J., 129, *164*
Catlin, A., 151, 153, *168*
Cattell, R.G.G., 100, *117*
Chakrabarti, S., 57, *83*
Chan, K., 129, *164*
Chanat, J., 124, *162*
Chandy, K., 151, *167*
Chapman, G., 133, *165*
Char, B., 151, *167*
Cheeseman, P., 140, *166*
Chen, H-C., 64, 69, *83*
Chen, W., *278*
Chou, A., 139, *166*
Clark, D.D., 65, *83*, 209, *232*
Classe, A., 54, *82*
Coiera, E., 155, *168*
Comerford, R., 51, *82*

Comiskey, J., 125, *163*
Condon, A., 173, 183, *183*
Corbalis, M.C., 51, *82*
Craven, M., 139, *166*
Crawford, A.K., 73, *84*
Crippen, R., 124, *162*
Cunningham, D.J., 6, *46*
Curry, J., 32, *47*
Curtis, B., 228, *232*
Cybenko, G., 69, *84*, 136, *165*

D

Damon, W., 78, *85*
Davari, B., 273, *279*
Davison, S., 153, *168*
Dean, C., 124, *162*
de Bernardis, P., 127, *163*
Demmel, J., 151, *168*
Denley, I., 214, *232*
Dennard, R.H., 242, 247, 273, *278*
Denning, D.E., 194, 197, *232*
Denning, D.E.R., 197, *232*
de Swaan, A., 76, *84, 85*
Dietz, R., 124, *162*
Diffie, W., 223, *232*
Diwan, S., 151, *168*
Djorgovski, S., 125, *163*
Dom, B.E., 57, *83*
Donald, B., 130, *164*
Donato, J., 122, *162*
Dongarra, J., 151, *168*
Downey, P.J., 197, *234*
Drashansky, T., 130, *164*
Drmac, Z., 122, *162*
Duffy, T., 6, *46*
Duffy, T.M., 6, *46*
Dumais, S., 122, *162*
DuMouchel, W., 122, 135, *162*
Dymond, R., 124, *162*
Dyson, E., 76, *85*
Dzeroski, S., 137, *166*

E

Earle, T., 73, *84*
Ebbsjo, I., 127, *164*
Eberling, 37, *47*
Edelsbrunner, H., 183, *183*

Ehrmann, S.C., 39, *47*
Eisenberg, M., 155, *168*
Ellisman, M., 151, *167*
Ellison, C., 224, *232*
Ellison, C.M., 224, *232*
Emerson, E.A., 183, *183*
Epstein, J., 201, *201, 232*
Estrin, D., 159, *169*

F

Faden, G., *202*
Fagin, R., 102, *117*
Fair, R.B., 270, *279*
Faloutsos, C., 122, 127, 135, *162, 163*
Farrara, J., 124, *162*
Fayyad, U., 125, 156, *163, 165*
Febvre, L., 59, *83*
Feenberg, A., 6, 10, *46*
Feigenbaum, J., 227, *232*
Feng, C., 138, *166*
Fenton, J.S., 197, *232*
Ferraiolo, D., 199, *233*
Fich, F., 173, *183*
Fierro, R., 122, *162*
Fischetti, M.V., 273, *279*
Flamm, R., 125, *163*
Foley, S.N., 212, *233*
Forbus, K., 130, *164*
Fortnow, L., 183, *183*
Fox, E.A., 64, 69, *83*
Fraim, L.J., 200, *233*
Frank, D.J., 250, 258, 266, 273, *278, 279*
Frantz, B., 224, *232*
Fraser, T., 208, *233*
Frazier, M., 143, *167*
Frederickson, G.N., 173, *183*
Friedl, M., 125, *163*
Friedman, J., 76, *85*
Friedman, T.L., 82, *85*
Froscher, J.N., 207, *233*
Fu, L., 121, 137, *162*
Fukunaga, K., 141, *166*
Fukuyama, F., 76, *85*

G

Gabriel, K., 130, *164*
Gaensslen, F.H., 242, 247, 273, *278*

Gage, P., 133, *165*
Galbraith, J.K., 76, 82, *85*
Gallman, J., 133, *165*
Gannon, D., 151, *168*
Ganti, V., 135, 141, *165, 166*
Garca-Molinia, H., 102, *117*
Gardarin, G., *et al.*, 113, *117*
Garland, I., 27, *47*
Garth, R.Y., 6, *46*
Gates, J.R., 65, 76, *83*
Gehrke, J., 135, 141, *165, 166*
Ghani, T., *et al.*, 268, *279*
Gibson, D., 141, *166*
Giunta, A., 152, *168*
Goel, A., 129, 130, 151, *164, 168*
Goeller, L., 57, *83*
Goguen, J.A., 197, *233*
Goldberg, A., 173, *183*
Gopalakrishnan, V., 159, *168, 169*
Gorski, K., 127, *163*
Govindan, D., 159, *169*
Govindaraju, M., 151, *168*
Grafton, A., 61, *83*
Graham, S., 151, *168*
Grama, A., 128, 139, 147, 148, 150, *164, 166, 167*
Graubart, R.D., 198, *233*
Gravano, L., 102, *117*
Griffin, J., 202, *231*
Grimson, J., 153, *168*
Grimson, W., 153, *168*
Gross, L., 125, *163*
Grosse, E., 151, *168*
Grossman, B., 151, 152, *168*
Gruser, J.-R., 113, *117*
Gubernick, 37, *47*

H

Haas, L.M., 113, *117*
Haas, P., 122, 135, *162*
Haber, S., 183, *183*
Hafner, K., 2, 45, 57, *83*
Haftka, R., 151, 152, *168*
Haghighat, S.A., 198, *231*
Halfant, M., 155, *168*
Han, E.-H., 135, 141, *165*
Han, J., 124, 135, 141, *162, 167*
Hanna, *47*

Harasim, L., 3, 6, 8, 9, 10, 16, 32, *45*, *46*
Hardman, V., 68, *84*
Hargittai, E., 78, *85*
Harrison, M.A., 198, *233*
Hart, K., 153, *168*
Hass, P.J., 139, *166*
Hasselbring, W., 153, *168*
Hau, D., 155, *168*
Haussler, D., 156, *165*
Hazen, B., 125, *163*
Heidemann, J., 159, *169*
Hellerstein, J., 122, 135, 139, *162*, *166*
Hellman, M.E., 223, *232*
Hennessy, D., 159, *168*, *169*
Hidber, C., 139, *166*
Hiltz, R., 2, 3, 5, 6, 10, 32, *45*, *46*
Hinshaw, G., 127, *163*
Holmes, W.N., 73, 80, *84*, *85*
Holzmann, G.J., 55, 56, *83*
Houstis, E., 130, 151, 153, *164*, *168*
Houston, A.L., 64, 69, *83*
Howes, T.A., 114, *118*
Hu, W., 127, *163*
Huang, K.-T., 90, *117*
Huang, T., 133, *165*
Huang, X., 123, 141, *162*, *166*
Huber, G., 201, *233*
Hut, P., 145, *167*

I

Ieona, M., 273, *279*
Imielinski, 142, *167*
Imielinski, T., 121, 138, *162*
Introna, L., 70, *84*
Investor's Business Daily, 19 June 2000, 13,
    47
Ioannidis, J., 227, *232*
Ioannidis, Y., 122, 135, *162*
Isaac, R.D., 270, *279*
Iscoe, N., 228, *232*

J

Jackson, P., 127, *163*
Jagadish, H., 122, 127, 135, *162*, *163*
Jessup, E., 122, *162*
Jiang, J., 122, *162*

Jin, W., 127, *164*
Johar, A., 150, *167*
Johns, A., 61, *83*
Johnson, A.W., 73, *84*
Johnson, C., 152, 153, *168*
Johnson, D.S., 173, *183*
Johnson, T., 122, 135, *162*
Jordan, M., 136, 137, *165*
Joy, B., 174, *183*

K

Kaelbling, L., 159, *169*
Kahn, B., 6, *46*
Kain, R.Y., 227, *232*
Kalia, R., 127, 128, 129, *164*
Kamke, F., 129, 130, *164*
Kang, M.H., 202, 207, *233*
Karger, P.A., 209, *233*
Karl, T.R., 51, *82*
Karp, R., 183, *183*
Karypis, G., 135, 141, *165*
Katzenelson, J., 155, *168*
Keegan, D., 4, *46*
Keegstra, P., 127, *163*
Kennedy, K., 174, *183*
Kennett, R., 203, *234*
Keromytis, A., 227, *232*
Khang, D., 238, *278*
Kibler, D., 124, *162*
Kida, S., 133, *165*
Kietz, J.-U., 143, *167*
King, P., 71, *84*
King, R., 137, 143, *166*, *167*
Kirk, T., 113, *117*
Kivinen, J., 159, *168*
Klaus, D., 255, *278*
Klein, W., 124, *162*
Kleinberg, J., 141, *166*
Kleinstreuer, L., 134, *165*
Knill, D., 152, *168*
Knorr, E., 135, *165*
Knudsen, C.M., 75, *84*
Knuth, R., 6, *46*
Kogut, A., 127, *163*
Kohl, John T., 216, *234*
Kolda, T., 150, *167*
Konopnicki, D., 114, *118*
Koperski, K., 124, *162*

Korn, F., 127, *163*
Kossmann, D., 113, *117*
Kouvelas, I., 68, *84*
Kovacs, G., 130, *164*
Krasner, H., 228, *232*
Kroo, I., 133, *165*
Kuhn, R., 199, *233*
Kuhn, T., 28, *47*
Kumar, S.R., 57, *83*
Kumar, V., 135, 141, 150, *165, 167*

L

Lacey, J., 227, *232*
Lakshmanan, L., 141, *167*
Lampson, B., 224, *232*
Lampson, B.W., 224, *234*
Lane, T., 71, *84*
Langley, P., 135, 136, *165*
LaPadula, L.J., 189, 193, *231*
Laux, S.E., 273, *279*
Lawton, G., 70, *84*
LeBlanc, A.R., 242, 247, 273, *278*
Lee, M., 127, *164*
Lee, A., *et al.*, 127, *163*
Lee, J.-H., 231, *231, 233*
Lee, Y.W., 90, *117*
Lei, M., 134, *165*
Leisawitz, D., 127, *163*
Leivant, D., 183, *183*
Letsche, T., 122, *162*
Levinson, P., 6, *46*
Levy, A.Y., 113, *117*
Li, C., 125, *163*
Lii, Y., 255, *278*
Lingam, S., 124, *162*
Lipton, R., 183, *183*
Littman, M., 159, *169*
Liu, S., 134, *165*
Livingston, J.D., 69, *84*
Lo, S.-H., 256, 271, *278*
Logan, R., 264, *278*
Lohani, V., 124, *162*
Lomas, M., 205, *233*
Lorenz, K., 217, 231, *233*
Loui, M., 183, *183*
Loui, M.C., 173, *183*
Luh, H.-K., 125, *163*
Lynch, C.A., 89, 114, *116*

Lynch, N., 183, *183*
Lynch, W.T., 263, *278*
Lyon, M., 2, *45*, 57, *83*

M

McCullough, D., 199, *233*
MacDonald, N., 130, *164*
Macedonia, M., 64, *83*
McHugh, J., 201, *232*
MacIntyre, R., 125, *163*
McKeough, J., 61, *83*
McLean, J., 198, *233*
Mahaney, S., 173, *183*
Manguel, A., 60, 63, *83*
Mann, S., 70, *84*
Mannila, H., 142, 159, *167, 168*
Manning, S., 35, *47*
Manor, J., 76, *85*
Marchionini, G., 64, 69, *83*
Marciano, R., 151, *167*
Marmor-Squires, A., 201, *232*
Martin, H-J., 59, *83*
Mason, W., 151, 152, *168*
Massey, C., 32, *47*
Mastro, J.G., 51, *82*
Mechoso, C., 124, *162*
Mendelzon, A.O., 100, *117*
Meseguer, J., 197, *233*
Mesrobian, E., 124, *162*
Mihaila, G., 90, 92, 100, 102, *117*
Mii, Y., 255, 274, *278, 279*
Mii, Y.J., 264, *278*
Milner, R., 202, *231*
Milo, T., 100, *117*
Minser, K., 125, *163*
Mitbander, B., 142, *167*
Mitchell, T., 121, 159, *162, 168*
Montrose, B., 202, *233*
Moore, A., 127, 157, 159, *164, 168, 169*
Moore, R., 151, *167*
Morik, K., 143, *167*
Moskowitz, I.S., 202, 207, *233*
Mowshowitz, A., 75, *84*
Moynihan, D.P., 206, *233*
Muggleton, S., 121, 137, 138, *162, 166*
Mukherjee, P., 203, *233*
Muntz, R., 124, *162*
Murthy, S., 130, *164*

N

Nakano, A., 127, 128, 129, 146, *164*, *167*
Nash, M., 203, *234*
Nash, M.J., 190, 211, *232*
Nayak, P., 130, *164*
Needham, R.M., 220, *234*, *235*
Neuman, C., 216, *234*
Ng, K.K., 263, *278*
Ng, R., 122, 124, 135, *162*, *165*
Ng, R.T., 141, *167*
Nguyen, T., 133, *165*
Nguyen, T.N., 246, 247, *278*
Ning, T.H., 242, 256, 260, 263, 265, 275, *278*
Nishida, T., 143, *167*
Nissenbaum, H., 70, *84*
Noor, A., 130, *164*
North, C., 202, *231*
Nowak, E.J., 266, *279*
Nuenschwander, E., 78, *85*

O

Oakley, B., II, 32, 35, *47*
O'Brien, G., 122, *162*
Ogden, W.F., 197, *234*, *235*
Oh, C.S., 273, *279*
O'Leary, D., 150, *167*
Olston, C., 139, *166*
Ong, K., 142, *167*
Opitz, D., 137, *166*
Ordonez, I., 141, *166*
Orman, H., 201, *232*
Ostrouchov, G., 122, *162*
Overton, C., 153, *168*
Oyen, E., 76, *85*

P

Packan, P., 268, *279*
Pallast, G., 74, *84*
Papadimitriou, C., 183, *183*
Papakonstantinou, Y., 113, *117*
Parberry, I., 183, *183*
Parker, S., 152, 153, *168*
Parkes, M.B., 62, *83*
Parsonese, J., 202, *233*
Pascale, R., 201, *201*, *232*

Pascucci, V., 147, *167*
Pehrson, B., 56, *83*
Peikert, R., 133, *164*
Pelton, J.N., 65, *83*
Petroski, H., 62, *83*
Phanouriou, C., 129, 130, *164*
Pieterse, J.N., 77, *85*
Pitt, L., 143, *167*
Pomeroy, B., 204, *234*
Poosala, V., 122, 135, *162*
Popek, G.J., 197, *234*
Post, F., 133, *165*
Postman, N., 64, *83*
Preparata, F.P., 109, *117*
Press, L., 68, *84*
Preston, E., 124, *162*
Prince, T., 151, *167*

R

Rabin, M., 183, *183*
Raghavan, P., 57, *83*, 141, *166*
Raghaven, P., 173, *183*
Rajagopalan, S., 57, *83*
Rajasekaar, A., 151, *167*
Ramakrishnan, N., 124, 130, 139, 150, 151,
    153, 154, 156, *162*, *164*, *166*, *167*, *168*
Ramakrishnan, R., 135, 141, *165*, *166*
Raman, V., 139, *166*
Randell, B., 198, *234*
Raschid, L., 90, 92, 100, 113, *117*, *118*
Raymond, E.S., 13, *47*
Reis, E.P., 76, *85*
Reynders, J., 151, *167*
Ribbens, C., 129, 130, 154, 156, *164*, *168*
Rice, J., 151, 153, 157, *166*, *168*
Rice, J.R., 130, *164*
Rideout, V.L., 242, 247, 273, *278*
Ridley, M., 131, 134, 138, 156, *164*
Riezenman, M.J., 65, *83*
Rivest, R., 136, *165*, 224, *232*
Rivest, R.L., 224, *234*
Roberts, L.G., 65, *84*
Roden, J., 125, *163*
Rolheiser, C., 6, *46*
Rolt, L.T.C., 51, 67, *82*
Rosenberg, A., 183, *183*
Rosenberg, J., 159, *168*
Ross, K., 122, 135, *162*

Rossignac, J., 147, *167*
Roth, M., 133, *164*
Roth, T., 139, *166*
Rounds, W.C., 197, *234, 235*
Royer, J., 183, *183*
Rubin, E., 124, *162*
Rundle, J., 124, 125, *162, 163*
Rushby, J., 198, *234*
Ruspini, E., 135, *165*
Ruth, P., 150, *167*
Ruzzo, W.L., 198, *233*

S

Sacks, E., 155, *168*
Sacks, J., 159, *168*
Sadarjoen, I., 133, *165*
Sagiv, Y., 113, *117*
Sah, C.T., 238, *278*
Sai-Halasz, G.A., 276, *279*
Saloman, G., 6, *46*
Saltz, J., 151, *168*
SaMartins, J., 124, *162*
Sameh, A., 133, *164*
Santos, J., 124, *162*
Sarin, V., 128, 133, 147, 148, *164*
Sasse, M.A., 68, *84*
Saul, J.R., 71, *84*
Savage, J., 183, *183*
Savage, J.E., 173, *183*
Savery, J.R., 6, *46*
Schell, R.R., 197, *234*
Schmandt-Besserat, D., 58, *83*
Schroeder, Michael, *234*
Schulten, K., 145, *167*
Schulze-Kremer, S., 135, *165*
Schürmann, A., 55, *83*
Selman, A., 173, 183, *183*
Semtner, A., 124, *162*
Sevcik, K., 122, 135, *162*
Shaffer, C., 124, 129, 130, 151, *162, 164, 168*
Sharan, S., 6, *46*
Sharan, Y., 6, *46*
Shavlik, J., 137, 139, *165, 166*
Shek, E., 124, *162*
Shen, W.-M., 142, *167*
Sherman, D.L., 198, *231*
Shmoys, D.B., 173, *183*
Shmueli, O., 114, *118*

Shneiderman, B., 82, *85*
Shumway, D.G., 197, *234, 235*
Simon, H., 135, 136, *165*
Slavin, 6, *46*
Smith, C., 10, *46*, 183, *183*
Smoot, G., 127, *163*
Sobieski, I., 133, *165*
Solomon, P.M., 258, *278*
Soria, J., 133, *165*
Speir, C., 124, *162*
Srinivasan, A., 137, 143, *166, 167*
Srivastava, D., 113, *117*
Stajano, F., 190, 217, 231, *234*
Standage, T., 56, *83*
Stavridou, V., 203, *233*
Stefik, M., 65, *83*
Stern, F., 258, *278*
Sterne, D.F., 198, *231*
Stewart, A., 61, *83*
Stoll, C., 66, *84*
Stolorz, P., 124, 156, *162, 165*
Stork, J.M.C., 270, *279*
Stough, T.M., 71, *84*
Strawn, G., 174, *183*
Streitfeld, D., 71, *84*
Stuckey, T., 151, *168*
Stutz, J., 140, *166*
Subrahmaniam, V.S., 113, *117*
Subramanian, D., 159, *168, 169*
Suh, J., 130, *164*
Sun, J.Y.-C., 273, *279*
Sussman, A., 151, *168*
Sussman, G., 155, *168*
Sutherland, D., 197, *234*
Swami, A., 121, 138, *162*
Szalay, A., 125, *163*
Szpankowski, W., 150, *167*

T

Tanaka, M., 133, *165*
Tardos, E., 183, *183*
Taubin, G., 147, *167*
Taur, Y., 242, 250, 255, 256, 260, 263, 264, 265, 266, 271, 273, 274, 275, *278, 279*
Tavani, H.T., 76, *85*
Teles, L., 3, 6, 32, *45*
Tester, J., 71, *84*
Thomas, B.M., 224, *232*

Thompson, S., 268, *279*
Tohline, J., 125, *163*
Toll, D.C., 209, *233*
Tomasic, A., 92, 100, 113, *117, 118*
Tomkins, A., 57, *83*
Towell, G., 137, *165*
Trenberth, K.E., 51, *82*
Turoff, M., 2, 3, 5, 6, 29, 30, 32, 44, *45, 47*

U

Ullman, J.D., 198, *233*

V

Valdés-Pérez, R., 139, *166*
Valduriez, P., 113, *118*
Vallas, S., 75, *84*
Vapnik, V., 135, *165*
Vashishta, P., 127, 128, 129, *164*
Venkatasubramanian, V., 129, *164*
Verykios, V., 151, 153, *168*
Vidal, M.E., 90, 113, *117*
Villacis, T., 151, *168*
Vitter, J., 183, *183*

W

Walker, K.M., 198, *231*
Walker, T.J., 80, *85*
Walter, K.G., 197, *234, 235*
Wan, M., 151, *167*
Wang, R.Y., 90, *117*
Wang, W., 256, 271, *278*
Wanlass, F., 238, *278*
Wann, C.H., 266, *279*
Ward, L., 35, *47*
Warnke, G., 54, *82*
Watson, L., 124, 129, 130, 151, 152, *162, 164,
    168*
Webb, J., 6, 9, *46*
Weir, N., 125, *163*
Welch, W., 159, *168*
Wellman, B., 6, *46*

Weston-Smith, S., 214, *232*
Wiederhold, G., 113, *118*
Wiessman, C., 197, 201, *235*
Wilkes, M.V., 220, *235*
Wilkinson, D., 127, *163*
Wilson, D.R., 209, *232*
Wimmers, E.L., 113, *117*
Wind, S., 255, 274, *278, 279*
Winkelmans, L.C., 9, *46*
Wisdom, J., 155, *168*
Wiseman, S., 204, *232, 234*
Wivell, H.W., 270, *279*
Wong, C.Y., 273, *279*
Wong, H.-S., 250, 258, 264, 273, *278, 279*
Wong, L., 153, *168*
Woodward, J.P.L., 198, *233, 235*
Wright, E., 127, *163*
Wright, P., 201, *235*
Wynn, H., 159, *168*

Y

Yang, D.-Y., 128, 147, 148, 150, *164, 167*
Yang, J., 113, *117*
Yang, S-K., 68, *84*
Yates, L., 133, *165*
Yeh, R.T., 109, *117*
Yesberg, J., 202, *231*
Yi, J., 124, *162*
Yip, K., 141, 155, *166, 168*
Yiu, K., 202, *231*
Ylonen, T., 224, *232*
Yu, H.N., 242, 247, 273, *278*
Yunus, M., 79, *85*

Z

Zaniolo, C., 142, *167*
Zhao, F., 123, 141, 154, *162, 165, 166, 168*
Zhao, Q., 143, *167*
Zhuang, G., 147, *167*
Zimmermann, P.R., 224, *235*
Zue, V., 52, *82*
Zwillinger, D., 159, *169*

Subject Index

A

Access Control List (ACL), 219–20
Active reading, 16
Active writing, 15
ADEPT-50, 197
Adjunct mode use of networks, 25
Aggregation, 205–6
Aircraft design, 158–9
Akamai, 175
Algorithms
  design and analysis, 181–2
  new theories, 182
Alta Vista, 72
Analyst Alice, 212
Anytime analysis, 161
ANZLIC, 90
Application incompatibility, 206
Arecibo Radio Telescope, 127
Astronomy, 179
Astrophysics, data mining, 126–7
Asynchronous transfer mode (ATM)
  networks, 175
Atmospheric Global Circulation Model
  (AGCM), 123
Automated compliance verification, 227–8
AXIOM, 178

B

B2B (business-to-business), 68
B2C (business-to-consumer), 68
BACON, 136
Bell-LaPadula (BLD) security policy model,
  189–99
Biba integrity model, 189, 207–9, 222
BiCMOS, 240
Bioinformatics, data mining, 131–2
Blacker encryption devices, 200–1
Blocking features, 123
BLP, 199, 203, 206–8, 210, 211, 219

BMA security policy, 190, 212–14
Books, 60–4
  content, 62
  manufacture, 61
  storage, 62–3
Boolean matrix, 222
BOOMERANG, 127
British National Lottery, 228–9
Brokers, 115
Buckets, 105–12, 116

C

Cambridge CAP machine, 220
Capability, 220–1
CCITT X.509 recommendation, 223
CD-ROM, 64
Centroids, 115
Certificates, 223
Certification practice statement, 225–6
CGI-based web applications, 17
Chemical engineering, data mining, 127–30
Children, 50, 64–75
  and Internet, 65–6
  and World Wide Web, 69–70
  digital divide, 73–5
  future, 73–5
  infancy divide, 75
Chinese Wall model, 190, 211–12, 222
CLARANS, 124
Clark-Wilson model, 190, 209–11, 221
Clustering, 124, 134–5, 140–1
CMC, 11
CMOS devices
  25-nm
    design, 266–73
    Monte Carlo simulations, 272–3
  band-to-band tunneling current density
    versus electric field, 270
  below 0.25 μm, 251–66
  channel profile design, 260–2

289

CMOS devices (*continued*)
  dopant number fluctuations, 264–6
  gate electrode, 258–60
  gate oxide, 256–8
  global wires, 276–8
  halo doping, 262
  interconnect issues, 273–8
  interconnect resistance, 275
  interconnect scaling, 273–5
  inversion layer quantization effect, 258
  low-temperature, 255
  polysilicon-gate depletion effects, 271–2
  power supply, 251–5
  power vs performance tradeoff, 254–5
  relative performance, 254
  retrograde doping, 260–1
  short-channel device design, 266–8
  source–drain doping requirements, 263–4,
    268–70
  standby power, 252
  threshold voltage, 251–5
CMOS inverter, 239, 273
CMOS technology, 239, 240
CMOS VLSI, 238–42
COBE, 127
Codewords, 192
Collaborative discourse, 15
Collaborative learning, 6–16, 24–5, 30
  online courses, 8
Combined recency, 112
Commerce and industry
  and Internet, 68
  and World Wide Web, 71–2
Commercial-off-the-shelf (COTS)
    components, 202
Common Criteria, 189, 200
Communication networks, 175
Communication technology, 50
Compartment, 192
Compartmented Mode Workstation (CMW),
    198, 201–2
Completeness, 96–7, 102
Composability, 199, 204
Computational biology, 178
Computational complexity, 180–1
Computational geometry, 175
Computational steering, 152
Computer-aided materials design (CAMD),
    129
Computer networking, 1–2

Computer simulation (QoSim), 43
Computer system, protection of, 187–8
Conferencing systems, 7
Configuration management, 189
CONQUEST, 124
Constant-field scaling, 242–5
  effect on circuit parameters, 244–5
  rules, 242–4
Constant-voltage scaling, 245–6
Constrained Data Item (CDI), 210, 222
Coordinating Communicating Systems
    (CCS), 176
CORBA, 113
Corporate email, 226–7
Cosmic background radiation (CMB), 126–7
Cosmology, data mining, 126–7
Covert channels, 205
Cryptography, 175

D

Dalton's equations, 136
Damage criteria, 191–2
DAMOCLES, 273
Dancing in Cyberspace, 27
DASL (DAV Searching and Locating), 114
Data diode, 200
Data management, 152–3
Data mining, 119–69
  applications, 122–34
    astrophysics and cosmology, 126–7
    bioinformatics, 131–2
    chemical and materials engineering,
      127–30
    flows, 133–4
    geological and geophysical, 123–6
  approximation, 122, 143–51
  best practices, 139–43, 147–51, 153–5
  compression, 121
    continuous attribute sets, 147–9
    data defined over geometry and
      topologies, 144
    particle position data, 148
  constructive induction, 138–9
  controlling the complexity of induction,
    141–2
  data is scarce, 156–9
  determining high-level structures, 140–1
  distributed environments, 160–1

evolution, 120
future directions, 161
future research issues, 156–61
induction, 121
inductive, 134–43
information integration, 153
integrated approaches, 139
integrating numeric, symbolic and
    geometric information, 155
interactive visualization, 151–2
inventing new features, 143
lossy compression, 143–51
motivating domains, 122–34
multiresolution phenomena, 144–6
"on-the-fly", 159–60
parallel environments, 160–1
querying, 121–2
rank reduction, 149–51
recommender systems, 151
spatial and temporal coherence coding,
    146–7
spatial coherence violations, 149
underlying principles, 134–9
Data modelling, 152–5
Data reduction techniques, 122
Data representation, 153–5
Data sources
    discovering, 100–1
    selecting and ranking, 101–4
Data storage, 64
Database management system (DBMS), 153
Dataquest, 11
de Boor's function, 157–8
Delayed communication, 50
Delphi effect, 44
Design of experiments, 159
DIF (Directory Interchange Format), 90
different time/different place interaction, 5
digital communications, 50
DIOM, 113
Diorama system, 113
Discipline-specific tools, 10
DISCO, 113
Discretionary access control, 193
Distance education
    key elements, 4
    traditional, 4
Distinguished Names, 223
DNA, 138
DNA sequences, 177–8

Domain definition table (DDT), 199–200
Domain theory, 178
Double-gate MOSFETs, 273
Downgrading, 206
Drain-induced barrier lowering (DIBL), 249
DRAMs, 241
Dublin Core, 114

E

ebXML, 72
E-commerce, 13
Educational environments, 12–15
Electrical telegraph, 56
Electronic books, 63–4
Electronic commerce, 68
Embedded systems, 161
Encapsulating, 222
Encoded signalling, 55
Encryption, 200–1
Entertainment industry
    and Internet, 67
    and World Wide Web, 70–1
Experiment management, 152–3

F

faculty concerns with online teaching, 14–15
Flows, data mining, 133–4
FOIL, 121
Foundational research, 179–80
Frequency of updates, 97
Fuzzy-body/implicit-integration/normal-mode
    (FIN), 146

G

Gene expression, biological variation, 132
Generalized noninterference, 198
Generic environments, 10
GENESYS, 129
Geological applications of data mining,
    123–6
Geophysical applications of data mining,
    123–6
Global enterprises, 68
Global wires, 276–8

Globalization, 78–9
Golem, 121
Google, 72
Granularity, 97, 102
Graph-drawing algorithms, 175
Group communication exchange, 7
Group interaction, 9
Group learning, 36

H

Harrison-Ruzzo-Ullman model, 198
Haskell, 177
Heuristics, new theories, 182
High-speed civil transport (HSCT), 151–2
HTML, 72, 89
HTTP, 72, 89
Human communication
  origins, 51–6
  recent development, 56–7
Human Genome Project, 153, 156
Hyperlinks, 57
Hypertext, 16

I

Immediate communication, 50
IMS (IEEE-LOM), 12
Inductive logic programming (ILP), 137–8,
  143
Information flow control, 193–4
Information Manager, 16
Information Manifold, 113
Integrated circuits (ICs), design, 237–79
Integrity verification procedures (IVP's),
  210
International networked communications,
  56–7
Internet, 1, 3–5, 11, 12, 49, 50, 127
  and children, 65–6
  and commerce and industry, 68
  and entertainment industry, 67
  development, 77–8
  exploiting standards, 79–80
  future, 65–9
  information from, 78
  overview, 51–7
  possibilities, 75–81

private use, 68–9
technical standards, 78–9
ISP (Internet service provider), 72

J

Jikzi, 190, 214–16, 222
Job loss, 14

K

Kepler's laws, 136
Key management policies, 223–6
KeyNote, 227–8
KSOS, 199

L

Language, 53
Lattice model, 197
Lattice solution, 111
LDAP, 114
Learning theory, 177–8
Libraries, 63
Life Forms, 27
Linus law, 44
Lithography, 240, 242
Local names, 224
Logical representations, 137–8
Logistics Information Technology Systems
  (LITS), 203
Logistics systems, 203
LOMAC, 208
Long-distance communication, 53–6
LSA system, 151

M

MaC Project, 155
Machine learning techniques, 134
Mail guards, 200
Mandatory access control, 193
Manufacturing, 179
Manuscripts, 58–9
Materials engineering, data mining, 127–30
Mathematics, 178

MAXIMA, 127
Maximal compatibility classes, 105
MDL (Minimum Description Length), 121
MECHEM, 139
Medical privacy, 212–14
Megacorp Inc security policy, 188
Message map analysis, 9
Messenger, signalling by, 54–5
Micro-Electro Mechanical Systems (MEMS),
    130, 133, 161
Microprocessor units (MPUs), 241
Mining scientific data. *See* Data mining
MLS, 196, 199, 201, 212
    future systems, 204
    polictical and economic issues, 206–7
Mobile telephones, 68–9
Modulation, 54
Molecular dynamics simulation, 128
MOSFET devices, 238–42
MOSFET scaling
    2-D scale length theory, 246–50
    theory, 242–50
MOSFET threshold voltage, 251
Multidisciplinary analysis and design (MAD),
    130
Multilevel security, 193, 197, 199–207
Multimedia, 64

N

NAND gates, 273
National Lottery system, 228–9
Net. *See* Internet
Network flow techniques, 179
network learning tools, 16
Networked learning, early findings, 9–10
Neural networks, 136–7
Neymann–Scott scheme, 124
nMOSFETs, 238–40, 257, 263, 264, 273
Noise, 143
Nondeducibility, 197–8
Noninterference, 197
NRL Pump, 202

O

Occam's Razor, 121
ODE, 159–60

Online courses, 8–9, 23, 26–7
Online educational environment, 7
Online interaction, attributes, 5–6
Online teaching, faculty concerns with, 14–15
Ontario Institute for Studies in Education
    (OISE), 8, 9
Open source advances, 12–15
Open source development, 13, 43
Orange book, 200
Overclassification, 206

P

P versus NP question, 180
Parallel computer architecture, 160–1, 176
Partially extended po-set, 112
PDE, 153–4, 156
Pedagogical design, 7
Plausible deniability, 227
pMOSFETs, 238–40, 257, 273
Pocket function, 157–8
Poisson equation, 245
Poisson process, 124
PolicyMaker, 227
Politics, 76
Polyinstantiation, 205
Polysilicon-gate depletion effects, 271–2
POSS-II, 126
Pretty Good Privacy (PGP), 224–6
Printing, 59–60
PROGOL, 121
Programming languages, 176–7
PROLOG, 138
Protection of computer system, 187–8
Protection profile, 189
Protective marking, 194
Public key cryptography, 223
Purple Penelope, 203–4
PYTHIA, 153–4

Q

qhull, 179
QoD applet, 102–3
QoD data parameters, 90
QoD metadata, 99–100
QoD parameters, 88, 90, 96–7, 101, 104, 115
QSIM, 155

QUAKEFINDER, 124
Quality of data. *See* QoD
Quality of service (QoS), 43

R

RC delay, 275–8
RDF, 114
Reactive fluid dynamics, 130
Recency, 97, 112
Reference monitor, 190
Remote teletype machines, 57
Restrictivenes, 198
Resurrecting Duckling, 190, 216–18
RJE (remote job entry) systems, 57
Role-based access control (RBAC), 199, 208,
    221

S

SAL interpreter, 142
SAL system, 141, 154, 155
Same time/different place interaction, 4–5
Sanity checks, 141
SAS/STAT, 143
Scientific function-finding, 135–6
SCOMP, 200
scqd's, 90–1, 96
    assessing combination, 108–12
    efficient manipulation, 104–12
    grouping using partially ordered sets,
        105–8
    model, 97–100
SDSI, 227
Secure computation, 175
Security labels, 192, 194, 195
Security policies, 185–235
    access control, 191, 219–27
    alternative formulations, 197–9
    automatic enforcement of information flow
        control, 193–4
    classifications and clearances, 191–3
    definition, 188–9
    formalising, 194–6
    model, 188
    origins, 189–90
    overview, 186–90
    tranquility, 196

Security state, 221–2
Security target, 189
Semantic Web, 89, 113
Semaphore systems, 56
Semi-discrete transforms (SDD), 150
SETI, 160
Shallow-trench oxide isolation (STI), 239
Short-channel MOSFET, 242, 246, 247
Signalling by code, 55–6
Silicon ICs, 238
Simple Public Key Infrastructure (SPKI), 224
Singular-value decomposition (SVD), 143
SKICAT, 126
Sloan Digital Sky Survey, 126, 179
Software development, 43
    bazaar approach, 13, 44
    cathedral style, 13, 44
Software environments, 10–11
Software systems, 176
SOIF records, 115
Sound waves, 54
Source content and quality metadata, 96–100
Source content quality descriptions. *See*
    scqd's
Source selection and ranking, 87–118
    example, 91
Speech, 51–3
    assisting, 53–4
SPKI, 227
SQL, 122
SRAM cells, 265, 273
SSL, 223
Standard ML (meta-language), 177
State machine abstraction, 195
Sub-markings, 194
Superbuckets, 106–8
Superhalo, 266
Synchronous communication, 4
System Z, 196, 197

T

Take-off gross weight (TOGW), 151
Technological design, 10–11
Technological developments, 12
Technological solutions, 11
Telelearning applications, 43
Telelearning environment support network,
    43

Telelearning initiative, 15–17
Telelearning Network of Centres of
    Excellence, 16, 42
Telelearning software, 43
Telephon, 54
Theoretical computer science, 171–83
  contributions to other disciplines,
      178–9
  history, 173–4
  prospects, 174
  role in practical computer science
      problems, 174–8
Thermodynamics, 130
Tranquility property, 196
Transformation procedures (TPs), 210
Transistors, 237–79
Trusted Computing Base (TCB), 190,
    211
Trusted X, 201–2
TSIMMIS, 113
Tumor protein $p53$ (TP_{53}), 131
Type enforcement model, 198

U

Uncertainty, 143
Unconstrained data item (UDI), 210, 222
Universal function approximators, 136–7
University of Illinois Online (UI-Online),
    35–6
University of Phoenix Online, 3
Unix, 12, 16
Upper Roanoke River Watershed, 125

V

Van der Pol relaxed system of dimension,
    159
Verisign, 223
ViewCat applet, 95–6
Virtual classrooms, 6–15
Virtual learner, 22–4
Virtual learning environment (VLE), 43
Virtual professor, 21–2
Virtual seminar, 10
Virtual-U, 15–27
  adjunct mode approaches, 25
  design principles and processes, 18

educational research and online
    educational tools and environments
    interface with open source
    programmers, 45
field trials, 21
instructors, 21–2
mixed mode, 25–6
online courses, 40
online mode, 26–7
overview, 15–18
professors, 21–2
research base, 15
security, 17
spatial metaphor, 18–19
tools, 19–20
Virtual university, 1–47
  best of breed, 37–8
  combined traditional and virtual university
      model, 35–6
  comparison with traditional university, 32
  costs, 30–1
  courses, 24–7
  defining, 31–9
  establishing, 27–31
  faculty credentials, 27–8
  fundamental role, 28–9
  group cohort model, 36–7
  group/semester model, 34–5
  implications for pedagogical and
      technological developments, 39
  network vs. consortium model, 37–8
  niche, 38–9
  number of courses and class size, 30
  pedagogic and administrative models, 32–9
  pedagogies and instructional design, 29
  potential, 29
  prestigious, 34–5
  professional, 36
  research directions and questions, 39–45
Visibility complex, 175
Visibility graphs, 175
VizCraft, 151
VLSI, 238–42
  design, 177
  performance, 275
  system performance, 273
VOD–(video on demand), 70
VU Research Database, 40
VUCat, 40, 41–5
VUDataMiner, 40–1, 45

W

W3QS, 114
Web. *See* World Wide Web
Web-based education software, 12
Web-based learning, 12
Web-based learning environments, 13
Web publishing, 12
WebDAV, 114
WebSemantics architecture, 87–118
  catalog, 95–6
  catalog layer, 92
  data source layer, 92
  data sources, 92
  future work, 115–16
  publishing and locating data sources, 92–6
  query processor, 92
  related research, 113–15
  World Wide Web layer, 92
  wrappers, 92
WebSemantics Query Language (WSQL),
    100, 104, 114
Whistled languages, 54
Whois++, 114
Wiretapping, 192
World Wide Web, 1, 11, 14, 49, 50, 87–8, 89,
    113
  and children, 69–70
  and commerce and industry, 71–2
  and entertainment industry, 70–1
  development, 80–1

  exploiting standards, 81
  future, 69–73
  origins, 58–60
  overview, 57–64
  possibilities, 75–81
  potential, 64
  private use, 72–3
  technical standards, 80–1
Wrappers, 113
WS-XML, 89, 92, 100, 113, 115
  catalog contents, 96
  publishing data sources, 93–5

X

X.509, 223
X Windows, 202
XML, 42, 89, 122
XMLSchema, 89, 114
XTS-300, 200

Y

Yahoo, 72

Z

Z39.50 protocol, 114

Contents of Volumes in This Series

Volume 40

Program Understanding: Models and Experiments
   A. VON MAYRHAUSER AND A. M. VANS
Software Prototyping
   ALAN M. DAVIS
Rapid Prototyping of Microelectronic Systems
   APOSTOLOS DOLLAS AND J. D. STERLING BABCOCK
Cache Coherence in Multiprocessors: A Survey
   MAZIN S. YOUSIF, M. J. THAZHUTHAVEETIL, and C. R. DAS
The Adequacy of Office Models
   CHANDRA S. AMARAVADI, JOEY F. GEORGE, OLIVIA R. LIU SHENG, AND JAY F. NUNAMAKER

Volume 41

Directions in Software Process Research
   H. DIETER ROMBACH AND MARTIN VERLAGE
The Experience Factory and Its Relationship to Other Quality Approaches
   VICTOR R. BASILI
CASE Adoption: A Process, Not an Event
   JOCK A. RADER
On the Necessary Conditions for the Composition of Integrated Software
Engineering Environments
   DAVID J. CARNEY AND ALAN W. BROWN
Software Quality, Software Process, and Software Testing
   DICK HAMLET
Advances in Benchmarking Techniques: New Standards and Quantitative Metrics
   THOMAS CONTE AND WEN-MEI W. HWU
An Evolutionary Path for Transaction Processing Systems
   CARLTON PU, AVRAHAM LEFF, AND SHU-WEI, F. CHEN

Volume 42

Nonfunctional Requirements of Real-Time Systems
   TEREZA G. KIRNER AND ALAN M. DAVIS
A Review of Software Inspections
   ADAM PORTER, HARVEY SIY, AND LAWRENCE VOTTA
Advances in Software Reliability Engineering
   JOHN D. MUSA AND WILLA EHRLICH
Network Interconnection and Protocol Conversion
   MING T. LIU
A Universal Model of Legged Locomotion Gaits
   S. T. VENKATARAMAN

297

Volume 43

Program Slicing
    DAVID W. BINKLEY AND KEITH BRIAN GALLAGHER
Language Features for the Interconnection of Software Components
    RENATE MOTSCHNIG-PITRIK AND ROLAND T. MITTERMEIR
Using Model Checking to Analyze Requirements and Designs
    JOANNE ATLEE, MARSHA CHECHIK, AND JOHN GANNON
Information Technology and Productivity: A Review of the Literature
    ERIK BRYNJOLFSSON AND SHINKYU YANG
The Complexity of Problems
    WILLIAM GASARCH
3-D Computer Vision Using Structured Light: Design, Calibration, and Implementation Issues
    FRED W. DEPIERO AND MOHAN M. TRIVEDI

Volume 44

Managing the Risks in Information Systems and Technology (IT)
    ROBERT N. CHARETTE
Software Cost Estimation: A Review of Models, Process and Practice
    FIONA WALKERDEN AND ROSS JEFFERY
Experimentation in Software Engineering
    SHARI LAWRENCE PFLEEGER
Parallel Computer Construction Outside the United States
    RALPH DUNCAN
Control of Information Distribution and Access
    RALF HAUSER
Asynchronous Transfer Mode: An Engineering Network Standard for High Speed Communications
    RONALD J. VETTER
Communication Complexity
    EYAL KUSHILEVITZ

Volume 45

Control in Multi-threaded Information Systems
    PABLO A. STRAUB AND CARLOS A. HURTADO
Parallelization of DOALL and DOACROSS Loops—a Survey
    A. R. HURSON, JOFORD T. LIM, KRISHNA M. KAVI, AND BEN LEE
Programming Irregular Applications: Runtime Support, Compilation and Tools
    JOEL SALTZ, GAGAN AGRAWAL, CHIALIN CHANG, RAJA DAS, GUY EDJLALI, PAUL HAVLAK,
    YUAN-SHIN HWANG, BONGKI MOON, RAVI PONNUSAMY, SHAMIK SHARMA, ALAN SUSSMAN
    AND MUSTAFA UYSAL
Optimization Via Evolutionary Processes
    SRILATA RAMAN AND L. M. PATNAIK
Software Reliability and Readiness Assessment Based on the Non-homogeneous Poisson Process
    AMRIT L. GOEL AND KUNE-ZANG YANG
Computer-supported Cooperative Work and Groupware
    JONATHAN GRUDIN AND STEVEN E. POLTROCK
Technology and Schools
    GLEN L. BULL

Volume 46

Software Process Appraisal and Improvement: Models and Standards
MARK C. PAULK
A Software Process Engineering Framework
JYRKI KONTIO
Gaining Business Value from IT Investments
PAMELA SIMMONS
Reliability Measurement, Analysis, and Improvement for Large Software Systems
JEFF TIAN
Role-based Access Control
RAVI SANDHU
Multithreaded Systems
KRISHNA M. KAVI, BEN LEE AND ALLI R. HURSON
COORDINATION MODELS AND LANGUAGES
GEORGE A. PAPADOPOULOS AND FARHAD ARBAB
Multidisciplinary Problem Solving Environments for Computational Science
ELIAS N. HOUSTIS, JOHN R. RICE AND NAREN RAMAKRISHNAN

Volume 47

Natural Language Processing: A Human–Computer Interaction Perspective
BILL MANARIS
Cognitive Adaptive Computer Help (COACH): A Case Study
EDWIN J. SELKER
Cellular Automata Models of Self-replicating Systems
JAMES A. REGGIA, HUI-HSIEN CHOU, AND JASON D. LOHN
Ultrasound Visualization
THOMAS R. NELSON
Patterns and System Development
BRANDON GOLDFEDDER
High Performance Digital Video Servers: Storage and Retrieval of Compressed Scalable Video
SEUNGYUP PAEK AND SHIH-FU CHANG
Software Acquisition: The Custom/Package and Insource/Outsource Dimensions
PAUL NELSON, ABRAHAM SEIDMANN, AND WILLIAM RICHMOND

Volume 48

Architectures and Patterns for Developing High-performance, Real-time ORB Endsystems
DOUGLAS C. SCHMIDT, DAVID L. LEVINE AND CHRIS CLEELAND
Heterogeneous Data Access in a Mobile Environment – Issues and Solutions
J. B. LIM AND A. R. HURSON
The World Wide Web
HAL BERGHEL AND DOUGLAS BLANK
Progress in Internet Security
RANDALL J. ATKINSON AND J. ERIC KLINKER
Digital Libraries: Social Issues and Technological Advances
HSINCHUN CHEN AND ANDREA L. HOUSTON
Architectures for Mobile Robot Control
JULIO K. ROSENBLATT AND JAMES A. HENDLER

Volume 49

A survey of Current Paradigms in Machine Translation
  BONNIE J. DORR, PAMELA W. JORDAN AND JOHN W. BENOIT
Formality in Specification and Modeling: Developments in Software Engineering Practice
  J. S. FITZGERALD
3-D Visualization of Software Structure
  MATHEW L. STAPLES AND JAMES M. BIEMAN
Using Domain Models for System Testing
  A. VON MAYRHAUSER AND R. MRAZ
Exception-handling Design Patterns
  WILLIAM G. BAIL
Managing Control Asynchrony on SIMD Machines—a Survey
  NAEL B. ABU-GHAZALEH AND PHILIP A. WILSEY
A Taxonomy of Distributed Real-time Control Systems
  J. R. AGRE, L. P. CLARE AND S. SASTRY

Volume 50

Index Part I
Subject Index, Volumes 1–49

Volume 51

Index Part II
Author Index
Cumulative list of Titles
Table of Contents, Volumes 1–49

Volume 52

Eras of Business Computing
  ALAN R. HEVNER AND DONALD J. BERNDT
Numerical Weather Prediction
  FERDINAND BAER
Machine Translation
  SERGEI NIRENBURG AND YORICK WILKS
The Games Computers (and People) Play
  JONATHAN SCHAEFFER
From Single Word to Natural Dialogue
  NEILS OLE BENSON AND LAILA DYBKJÆR
Embedded Microprocessors: Evolution, Trends and Challenges
  MANFRED SCHLETT

Volume 53

Shared-Memory Multiprocessing: Current State and Future Directions
  PER STEUSTRÖM, ERIK HAGERSTEU, DAVID I. LITA, MARGARET MARTONOSI and MADAN VERNGOPAL

Shared Memory and Distributed Shared Memory Systems: A Survey
KRISHNA KAUI, HYONG-SHIK KIM, BEU LEE and A. R. HURSON
Resource-Aware Meta Computing
JEFFREY K. HOLLINGSWORTH, PETER J. KELCHER and KYUNG D. RYU
Knowledge Management
WILLIAM W. AGRESTI
A Methodology for Evaluating Predictive Metrics
JASRETT ROSENBERG
An Empirical Review of Software Process Assessments
KHALED EL EMAM and DENNIS R. GOLDENSON
State of the Art in Electronic Payment Systems
N. ASOKAN, P. JANSON, M. STEIVES and M. WAIDNES
Defective Software: An Overview of Legal Remedies and Technical Measures Available to Consumers
COLLEEN KOTYK VOSSLER and JEFFREY VOAS

Volume 54

An Overview of Components and Component-Based Development
ALAN W. BROWN
Working with UML: A Software Design Process Based on Inspections for the Unified Modeling Language
GUILHERME H. TRAVASSOS, FORREST SHULL AND JEFFREY CARVER
Enterprise JavaBeans and Microsoft Transaction Server: Frameworks for Distributed Enterprise Components
AVRAHAM LEFF, JOHN PROKOPEK, JAMES T. RAYFIELD AND IGNACIO SILVA-LEPE
Maintenance Process and Product Evaluation Using Reliability, Risk, and Test Metrics
NORMAN F. SCHNEIDEWIND
Computer Technology Changes and Purchasing Strategies
GERALD V. POST
Secure Outsourcing of Scientific Computations
MIKHAIL J. ATALLAH, K.N. PANTAZOPOULOS, JOHN R. RICE AND EUGENE SPAFFORD

Printed and bound by CPI Group (UK) Ltd, Croydon, CR0 4YY

03/10/2024

01040412-0005